Merriam-Webster Dictionary of Synonyms and Antonyms

A Merriam-Webster®

MERRIAM-WEBSTER, INC., *Publishers*
Springfield, Massachusetts

A GENUINE MERRIAM-WEBSTER

The name *Webster* alone is no guarantee of excellence. It is used by a number of publishers and may serve mainly to mislead an unwary buyer.

A Merriam-Webster© is the registered trademark you should look for when you consider the purchase of dictionaries or other fine reference books. It carries the reputation of a company that has been publishing since 1831 and is your assurance of quality and authority.

First Indian edition 2005
ISBN: 0-87779-842-7
This special low-price edition is for sale in
India, Nepal, Pakistan, Bangladesh, Sri Lanka,
Bhutan, Myanmar and Maldives only.
It is the only authorized, complete and unabridged reprint of the latest original edition.

Distributed in the Indian Subcontinent by
GOYAL Publishers & Distributors Pvt. Ltd.
86 U.B. Jawahar Nagar, Delhi – 110007, India.
Tel : 011 - 23852986, 23858362 Fax: 23850961
E-mail: goyal@vsnl.com
Printed in India by Gopsons Papers Limited.
1234GPL060504

PREFACE

The Merriam-Webster Dictionary of Synonyms and Antonyms is a concise guide to the understanding and use of synonyms. It is intended for people who wish to appreciate the shades of difference that exist among English words having the same or nearly the same meaning and who wish to be able to choose the precisely suitable word for a particular purpose.

The bulk of this book is made up of a collection of articles in which distinctions are drawn from among a group of synonyms. The distinctions usually fall into one of three peripheral areas of meaning: implication, connotation, or application. Implications are the usually minor ideas involved in the meaning of a word. Connotations are the ideas which color the meaning of a word and are the product of various factors, such as etymology and historical and literary associations. Applications are the restrictions on a word's use established by current idiom.

Each main entry begins with a list of words that are discussed in that article. Following the list is a concise statement of the element of meaning that the synonyms have in common:

abdicate, renounce, resign mean to give up formally and definitely.

After this initial sentence, there is a series of statements describing the differences that distinguish the synonyms from one another. The statements are supplemented and clarified by examples, set in angle brackets, that illustrate typical ways in which the word may be used. When the word being discriminated has an antonym, the antonym appears following the bracketed example:

Abdicate implies a giving up of sovereign power <the king was forced to *abdicate*> or sometimes an evading of responsibility <by walking out he *abdicated* his rights as a father>. **ant** assume, usurp

In addition, the book also contains thousands of cross-reference entries. By means of these entries, every word discussed in each article is entered at its own alphabetical place, followed by a cross-reference to the main entry where it is discussed:

desert see ABANDON.

When a word is discussed at more than one entry and is treated as the same part of speech at each entry, numbered cross-references list all of the entries at which that word is treated:

casual 1. see ACCIDENTAL. **2.** see RANDOM.

abandon *vb* **Abandon, desert, forsake** mean to leave without intending to return . . . .
2. see RELINQUISH.

When a word is discussed at more than one entry and as a different part of speech, separate cross-reference entries appear:

humor *vb* see INDULGE.
humor *n* **1.** see WIT. **2.** see INDULGE.

need *n* **Need, necessity, exigency** mean a pressing lack of something essential . . . .
need *vb* see LACK.

In the entries listed above, the entry word is followed by an italic part-of-speech label. Such a part-of-speech label appears whenever the same entry word is listed more than once and is intended to help the reader identify the appropriate entry and reference. The meanings of the abbreviations used in part-of-speech labels in this book are as follows:

adj adjective *n* noun *adv* adverb *vb* verb

Some cross-references are followed by a number or a part-of-speech label. References like this direct the reader to the desired article when the same word serves as a main-entry word for more than one article:

adventitious see ACCIDENTAL 2.
alternative see CHOICE *n*.
correlate see PARALLEL *n* 2.

This book draws on materials that appear in various Merriam-Webster® publications, especially *Webster's Compact Dictionary of Synonyms,* and so is based on work done by the writers and editors of those books. The manuscript for this book was prepared by Dr. Mary W. Cornog, working in consultation with members of the Merriam-Webster Editorial Department. Proofreading and copyediting was done by Eileen M. Haraty. Data entry was done by Georgette B. Boucher and Marjorie C. Kochanowicz. Frederick C. Mish, Editorial Director, helped to prepare the plan for this book. Overall project coordination was provided by John M. Morse, Executive Editor.

A

abandon *vb* **1. Abandon, desert, forsake** mean to give up completely.

Abandon can suggest complete disinterest in the future of what is given up <they *abandoned* their cat at the end of the summer>. ***ant*** reclaim

Desert implies a relationship (as of occupancy or guardianship); it can suggest desolation <*deserted* farms growing up to brush> or culpability <soldiers who *desert* their posts>. ***ant*** cleave to, stick to

Forsake implies a breaking of a close association by repudiation or renunciation <she *forsook* her husband for a career>. ***ant*** return to, revert to

2. see RELINQUISH.

abandon *n* see UNCONSTRAINT.

abase, demean, debase, degrade, humble, humiliate mean to lessen in dignity or status.

Abase suggests losing or voluntarily yielding up dignity or prestige <a fine stage actor who *abased* himself by turning to television>. ***ant*** exalt, extol

Demean suggests unsuitable behavior or association as the cause of loss of status <commercial endorsements *demean* the Olympics>.

Debase emphasizes loss of worth or quality <*debase* a currency> and especially deterioration of moral standards <drunkenness has *debased* the Mardi Gras>.

Degrade suggests a downward step, sometimes in rank, more often in ethical stature, and typically implies a shameful or corrupt end <the public altercation *degraded* both candidates>. ***ant*** uplift

Humble frequently replaces *degrade* when the disgrace of a reduction in status is to be emphasized <they were delighted to see the bully *humbled* by a boy half his size>.

Humiliate implies the severe wounding of one's pride and the causing of deep shame <*humiliated* by his suggestive remarks>.

abash see EMBARRASS.

abate 1. see DECREASE.

2. Abate, subside, wane, ebb mean to die down in force or intensity.

Abate stresses a progressive diminishing <waited until the storm *abated*>. ***ant*** rise, revive

Subside suggests a falling to a low level and an easing of turbulence <the protests subsided after a few days>.

Wane adds to *abate* an implication of fading or weakening <a *waning* moon> and is often used of something impressive or intense <the public's *waning* interest in spaceflight>. ***ant*** wax

Ebb suggests a gradual waning, especially of something that commonly comes and goes <vitality often *ebbs* with illness>. ***ant*** flow *(as the tide)*

abbey see CLOISTER.

abbreviate see SHORTEN.

abdicate, renounce, resign mean to give up formally or definitely.

Abdicate implies a giving up of sovereign power <the king was forced to *abdicate*> or sometimes an evading of responsibility such as that of a parent <by walking out he *abdicated* his rights as a father>. ***ant*** assume, usurp

Renounce may be chosen when the sacrifice, especially to some higher or moral end, is stressed <the king *renounced* his throne to obtain peace>. ***ant*** arrogate, covet

Resign applies especially to the giving up of an unexpired office or trust <forced to *resign* from office>.

aberrant see ABNORMAL.

abet see INCITE.

abeyant see LATENT.

abhor see HATE.

abhorrent 1. see HATEFUL. **2.** see REPUGNANT.

abide 1. see BEAR. **2.** see CONTINUE. **3.** see STAY 1.

abject see MEAN.

abjure, renounce, forswear, recant, retract mean to withdraw one's word or professed belief.

Abjure implies a firm and final rejecting or abandoning under oath <candidates for citizenship must *abjure* allegiance to any foreign power>. ***ant*** pledge *(as allegiance)*, elect *(as a way of life)*

Renounce often equals *abjure* but may carry the meaning of *disclaim* or *disown* <willing to *renounce* his lifelong friends>.

Forswear may add to *abjure* an implication of perjury or betrayal <cannot *forswear* my principles to win votes>.

Recant stresses the withdrawing or denying of something professed or taught <the suspect *recanted* his confession and professed his innocence>.

Retract applies to the withdrawing of a promise, an offer, or an accusation <under threat of lawsuit the paper *retracted* the statement>.

able, capable, competent, qualified mean having power or fitness for work.

Able suggests ability above the average as revealed in actual performance <proved that she is an *able* Shakespearean actress>. ***ant*** inept, unable

Capable stresses the having of qualities fitting one for work but does not imply outstanding ability <*capable* of doing simple tasks under supervision>. ***ant*** incapable

Competent and ***qualified*** imply having the experience or training for adequate performance <a leap that any *competent* ballet dancer can execute> <seek help from a *qualified* medical professional>. ***ant*** incompetent, unqualified

abnegation see RENUNCIATION.

abnormal, atypical, aberrant mean deviating markedly from the rule or standard of its kind.

Abnormal frequently suggests strangeness and sometimes deformity or monstrosity <a classic study of *abnormal* personalities>. ***ant*** normal

Atypical stresses divergence upward or downward from some established norm <a markedly *atypical* reaction to a drug>. ***ant*** typical, representative

Aberrant implies a departure from the usual or natural type <that joyriding incident must be regarded as an *aberrant* episode in his life>. ***ant*** true *(to a type)*

abolish, annihilate, extinguish mean to make nonexistent.

Abolish implies a putting to an end chiefly of things that are the outgrowth of law, customs, and conditions of existence <*abolish* a poll tax>. ***ant*** establish, institute

Annihilate suggests a complete wiping out of existence of something material or immaterial <homes and cities *annihilated* by enemy attack>.

Extinguish is likely to suggest a complete but gradual ending (as by stifling, choking, or smothering) <a religion that was thoroughly *extinguished* by governmental oppression>.

abominable see HATEFUL.

abominate see HATE.

abomination, anathema, bugbear, bête noire mean a person or thing that arouses intense dislike.

Abomination suggests the arousal of loathing, disgust, and extreme displeasure <in her opinion all of modern art is an *abomination*>.

Anathema suggests that something is so odious that it is dismissed or rejected out of hand <anything that was Yankee was *anathema* to my Southern aunt>.

Bugbear suggests something so dreaded that one seeks continually to avoid it <the deficit became an annual congressional *bugbear*>.

Bête noire suggests a pet aversion that one habitually or especially avoids <his mooching brother-in-law was the *bête noire* of his life>.

aboriginal see NATIVE.

abortive see FUTILE.

abound see TEEM.
aboveboard see STRAIGHTFORWARD.
abridge see SHORTEN.
abridgment, abstract, synopsis, conspectus, epitome mean a condensed treatment.
Abridgment implies reduction in compass with retention of relative completeness <an *abridgment* of a dictionary>. *ant* expansion
Abstract applies to a summary of points (as of a treatise, document, or proposed treatment) <a published *abstract* of a medical paper>. *ant* amplification
Synopsis implies a skeletal presentation of an article or narrative suitable for rapid examination <read a *synopsis* of the screenplay>.
Conspectus suggests a quick overall view of a large detailed subject <the book is a *conspectus* of modern American history>.
Epitome suggests the briefest possible presentation of a complex whole as an ideal example <"know thyself" was the *epitome* of Greek philosophy>.
abrogate see NULLIFY.
abrupt 1. see PRECIPITATE. **2.** see STEEP.
absolute, autocratic, arbitrary, despotic, tyrannical mean exercising power or authority without restraint.
Absolute implies that one is not bound by legal constraints or the control of another <King Louis XIV was an *absolute* monarch>.
Autocratic suggests the egotistical, self-conscious use of power or the haughty imposition of one's own will <the flamboyant, *autocratic* director of the ballet company>.
Arbitrary implies the exercise and usually the abuse of power according to one's momentary inclination <his high-handed, *arbitrary* way of running his department>. *ant* legitimate
Despotic implies the arbitrary and imperious exercise of absolute power or control <the most decadent and *despotic* of the Roman emperors>.
Tyrannical implies the abuse of absolute power and harsh or oppressive rule <a new regime as *tyrannical* as the one it had deposed>.
absolution see PARDON.
absolve see EXCULPATE.
absorb 1. Absorb, imbibe, assimilate mean to take something in so as to become imbued with it.
Absorb is likely to suggest a loss of identity in what is taken in or an enrichment of what takes in <a lotion *absorbed* quickly by the skin>. *ant* dissipate *(as time, energies)*
Imbibe implies a drinking in and may imply an unconscious

taking in whose effect may be significant or profound <children *imbibe* the values of their parents>. ***ant*** ooze, exude

Assimilate stresses an incorporation into the substance of the body or mind <asked to *assimiliate* a mass of material in a brief time>.

2. see MONOPOLIZE.

abstain see REFRAIN.

abstemiousness see TEMPERANCE.

abstinence see TEMPERANCE.

abstract see ABRIDGMENT.

abundant see PLENTIFUL.

abuse, vituperation, invective, obloquy, scurrility, billingsgate mean vehemently expressed condemnation or disapproval.

Abuse implies the anger of the speaker and stresses the harshness of the language <charged her husband with verbal *abuse*>. ***ant*** adulation

Vituperation implies fluent and sustained abuse <subjected his aide to a torrent of *vituperation*>. ***ant*** acclaim, praise

Invective implies a comparable vehemence but suggests greater verbal and rhetorical skill and may apply to a public denunciation <a politician known for his blistering *invective*>.

Obloquy suggests defamation and consequent shame and disgrace <silently endured the *obloquy* of his former friend>.

Scurrility implies viciousness of attack and coarseness or foulness of language <a debate that was not an exchange of ideas but an exercise in *scurrility*>.

Billingsgate implies practiced fluency and variety of profane or obscene abuse <a *billingsgate* that would make a drunken sailor blush>.

abutting see ADJACENT.

abysmal see DEEP 2.

academic 1. see PEDANTIC. **2.** see THEORETICAL.

accede see ASSENT.

accept see RECEIVE.

acceptation see MEANING.

access see FIT *n*.

accession see FIT *n*.

accident see CHANCE *n*.

accidental 1. Accidental, fortuitous, casual, contingent mean happening by chance.

Accidental stresses chance or unexpected occurrence <any resemblance to actual persons is entirely *accidental*>. ***ant*** planned

Fortuitous so strongly suggests chance that it often connotes entire absence of cause <believes that life is more than a series of *fortuitous* events>. ***ant*** deliberate

Casual stresses lack of real or apparent premeditation or intent <a *casual* encounter between two acquaintances>.

Contingent suggests possibility of happening but stresses uncertainty and dependence on other future events <the *contingent* effects of a proposed amendment to the constitution>.

2. Accidental, incidental, adventitious mean not being part of the real or essential nature of something.

Accidental retains its basic notion of chance occurrence but may also imply nonessential character <the essential and *accidental* values of an education>. ***ant*** essential

Incidental suggests a real, sometimes a designed, relationship but one which is secondary and nonessential <expenses *incidental* to the performance of her job>. ***ant*** essential

Adventitious implies a lack of essential relationships and may suggest casual addition or irrelevance <avoided elaborate designs with superfluous or *adventitious* elements>. ***ant*** inherent

accommodate **1.** see ADAPT. **2.** see OBLIGE. **3.** see CONTAIN.

accompany, attend, escort mean to go along with.

Accompany when referring to persons, usually implies equality of status <*accompanied* his wife to the theater>.

Attend implies a waiting upon in order to serve usually as a subordinate <will *attend* the President at the summit meeting>.

Escort adds to *accompany* implications of protection, ceremony, or courtesy <a motorcade *escorted* the visiting queen>.

accomplish see PERFORM.

accomplishment see ACQUIREMENT.

accord *vb* **1.** see AGREE 3. **2.** see GRANT.

accord *n* see HARMONY.

accordingly see THEREFORE.

accountable see RESPONSIBLE.

accoutre see FURNISH.

accredit see APPROVE.

accumulative see CUMULATIVE.

accurate see CORRECT *adj*.

accuse, charge, indict, impeach mean to declare a person guilty of a fault or offense.

Accuse implies a direct, personal declaration <*accused* him of trying to steal his wallet>. ***ant*** exculpate

Charge usually implies a formal declaration of a serious offense <an athlete *charged* with taking illegal drugs before the race>. ***ant*** absolve

Indict is usually used in a legal context and implies a formal consideration of evidence prior to a trial <*indicted* by a grand jury for first-degree murder>.

Impeach technically refers to a formal charge of malfeasance in office on the part of a public official <the House of Representatives *impeached* President Andrew Johnson for high crimes and misdemeanors>.

accustomed see USUAL.

acerbity see ACRIMONY.

achieve 1. see PERFORM. **2.** see REACH *vb*.

achievement see FEAT.

acknowledge, admit, own, avow, confess mean to disclose against one's will or inclination.

Acknowledge implies the disclosing of something that has been or might be concealed <*acknowledged* a lie>. ***ant*** deny

Admit stresses reluctance to disclose, grant, or concede and refers usually to facts rather than their implications <*admitted* that the project was over budget>. ***ant*** gainsay, disclaim.

Own implies acknowledging something in close relation to oneself <must *own* that I know little about computers>. ***ant*** disown, repudiate

Avow implies boldly declaring what one might be expected to be silent about <*avowed* hostility toward his parents>. ***ant*** disavow

Confess may apply to an admission of a weakness, failure, omission, or guilt <*confessed* that she had a weakness for sweets>. ***ant*** renounce *(one's beliefs, principles)*

acme see SUMMIT.

acquaint see INFORM.

acquiesce see ASSENT.

acquire see GET.

acquirement, acquisition, attainment, accomplishment mean a power or skill won through exertion or effort.

Acquirement suggests the result of continued endeavor to cultivate oneself <an appreciation of good music was not one of his *acquirements*>.

Acquisition stresses the effort involved and the inherent value of what is gained <the ability to concentrate is a valuable *acquisition*>.

Attainment implies a distinguished achievement (in the arts or sciences) and suggests fully developed talents <honored as woman of the year for her many *attainments*>.

Accomplishment implies a socially useful skill <mastery of a foreign language is an admirable *accomplishment*>.

acquisition see ACQUIREMENT.

acquisitive see COVETOUS.

acquit 1. see BEHAVE. **2.** see EXCULPATE.

acrid see CAUSTIC.

acrimony, acerbity, asperity mean temper or language marked by irritation, anger, or resentment.

Acrimony implies feelings of bitterness and a stinging verbal attack <a campaign marked by verbal exchanges of intense *acrimony*>. ***ant*** suavity

Acerbity suggests sourness as well as bitterness and applies especially to mood or temperament <an inbred *acerbity* that pervades even his personal letters>. ***ant*** mellowness

Asperity suggests quickness of temper and sharpness of resentment, usually without bitterness <told him with some *asperity* to mind his own business>. ***ant*** amenity

action see BATTLE.

activate see VITALIZE.

actual see REAL.

actuate see MOVE.

acumen see DISCERNMENT.

acute 1. see SHARP.

2. Acute, critical, crucial mean full of uncertainty as to outcome.

Acute stresses intensification of conditions leading to a culmination or breaking point <the housing shortage is becoming *acute*>.

Critical adds to *acute* implications of imminent change, of attendant suspense, and of decisiveness in the outcome <the war has entered a *critical* phase>.

Crucial suggests a dividing of the ways and often implies a test or trial involving the determination of a future course or direction <for the campaign, the coming weeks will be *crucial*>.

adamant see INFLEXIBLE.

adapt, adjust, accommodate, conform, reconcile mean to bring one thing into correspondence with another.

Adapt implies a ready modification to changing circumstances <they *adapted* themselves to the warmer climate>.

Adjust suggests bringing into a close and exact correspondence or harmony as exists between the parts of a mechanism, often by the use of tact or ingenuity <*adjusted* the budget to allow for inflation>.

Accommodate may suggest yielding or compromising in order to achieve a correspondence <*accommodated* his political beliefs to those of the majority>. ***ant*** constrain

Conform applies to bringing into harmony or accordance with a pattern, example, or principle <refused to *conform* to society's idea of woman's proper role>.

Reconcile implies the demonstration of the underlying consistency or congruity of things that seem to be incompatible <tried to *reconcile* what they said with what I knew>.

adaptable see PLASTIC.

additive see CUMULATIVE.

address see TACT.

adduce see CITE.

adept see PROFICIENT.

adequate see SUFFICIENT.

adhere see STICK.

adherence, adhesion mean a sticking to or together.

Adherence suggests a mental or moral attachment <*adherence* to the principles of reform>. ***ant*** nonadherence

Adhesion implies a physical attachment <the *adhesion* of paint to a surface>.

adherent see FOLLOWER.

adhesion see ADHERENCE.

adjacent, adjoining, contiguous, abutting, tangent, conterminous, juxtaposed mean being in close proximity.

Adjacent may or may not imply contact but always implies absence of anything of the same kind in between <the price of the house and the *adjacent* garage>. ***ant*** nonadjacent

Adjoining definitely implies meeting and touching at some point or line <assigned *adjoining* rooms at the hotel>. ***ant*** detached, disjoined

Contiguous implies having contact on all or most of one side <offices in all 48 *contiguous* states>.

Abutting stresses the termination of one thing along a line of contact with another <land *abutting* on the road>.

Tangent implies contact at a single point <a line *tangent* to a curve>.

Conterminous applies to objects bordering on each other <crossing the *conterminous* border of France and Germany> or having the same bounds, limits, or ends <the several *conterminous* civil and ecclesiastical parishes of England>.

Juxtaposed means placed side by side esp. so as to permit comparison and contrast <an ultramodern office building *juxtaposed* to a Gothic church>.

adjoining see ADJACENT.

adjourn, prorogue, dissolve mean to terminate the activities of (as a legislature or meeting).

Adjourn implies suspension until an appointed time or indefinitely <*adjourn* a meeting>. ***ant*** convene, convoke

Prorogue applies especially to action of the British crown or its representative by which a parliament is adjourned <the king's hasty decision to *prorogue* the parliamentary session>.

Dissolve implies permanency and suggests that the body ceases to exist as presently constituted so that an election must be held in order to reconstitute it <the president's decision *dissolved* the committee>.

adjure see BEG.

adjust see ADAPT.

administer see EXECUTE.

admire see REGARD.

admission see ADMITTANCE.
admit 1. see ACKNOWLEDGE. **2.** see RECEIVE.
admittance, admission mean permitted entrance.
Admittance is usually applied to mere physical entrance to a locality or a building <members must show their cards upon *admittance* to the club>.
Admission applies to entrance or formal acceptance (as into a club) that carries with it rights, privileges, standing, or membership <candidates for *admission* must submit recommendations from two club members>.
admixture see MIXTURE.
admonish see REPROVE.
ado see STIR.
adopt, embrace, espouse mean to take an opinion, policy, or practice as one's own.
Adopt implies accepting something created by another or foreign to one's nature <forced to *adopt* the procedures of the new parent company>. ***ant*** repudiate, discard
Embrace implies a ready or happy acceptance <eagerly *embraced* the ways and customs of their new homeland>. ***ant*** spurn
Espouse adds an implication of close attachment to a cause and a sharing of its fortunes <spent her lifetime *espousing* equal rights for women>.
adore see REVERE.
adorn, decorate, ornament, embellish, beautify, deck, bedeck, garnish mean to enhance the appearance of something by adding something unessential.
Adorn implies an enhancing by something beautiful in itself <a diamond necklace *adorned* her neck>. ***ant*** disfigure
Decorate suggests the addition of color or interest to what is dull or monotonous <*decorate* a birthday cake with colored frosting>.
Ornament implies the adding of something extraneous to heighten or set off the original <a white house *ornamented* with green shutters>.
Embellish often stresses the adding of a superfluous or adventitious element <*embellish* a page with floral borders>.
Beautify suggests a counteracting of a plainness or ugliness <will *beautify* the park with flower beds>. ***ant*** uglify
Deck and ***bedeck*** imply the addition of something that contributes to gaiety, splendor, or showiness <a house all *decked* out for the holidays> <*bedecked* with garlands>.
Garnish suggests decorating with a small final touch and is used especially in referring to the serving of food <airline food invariably *garnished* with parsley>.
adroit 1. see CLEVER. **2.** see DEXTEROUS.

adult see MATURE.

adultery, fornication, incest mean illicit sexual intercourse.

Adultery implies unfaithfulness to one's spouse and therefore can be applied only to sexual intercourse between a married person and a partner other than his or her wife or husband <listed *adultery* as grounds for divorce>.

Fornication designates sexual intercourse on the part of an unmarried person <religious laws strictly forbidding *fornication*>.

Incest refers to sexual intercourse between persons proscribed from marrying on the basis of kinship ties <*incest* involving father and daughter is the most common>.

advance 1. Advance, promote, forward, further mean to help (someone or something) to move ahead.

Advance stresses effective assistance in hastening a process or bringing about a desired end <a gesture intended to *advance* the cause of peace>. ***ant*** retard, check

Promote suggests an open encouraging or fostering <a company trying to *promote* better health among employees> and may denote an increase in status or rank <a student *promoted* to third grade>. ***ant*** demote

Forward implies an impetus or moral force moving something ahead <a wage increase would *forward* productivity>. ***ant*** hinder, balk

Further suggests a removing of obstacles in the way of a desired advance <used the marriage to *further* his career>. ***ant*** hinder, retard

2. see CITE.

advanced see LIBERAL 2.

advantageous see BENEFICIAL.

advent see ARRIVAL.

adventitious see ACCIDENTAL 2.

adventurous, venturesome, daring, daredevil, rash, reckless, foolhardy mean exposing oneself to danger more than dictated by good sense.

Adventurous implies a willingness to accept risks but not necessarily imprudence <*adventurous* pioneers opened the West>. ***ant*** unadventurous, cautious

Venturesome Implies a jaunty eagerness for perilous undertakings <*venturesome* pilots became popular heroes>.

Daring heightens the implication of fearlessness or boldness in courting danger <mountain climbing attracts the *daring* types>.

Daredevil stresses ostentation in daring <*daredevil* motorcyclists performing stunts>.

Rash suggests imprudence, haste, and lack of forethought <a *rash* decision that you will regret later>. ***ant*** calculating

Reckless implies heedlessness of probable consequences <a *reckless* driver who endangers others>. ***ant*** calculating

Foolhardy suggests a recklessness that is inconsistent with good sense <only a *foolhardy* sailor would venture into this storm>. ***ant*** wary

adversary see OPPONENT.

adverse, antagonistic, counter, counteractive mean so opposed as to cause often harmful interference.

Adverse applies to what is unfavorable, harmful, or detrimental <very sensitive to *adverse* criticism>. ***ant*** propitious

Antagonistic usually implies mutual opposition and either hostility or incompatibility <neighboring countries were *antagonistic* to the new nation>. ***ant*** favoring, favorable

Counter applies to forces coming from opposite directions with resulting conflict or tension <the *counter* demands of family and career>.

Counteractive implies an opposition between two things that nullifies the effect of one or both <poor eating habits will have a *counteractive* effect on any gains from exercise>.

adversity see MISFORTUNE.

advert see REFER 3.

advertise see DECLARE.

advice, counsel mean a recommendation as to a decision or a course of conduct.

Advice implies real or pretended knowledge or experience, often professional or technical, on the part of the one who advises <a book of *advice* for would-be entrepreneurs>.

Counsel often stresses the fruit of wisdom or deliberation and may presuppose a weightier occasion, or more authority, or more personal concern on the part of the one giving counsel <the benefit of a father's *counsel*>.

advisable see EXPEDIENT.

advise see CONFER.

advocate *vb* see SUPPORT.

advocate *n* see LAWYER.

affable see GRACIOUS.

affair 1. Affair, business, concern, matter, thing mean in general terms something done or dealt with.

Affair suggests action or performance and may imply a process, an operation, a proceeding, an undertaking, or a transaction <the resounding success of the whole *affair*>.

Business stresses duty or office and implies an imposed task <concern for quality is everybody's *business*>.

Concern suggests personal or direct relationship to something that has bearing on one's welfare, success, or interests <viewed the issue as of no *concern* to them>.

Matter generally refers to something being considered or being dealt with <the one remaining *matter* in dispute>.

Thing is often used when there is a desire to be vague or inexplicit <a promise to see the *thing* through>.

2. see AMOUR.

affect 1. Affect, influence, touch, impress, strike, sway mean to produce or have an effect upon.

Affect implies the action of a stimulus that can produce a response or reaction <the sight *affected* him deeply>.

Influence implies a force that brings about a change (as in nature or behavior) <our beliefs are *influenced* by our upbringing> <a drug that *influences* growth rates>.

Touch may carry a vivid suggestion of close contact and may connote stirring, arousing, or harming <plants *touched* by frost> <his emotions were *touched* by her distress>.

Impress stresses the depth and persistence of the effect <only one of the plans *impressed* him>.

Strike may convey the notion of sudden sharp perception or appreciation <*struck* by the solemnity of the occasion>.

Sway implies the acting of influences that are not resisted or are irresistible, with resulting change in character or course of action <politicians who are *swayed* by popular opinion>.

2. see ASSUME.

affectation see POSE.

affecting see MOVING.

affection see FEELING.

affiliated see RELATED.

affinity 1. see ATTRACTION. **2.** see LIKENESS.

affirm see ASSERT.

affix see FASTEN.

afflict, try, torment, torture, rack mean to inflict on a person something that is hard to bear.

Afflict applies to the causing of any pain or suffering or of acute annoyance, embarrassment, or any distress <many aged persons who are *afflicted* with blindness>. ***ant*** comfort

Try suggests an imposing of something that strains the powers of endurance or self-control <young children often *try* their parent's patience>.

Torment suggests persecution or the repeated inflicting of suffering or annoyance <the horses are *tormented* by flies>.

Torture implies the unbearable pain or suffering <*tortured* his captive by withholding food>.

Rack stresses straining or wrenching <a mind *racked* by guilt>.

affluent see RICH.

afford see GIVE.

affront see OFFEND.

afraid see FEARFUL.
age *n* see PERIOD.
age *vb* see MATURE *vb.*
agent see MEAN *n* 2.
aggravate **1.** see INTENSIFY. **2.** see IRRITATE.
aggregate see SUM.
aggression see ATTACK *n* 2.
aggressive, militant, assertive, self-assertive, pushing, pushy mean obtrusively energetic especially in pursuing particular goals.

Aggressive implies a disposition to dominate often in disregard of others' rights or in determined and energetic pursuit of one's ends <*aggressive* and successful in the business world>.

Militant suggests not self-seeking but devotion to a cause, movement, or principle <*militant* environmentalists staged a protest>.

Assertive suggests bold self-confidence in expression of opinion <*assertive* speakers dominated the open forum>. ***ant*** retiring, acquiescent

Self-assertive connotes forwardness or brash self-confidence <a *self-assertive* young executive climbing the corporate ladder>.

Pushing and ***pushy*** may apply to ambition or enterprise or to snobbish and crude intrusiveness or officiousness <*pushing* salespeople using high-pressure tactics> <*pushy* people breaking into the line for tickets>.

aggrieve see WRONG.
agile, nimble, brisk, spry mean acting or moving with easy quickness.

Agile implies dexterity and ease in physical or mental actions <*agile* at answering questions on a variety of issues>. ***ant*** torpid

Nimble stresses lightness and swiftness of action or thought <a *nimble* tennis player>.

Brisk suggests liveliness, animation, or vigor of movement sometimes with a suggestion of hurry <a *brisk* cleaning-up before the relatives arrived>. ***ant*** sluggish

Spry stresses an ability for quick action that is unexpected because of age or known infirmity <*spry* older players beating younger opponents>. ***ant*** doddering

agitate **1.** see DISCOMPOSE. **2.** see SHAKE.
agony see DISTRESS.
agree **1. Agree, concur, coincide** mean to come into or be in harmony regarding a matter of opinion.

Agree implies complete accord usually attained by discussion and adjustment of differences <on some points we all can *agree*>. ***ant*** differ, disagree

Concur tends to suggest cooperative thinking or acting toward an end but sometimes implies no more than approval (as of a decision reached by others) <members of the committee *concurred* with his decision>. ***ant*** contend, altercate

Coincide used more often of opinions, judgments, wishes, or interests than of people, implies an agreement amounting to identity <their wishes *coincide* exactly with my desire>.

2. see ASSENT.

3. Agree, tally, square, conform, accord, comport, harmonize, correspond, jibe mean to go or exist together without conflict or incongruity.

Agree applies to any precise going, existing, or fitting together <the conclusion *agrees* with the evidence>. ***ant*** differ *(from)*

Tally implies an agreement between two correct accounts that match not only in overall conclusions but detail by detail <your story *tallies* with earlier accounts>.

Square suggests a precise or mathematically exact agreement <force facts to *square* with theory>.

Conform implies a fundamental likeness in form, nature, or essential quality <*conform* to local customs>. ***ant*** diverge

Accord implies perfect fitness in a relation or association (as in character, spirit, quality, or tone) <the speaker's remarks did not *accord* with the sentiments of his listeners>. ***ant*** conflict

Comport, like *accord,* stresses the fitness or suitability of a relationship <acts that *comport* with ideals>.

Harmonize stresses the blending of dissimilar things to form a congruous or pleasing whole <*harmonize* the conflicting colors through the use of blue>. ***ant*** clash, conflict

Correspond stresses the way in which dissimilar elements match, complement, or answer to each other <fulfillment seldom *corresponds* to anticipation>.

Jibe may sometimes be closely equivalent to *agree,* sometimes to *harmonize,* and sometimes to *accord* <his actions do not *jibe* with his words>.

agreeable see PLEASANT.

aid *vb* see HELP.

aid *n* see ASSISTANT.

aide see ASSISTANT.

aide-de-camp see ASSISTANT.

ail see TROUBLE.

aim see INTENTION.

air *vb* see EXPRESS.

air *n* **1. Air, atmosphere, ether, ozone** mean the invisible mixture of gases which surrounds the earth.

Air refers to the impalpable breathable substance essential to life <the *air* we breathe> or that substance mixed with others <smoggy *air*>.

Atmosphere suggests the gaseous layers surrounding the earth or another celestial body <the poisonous *atmosphere* of Venus> or the air which fills a particular place or is in a particular state <the room's stagnant *atmosphere*>.

Ether implies a more rarefied or more delicate or subtle medium which was formerly said to fill the upper regions or interstellar space <gods who dwelled in the *ether*> and is used technically to denote a hypothetical medium in space suitable for the transmission of transverse waves <broadcast into the *ether* in hopes someone would hear>.

Ozone denotes generally air that is notably pure and refreshing <the vivifying *ozone* of a thunderstorm>.

2. see POSE.

3. see MELODY.

airs see POSE.

akin see SIMILAR.

alacrity see CELERITY.

alarm see FEAR.

albeit see THOUGH.

alert 1. see INTELLIGENT. **2.** see WATCHFUL.

alibi see APOLOGY.

alien see EXTRINSIC.

alienate see ESTRANGE.

align see LINE.

alike see SIMILAR.

alive 1. see AWARE. **2.** see LIVING.

all see WHOLE.

all-around see VERSATILE.

allay see RELIEVE.

allege see CITE.

allegiance see FIDELITY.

alleviate see RELIEVE.

alliance, league, coalition, confederation, federation mean an association to further the common interests of its members.

Alliance applies to an association formed for the mutual benefit of its members <an *alliance* between feminist and religious groups against pornography>.

League suggests a more formal compact often with a definite goal <the *League* of Nations> and may be used to suggest association for a bad end <in *league* with the devil>.

Coalition applies to a temporary association of parties often of opposing interests <formed a *coalition* government with two other parties>.

Confederation applies to a union of independent states under a central government to which powers dealing with common external relations are delegated <the *confederation* formed by the American colonies>.

Federation implies any union under the terms of a league or covenant, and specifically a sovereign power formed by a union of states and having a central government and several state and local governments <the United States of America constitutes a *federation*>.

allied see RELATED.

allocate see ALLOT.

allot, assign, apportion, allocate mean to give as a share, portion, role, or lot.

Allot implies haphazard or arbitrary distribution with no suggestion of fairness or equality <each child was *alloted* a portion of pie>.

Assign stresses an authoritative and fixed allotment but carries no clear implication of an even division <each employee is *assigned* a parking space>.

Apportion implies a dividing according to some principle of equal or proportionate distribution <profits were *apportioned* according to a predetermined ratio>.

Allocate suggests a fixed appropriation of money, property, territory, or powers to a person or group for a particular use <*allocated* $50,000 for park improvements>.

allow see LET.

allowance see RATION.

allude see REFER.

allure see ATTRACT 2.

ally see PARTNER.

almost see NEARLY.

alone, solitary, lonely, lonesome, lone, forlorn, desolate mean isolated from others.

Alone suggests the objective fact of being by oneself with a slight notion of emotional involvement <happier when left *alone* occasionally>. ***ant*** accompanied

Solitary may indicate isolation as a chosen course <glorying in the calm of her *solitary* life> but more often it suggests sadness and a sense of loss <left *solitary* by the death of his wife>.

Lonely adds a suggestion of longing for companionship <felt *lonely* and forsaken>.

Lonesome heightens the suggestion of the sadness and poignancy of separation <an only child sometimes leads a *lonesome* life>.

Lone may replace *lonely* or *lonesome* but typically is as objective as *alone* <a *lone* robin pecking at the lawn>.

Forlorn stresses dejection, woe, and listlessness at separation from someone or something dear <a child lost and *forlorn*>.

Desolate implies inconsolable grief at isolation caused by loss or bereavement <her brother's death now left her completely *desolate*>.

aloof see INDIFFERENT.
alter see CHANGE.
altercation see QUARREL.
alternate *adj* see INTERMITTENT.
alternate *vb* see ROTATE.
alternative see CHOICE ***n.***
although see THOUGH.
altitude see HEIGHT.
amalgam see MIXTURE.
amalgamate see MIX.
amateur, dilettante, dabbler, tyro mean a person who follows a pursuit without attaining proficiency or professional status.

Amateur often applies to one practicing an art without mastery of its essentials <a painting obviously done by an *amateur*>, and in sports it may also suggest not so much lack of skill but avoidance of direct remuneration <must remain an *amateur* in order to qualify for the Olympics>. ***ant*** expert, professional

Dilettante may apply to the lover of an art rather than its skilled practitioner but usually implies elegant trifling in the arts and an absence of serious commitment <a serious art teacher with no patience for *dilettantes*>.

Dabbler suggests a lack of serious purpose, desultory habits of work, and lack of persistence <a *dabbler* who never finished a single novel>.

Tyro implies inexperience and the attendant incompetence often combined with audacity resulting in crudeness or blundering <a *tyro* who has yet to master the basics of playwriting>.

amaze see SURPRISE 2.
ambiguity, equivocation, tergiversation, double entendre mean an expression capable of more than one interpretation.

Ambiguity usually refers to the use of a word or phrase in such a way that it may be taken in either of two senses <the *ambiguity* in the directive's wording caused much confusion>. ***ant*** lucidity, explicitness

Equivocation suggests that the ambiguity is intentional and the intent is to mislead <a report on the nuclear accident filled with *equivocations*>. ***ant*** explicitness

Tergiversation stresses the shifting of senses during the course of one's argument and usually suggests evasion or looseness of thought and intentional subterfuge <a thesis that relies on several *tergiversations* of the word "society">.

Double entendre refers to a word or expression allowing two interpretations, one of them being a cover for a subtle, indelicate, or risqué implication <the *double entendres* rife in any bedroom farce>.

ambiguous see OBSCURE.

ambition, aspiration, pretension mean strong desire for advancement or success.

Ambition applies to the desire for personal advancement or preferment and may suggest equally a praiseworthy or an inordinate desire <driven by the *ambition* to be very rich>.

Aspiration implies a striving after something higher than oneself and usually implies that the striver is thereby ennobled or uplifted <an *aspiration* to become President someday>.

Pretension suggests ardent desire for recognition of accomplishment without actual possession of the necessary ability or qualifications and therefore implies presumption or folly <people with literary *pretensions* frequenting her salon>.

amble see SAUNTER.

ambush see SURPRISE 1.

ameliorate see IMPROVE.

amenable **1.** see OBEDIENT. **2.** see RESPONSIBLE.

amend see CORRECT.

amerce see PENALIZE.

amiable, good-natured, obliging, complaisant mean having the desire or disposition to please.

Amiable implies having qualities that make one liked and easy to deal with <a travel club that attracts *amiable* types>. ***ant*** unamiable

Good-natured implies a cheerful willingness to please or to be helpful and sometimes to permit imposition <a *good-natured* boy always willing to pitch in>. ***ant*** contrary

Obliging stresses a friendly readiness to be helpful or to accommodate to the wishes of others <our *obliging* innkeeper granted our request>. ***ant*** disobliging, inconsiderate

Complaisant often implies passivity or a weakly amiable willingness to yield to others through a desire to please or to be agreeable <*complaisant* people who only say what others want to hear>. ***ant*** contrary, perverse

amicable, neighborly, friendly mean exhibiting goodwill and an absence of antagonism.

Amicable implies a state of peace and a desire on the part of the parties not to quarrel <maintained *amicable* relations even after the divorce>. ***ant*** antagonistic

Neighborly implies a disposition to live on good terms with others in necessary proximity and to be helpful and kindly on principle <prompted by *neighborly* concern to inquire about her health>. ***ant*** unneighborly, ill-disposed

Friendly stresses cordiality and often warmth or intimacy of personal relations <sought his *friendly* advice on this important matter>. ***ant*** unfriendly, belligerent

amnesty see PARDON.

amoral see IMMORAL.
amount see SUM.
amour, liaison, intrigue, affair mean an instance of illicit sexual relationship.
Amour stresses passion as the motivating force and often connotes transcience <went from one *amour* to another>.
Liaison implies duration but not necessarily permanence of the attachment <known for her *liaison* with a powerful senator>.
Intrigue emphasizes the clandestine element in the relationship <frequently drawn to complicated *intrigues*>.
Affair is the least specific term and suggests something equivocal rather than definitely illicit about the relationship <had a series of *affairs* after his divorce>.
ample 1. see PLENTIFUL. **2.** see SPACIOUS.
amplify see EXPAND.
amulet see FETISH.
amuse, divert, entertain mean to pass or cause to pass the time pleasantly.
Amuse suggests that the attention is engaged lightly or frivolously <*amuse* yourselves while I prepare dinner>. ***ant*** bore
Divert implies the distracting of the attention from worry or duty especially by something different, often something light <tired businessmen looking for a comedy to *divert* them>.
Entertain suggests supplying amusement or diversion by specially prepared or contrived methods <comedians and pretty girls to *entertain* the troops>.
analgesic see ANODYNE 1.
analogous see SIMILAR.
analogue see PARALLEL.
analogy see LIKENESS.
analytic *or* **analytical** see LOGICAL.
analyze, resolve, dissect, break down mean to divide a complex whole into its parts or elements.
Analyze suggests separating or distinguishing the component parts of something (as a substance, a process, or a situation) so as to discover its true nature or inner relationships <*analyzed* the current problem of trade imbalances to discover its basis>. ***ant*** compose, compound, construct
Resolve often suggests only the separation or division into elements or parts <matter *resolved* by the microscope into distinct cells> or its change of form or metamorphosis <hatred *resolved* by suffering into tenderness>. ***ant*** blend
Dissect suggests a searching analysis by laying bare parts or pieces for individual scrutiny <commentators *dissected* every word of the President's statement>.
Break down implies a methodical reducing of a complex whole

to simpler parts or divisions <*break down* the budget to see where the money is going>.

anathema see ABOMINATION.

anathematize see EXECRATE.

anatomy see STRUCTURE.

ancient see OLD.

anesthetic see ANODYNE 1.

anecdote see STORY.

anemic see PALE 2.

anger, ire, rage, fury, indignation, wrath mean emotional excitement induced by intense displeasure.

Anger, the most general term, names the emotional reaction but in itself conveys nothing about intensity or justification or manifestation of the state <tried to hide his *anger* at their behavior>. ***ant*** pleasure, gratification, forbearance

Ire, more frequent in literary contexts, may suggest greater intensity than anger, often with a display of feeling <cheeks flushed dark with *ire*>.

Rage suggests loss of self-control from violence of emotion often with an outward display <screaming with *rage*>.

Fury implies overmastering destructive rage verging on madness <in her *fury* she hurled abuse in all directions>.

Indignation stresses righteous anger at what one considers unfair, mean, outrageous, or shameful <high-handed behavior that caused general *indignation*>.

Wrath is likely to suggest rage or indignation accompanied by a desire or intent to avenge or punish <rose in his *wrath* and struck his tormentor to the floor>.

angle see PHASE.

anguish see SORROW.

animadvert see REMARK.

animal see CARNAL.

animate *adj* see LIVING.

animate *vb* see QUICKEN.

animated 1. see LIVELY. **2.** see LIVING.

animosity see ENMITY.

animus see ENMITY.

annals see HISTORY.

annihilate see ABOLISH.

announce see DECLARE.

annoy 1. Annoy, vex, irk, bother mean to upset a person's composure.

Annoy implies a wearing on the nerves by persistent and often petty unpleasantness <his constant complaining *annoys* us>. ***ant*** soothe

Vex implies greater provocation and stronger disturbance and usually connotes anger but sometimes perplexity or anxiety <a problem that *vexes* cancer researchers>. ***ant*** please, regale

Irk stresses difficulty in enduring and the resulting weariness or impatience <his chronic tardiness *irks* his colleagues>.

Bother suggests bewildering or upsetting interference with comfort or peace of mind <that discrepancy *bothers* me>. ***ant*** comfort

2. see WORRY.

annul see NULLIFY.

anodyne 1. Anodyne, analgesic, anesthetic mean something used to relieve or prevent pain.

Anodyne may be applied to any agent used primarily to relieve pain whether by dulling the perception of pain or by altering the situation and has a literary rather than a medical connotation <took a long, hard walk as an *anodyne* for disappointment>.

Analgesic applies especially to a medicinal preparation used locally or systematically to dull the sensation of pain <used liniment as an *analgesic* for stiff joints>. ***ant*** irritant

Anesthetic implies a medicinal agent that causes insensibility to pain and other sensations either locally or generally <given an *anesthetic* by the dentist before her tooth was pulled>. ***ant*** stimulant

2. Anodyne, opiate, narcotic, nepenthe mean something used to dull or deaden the senses or sensibilities.

Anodyne usually suggests something that soothes or calms often by inducing forgetfulness or oblivion <the *anodyne* of religious fervor>. ***ant*** stimulant, irritant

Opiate implies a substance that causes a dream state and a delusion of happiness and suggests an indifference and false sense of security or well-being <price supports that were an *opiate* for distressed industries>.

Narcotic applies to something that literally or figuratively produces sleep, stupor, or lulling drowsiness <beautiful music used as a *narcotic* to escape from the pressures of work>.

Nepenthe connotes something sweet and pleasurable that is substituted for something painful <the *nepenthe* of rest after a hard day's work>.

anomalous see IRREGULAR.

answer 1. Answer, respond, reply, rejoin, retort mean to say, write, or do something in return.

Answer implies the satisfying of a question, demand, call, or need <*answered* all the questions on the form>.

Respond may suggest a willing or spontaneous and often quick reaction <chose not to *respond* to that comment>.

Reply implies making a return commensurate with the original question or demand <an invitation that requires you to *reply* at once>.

Rejoin often implies sharpness or pointedness in answering <she *rejoined* quickly to his criticism>.

Retort suggests responding to an explicit charge or criticism by way of retaliation <he *retorted* to her every charge with biting sarcasm>.

2. see SATISFY 3.

answerable see RESPONSIBLE.

antagonism see ENMITY.

antagonist see OPPONENT.

antagonistic see ADVERSE.

antagonize see OPPOSE.

antecedent *n* see CAUSE.

antecedent *adj* see PRECEDING.

antediluvian see OLD.

anterior see PRECEDING.

anticipate 1. see FORESEE. **2.** see PREVENT.

anticipation see PROSPECT.

antipathy see ENMITY.

antiquated see OLD.

antique see OLD.

antisocial see UNSOCIAL.

antithetical see OPPOSITE.

anxiety see CARE.

anxious see EAGER.

apathetic see IMPASSIVE.

ape see COPY.

aperture, interstice, orifice mean an opening that allows passage through or in and out.

Aperture applies to an opening in an otherwise closed or solid surface or structure <light entered through an *aperture* in the castle wall>.

Interstice implies an unfilled space or break in a continuous substance or fabric, especially in something loosely woven, coarse-grained, piled, or layered <moss growing in the *interstices* of an old stone wall.

Orifice suggests an opening that functions as a mouth or vent <the *orifice* of the bladder>.

apex see SUMMIT.

aplomb see CONFIDENCE.

apocryphal see FICTITIOUS.

apologia see APOLOGY.

apology, apologia, excuse, plea, pretext, alibi mean matter offered in explanation or defense.

Apology usually applies to an expression of regret for a mistake or wrong with implied admission of guilt or fault and with or without reference to extenuating circumstances <said by way of *apology* that he would have met them if he could>.

Apologia, and sometimes *apology,* implies not admission of guilt or regret but a desire to make clear the grounds for some course, belief, or position <the speech was an effective *apologia* for his foreign policy>.

Excuse implies an intent to avoid or remove blame or censure <used his illness as an *excuse* for missing the meeting>.

Plea stresses argument or appeal for understanding or sympathy or mercy <her usual *plea* that she was nearsighted>.

Pretext suggests subterfuge and the offering of false reasons or motives in excuse or explanation <used any *pretext* to get out of work>.

Alibi implies a desire to shift blame or evade punishment and imputes plausibility rather than truth to the explanation offered <his *alibi* failed to withstand scrutiny>.

appall see DISMAY.

appalling see FEARFUL 2.

apparent 1. Apparent, illusory, seeming, ostensible mean not actually being what appearance indicates.

Apparent suggests appearance to unaided senses that is not or may not be proven by more rigorous examination or greater knowledge <the *apparent* cause of the train wreck>. ***ant*** real

Illusory implies a false impression based on deceptive resemblance or faulty observation, or influenced by emotions that prevent a clear view <the *illusory* happiness of a new infatuation>. ***ant*** factual, matter-of-fact

Seeming implies a character in the thing observed that gives it the appearance, sometimes through intent, of something else <the *seeming* simplicity of the story>.

Ostensible suggests a discrepancy between an openly declared or logically implied aim or reason and the true one <business was the *ostensible* reason for their visit>.

2. see EVIDENT.

appear see SEEM.

appease see PACIFY.

apperception see RECOGNITION.

appetizing see PALATABLE.

appliance see IMPLEMENT.

applicable see RELEVANT.

apply 1. see USE *vb.* **2.** see RESORT.

appoint see FURNISH.

apportion see ALLOT.

apposite see RELEVANT.

appraise see ESTIMATE.

appreciable see PERCEPTIBLE.

appreciate 1. Appreciate, value, prize, treasure, cherish mean to hold in high estimation.
Appreciate often connotes understanding sufficient to allow enjoyment or admiration of a thing's excellence <*appreciates* fine wine>. ***ant*** despise
Value implies rating a thing highly for its intrinsic worth <*values* our friendship>.
Prize implies taking a deep pride in or setting great store by something one possesses <all people *prize* their freedom>.
Treasure emphasizes jealously safeguarding something considered precious <*treasured* mementos of her youth>.
Cherish implies a special love and care for an object of attachment <*cherishes* her children above all>. ***ant*** neglect
2. see UNDERSTAND.

apprehend see FORESEE.

apprehension, foreboding, misgiving, presentiment mean a feeling that something undesirable will or is about to happen.
Apprehension implies a mind preoccupied with fear and anxiety <approached the dangerous undertaking with great *apprehension*>. ***ant*** confidence
Foreboding suggests fear that is oppressive, unreasoning, or indefinable <the deserted streets filled me with strange *forebodings*>.
Misgiving suggests uneasiness and mistrust <had my *misgivings* about her from the start>.
Presentiment implies a vague or uncanny sense that something, often unpleasant, is bound to happen <a *presentiment* that some of our group would not survive>.

apprehensive see FEARFUL 1.

apprentice see NOVICE.

apprise see INFORM.

approach see MATCH.

appropriate *vb* **Appropriate, preempt, arrogate, usurp, confiscate** mean to seize high-handedly.
Appropriate suggests making something one's own or converting to one's own use without authority or with questionable right <just *appropriated* the tools meant to be shared by all>.
Preempt implies beforehandedness in taking something desired or needed by others <news of the crisis *preempted* much of the regular programming>.
Arrogate implies insolence, presumption, and exclusion of others in seizing rights, powers, or functions <White House staffers *arrogated* powers belonging to cabinet members>. ***ant*** renounce, yield
Usurp implies unlawful or unwarranted intrusion into the place of another and seizure of what is his by custom, right, or law

<her new stepmother had *usurped* her place in the household>. ***ant*** abdicate

Confiscate always implies seizure through exercise of authority <customs officers *confiscate* all contraband>.

appropriate *adj* see FIT *adj.*

approve, endorse, sanction, accredit, certify mean to have or express a favorable opinion of or about someone or something.

Approve implies commendation or agreement and may suggest a judicious attitude <the parents *approve* of the marriage>. ***ant*** disapprove

Endorse suggests an explicit statement of support <publicly *endorsed* her for Senator>.

Sanction implies both approval and authorization and may suggest the providing of a standard <the President *sanctioned* covert operations>. ***ant*** interdict

Accredit and ***certify*** usually imply official endorsement attesting conformity to set standards <the board voted to *accredit* the college> <must be *certified* to teach>.

approximately see NEARLY.

apropos see RELEVANT.

apt 1. see FIT *adj.* **2.** see QUICK.

aptitude see GIFT.

arbitrary see ABSOLUTE.

archaic see OLD.

arcane see MYSTERIOUS.

arch see SAUCY.

ardent see IMPASSIONED.

ardor see PASSION.

arduous see HARD.

argot see DIALECT.

argue see DISCUSS.

arid see DRY.

arise 1. see SPRING. **2.** see RISE 2.

aristocracy 1. see OLIGARCHY.

2. Aristocracy, nobility, gentry, elite, society mean a body of people constituting a socially superior caste.

Aristocracy usually refers to those persons of superior birth, breeding, and social station <plantation families constituted the *aristocracy* of the antebellum South> or to an ideally superior caste without reference to a definite group <the *aristocracy* of intellectuals>. ***ant*** people, proletariat

Nobility refers to persons of a privileged and titled class that ranks just below royalty <the duke ranks highest in British *nobility*>.

Gentry refers to a class of leisured, well-bred persons who are considered gentlefolk but are without hereditary titles <a private school favored by generations of the *gentry*>.

Elite refers to the members of any group or class who are judged highest by social or cultural standards <acknowledged to be among the *elite* few of the artistic set>. ***ant*** rabble

Society refers to that class of people who are celebrated for their active social life, conspicuous leisure, and fashionable sports and clothes <the famed lavish balls of Newport *society*>.

arm see FURNISH.

aroma see SMELL.

aromatic see ODOROUS.

arouse see STIR.

arrange 1. see NEGOTIATE. **2.** see ORDER.

arrant see OUTRIGHT.

array see LINE.

arrival, advent mean the reaching of a destination.

Arrival emphasizes the preceding travel or movement <an *arrival* delayed by fog and ice>. ***ant*** departure

Advent applies to a momentous or conspicuous arrival or an appearance upon a scene especially for the first time <the *advent* of a new age in space travel>. ***ant*** exit

arrogant see PROUD.

arrogate see APPROPRIATE *vb*.

art, skill, cunning, artifice, craft mean the faculty of executing expertly what one has planned or devised.

Art distinctively implies a personal, unanalyzable creative power <an *art* for saying the right thing>.

Skill stresses technical knowledge and proficiency <the *skills* required of a surgeon>.

Cunning suggests ingenuity and subtlety in devising, inventing, or executing <a mystery thriller written with great *cunning*>.

Artifice suggests mechanical skill especially in imitating things in nature but implies a lack of real creative power and a degree of artificiality <a painter with much of the *artifice* of Rubens and none of the art>.

Craft may imply ingenuity and skill but tends to suggest expertness in workmanship and facility in the use of tools <a saltcellar wrought with *craft* worthy of Cellini>.

artful see SLY.

article see THING.

articulate see VOCAL 1, 2.

articulation see JOINT.

artifice 1. see ART. **2.** see TRICK.

artificial, factitious, synthetic, ersatz mean brought into being not by nature but by human art or effort.

Artificial is applicable to anything that is not the result of natural processes or conditions <the state is an *artificial* society> but especially to something that has a counterpart in nature or imitates something natural <*artificial* teeth>. ***ant*** natural

Factitious applies chiefly to emotions or states of mind not naturally caused or spontaneously aroused but artfully produced to serve some end <created a *factitious* demand for the product>. ***ant*** bonafide, veritable

Synthetic applies especially to a manufactured substance or to a natural substance so treated that it acquires the appearance or qualities of another and may substitute for it <*synthetic* furs>.

Ersatz often implies the use of an inferior substitute for a natural product <served *ersatz* cream with the coffee>. ***ant*** genuine

artless see NATURAL.

ascend 1. Ascend, mount, climb, scale mean to move upward or toward a summit.

Ascend implies progressive upward movement <the car *ascended* the steep grade>. ***ant*** descend

Mount suggests a getting up upon something raised <*mount* a horse>. ***ant*** dismount

Climb connotes the effort involved in upward movement and is used when difficulty is implicit in the situation <*climb* a tree to rescue a cat>. ***ant*** descend

Scale suggests skill and adroitness in upward movement <*scale* a high wall to freedom>.

2. see RISE.

ascendancy see SUPREMACY.

ascertain see DISCOVER.

ascetic see SEVERE.

ascribe, attribute, assign, impute, credit, charge mean to lay something to the account of a person or thing.

Ascribe suggests an inferring or conjecturing of a cause, quality, or authorship not outwardly apparent <none of the frivolity commonly *ascribed* to teenagers>.

Attribute may suggest the plausibility and appropriateness of the indicated relation <*attribute* the project's failure to poor planning>.

Assign implies ascribing with certainty or after deliberation <an investigatory panel *assigned* blame to top officials>.

Impute suggests ascribing something that brings discredit by way of accusation or blame <tried to *impute* sinister motives to my actions>.

Credit implies ascribing a thing or especially an action to a person or other thing as its agent, source, or explanation <*credited* his insecurities to an unhappy childhood>.

Charge implies a fixing upon a person or thing of the responsibility for a fault, crime, or evil <*charged* with the crime of murder>.

ashen see PALE 1.
ashy see PALE 1.
asinine see SIMPLE.
ask 1. Ask, question, interrogate, query, inquire mean to address a person in order to acquire information.
Ask implies no more than the putting of a question <*ask* for directions>.
Question usually suggests the asking of a series of questions <*questioned* them about every detail of the trip>. ***ant*** answer
Interrogate suggests formal or official systematic questioning <the prosecutor *interrogated* the witness all day>.
Query implies a desire for authoritative information or confirmation <*queried* the reference librarian about the book>.
Inquire implies a searching for facts or for truth often specifically by asking questions <began to *inquire* into the charges of espionage>.
2. Ask, request, solicit mean to seek to obtain by making one's wants known.
Ask implies no more than the statement of the desire <*ask* a favor of a friend>.
Request implies greater formality and courtesy <*requests* the pleasure of your company at the ball>.
Solicit suggests a calling attention to one's wants or desires, often publicly, in the hope of having them satisfied <a classified ad that *solicits* a situation as a babysitter>.
asocial see UNSOCIAL.
aspect see PHASE.
asperity see ACRIMONY.
asperse see MALIGN *vb*.
asphyxiate see SUFFOCATE.
aspiration see AMBITION.
assail see ATTACK *vb*.
assassinate see KILL.
assault *n* see ATTACK *n* 1.
assault *vb* see ATTACK *vb*.
assemble see GATHER 1.
assent, consent, accede, acquiesce, agree, subscribe mean to concur with what has been proposed.
Assent implies an act involving the understanding or judgment and applies to propositions or opinions <potential members must *assent* to the organization's credo>. ***ant*** dissent
Consent involves the will or feelings and indicates compliance with what is requested or desired <*consented* to their daughter's wish to go on the trip>. ***ant*** dissent
Accede implies a yielding, often under pressure, of assent or concession <officials *acceded* to every demand of the prisoners>. ***ant*** demur

Acquiesce implies tacit acceptance or forbearance of opposition <usually *acquiesces* to his wife's wishes>. ***ant*** object

Agree sometimes implies previous difference of opinion or attempts at persuasion, negotiation, or discussion <finally *agreed* to give him a raise>. ***ant*** protest (*against*), differ (*with*)

Subscribe implies not only consent or assent but hearty approval and willingness to go on record <totally *subscribed* to the free enterprise system>. ***ant*** boggle

assert 1. Assert, declare, affirm, protest, avow mean to state positively usually in anticipation or in the face of denial or objection.

Assert implies stating confidently or even brashly without need for proof or regard for evidence <*asserted* that modern music is just noise>. ***ant*** deny, controvert

Declare stresses the making of an open or public statement <the jury *declared* the defendant guilty>.

Affirm implies conviction and willingness to stand by one's statement because of evidence, experience, or faith <*affirmed* the existence of an afterlife>. ***ant*** deny

Protest stresses affirmation, especially in the face of denial or doubt <*protested* that he had never had a more splendid meal>.

Avow stresses frank declaration and acknowledgment of personal responsibility for what is declared <*avowed* that all investors would be repaid in full>.

2. see MAINTAIN.

assertive see AGGRESSIVE.

assess see ESTIMATE.

assiduous see BUSY.

assign 1. see ALLOT. **2.** see ASCRIBE. **3.** see PRESCRIBE.

assignment see TASK.

assimilate see ABSORB.

assimilation see RECOGNITION.

assist see HELP.

assistant, helper, coadjutor, aid, aide, aide-de-camp mean a person who takes over part of the duties of another, especially in a subordinate capacity.

Assistant applies to such a person, regardless of the status of the work <a carpenter's *assistant*>.

Helper often implies apprenticeship in a trade or status as an unskilled laborer <a mother's *helper* who performs the duties of a nursemaid>.

Coadjutor implies equality except in authority and may be used of a coworker or a volunteer <viewed the librarian as *coadjutor* of her researches>.

Aid and ***aide*** are often interchangeable <a nurse's *aid*> <a

teacher's *aide*>, but *aide* frequently and *aid* rarely denotes a special, highly qualified assistant who acts as an advisor <the President and his chief *aides* formulating domestic policy>.

Aide and ***aide-de-camp*** designate specifically a military officer who personally attends a general, a sovereign, a president, or a governor, often as an escort but sometimes with definite duties <instructed his *aide-de-camp* to keep the press away>.

associate see JOIN.

assorted see MISCELLANEOUS.

assuage see RELIEVE.

assume 1. Assume, affect, pretend, simulate, feign, counterfeit, sham mean to put on a false or deceptive appearance.

Assume often implies a justifiable motive rather than an intent to deceive <*assumed* an air of cheerfulness for the sake of the patient>.

Affect implies making a false show of possessing, using, or feeling something, usually for effect <willing to *affect* an interest in art in order to impress her>.

Pretend implies an overt and sustained false profession of what is <*pretended* not to know about her husband's affair>.

Simulate suggests an assumption of the characteristics of something else by a close imitation <the training chamber *simulates* a weightless atmosphere>.

Feign implies more artful invention than *pretend,* less specific imitation than *simulate* <*feigned* sickness in order to stay home from school>.

Counterfeit implies imitation that achieves an extremely high degree of verisimilitude <*counterfeited* drunkenness so perfectly that many forgot he was acting>.

Sham stresses an obvious intent to deceive with falseness that fools only the gullible <*shammed* a most unconvincing limp>.

2. see PRESUPPOSE.

assurance 1. see CERTAINTY. **2.** see CONFIDENCE.

assure see ENSURE.

astonish see SURPRISE 2.

astound see SURPRISE 2.

astute see SHREWD.

asylum see SHELTER.

athirst see EAGER.

athletics, sports, games mean physical activities engaged in for exercise or play.

Athletics is a collective term applied to exercises for which one acquires and maintains agility, skill, and stamina usually in order to compete as an individual or a member of a team <played amateur and professional *athletics*>.

Sports implies forms of physical activity that give pleasure or diversion, and sometimes lacks the connotation of vigorous skill, training, and competition <finds more opportunity for *sports* in the summer>.

Games suggests athletic or sports contests that require extensive rules <the intricate rules of *games* that use a ball or puck> or denotes a meet held for competition chiefly in track-and-field events <winners from the Pan-American and Pan-African *games*>.

atmosphere **1.** see AIR.

2. Atmosphere, feeling, aura mean an intangible quality that gives something an individual and distinctly recognizable character.

Atmosphere implies a quality that accrues to something or that pervades it as a whole and that determines the impression given by that thing <a country inn with a warm and friendly *atmosphere*>.

Feeling implies that something has distinctive qualities that create a definite if unanalyzable impression <a garden with a definite country *feeling*>.

Aura suggests an ethereal or mysterious quality that seems to emanate from a person or thing <a movie queen with an unmistakable *aura* of glamour>.

atom see PARTICLE.

atrocious see OUTRAGEOUS.

attach see FASTEN.

attack *n* **1. Attack, assault, onslaught, onset** mean an attempt to injure, destroy, or defame.

Attack, whether on person or character, suggests animosity or enmity as its cause but may imply such motives as cruelty, partisanship, or criticism <a speech *attacking* governmental policies>.

Assault implies more violence and malice or viciousness and often the infliction of greater damage than *attack,* sometimes with specific legal or military connotations <a victim of a brutal *assault*>.

Onslaught suggests a vigorous, destructive attempt to overwhelm by force of momentum or numbers or intensity <succumbed to the *onslaught* of the disease>.

Onset applies both to the initial attack and to any successive renewal of vigor in the attack <troops preparing for a fresh *onset* from the enemy>.

2. Attack, aggression, offense, offensive mean action in a struggle for supremacy, either military or athletic, which must be defended against.

Attack implies the initiation of action, often sudden and violent <sustained running *attack* resulting in an early touchdown>.

Aggression stresses a lack of provocation and a desire for conquest or domination, chiefly by military invasion of another's territory <pledged never to fight a war of *aggression*>. ***ant*** resistance

Offense characterizes the position or methods of the attackers with specific reference to their desire for supremacy <went on the *offense* to gain as much ground as possible>.

Offensive implies vigorously aggressive action, especially in war, or it denotes a particular episode marked by such action <launched an economic *offensive* to stave off a recession>.

3. see FIT *n.*

attack *vb* **Attack, assault, assail, bombard, storm** mean to make a more or less violent onset upon.

Attack implies aggressively taking the initiative in a struggle <seek new ways to *attack* the problem of poverty>.

Assail implies attempting to conquer or break down resistance by repeated blows or shots <*assailed* the enemy with artillery fire>.

Assault suggests a direct attempt to overpower by suddenness and violence of onslaught in a direct confrontation <commando troops *assaulted* the building from all sides>.

Bombard applies to attacking continuously and devastatingly with bombs or shells <*bombarded* the city nightly>.

Storm implies an attempt to sweep from its path every obstacle to victory <a fortress that has never been *stormed*>.

attain see REACH.

attainment see ACQUIREMENT.

attempt, try, endeavor, essay, strive mean to make an effort to accomplish an end.

Attempt stresses the initiation or beginning of an effort and often suggests the strong possibility of failure <will *attempt* to photograph the rare bird>.

Try stresses effort or experiment made to test or prove something <*tried* several times to find a solution>.

Endeavor heightens the implications of exertion and difficulty and connotes a striving to fulfill a duty <*endeavored* to find survivors of the crash>.

Essay implies difficulty but also suggests tentative trying or experimenting <had *essayed* dramatic roles on two earlier occasions>.

Strive implies exertion against great difficulty and specifically suggests persistent effort <continues to *strive* for a lasting peaceful solution>.

attend 1. see ACCOMPANY. **2.** see TEND.

attentive see THOUGHTFUL 2.

attest see CERTIFY.

attitude see POSITION 1.

attorney see LAWYER.

attract, allure, charm, captivate, fascinate, bewitch, enchant mean to draw another by exerting an irresistible or powerful influence.

Attract applies to any degree or kind of ability to exert influence to draw <a university that *attracts* students from around the world>. ***ant*** repel

Allure implies an enticing by what is fair, pleasing, or seductive <the excitement of the city *allures* young people>. ***ant*** repel

Charm may suggest magic and implies a power to evoke or attract admiration <*charmed* by the beauty of that serene isle>. ***ant*** disgust

Captivate implies an often transitory capturing of the fancy or feelings <her grace and beauty *captivated* us all>. ***ant*** repulse

Fascinate suggests a magical influence and tends to stress the ineffectiveness of attempts to resist or escape <a story that continues to *fascinate* children>.

Bewitch implies exertion of an overwhelming power of attraction <*bewitched* by the promise of great wealth>.

Enchant stresses the power to evoke delight or joy or ecstatic admiration in the one affected <hopelessly *enchanted* by his dashing looks and deep voice>. ***ant*** disenchant

attraction, affinity, sympathy mean the relationship existing between things or persons that are naturally or involuntarily drawn together.

Attraction implies the possession by one thing of a quality that tends to draw another to it <a curious *attraction* between people of opposite temperaments>.

Affinity implies a susceptibility or predisposition on the part of the one attracted <a student with an *affinity* for mathematics>.

Sympathy implies a reciprocal relation between two things that are both susceptible to the same influence <shared a glance of mutual *sympathy*>. ***ant*** antipathy

attribute *vb* see ASCRIBE.

attribute *n* **1.** see QUALITY. **2.** see SYMBOL.

atypical see ABNORMAL.

audacity see TEMERITY.

augment see INCREASE.

aura see ATMOSPHERE.

auspicious see FAVORABLE.

austere see SEVERE.

authentic, genuine, veritable, bona fide mean being actually and exactly what is claimed.

Authentic implies being fully trustworthy as according with fact or actuality <the *authentic* story>. ***ant*** spurious

Genuine implies accordance with an original or a type without counterfeiting, admixture, or adulteration <*genuine* maple syrup>, or it may stress sincerity <*genuine* piety>. ***ant*** counterfeit, fraudulent

Veritable implies a correspondence with truth and typically conveys a suggestion of affirmation <in the grip of anxiety that drove him into a *veritable* trance> or asserts the suitability of a metaphor <*veritable* hail of questions>. ***ant*** factitious

Bona fide can apply when sincerity of intention is in question <*bona fide* sale of securities>. ***ant*** counterfeit, bogus

authenticate see CONFIRM.

author see MAKER.

authority **1.** see INFLUENCE. **2.** see POWER 3.

autocratic see ABSOLUTE.

automatic see SPONTANEOUS.

autonomous see FREE *adj.*

avaricious see COVETOUS.

avenge, revenge mean to punish a person who has wronged oneself or another.

Avenge suggests that the ends of justice are being served or another is being vindicated or a merited punishment is being administered <*avenged* the insult to his honor>.

Revenge implies a desire to retaliate or get even and therefore connotes states of malice, spite, or unwillingness to forgive <angry determination to *revenge* herself for the slight>.

average, mean, median, norm mean something that represents a middle point between extremes.

Average is exactly or approximately the quotient obtained by dividing the sum total of a set of figures by the number of figures <scored an *average* of 85 in a series of five tests>. ***ant*** maximum, minimum

Mean may be an average, or it may represent value midway between two extremes <annual temperature *mean* of 50°> <the tranquil *mean* between misery and ecstasy>.

Median applies to the value that represents the point at which there are as many instances above as there are below <the *average* of a group of persons earning 3, 4, 5, 8, and 10 dollars a day is 6 dollars, whereas the *median* is 5 dollars>.

Norm denotes the computed or estimated average of performance of a significantly large group, class, or grade and implies a standard of reference <scores about the *norm* for 5th grade arithmetic>.

averse see DISINCLINED.

avert see PREVENT 2.

avid see EAGER.

avoid see ESCAPE.

avow **1.** see ACKNOWLEDGE. **2.** see ASSERT.

await see EXPECT.
awake see AWARE.
awaken see STIR *vb.*
award see GRANT.
aware, cognizant, conscious, sensible, alive, awake mean having knowledge of something.

Aware implies vigilance in observing or alertness in drawing inferences from what is observed <*aware* of a greater number of police officers out and about>. ***ant*** unaware

Cognizant implies possession of special or certain knowledge as from firsthand sources <as yet, not fully *cognizant* of all the facts>. ***ant*** ignorant

Conscious implies that one is focusing one's attention on something already perceptible to the mind or senses <*conscious* that my heart was pounding away>. ***ant*** unconscious

Sensible implies direct or intuitive perception especially of intangibles or of emotional states or qualities <a doctor who was *sensible* of the woman's deep depression>. ***ant*** insensible (*of* or *to*)

Alive suggests vivid awareness of or acute sensitivity to something <we were fully *alive* to the momentousness of the occasion>. ***ant*** blind (*to*)

Awake implies that one has become alive to something and is on the alert < a country not *awake* to the dangers of persistent inflation>.

awe see REVERENCE.
awful see FEARFUL 2.
awkward, clumsy, maladroit, inept, gauche mean not marked by ease and smoothness (as of performance or movement).

Awkward is widely applicable and may suggest unhandiness, inconvenience, lack of control, embarrassment, or lack of tact <a dinner party marked by periods of *awkward* silence>. ***ant*** handy, deft, graceful

Clumsy implies stiffness and heaviness and so may connote inflexibility, unwieldiness, ponderousness, or lack of ordinary skill <a writer with a persistently *clumsy* style>. ***ant*** dexterous, adroit, facile

Maladroit suggests a deficiency of tact and a tendency to create awkward situations <a *maladroit* handling of a delicate situation>. ***ant*** adroit

Inept often implies inappropriateness, futility, and absurdity <blamed the conviction on his *inept* defense attorney>. ***ant*** apt, adept, able

Gauche implies the effects of shyness, inexperience, or ill breeding <always felt *gauche* and unsophisticated at formal parties>.

B

babel see DIN.
baby see INDULGE.
back 1. see RECEDE. **2.** see SUPPORT.
backbone see FORTITUDE.
background, setting, environment, milieu, mise-en-scène mean the place, time, and circumstances in which something occurs.

Background refers to those aspects of a stage or picture most remote from the viewer and against or in front of which the actions or figures are set <city streets visible in the *background*> and by extension often refers to the circumstances or events that precede a phenomenon or development <a *background* that prepared her well for the task>.

Setting describes the time, place, and conditions in which the characters act in a piece of literature, art, or drama <chose a 19th-century *setting* for her novel> and suggests that one is looking at a real-life situation as though it were a dramatic or literary representation <a social reformer who was born into the most unlikely social *setting*>.

Environment applies to all the external factors that have a formative influence on one's physical, mental, or moral development <the kind of *environment* that produces juvenile delinquents>.

Milieu applies especially to the physical and social surroundings of a person or group of persons <an intellectual *milieu* conducive to bold experimentation in the arts>.

Mise-en-scène strongly suggests the use of properties to achieve a particular atmosphere or theatrical effect <a tale of the occult with a carefully crafted *mise-en-scène*>.

backslide see LAPSE *vb*.
bad, evil, ill, wicked, naughty mean not morally good or ethically acceptable.

Bad may apply to any degree or kind of reprehensibility <the *bad* guys in a Western>. ***ant*** good

Evil is a stronger term than *bad* and usually carries a baleful or sinister connotation <*evil* men who would even commit murder>. ***ant*** exemplary, salutary

Ill may imply malevolence or vice <paid dearly for his *ill* deeds>. ***ant*** good

Wicked usually connotes malice and malevolence <a *wicked* person who delighted in the suffering of others>.

Naughty applies either to trivial misdeeds or to matters impolite or amusingly risqué <looked up all the *naughty* words in the dictionary>.

badger see BAIT.

baffle see FRUSTRATE.

bag see CATCH.

bait, badger, heckle, hector, chivy, hound mean to harass persistently or annoyingly by efforts to break down.

Bait implies wanton cruelty or delight in persecuting a helpless victim <siblings *baited* each other constantly>.

Badger implies pestering so as to drive a person to confusion or frenzy <*badgered* her father for a raise in her allowance>.

Heckle implies persistent interruptive questioning of a speaker in order to confuse or discomfit <drunks *heckled* the stand-up comic>.

Hector carries an implication of bullying, scolding, and domineering that breaks the spirit <as a child he had been *hectored* by his father>.

Chivy suggests persecution by teasing or nagging <*chivied* her husband to the breaking point>.

Hound implies unrelenting pursuit and persecution <*hounded* on all sides by creditors>.

balance *vb* see COMPENSATE.

balance *n* see SYMMETRY.

bald see BARE.

baleful see SINISTER.

balk see FRUSTRATE.

balky see CONTRARY.

balmy 1. see SOFT. **2.** see ODOROUS.

ban see FORBID.

banal see INSIPID.

bane see POISON.

baneful see PERNICIOUS.

banish, exile, deport, transport mean to remove by authority or force from a state or country.

Banish implies compulsory removal from a country not necessarily one's own <a country that once *banished* the Jesuits>.

Exile may imply compulsory removal or an enforced or voluntary absence from one's own country <a writer who *exiled* himself from South Africa>.

Deport implies a sending out of a country, often back to his or her country of origin, an alien who has illegally entered or whose presence is judged inimical to the public welfare <*deported* many foreign criminals>.

Transport implies a sending of a convicted criminal to a particular place, often an overseas penal colony <a convict who was *transported* to Australia>.

bank see RELY.

bankrupt see DEPLETE.

barbarian, barbaric, barbarous, savage mean characteristic of uncivilized people.

Barbarian often implies a state midway between tribal savagery and full civilization <traded with *barbarian* peoples to the north>. ***ant*** civilized

Barbaric tends to imply a wild profusion and lack of restraint that is indicative of crudity of taste and lack of self-restraint <punished the animal with *barbaric* cruelty>. ***ant*** restrained, refined, subdued

Barbarous is more likely to imply uncivilized cruelty or ruthlessness or sometimes complete lack of cultivated taste and refinement <outlawed the *barbarous* practices of war>. ***ant*** civilized, humane

Savage in its basic use implies less advance toward civilization than *barbarian* <a *savage* tribe with a gathering economy> and in its extended use is ordinarily very close to *barbarous* <a *savage* attack>. ***ant*** civilized

barbaric see BARBARIAN.

barbarous 1. see BARBARIAN. **2.** see FIERCE.

bare, naked, nude, bald, barren mean deprived of naturally or conventionally appropriate covering.

Bare implies the absence of what is additional, superfluous, ornamental, or dispensable <a bleak apartment with *bare* walls>. ***ant*** covered

Naked suggests complete absence of protective or ornamental covering but may imply a state of nature, of destitution, of defenselessness, or of simple beauty <poor, half-*naked* children shivering in the cold>.

Nude applies especially to the unclothed human figure <a *nude* model posing for art students>. ***ant*** clothed

Bald implies actual or seeming absence of natural covering and may suggest a severe plainness or lack of adornment <a *bald* mountain peak>.

Barren often suggests aridity or impoverishment or sterility through absence of natural or appropriate covering <*barren* plains with few shrubs and no trees>.

barefaced see SHAMELESS.

barren 1. see BARE. **2.** see STERILE.

barrister see LAWYER.

base *n* **Base, basis, foundation, ground, groundwork** mean something on which another thing is built up and by which it is supported.

Base implies an underlying element that supports or seems to support something material or immaterial <the *base* of a column>. ***ant*** top

Basis, similar in meaning, is rarely used of material things and usually carries a more definite implication of support <used those facts as the *basis* of her argument>.

Foundation tends to imply solidity in what underlies and supports and fixity or stability in what is supported <the beliefs rested on a *foundation* of firm conviction>. ***ant*** superstructure

Ground suggests solidity and is likely to imply a substratum comparable to the earth in its capacity to support and sometimes to justify <behavior that was *ground* for dismissal>.

Groundwork can apply to a substructure but is used chiefly in a figurative sense <laid the *groundwork* for future negotiations>. ***ant*** superstructure

base *adj* **Base, low, vile** mean deserving of contempt because beneath what is expected of the average person.

Base stresses the ignoble and may suggest cruelty, treachery, greed, or grossness <real estate developers with *base* motives>. ***ant*** noble

Low may connote crafty cunning, vulgarity, or immorality and regularly implies an outraging of one's sense of decency or propriety <refused to listen to such *low* talk>.

Vile, the strongest of these words, tends to suggest disgusting depravity or foulness <a *vile* remark> <the *vilest* of crimes>.

bashful see SHY.

basis see BASE.

bathos see PATHOS.

batter see MAIM.

battle, engagement, action mean a meeting, often military, between opposing forces.

Battle describes general and prolonged combat or can imply a major extended struggle or controversy <fighting a losing *battle* for basic civility>.

Engagement stresses actual combat between forces and may apply to a major battle or a minor skirmish; in extended uses it tends to replace the suggestion of hostility with one of interaction <sought to create an *engagement* between students and teachers>.

Action stresses the active give-and-take of offensive and defensive efforts or of attaining an end or resisting a pressure <sounded the call to *action* on behalf of environmentalists>.

bear 1. see CARRY.

2. Bear, suffer, endure, abide, tolerate, brook, stand mean to put up with something trying or painful.

Bear usually implies the power to sustain what is distressing or hurtful without flinching or breaking <forced to *bear* one personal tragedy after another>.

Suffer often suggests acceptance or passivity rather than courage or patience in bearing <never *suffered* a single insult to go unchallenged>.

Endure implies meeting trials and difficulties with continued firm resolution <*endured* years of rejection and neglect>.

Abide suggests acceptance without resistance or protest <I cannot *abide* her chronic rudeness>.

Tolerate suggests overcoming or successfully controlling an impulse to resist, avoid, or resent something injurious or distasteful <*tolerated* his affairs for the sake of the children>.

Brook implies self-assertion and defiance <will not *brook* restraint>.

Stand emphasizes even more strongly the ability to bear without discomposure or flinching <she cannot *stand* teasing>.

bearing, deportment, demeanor, mien, manner, carriage mean the outward manifestation of personality or attitude.

Bearing is the most general of these words but now usually implies characteristic posture <a woman of regal *bearing*>.

Deportment suggests actions or behavior as formed by breeding or training in regard to the amenities of life <a child with atrocious *deportment*>.

Demeanor suggests one's attitude as expressed by behavior among others <the haughty *demeanor* of a head waiter>.

Mien refers both to bearing and demeanor often as indicative of mood <a *mien* of supreme self-satisfaction>.

Manner implies characteristic or customary way of moving and gesturing in a social context <the imperious *manner* of a man used to giving orders>.

Carriage applies chiefly to habitual posture in standing or walking <the kind of *carriage* learned at elite private schools>.

beat see CONQUER.

beautiful, lovely, handsome, pretty, comely, fair mean sensuously or aesthetically pleasing.

Beautiful applies to whatever excites the keenest of pleasure to the senses and stirs intellectual or spiritual emotion <*beautiful* mountain scenery>. ***ant*** ugly

Lovely applies to a narrower range of emotional excitation rather than to intellectual or spiritual pleasure <a *lovely* melody>. ***ant*** unlovely, plain

Handsome suggests aesthetic pleasure resulting from proportion, symmetry, or elegance <a *handsome* Georgian mansion>.

Pretty applies to superficial or insubstantial attractiveness that pleases by its delicacy, grace, or charm <a painter of conventionally *pretty* scenes>.

Comely is like *handsome* in suggesting cool approval rather than emotional response <the *comely* grace of a dancer>. ***ant*** homely

Fair suggests beauty based on purity, flawlessness, or freshness <looking for fashion models with *fair* faces>. ***ant*** foul, ill-favored

beautify see ADORN.

bedeck see ADORN.

beg, entreat, beseech, implore, supplicate, adjure, importune mean to ask or request urgently.

Beg suggests earnestness or insistence especially in asking for a favor <children *begging* to stay up later>.

Entreat implies an effort to persuade or to overcome resistance in another <*entreated* him to change his mind>.

Beseech implies eagerness, anxiety, or solicitude <I *beseech* you to have mercy>.

Implore adds a suggestion of greater urgency or anguished appeal <*implored* her not to leave him>.

Supplicate suggests a posture of humility <with bowed heads they *supplicated* their lord>.

Adjure implies advising as well as pleading and suggests the involving of something sacred <in God's name I *adjure* you to cease>.

Importune suggests an annoying persistence in trying to break down resistance to a request <*importuned* his mother nearly every day to buy him a new bike>.

begin, commence, start, initiate, inaugurate mean to take the first step in a course, process, or operation.

Begin is the most general and applies especially to less formal contexts <school *begins* at eight> <*began* to wash the dishes>. ***ant*** end

Commence suggests greater formality <let the games *commence*>. ***ant*** conclude

Start suggests a getting or setting into motion <the procession *started* out slowly>. ***ant*** stop

Initiate suggests the taking of a first step of a process or series <*initiated* the custom of annual gift giving>. ***ant*** consummate

Inaugurate implies a ceremonial beginning <the discovery of penicillin *inaugurated* a new medical age>.

beguile see DECEIVE.

behave, conduct, deport, comport, acquit mean to act or to cause or allow oneself to do something in a certain way.

Behave may apply to the meeting of a standard of what is proper or decorous <*behaved* very badly throughout the affair>. ***ant*** misbehave

Conduct implies action or behavior that shows one's capacity to control or direct oneself <*conducted* herself with unfailing good humor>. ***ant*** misconduct

Deport implies behaving in conformity with conventional rules of discipline or propriety <an ingenue who *deports* herself in the best tradition>.

Comport suggests conduct measured by what is expected or required of one in a certain class or position <*comported* themselves as the gentlemen they were>.

Acquit applies to action under stress that deserves praise or meets expectations <*acquitted* himself well in his first battle>.

behindhand see TARDY.

behold see SEE 1.

beholder see SPECTATOR.

belie see MISREPRESENT.

belief 1. Belief, faith, credence, credit mean an assent to the truth of something offered for acceptance.

Belief suggests mental acceptance but may or may not imply certitude in the believer <my *belief* that I had caught all the errors>. ***ant*** unbelief, disbelief

Faith always suggests certitude even where there is no evidence or proof <an unshakable *faith* in God>. ***ant*** doubt

Credence suggests intellectual assent without implying anything about the validity of the grounds for assent <a theory given little *credence* by scientists>.

Credit implies assent on grounds other than direct proof <give no *credit* to idle rumors>.

2. see OPINION.

believable see PLAUSIBLE.

believe see KNOW.

belittle see DECRY.

bellicose see BELLIGERENT.

belligerent, bellicose, pugnacious, combative, quarrelsome, contentious mean having an aggressive or truculent attitude.

Belligerent implies being actively at war or engaged in hostilities <*belligerent* nations respected the country's neutrality>. ***ant*** friendly

Bellicose suggests a disposition to fight <an intoxicated person in a *bellicose* mood>. ***ant*** pacific, amicable

Pugnacious suggests a disposition that takes pleasure in personal combat <a *pugnacious* student always getting into scraps>. ***ant*** pacific

Combative, like *pugnacious,* connotes readiness to fight on the basis of a genuine cause <assumed a *combative* stance under questioning>. ***ant*** pacifistic

Quarrelsome stresses an ill-natured readiness to fight without good cause <the stifling heat made us all *quarrelsome*>.

Contentious implies perverse and irritating fondness for arguing and quarreling <wearied by her *contentious* disposition>. ***ant*** peaceable

bemoan see DEPLORE.

bend see CURVE.

beneficial, advantageous, profitable mean bringing good or gain.

Beneficial implies especially promoting health or well-being <legislation that would be *beneficial* to the elderly>. ***ant*** harmful, detrimental

Advantageous stresses a choice or preference that brings superiority or greater success in attaining an end <took up a more *advantageous* position>. ***ant*** disadvantageous

Profitable implies the yielding of useful or lucrative returns <seeking *profitable* ways to use their time>. ***ant*** unprofitable

benign see KIND.
benignant see KIND.
bent see GIFT.
berate see SCOLD.
beseech see BEG.
bestow see GIVE.
bête noire see ABOMINATION.
betray see REVEAL.
better see IMPROVE.
bewail see DEPLORE.
bewilder see PUZZLE.
bewitch see ATTRACT.
bias *n* see PREDILECTION.
bias *vb* see INCLINE.
bid 1. see COMMAND. **2.** see INVITE.
big see LARGE.
billingsgate see ABUSE.
bind see TIE.
birthright see HERITAGE.
biting see INCISIVE.
bit see PARTICLE.
bizarre see FANTASTIC.
blamable see BLAMEWORTHY.
blame see CRITICIZE.

blameworthy, blamable, guilty, culpable mean deserving reproach or punishment.

Blameworthy and *blamable* acknowledge the censurable quality of the act or the agent but imply nothing about the degree of reprehensibility <conduct adjudged *blameworthy* by a military court> <an accident for which no one is *blamable*>. ***ant*** blameless

Guilty implies responsibility for or consciousness of crime, sin, or, at least, grave error or misdoing <the defendant was found *guilty*>. ***ant*** innocent

Culpable is weaker than *guilty* and is likely to connote malfeasance or errors of ignorance, omission, or negligence <a clear case of *culpable* neglect on the part of the landlord>.

blanch see WHITEN.
bland 1. see SOFT. **2.** see SUAVE.
blandish see COAX.
blank see EMPTY.
blasé see SOPHISTICATED.
blatant see VOCIFEROUS.
blaze, flame, flare, glare, glow mean a brightly burning light or fire or something suggesting this.

Blaze implies rapidity in kindling of material and the radiation of intense heat and light <the crackle and *blaze* of dry oak logs> <the angry *blaze* of her eyes>.

Flame suggests a darting tongue or tongues of fire <the *flames* rose above the burning building>.

Flare stresses a sudden rapid burst of fire or flame against a dark background (as of a dying fire) <the sudden *flare* of a match> and implies both suddenness and intensity <a *flare* of temper>.

Glare is likely to connote unendurable brilliance <the *glare* of a searchlight>.

Glow is more likely to suggest a temperate burning that yields light without flame or glare, or gentle warmth and radiance <the comforting *glow* of coals on the hearth>.

bleach see WHITEN.
bleak see DISMAL.
blemish, defect, flaw mean an imperfection that mars or damages.

Blemish suggests something that affects only the surface or appearance <fair skin completely devoid of *blemishes*>. ***ant*** immaculateness

Defect implies a lack, often hidden, of something that is essential to completeness or perfect functioning <the smoke detector failed because of a mechanical *defect*>.

Flaw suggests a small defect in continuity or cohesion that is likely to cause failure under stress <a *flaw* in a pane of glass>.

blench see RECOIL.
blend see MIXTURE.
blithe see MERRY.
block see HINDER.
bloodless see PALE 2.
bloody, sanguinary, sanguine, gory mean affected by or involving the shedding of blood.

Bloody is applied especially to things that are actually covered with blood or are made up of blood <*bloody* hands>.

Sanguinary applies especially to something attended by, or someone bent on, bloodshed <the Civil War was America's most *sanguinary* conflict>.

Sanguine is applied specifically to bleeding, bloodthirstiness, or the color of blood <one of the most *sanguine* of the Jacobean revenge tragedies>. ***ant*** bloodless

Gory suggests a profusion of blood and slaughter <exceptionally *gory*, even for a teenage horror movie>.

blot see STIGMA.

blot out see ERASE.

blowsy see SLATTERNLY.

bluff, blunt, brusque, curt, crusty, gruff mean abrupt and unceremonious in speech or manner.

Bluff connotes a good-natured outspokenness and unconventionality <a bartender with a *bluff* manner>. ***ant*** smooth, suave

Blunt suggests directness of expression in disregard of others' feelings <a *blunt* appraisal of the performance>. ***ant*** tactful, subtle

Brusque applies to an abrupt sharpness or ungraciousness <a *brusque* response to a civil question>. ***ant*** unctuous, bland

Curt implies disconcerting shortness or rude conciseness <a *curt* comment about the cause of the foul-up>. ***ant*** voluble

Crusty suggests a harsh or surly manner that may conceal an inner kindliness <a *crusty* exterior that conceals a heart of gold>.

Gruff suggests a hoarse or husky speech which may imply bad temper but more often implies embarrassment or shyness <puts on a *gruff* pose in front of strangers>.

blunder see ERROR.

blunt 1. see BLUFF. **2.** see DULL.

board see HARBOR.

boast, brag, vaunt, crow mean to express in speech pride in oneself or one's accomplishments.

Boast often suggests ostentation and exaggeration <ready to *boast* of every trivial success>, but it may imply proper and justifiable pride <the town *boasts* one of the best hospitals in the area>. ***ant*** depreciate

Brag suggests conceit, crudity, and artlessness in glorifying oneself <boys *bragging* to each other>. ***ant*** apologize

Vaunt usually connotes more pomp and bombast than *boast* and less crudity or naïveté than *brag* <used the occasion to *vaunt* the country's military might>.

Crow usually implies exultant boasting or blatant bragging <loved to *crow* about his triumphs>.

boat, vessel, ship, craft mean a floating structure designed to carry persons or goods over water.

Boat is sometimes applied generally to all such structures, but more specifically denotes a small, typically open structure operated by oars, paddles, poles, sails, or a motor <took the *boat* out without any paddles>.

Vessel suggests chiefly a large seagoing boat used to contain or

transport persons or commodities or to serve as a base of operations <a fleet of fishing *vessels*>.
Ship stresses the navigational aspect of a large seagoing vessel and has connotations of individuality and romance <the beauty of the great sailing *ships*>.
Craft applies to any boat or ship that plies the water and is often a vague or general term <small *craft* darting in all directions>.

bodily, physical, corporeal, corporal, somatic mean of or relating to the human body.
Bodily suggests contrast with *mental* or *spiritual* <an intellectual who had *bodily* needs>.
Physical suggests less explicitly an organic structure <their ordeal left them at the point of *physical* exhaustion>.
Corporeal suggests the substance of which the body is composed <a divinity who assumed *corporeal* existence>.
Corporal applies chiefly to things that affect or involve the body <a teacher who still used *corporal* punishment>.
Somatic implies contrast with *psychical* and is free of theological and poetic connotations <*somatic* reactions to the drug>.

boisterous see VOCIFEROUS.

bombard see ATTACK *vb*.

bombast, rhapsody, rant, fustian mean speech or writing characterized by high-flown pomposity or pretentiousness.
Bombast implies verbose grandiosity or inflation of style disproportionate to the thought <pedestrian ideas dressed up with *bombast*>.
Rhapsody applies to an ecstatic or effusive utterance governed more by the feelings than by logical thought and may specifically describe an excess of more or less incoherent praise <she went into *rhapsodies* over their new house>.
Rant stresses extravagance or violence in expressing something <the *rants* and ravings of political fanatics>.
Fustian stresses the banality of what is expressed <dimestore novels bursting with romantic *fustian*>.

bona fide see AUTHENTIC.

bondage see SERVITUDE.

bon vivant see EPICURE.

bookish see PEDANTIC.

boorish, churlish, loutish, clownish mean uncouth in manner or appearance.
Boorish implies rudeness of manner due to lack of culture, insensitiveness to others' feelings, or unwillingness to be agreeable <your *boorish* behavior at the wedding reception>. ***ant*** gentlemanly
Churlish suggests surliness, unresponsiveness, and ungra-

ciousness <*churlish* remarks made during a television interview>. ***ant*** courtly

Loutish implies bodily awkwardness together with crude stupidity <her *loutish* boyfriend spoiled the cocktail party>.

Clownish suggests ill-bred awkwardness, ignorance or stupidity, ungainliness, and often a propensity for absurd antics <*clownish* conduct that was out of keeping with the solemn occasion>. ***ant*** urbane

boost see LIFT.

bootleg see SMUGGLED.

bootless see FUTILE.

booty see SPOIL.

border, margin, verge, edge, rim, brim, brink mean a line or outer part that marks the limit of something.

Border refers to the part of a surface just within a boundary <the magazine cover's red *border*> or to the boundary itself <across international *borders*>.

Margin denotes a border or definite width or distinguishing character <a *margin* of one inch on the page's left side>.

Verge applies to the line marking an extreme limit or termination of something <an empire that extended to the *verge* of the known world>.

Edge denotes the line of termination made by two converging surfaces as of a blade or a box <the *edge* of a table>.

Rim applies to an edge of something circular or curving <the *rim* of a wagon wheel>.

Brim applies to the upper inner rim of something hollow <fill the cup to the *brim*>.

Brink denotes the edge of something that falls away steeply <walked to the *brink* of the cliff> and may imply abrupt transition <nations on the *brink* of peace>.

boredom see TEDIUM.

bother see ANNOY.

bough see SHOOT.

bountiful see LIBERAL 1.

bouquet see FRAGRANCE.

box see STRIKE 2.

brag see BOAST.

branch see SHOOT.

brand see STIGMA.

brandish see SWING 1.

brash see SHAMELESS.

brave, courageous, unafraid, fearless, intrepid, valiant, valorous, dauntless mean having or showing no fear when faced with something dangerous, difficult, or unknown.

Brave indicates lack of fear in alarming or difficult circumstances <a *brave* kitten hissing at the much bigger dog>. ***ant*** craven

Courageous implies temperamental stoutheartedness and readiness to meet danger or difficulties <*courageous* stance before the unruly crowd>. ***ant*** pusillanimous

Unafraid indicates simple lack of fright or fear <faced the future *unafraid*>. ***ant*** afraid

Fearless may indicate lack of fear or, more positively, undismayed resolution <took a *fearless* stance against powerful opponents>. ***ant*** fearful

Intrepid suggests daring in meeting danger or fortitude in enduring it <*intrepid* pioneers struggling westward>.

Valiant implies resolute courage and fortitude whether in facing danger or attaining some end <her *valiant* efforts to perfect her technique>. ***ant*** timid, dastardly

Valorous suggests illustrious accomplishments <the *valorous* deeds of King Arthur's knights>.

Dauntless emphasizes determination, resolution, and fearlessness <held their *dauntless* position to the end>. ***ant*** poltroon

brazen see SHAMELESS.

breach, infraction, violation, transgression, trespass, infringement mean the breaking of a law, duty, or obligation.

Breach implies failure to keep a promise <sued for *breach* of contract>. ***ant*** observance

Infraction usually implies the breaking of a law or obligation <an *infraction* of the school rules>. ***ant*** observance

Violation implies the flagrant disregard of the law or the rights of others and often suggests the exercise of force or violence <the police interference was a *violation* of the right to free assembly>.

Transgression, often with a moral connotation, applies to any act that goes beyond the limits prescribed by law, rule, or order <censured for repeated financial *transgressions*>.

Trespass implies an encroachment upon the rights, the comfort, or the property of others <a would-be burglar who was arrested for *trespass*>.

Infringement implies an encroachment upon a legally protected right or privilege <any unauthorized reproduction constitutes an *infringement* of the book's copyright>.

break down see ANALYZE.

bridle 1. see RESTRAIN. **2.** see STRUT.

brief, short mean lacking length.

Brief applies primarily to duration and may imply condensation, conciseness, or occasionally intensity <a *brief* speech>. ***ant*** prolonged, protracted

Short may imply sudden stoppage or incompleteness <the interview was rather *short*>. ***ant*** long

bright 1. Bright, brilliant, radiant, luminous, lustrous mean shining or glowing with light.

Bright implies emitting or reflecting a high degree of light <one of the *brightest* stars in the sky>. ***ant*** dull, dim

Brilliant implies intense often sparkling brightness <*brilliant* diamonds>. ***ant*** subdued

Radiant stresses the emission or seeming emission of rays of light <an imposing figure in *radiant* armor>.

Luminous implies emission of steady, suffused, glowing light by reflection or in surrounding darkness <*luminous* white houses dot the shore>.

Lustrous stresses an even, rich light from a surface that reflects brightly without sparkling or glittering <the *lustrous* sheen of fine satin>.

2. see INTELLIGENT.

brilliant 1. see BRIGHT. **2.** see INTELLIGENT.

brim see BORDER.

brink see BORDER.

brisk see AGILE.

bristle see STRUT.

brittle see FRAGILE.

broach see EXPRESS.

broad, wide, deep mean having horizontal extent.

Broad is preferred when full horizontal extent is considered <*broad* shoulders>. ***ant*** narrow

Wide is more common when units of measurement are mentioned <rugs eight feet *wide*> or applied to unfilled space between limits <a *wide* doorway>. ***ant*** strait

Deep may indicate horizontal extent away from the observer or from a front or peripheral point <a *deep* cupboard> <*deep* woods>. ***ant*** shallow

brook see BEAR.

browbeat see INTIMIDATE.

brusque see BLUFF.

bucolic see RURAL

bugbear see ABOMINATION.

build see PHYSIQUE.

bulge see PROJECTION.

bulk, mass, volume mean the aggregate that forms a body or unit.

Bulk implies an aggregate that is impressively large, heavy, or numerous <the darkened *bulks* of skyscrapers towered over him>.

Mass suggests an aggregate made by piling together things of the same kind <the cave held a *mass* of pottery>.

Volume applies to an aggregate without shape or outline and capable of flowing or fluctuating <a tremendous *volume* of water>.

bulldoze see INTIMIDATE.

bully see INTIMIDATE.

bunch see GROUP.

burdensome see ONEROUS.

burglary see THEFT.

burlesque see CARICATURE.

bury see HIDE.

business 1. Business, commerce, trade, industry, traffic mean activity concerned with the supplying and distribution of commodities.

Business may be an inclusive term but specifically designates the activities of those engaged in the purchase or sale of commodities or in related financial transactions <the *business* section of the newspaper>.

Commerce and ***trade*** imply the exchange and transportation of commodities especially on a large scale <full power to regulate interstate *commerce*> <seek ways to increase foreign *trade*>.

Industry applies to the producing of commodities, especially by manufacturing or processing <*industry* has overtaken agriculture in the South>.

Traffic applies to the operation and functioning of public carriers of goods and persons <*traffic* managers have rediscovered the railroads> or to the activities of those engaged in the exchange of commodities <*traffic* in contraband goods>.

2. see WORK 2.

3. see AFFAIR 1.

bustle see STIR *n.*

busy, industrious, diligent, assiduous, sedulous mean actively engaged or occupied.

Busy chiefly stresses activity as opposed to idleness or leisure <too *busy* to spend time with the children>. ***ant*** idle, unoccupied

Industrious implies characteristic or habitual devotion to work <they are by nature an *industrious* people>. ***ant*** slothful, indolent

Diligent suggests earnest application to some specific object or pursuit <very *diligent* in her pursuit of a degree>. ***ant*** dilatory

Assiduous stresses careful and unremitting application <mastered the piano only after *assiduous* practice>. ***ant*** desultory

Sedulous implies painstaking and persevering application <a *sedulous* reconstruction of the events of that night>.

butchery see MASSACRE.

butt in see INTRUDE.

bystander see SPECTATOR.

C

cabal see PLOT.
cadence see RHYTHM.
cajole see COAX.
calamity see DISASTER.
calculate, compute, estimate, reckon mean to determine something mathematically.
Calculate is usually preferred in reference to highly intricate and precise processes that produce a result not readily proven by physical confirmation <*calculated* when the comet would next appear>.
Compute is the term for reaching an exact result by simpler though often lengthy arithmetic processes <*computed* the interest at a quarterly rate>.
Estimate applies chiefly to the forecasting of costs or trends and suggests a seeking of usable but tentative and approximate results <the mechanic *estimated* the cost of repairs>.
Reckon usually suggests the simpler arithmetical processes or the use of methods such as can be carried in one's head <*reckoned* the number of yards of fabric needed>.
caliber see QUALITY 2.
call *vb* see SUMMON.
call *n* see VISIT.
calling see WORK 2.
callow see RUDE.
calm, tranquil, serene, placid, peaceful mean quiet and free from disturbance or harm.
Calm often implies a contrast with a foregoing or nearby state of agitation or violence <the protests ended, and the streets were *calm* again>. ***ant*** stormy, agitated
Tranquil suggests a deep quietude or composure <the *tranquil* beauty of a formal garden>. ***ant*** troubled
Serene stresses an unclouded and lofty tranquility <a woman of *serene* beauty>.
Placid suggests lack of excitement or agitation and an equable temper and may imply a degree of complacency <led a very *placid* existence>. ***ant*** choleric
Peaceful implies a state of repose often in contrast with or following strife or turmoil <a former firebrand grown *peaceful* in his old age>. ***ant*** turbulent.
calumniate see MALIGN.
cancel see ERASE.
cancer see TUMOR.
candid see FRANK.

canon see LAW.
cant see DIALECT.
canting see HYPOCRITICAL.
capable see ABLE.
capacious see SPACIOUS.
capitulate see YIELD.
capitulation see SURRENDER.
caprice, freak, whim, vagary, crotchet mean an irrational, fanciful, or impractical idea or desire.

Caprice stresses lack of apparent motivation and suggests willfulness <by sheer *caprice* she quit her job>.

Freak implies an impulsive change of mind made apparently without cause <struck by a *freak* notion>.

Whim implies a fantastic, humorous turn of mind or inclination <an odd antique that was bought on a *whim*>.

Vagary stresses the erratic, irresponsible, or extravagant character of the notion or desire <recently he had been prone to strange *vagaries* of taste>.

Crochet implies perversely eccentric opinion or preference especially on trivial matters <a serious scientist equally known for his bizarre *crotchets*>.

capricious see INCONSTANT.
captious see CRITICAL.
captivate see ATTRACT.
capture see CATCH.
cardinal see ESSENTIAL.
care, concern, solicitude, anxiety, worry mean a troubled or engrossed state of mind or the thing that causes this.

Care implies oppression of the mind by responsibility or apprehension <a face worn by a host of *cares*>.

Concern implies a troubled state of mind and the interest, relation, affection, or responsibility that produces it <your happiness is my only *concern*>. ***ant*** unconcern

Solicitude implies great concern or apprehension and connotes either thoughtful or hovering attentiveness <behaved with typical maternal *solicitude*>. ***ant*** neglectfulness, unmindfulness

Anxiety stresses anguished uncertainty or fear of misfortune or failure <plagued by *anxiety* and self-doubt>. ***ant*** security

Worry suggests prolonged fretting over matters that may or may not be real cause for anxiety <a businessman's endless list of *worries*>.

careful, meticulous, scrupulous, puntilious mean showing close attention to detail.

Careful implies great concern for persons or matters in one's charge and attentiveness and cautiousness in avoiding mistakes <a *careful* worker>. ***ant*** careless

Meticulous may imply either extreme carefulness or a finicky caution over small points <*meticulous* scholarship>.

Scrupulous applies to what is proper, fitting, or ethical <*scrupulous* honesty>. ***ant*** remiss

Punctilious implies minute, even excessive attention to fine points <*punctilious* observance of ritual>.

caress, fondle, pet, cuddle mean to show affection by touching or handling.

Caress implies expression of affection by gentle stroking or patting <the *caress* of a soft breeze>.

Fondle implies doting fondness and sometimes lack of dignity; it may suggest more intimacy and less gentleness than *caress* <*fondle* a baby>.

Pet applies to caressing or fondling children or animals <*pet* a cat> but may also apply to excessive indulgence <a spoiled *petted* child> or to amorous fondling in which it may suggest undue familiarity <decided not to *pet* with her boyfriend>.

Cuddle applies to a close but gentle embracing designed to soothe and comfort <*cuddle* a frightened puppy>.

caricature, burlesque, parody, travesty mean a comic or grotesque imitation.

Caricature implies ludicrous exaggeration of the characteristic or peculiar features of a subject <the movie is a *caricature* of the novel>.

Burlesque implies mockery either through treating a trivial subject in a mock-heroic style or through giving a serious or lofty subject a frivolous treatment <a *burlesque* that treats a petty quarrel as a great battle>.

Parody applies especially to treatment of a subject in the style of a well-known author or work through subtle and sustained exaggeration or distortion <a witty *parody* of a popular soap opera>.

Travesty implies use of an extravagant or absurd style that at once demeans the user and the topic <this production is a *travesty* of a classic opera>.

carnage see MASSACRE.

carnal, fleshly, sensual, animal mean having a physical orientation or origin.

Carnal may mean only this but more often carries a derogatory connotation of an action or manifestation of a person's lower nature <a woman who was victimized by her own *carnal* appetites>. ***ant*** spiritual, intellectual

Fleshly, similar in meaning, is somewhat less derogatory than *carnal* <a saint who wrote at length on his *fleshly* temptations>.

Sensual may apply to any gratification of a bodily desire or pleasure but commonly implies sexual appetite or bodily sat-

isfaction <a place infamous for providing *sensual* delight>.
Animal stresses a relation to physical as distinguished from rational nature <led a mindless, *animal* existence>. ***ant*** rational

carping see CRITICAL.
carriage see BEARING.
carry, bear, convey, transport mean to move something from one place to another.
Carry tends to emphasize the means by which something is moved or the fact of supporting off the ground while moving <*carried* the basket on her head>.
Bear stresses the effort of sustaining or the importance of what is carried <*bear* the banner aloft>.
Convey suggests the continuous movement of something in mass <the pipeline *conveys* oil for more than a thousand miles>.
Transport implies the orderly moving of something often over great distances to its destination <trucks *transporting* farm produce to market>.

cartel see MONOPOLY.
case see INSTANCE.
cast 1. see DISCARD. **2.** see THROW.
castigate see PUNISH.
casual 1. see ACCIDENTAL. **2.** see RANDOM.
cataclysm see DISASTER.
catastrophe see DISASTER.
catch 1. Catch, capture, trap, snare, entrap, ensnare, bag mean to come to possess or control by or as if by seizing.
Catch implies the seizing of something that has been in motion or in flight or in hiding <*caught* the dog as it ran by>. ***ant*** miss
Capture suggests taking by overcoming resistance or difficulty <*capture* an enemy stronghold>.
Trap, snare, entrap, ensnare imply seizing by some device that holds the one caught at the mercy of one's captor. *Trap* and *snare* apply more commonly to physical seizing <*trap* animals> <*snared* butterflies with a net>. *Entrap* and *ensnare* more often are figurative <*entrapped* the witness with a trick question> <a sting operation that *ensnared* burglars>.
Bag implies success in seizing a difficult quarry by skill, stealth, or artifice, often with the suggestion of a hunter's craft <*bagged* a brace of pheasants>.
2. see INCUR.

cause, determinant, antecedent, reason, occasion mean something that produces an effect or result.
Cause applies to any event, circumstance, or condition that brings about or helps bring about a result <an icy road was the *cause* of the accident>.

Determinant applies to a cause that fixes the nature of what results <heredity may be a *determinant* of heart disease>.
Antecedent applies to that which has preceded and may therefore be in some degree responsible for what follows <the *antecedents* of the famine>. ***ant*** consequence
Reason applies to a traceable or explainable cause of a known effect <the *reason* I was late was that my car would not start>.
Occasion applies to a particular time or situation at which underlying causes become effective <the assassination was the *occasion* of the war>.

caustic, mordant, acrid, scathing mean stingingly incisive.
Caustic suggests a biting wit <*caustic* comments about her singing ability>. ***ant*** genial
Mordant suggests a wit that is used with deadly effectiveness <*mordant* reviews put the play out of its misery>.
Acrid implies bitterness and often malevolence <a speech marked by *acrid* invective>. ***ant*** benign, kindly
Scathing implies indignant attacks delivered with fierce or withering severity <a *scathing* satire of corporate life>.

caution see WARN.

cautious, circumspect, wary, chary mean prudently watchful and discreet in the face of danger or risk.
Cautious implies the exercise of forethought or prudence usually prompted by fear of danger <a *cautious* driver>. ***ant*** adventurous, temerarious
Circumspect stresses prudence, discretion, vigilance, and the surveying of all possible consequences before acting or deciding <the panel must be *circumspect* in assigning blame>. ***ant*** audacious
Wary emphasizes suspiciousness and alertness in watching for danger and cunning in escaping it <be *wary* of those claiming to have all the answers>. ***ant*** foolhardy, brash
Chary implies a cautious reluctance to give, act, or speak freely <I am *chary* of signing papers I have not read>.

cease see STOP.

celebrate see KEEP.

celebrated see FAMOUS.

celerity, alacrity mean quickness in movement or action.
Celerity implies speed in working <got dinner ready with remarkable *celerity*>. ***ant*** leisureliness
Alacrity stresses eager promptness in response to suggestion or command <the students volunteered with surprising *alacrity*>. ***ant*** languor

censorious see CRITICAL.

censure see CRITICIZE.

ceremonial, ceremonious, formal, conventional mean marked by attention to or adhering strictly to prescribed forms.

Ceremonial and ***ceremonious*** both imply strict attention to what is prescribed by custom or by ritual, but *ceremonial* applies to things that are associated with ceremonies <a *ceremonial* offering>, *ceremonious* to persons given to ceremony or to acts attended by ceremony <a *ceremonious* old man>. ***ant*** unceremonious, informal

Formal applies both to things prescribed by and to persons obedient to custom and may suggest stiff, restrained, or old-fashioned behavior <a *formal* report on the summit meeting> <a *formal* manner>. ***ant*** informal

Conventional implies accord with general custom and usage and may suggest a lack of originality or independence <*conventional* courtesy> <*conventional* standards of beauty>. ***ant*** unconventional

ceremonious see CEREMONIAL.

certain see SURE.

certainty, certitude, assurance, conviction mean a state of being free from doubt.

Certainty may stress the existence of objective proof <claims that cannot be confirmed with any scientific *certainty*>. ***ant*** uncertainty

Certitude may emphasize a faith strong enough to resist all attack <believed in his innocence with a fair degree of *certitude*>. ***ant*** doubt

Assurance implies confidence rather than certainty and implies reliance on one's own powers or methods, or trust in another <as much *assurance* as is ever possible where hurricanes are concerned>. ***ant*** mistrust, dubiousness

Conviction usually implies previous doubt or uncertainty and stresses a subjective, rational reaction to evidence <holds firm *convictions* about everything>.

certify 1. Certify, attest, witness, vouch mean to testify to the truth or genuineness of something.

Certify usually applies to a written statement, especially one carrying a signature or seal <*certified* that the candidate had met all requirements>.

Attest applies to oral or written testimony usually from experts or witnesses and often under oath or by word of honor <*attested* the authenticity of the document>.

Witness applies to the subscribing of one's own name as evidence of the genuineness of a document <two persons who *witnessed* the signing of the will>.

Vouch suggests that the one who testifies is a competent authority or a reliable person who will stand behind an affirmation <willing to *vouch* for the woman's integrity>.

2. see APPROVE.

certitude see CERTAINTY.

champion see SUPPORT.

chance *n* **Chance, accident, fortune, luck, hap, hazard** mean something that happens without an apparent cause or as a result of unpredictable forces.

Chance is the most general term and may imply determination by irrational, uncontrollable forces <left things to *chance*> or degree of probability <a *chance* of one in ten>. ***ant*** law

Accident emphasizes lack of intention <met by happy *accident*>. ***ant*** design, intent

Fortune often refers to the hypothetical cause of what happens fortuitously <favored by *fortune*> or the outcome of a problematical undertaking <the *fortunes* of war>.

Luck, less dignified than *fortune,* has connotations of gambling <her good *luck* held> and can imply success or a happy outcome <I wish you *luck*>.

Hap usually denotes what falls or has already fallen to one's lot <a position won by *hap*>.

Hazard is used when the influence of existing conditions or accompanying circumstances is present but not predictable <partners chosen by *hazard*>.

chance *vb* see HAPPEN.

chance *adj* see RANDOM.

change, alter, vary, modify mean to make or become different.

Change implies making either an essential difference often amounting to a loss of original identity or a substitution of one thing for another <*changed* the shirt for a larger size>.

Alter implies the making of a difference in some particular respect without suggesting loss of identity <slightly *altered* the original design>. ***ant*** fix

Vary stresses a breaking away from sameness, duplication, or exact repetition <you can *vary* the speed of the conveyor belt>.

Modify suggests a difference that limits, restricts, or adapts to a new purpose <*modified* the building for use by the handicapped>.

character 1. see DISPOSITION. **2.** see QUALITY. **3.** see TYPE.

characteristic, individual, peculiar, distinctive mean revealing a special quality or identity.

Characteristic applies to something that distinguishes or identifies a person, thing, or class <responded with his *characteristic* wit>.

Individual stresses qualities that distinguish one from other members of the same group or class <a highly *individual* writing style>. ***ant*** common

Peculiar stresses the rarity or uniqueness of qualities possessed by a particular individual or class or kind <an eccentricity that is *peculiar* to the British>.

Distinctive indicates qualities distinguishing and uncommon and often worthy of recognition or praise <her *distinctive* aura of grace and elegance>. ***ant*** typical

charge *vb* **1.** see ACCUSE. **2.** see COMMAND. **3.** see ASCRIBE.

charge *n* see PRICE.

charity see MERCY.

charm *vb* see ATTRACT.

charm *n* see FETISH.

charter see HIRE.

chary see CAUTIOUS.

chase see FOLLOW 2.

chaste, pure, modest, decent mean free from all taint of what is lewd or salacious.

Chaste primarily implies a refraining from acts or even thoughts or desires that are not virginal or not sanctioned by marriage vows <maintained *chaste* relations until marriage>. ***ant*** lewd, wanton, immoral

Pure implies innocence and absence of temptation rather than control of one's impulses and actions <the *pure* of heart>. ***ant*** impure, immoral

Modest stresses absence of characteristics of dress or behavior unbefitting one who is pure and chaste <her dress was always modest>. ***ant*** immodest

Decent stresses regard for what is considered seemly or proper <*decent* people didn't go to such movies>. ***ant*** indecent, obscene

chasten see PUNISH.

chastise see PUNISH.

cheap see CONTEMPTIBLE.

cheat, cozen, defraud, swindle mean to get something by dishonesty or deception.

Cheat suggests using deceit or trickery that is intended to escape observation <*cheated* on the written examination>.

Cozen implies artful persuading or flattering to attain a thing or a purpose <always able to *cozen* her doting grandfather out of a few dollars>.

Defraud stresses depriving someone of what is rightfully his or her own and usually connotes deliberate perversion of the truth <her own lawyer *defrauded* her of her inheritance>.

Swindle implies large-scale cheating by means of misrepresentation or abuse of confidence chiefly in order to obtain money <widows *swindled* of their savings by con artists>.

check see RESTRAIN.

cheek see TEMERITY.

cheerful see GLAD.

cheerless see DISMAL.

cherish see APPRECIATE.

chide see REPROVE.
chimerical see IMAGINARY.
chivalrous see CIVIL.
chivy see BAIT.
choice *n* **Choice, option, alternative, preference, selection, election** mean the act or opportunity of choosing or the thing chosen.

Choice suggests the opportunity or privilege to choose freely from a number of alternatives <total freedom of *choice* in the matter>.

Option implies a specifically given power to choose among mutually exclusive items <the *option* of paying now or later>.

Alternative implies a necessity to choose one and reject another possibility <the *alternatives* were peace with dishonor or war>.

Preference suggests personal bias and predilection as a basis of choice <stated a *preference* for red-haired women>.

Selection implies a wide range of choice and often the need of thought or discrimination in choosing <a store offering a wide *selection* of furniture>.

Election implies a formal choosing, typically for an explicit role, duty, or function <the careful *election* of college courses>.

choice *adj* **Choice, exquisite, elegant, rare, dainty, delicate** mean having qualities that appeal to a cultivated taste.

Choice stresses preeminence in quality or kind <a *choice* bit of gossip>. ***ant*** indifferent

Exquisite implies a perfection in workmanship or design that appeals only to very sensitive taste <an *exquisite* gold bracelet>.

Elegant applies to what is rich and luxurious but restrained by good taste <an *elegant* dining room with genuine French antiques>.

Rare suggests a uncommon excellence <refuses to drink any but the *rarest* of wines>.

Delicate implies exquisiteness, subtlety, or fragility <the play's *delicate* charm was lost on screen>. ***ant*** gross

Dainty suggests smallness coupled with exquisiteness <precious, *dainty* food that leaves you hungry>. ***ant*** gross

choke see SUFFOCATE.
choleric see IRASCIBLE.
chore see TASK.
chronic see INVETERATE.
chronicle see HISTORY.
chunky see STOCKY.
churlish see BOORISH.
chutzpah see TEMERITY.

circadian see DAILY.
circle see SET *n*.
circuit see PERIMETER.
circumference see PERIMETER.
circumscribe see LIMIT.
circumspect see CAUTIOUS.
circumstance see OCCURRENCE.
circumstantial, minute, particular, detailed mean dealing with a matter fully and usually point by point.
Circumstantial implies a description, narrative, or report that fixes something in time and space with precise details and happenings <a *circumstantial* account of our visit>. ***ant*** abridged, summary
Minute implies thorough and meticulous attention to the smallest details <a *minute* examination of a fossil>.
Particular implies zealous attention to every detail <a *particular* description of the scene of the crime>.
Detailed stresses abundance rather than completeness of detail <a *detailed* description of the event>.
circumvent see FRUSTRATE.
citation see ENCOMIUM.
cite 1. see SUMMON.
2. see QUOTE.
3. Cite, advance, allege, adduce mean to bring forward as in explanation, proof, or illustration.
Cite implies a bringing forward of something as relevant or specific to an inquiry or discussion <asked to *cite* a single piece of legislation enacted to relieve the situation>.
Advance stresses the notion of bringing forward for consideration or study <the idea has been *advanced* as a theoretical possibility>.
Allege often carries a strong suggestion of doubt about the validity of what is brought forward <tried the *alleged* perpetrator> and sometimes amounts to a disclaimer of responsibility for the assertion <the existence, real or *alleged*, of ghosts>.
Adduce more specifically applies to a bringing forth of evidence, facts, instances, or arguments in support of a position or contention <reasons *adduced* by those who doubt the reality of UFOs>.
citizen, subject, national mean a person owing allegiance to and entitled to the protection of a sovereign state.
Citizen is preferred for one who owes allegiance to a state in which sovereign power is retained by the people and who shares in the political rights of those people <the inalienable rights of a free *citizen*>. ***ant*** alien
Subject implies allegiance to a personal sovereign such as a

monarch <the king enjoys the loyalty of his *subjects*>. ***ant*** sovereign

National designates one who may claim the protection of a state and applies especially to one living or traveling outside that state <American *nationals* currently in Europe>.

civil, polite, courteous, gallant, chivalrous mean observant of the forms required by good breeding.

Civil often suggests little more than the avoidance of overt rudeness <a *civil* reply that showed a lack of real enthusiasm>. ***ant*** uncivil, rude

Polite commonly implies polish of speech and manners with sometimes an absence of cordiality <a conversation as *polite* as it was condescending>. ***ant*** impolite

Courteous implies more actively considerate or dignified politeness <clerks who were unfailingly *courteous* to customers>. ***ant*** discourteous

Gallant suggests spirited and dashing behavior and ornate expressions of courtesy <a *gallant* suitor of the old school>. ***ant*** ungallant

Chivalrous suggests high-minded and self-sacrificing attentions <a *chilvarous* display of duty>. ***ant*** churlish

claim see DEMAND.

clamor see DIN.

clamorous see VOCIFEROUS.

clandestine see SECRET.

clear 1. Clear, transparent, translucent, limpid mean capable of being seen through.

Clear implies absence of cloudiness, haziness, or muddiness <*clear* water>. ***ant*** turbid

Transparent applies to whatever can be seen through clearly and sharply <a *transparent* sheet of film>. ***ant*** opaque

Translucent applies to what permits the passage of light but not a clear view of what lies beyond <*translucent* frosted glass>.

Limpid suggests the soft clearness of pure water <*limpid* blue eyes>. ***ant*** turbid

2. Clear, perspicuous, lucid mean quickly and easily understood.

Clear implies freedom from obscurity, ambiguity, or undue complexity <the instructions were perfectly *clear*>. ***ant*** unintelligible, obscure

Perspicuous applies to a style that is simple and elegant as well as clear <the *perspicuous* beauty of Shakespeare's sonnets>.

Lucid suggests a clear logical coherence and evident order of arrangement <an amazingly *lucid* description of nuclear physics>. ***ant*** obscure, vague, dark

3. see EVIDENT.

clear-cut see INCISIVE.
cleave 1. see STICK. **2.** see TEAR.
clemency see MERCY.
clever 1. see INTELLIGENT.

2. Clever, adroit, cunning, ingenious mean having or showing practical wit or skill in contriving.

Clever stresses physical or mental quickness, deftness, or aptitude <a person *clever* with horses>.

Adroit often implies a shrewd or skillful use of expedients to achieve one's purpose <an *adroit* negotiator of business deals>. ***ant*** maladroit

Cunning implies great skill in constructing or creating <a writer who is *cunning* in his manipulation of the reader>.

Ingenious suggests brilliance or cleverness in inventing or discovering <an *ingenious* computer engineer>.

climax see SUMMIT.
climb see ASCEND.
cling see STICK.
clique see SET *n*.
cloak see DISGUISE.
clog see HAMPER.
cloister, convent, monastery, nunnery, abbey, priory mean a place of retirement from the world for members of a religious community.

Cloister stresses the idea of seclusion from the world for either sex <kept a strict silence within the *cloister* walls>.

Convent may refer to a retreat for either sex or may refer to a retreat for nuns and stresses the idea of community of living <the shared labor of life within the *convent*>.

Monastery refers to a cloister for monks and may indicate a community that combines the cloistered life with teaching, preaching, or other work <left his job on Wall Street and entered a *monastery*>.

Nunnery, often interchangeable with *convent*, refers to a cloister for nuns <found life in a *nunnery* too restrictive>.

Abbey denotes a monastery or a nunnery governed by an abbot or an abbess <took the message to the abbot at the *abbey*>.

Priory indicates a community governed by a prior or prioress <summoned the inhabitants of the *priory* for matins>.

close *vb* **Close, end, conclude, finish, complete, terminate** mean to bring or come to a stopping point or limit.

Close usually implies that something has been in some way open as well as unfinished <*close* a debate>.

End conveys a strong sense of finality and implies a development which has been carried through <*ended* his life>. ***ant*** begin

Conclude may imply a formal closing (as of a meeting) <the service *concluded* with a blessing>. ***ant*** open

Finish may stress completion of a final step in a process <after it is painted, the house will be *finished*>.

Complete implies the removal of all deficiencies or a successful finishing of what has been undertaken <the resolving of this last issue *completes* the agreement>.

Terminate implies the setting of a limit in time or space <your employment *terminates* after three months>. ***ant*** initiate

close *adj* **1. Close, dense, compact, thick** mean massed tightly together.

Close applies to something made up of separate items that are or seem pressed together <paintings hung *close* together>. ***ant*** open

Dense implies compression of parts or elements so close as to be almost impenetrable <the *dense* growth in a tropical rain forest>. ***ant*** sparse

Compact suggests a firm, neat union or effective consolidation of parts within a small compass <a *compact*, muscular body>.

Thick implies a concentrated condensed abundance of parts or units <a *thick* head of hair>.

2. see STINGY.

clownish see BOORISH.

cloy see SATIATE.

clumsy see AWKWARD.

cluster see GROUP.

clutch *vb* see TAKE.

clutch *n* see HOLD.

coadjutor see ASSISTANT.

coalesce see MIX.

coalition see ALLIANCE.

coarse, vulgar, gross, obscene, ribald mean offensive to good taste or moral principles.

Coarse implies roughness, rudeness, crudeness, or insensitivity of spirit, behavior, or language <found the *coarse* humor of her coworkers offensive>. ***ant*** fine, refined

Vulgar often implies boorishness or ill-breeding <a loud, *vulgar* laugh>.

Gross stresses crude animal inclinations and lack of refinement <*gross* eating habits make others lose their appetites>. ***ant*** delicate, dainty, ethereal

Obscene stresses impropriety, indecency, or nasty obnoxiousness <*obscene* language that violated the broadcasters' code>. ***ant*** decent

Ribald applies to what is amusingly or picturesquely vulgar or indecent or crudely earthy <entertained the campers with *ribald* songs>.

coax, cajole, wheedle, blandish mean to influence or gently urge by caressing or flattering.

Coax suggests an artful, gentle pleading in an attempt to gain one's ends <*coaxed* their friends into staying for dinner>. ***ant*** bully

Cajole suggests enticing or alluring through beguilement <*cajoled* by his friend into trying the exotic dish>.

Wheedle stresses the use of soft words, artful flattery, or seductive appeal <*wheedled* the old man out of his money>.

Blandish suggests open flattery and the obvious use of charm in an effort to win over <a salesclerk not above shamelessly *blandishing* customers>.

cocksure see SURE.

coerce see FORCE.

coeval see CONTEMPORARY.

cogent see VALID.

cogitate see THINK 2.

cognate see RELATED.

cognizant see AWARE.

cohere see STICK.

coincide see AGREE 1.

coincident see CONTEMPORARY.

collate see COMPARE.

colleague see PARTNER.

collect see GATHER.

collected see COOL.

color, hue, shade, tint, tinge mean a property of a visible thing that is recognizable in the light and is distinguished from other properties, such as shape, size, and texture.

Color is the ordinary and generic term for this property and specifically applies to the property of things seen as red, yellow, blue, and so on as distinguished from gray, black, or white <gave the white room touches of *color*>.

Hue may be a close synonym of *color* <flowers of many *hues*> but suggests gradation or modification of colors <the many green *hues* of spring>.

Shade more usually indicates a gradation of a color or hue according to lightness or brightness <use a paler *shade* of blue for the curtains>.

Tint usually applies to color that is pale or faint or diluted (as with white) <the rose *tints* of the evening sky>.

Tinge distinctively applies to color that modifies other color by mingling with or overlaying <embarrassment brought a *tinge* of red to her pale cheeks>.

colorable see PLAUSIBLE.

colossal see ENORMOUS.

combat see OPPOSE.

combative see BELLIGERENT.
combine see JOIN.
comely see BEAUTIFUL.
comfort, console, solace mean to give or offer help in relieving suffering or sorrow.

Comfort implies imparting cheer, strength, or encouragement as well as lessening pain <a message intended to *comfort* the grieving family>. ***ant*** afflict, bother

Console emphasizes the alleviating of grief or the mitigating of the sense of loss <*consoled* herself by remembering the good times>.

Solace suggests a lifting of spirits often from loneliness or boredom as well as from pain or grief <*solaced* himself by reading books and writing poetry>.

comfortable, cozy, snug, easy, restful mean enjoying or providing circumstances of contentment and security.

Comfortable applies to anything that encourages serenity, well-being, or complacency as well as physical ease <began to feel *comfortable* in her new surroundings>. ***ant*** uncomfortable, miserable

Cozy suggests comfortableness derived from warmth, shelter, ease, and friendliness <a *cozy* neighborhood coffee shop>.

Snug suggests having just enough of something for comfort and safety but no more <a *snug* little cottage>.

Easy implies relief from or absence of anything likely to cause physical or mental discomfort or constraint <our host had a warm, *easy* manner>. ***ant*** disquieting, disquieted

Restful applies to whatever induces or contributes to rest or relaxation <a quiet *restful* inn where indolence is encouraged>.

comic see LAUGHABLE.
comical see LAUGHABLE.
command *vb* **Command, order, bid, enjoin, direct, instruct, charge** mean to issue orders.

Command implies authority and some degree of formality and impersonality in the official exercise of authority <when his superior *commands*, a soldier obeys>. ***ant*** comply, obey

Order may add the notion of the peremptory or arbitrary exercise of power <*ordered* his men about like slaves>.

Bid suggests giving orders directly and orally <*bade* her fix a drink for him>. ***ant*** forbid

Enjoin implies the giving of an order or direction authoritatively and urgently and often with admonition or solicitude <our guide *enjoined* us to be quiet in the cathedral>.

Direct connotes expectation of obedience and usually concerns specific points of procedure or method <*directed* her assistant to hold all calls>.

Instruct sometimes implies greater explicitness or formality <the judge *instructed* the jury to ignore the remark>.

Charge adds to *enjoin* an implication of imposing as a duty or responsibility <*charged* by the President with a covert mission>.

command *n* see POWER 3.

commemorate see KEEP.

commence see BEGIN.

commensurable see PROPORTIONAL.

commensurate see PROPORTIONAL.

comment see REMARK.

commentate see REMARK.

commerce see BUSINESS.

commingle see MIX.

commit, entrust, confide, consign, relegate mean to assign to a person or place especially for safekeeping.

Commit may express the general idea of delivering into another's charge <*commit* his child to the sitter> or the special sense of transferring to a superior power or to a place of custody <*committed* the person to prison>.

Entrust implies committing with trust and confidence <the president is *entrusted* with broad powers>.

Confide implies entrusting with assurance or reliance <*confided* all power over my financial affairs to my attorney>.

Consign suggests a transferring that removes something from one's immediate control <*consigned* my paintings to a gallery for sale>.

Relegate implies a consigning to a particular class, position, or sphere, often with a suggestion of getting rid of <*relegated* to an obscure position in the company>.

commodious see SPACIOUS.

common, ordinary, plain, familiar, popular, vulgar mean generally met with and not in any way special, strange, or unusual.

Common implies usual everyday quality or frequency of occurrence <a *common* error> <lacked *common* honesty> and may additionally suggest inferiority or coarseness <his *common* manners shocked her family>. ***ant*** uncommon, exceptional

Ordinary stresses accordance in quality or kind with the regular order of things <an *ordinary* pleasant summer day> <a very *ordinary* sort of man>. ***ant*** extraordinary

Plain suggests ordinariness and homely simplicity <she comes from *plain*, hard-working stock>. ***ant*** fancy, ornamental

Familiar stresses the fact of being generally known and easily recognized <a *familiar* melody>. ***ant*** unfamiliar, strange

Popular applies to what is accepted by or prevalent among people in general sometimes in contrast to upper classes or special groups <a hero typically found in *popular* fiction>. ***ant*** unpopular, esoteric

Vulgar, otherwise similar to *popular*, is likely to carry derogatory connotations of inferiority or coarseness <goods designed to appeal to the *vulgar* taste>.

2. see RECIPROCAL.

common sense see SENSE.

commotion, tumult, turmoil, upheaval mean great physical, mental, or emotional excitement.

Commotion suggests disturbing, sometimes violent, bustle or hubbub <the unexpected dinner guests caused quite a *commotion*>.

Tumult suggests a shaking up or stirring up that is accompanied by uproar, din, or great disorder <the town was in a *tumult* over the war news>.

Turmoil suggests a state devoid of calm and seething with excitement <a well-ordered life that was suddenly thrown into great *turmoil*>.

Upheaval suggests a violent and forceful thrusting that results in a heaving up or an overthrowing <a nation in need of peace after years of *upheaval*>.

compact see CLOSE *adj*.

compare, contrast, collate mean to set side by side in order to show likenesses and differences.

Compare implies an aim of showing relative values or excellences by bringing out characteristic qualities whether similar or divergent <wanted to *compare* the convention facilities of the two cities>.

Contrast implies an aim of emphasizing differences <*contrasted* the computerized system with the old filing cards>.

Collate implies minute and critical comparison in order to note points of agreement or divergence <data from police districts across the country will be *collated*>.

compass *vb* see REACH.

compass *n* **1.** see PERIMETER. **2.** see RANGE.

compassion see SYMPATHY.

compatible see CONSONANT.

compel see FORCE.

compendious see CONCISE.

compendium, syllabus, digest, survey, sketch, précis mean a brief treatment of a subject or topic.

A ***compendium*** gathers together and presents in concise or outline form all the essential facts and details of a subject <a *compendium* of computer technology>.

A ***syllabus*** gives the material necessary for a comprehensive view of a whole subject often in the form of a series of heads or propositions <a *syllabus* for a college history course>.

A ***digest*** presents material gathered from many sources and arranged for ready and convenient accessibility <a *digest* of world opinion on the Central America question>.

A ***survey*** is a brief but comprehensive treatment presented often as a preliminary to further study or discussion <a *survey* of current trends in higher education>.

A ***sketch*** is a slight and tentative treatment subject to later change and amplification <a *sketch* of the proposal>.

A ***précis*** is a concise statement of essential facts or points, often in the style or tone of the original <a *précis* of the lengthy article>.

compensate 1. Compensate, countervail, balance, offset mean to make up for what is excessive or deficient, helpful or harmful in another.

Compensate implies making up a lack or making amends for loss or injury <*compensated* for an injury on the job>.

Countervail suggests counteracting a bad or harmful influence or overcoming the damage suffered through it <a compassionate heart *countervailed* his short temper>.

Balance implies the equalizing or adjusting of two or more things that are contrary or opposed so that no one outweighs the other in effect <in sentencing prisoners, the judge *balanced* justice and mercy>.

Offset implies neutralizing one thing's good or evil effect by the contrary effect of another <overeating will *offset* the benefits of exercise>.

2. see PAY.

compete 1. Compete, contend, contest mean to strive to gain the mastery or upper hand.

Compete implies a struggle to overcome or get the better of in an activity involving rivalry between or among two or more participants and may sometimes connote an incentive or inducement <teams *competed* for the championship>.

Contend stresses the need for fighting or struggling against opposition that has equal or better chances of succeeding <hope *contended* with despair>.

Contest implies a competing or a contending in a debate, dispute, or controversy, an athletic competition, or a physical struggle in an effort to prove one's mastery or superiority <a hotly *contested* election>.

2. see RIVAL.

competent 1. see ABLE. **2.** see SUFFICIENT.

complaisant see AMIABLE.

complete *vb* see CLOSE *vb*.

complete *adj* see FULL.

complex, complicated, intricate, involved, knotty mean having confusingly interrelated parts.
Complex suggests the unavoidable result of bringing together various parts, notions, or details and does not imply a fault or failure <a *complex* problem that calls for a *complex* solution>. ***ant*** simple
Complicated applies to what offers difficulty in understanding, solving, or dealing with <baffled by the *complicated* budgetary procedures>. ***ant*** simple
Intricate suggests difficulty of understanding or appreciating quickly because of perplexing interweaving or interacting of parts <the *intricate* balance of power among nations>.
Involved implies extreme complication and often disorder <an *involved* explanation that clarifies nothing>.
Knotty suggests complication and entanglement that make solution or understanding improbable <*knotty* questions concerning free expression and censorship>.

complexion see DISPOSITION.
complicated see COMPLEX.
comply see OBEY.
component see ELEMENT.
comport 1. see AGREE 3. **2.** see BEHAVE.
composed see COOL.
composite see MIXTURE.
composure see EQUANIMITY.
compound see MIXTURE.
comprehend 1. see INCLUDE. **2.** see UNDERSTAND.
compress see CONTRACT.
compunction 1. see PENITENCE. **2.** see QUALM.
compute see CALCULATE.
conceal see HIDE.
concede see GRANT.
conceive see THINK 1.
concept see IDEA.
conception see IDEA.
concern 1. see AFFAIR 1. **2.** see CARE.
conciliate see PACIFY.

concise, terse, succinct, laconic, summary, pithy, compendious mean very brief in statement or expression.
Concise suggests the removal of whatever is superfluous or elaborative <a *concise* study of the situation>. ***ant*** redundant
Terse implies pointed, elegant conciseness <a *terse* reply that ended the conversation>.
Succinct implies precise expression without waste of words <a *succinct* letter of resignation>. ***ant*** discursive
Laconic implies brevity to the point of seeming rude, indif-

ferent, or mysterious <a *laconic* people who are cold to strangers>. ***ant*** verbose

Summary suggests the statement of main points with no elaboration or explanation <a *summary* listing of the year's main events>. ***ant*** circumstantial

Pithy adds to *succinct* or *terse* the implication of richness of meaning or substance <the play's dialogue is studded with *pithy* one-liners>.

Compendious applies to a treatment at once full in scope and brief and concise in treatment <a *compendious* report giving all that is known about the disease>.

conclude 1. see CLOSE *vb*. **2.** see INFER.

conclusive, decisive, determinative, definitive mean bringing to an end.

Conclusive applies to reasoning or logical proof that puts an end to debate or questioning <*conclusive* evidence of criminal guilt>. ***ant*** inconclusive

Decisive may apply to something that ends a controversy, a contest, or any uncertainty <the *decisive* battle of the war>. ***ant*** indecisive

Determinative adds an implication of giving a fixed character, course, or direction <the *determinative* influence in her life>.

Definitive applies to what is put forth as final and permanent <the *definitive* biography of Jefferson>. ***ant*** tentative, provisional

concoct see CONTRIVE.

concord see HARMONY.

concourse see JUNCTURE.

concur see AGREE 1.

condemn see CRITICIZE.

condense see CONTRACT.

condescend see STOOP.

condition *n* see STATE.

condition *vb* see PREPARE.

condone see EXCUSE.

conduce, contribute, redound mean to lead to an end.

Conduce implies having a predictable tendency to further an end <a country setting that *conduces* to relexation>. ***ant*** ward off

Contribute applies to one factor out of a group of influential factors that furthers an end or produces a result <their studies *contributed* much to our knowledge of the past>.

Redound implies a leading to an unplanned end or state by a flow of consequences <such good results can only *redound* to our credit>.

conduct 1. Conduct, manage, control, direct mean to use one's powers to lead, guide, or dominate.

Conduct implies a leader's taking responsibility for or supervising the acts and achievements of a group <in charge of *conducting* the negotiations>.

Manage implies direct handling and manipulating or maneuvering toward a desired result <*manages* the financial affairs of the company>.

Control implies a regulating or restraining in order to keep within bounds or on a course <try to *control* the number of people using the park>.

Direct implies constant guiding and regulating so as to achieve smooth operation <*directs* the day-to-day running of the store>.

2. see BEHAVE.

confederate see PARTNER.

confederation see ALLIANCE.

confer 1. Confer, consult, advise, parley, treat, negotiate mean to engage in discussion in order to reach a decision or settlement.

Confer implies comparison of views or opinions and usually an equality between participants <the executives *confer* weekly about current business problems>.

Consult adds to *confer* the implication of seeking or taking counsel <before acting, the president *consulted* with his aides>.

Advise applies especially to the seeking and giving of opinions regarding personal matters <before deciding to run, he *advised* with friends>.

Parley implies a conference for the sake of settling differences <the government refusing to *parley* with the rebels>.

Treat implies the existence of a common will to adjust differences or a need for diplomacy <warring nations ready to *treat* for peace>.

Negotiate suggests compromise or bargaining <unwilling to *negotiate* with terrorists>.

2. see GIVE.

confess see ACKNOWLEDGE.

confide see COMMIT.

confidence, assurance, self-possession, aplomb mean a state of mind or a manner marked by easy coolness and freedom from uncertainty, diffidence, or embarrassment.

Confidence stresses faith in oneself and one's powers without any suggestion of conceit or arrogance <had the *confidence* that comes only from long experience>. ***ant*** diffidence

Assurance carries a stronger implication of certainty and may suggest arrogance or lack of objectivity in assessing one's own powers <moved among the guests with great *assurance*>. ***ant*** diffidence, alarm

Self-possession implies an ease or coolness under stress that reflects perfect self-control and command of one's powers <she answered the insolent question with complete *self-possession*>.

Aplomb implies a manifest self-possession in trying or challenging situations <handled the horde of reporters with great *aplomb*>. ***ant*** shyness

configuration see FORM.

confine see LIMIT.

confirm, corroborate, substantiate, verify, authenticate, validate mean to attest to the truth or validity of something.

Confirm implies the removing of doubts by an authoritative statement or indisputable fact <*confirmed* reports of troop movements>. ***ant*** deny

Corroborate suggests the strengthening of evidence that is already partly established or accepted <witnesses *corroborated* his story>. ***ant*** contradict

Substantiate implies the offering of evidence that demonstrates or proves a contention <claims that have yet to be *substantiated*>.

Verify implies the establishment of correspondence of actual facts or details with those proposed or guessed at <all statements of fact in the article have been *verified*>.

Authenticate implies establishing genuineness by adducing legal or official documents or expert opinion <handwriting experts *authenticated* the diaries>. ***ant*** impugn

Validate implies establishing validity by authoritative affirmation or certification or by factual proof <*validate* a passport>. ***ant*** invalidate

confirmed see INVETERATE.

confiscate see APPROPRIATE *vb*.

conflict see DISCORD.

confluence see JUNCTURE.

conform 1. see ADAPT. **2.** see AGREE 3.

conformation see FORM.

confound 1. see PUZZLE. **2.** see MISTAKE.

confuse see MISTAKE.

confute see DISPROVE.

congenial see CONSONANT.

congenital see INNATE.

congratulate, felicitate mean to express pleasure in the joy, success, or prospects of another.

Congratulate, the more common and more intimate term, implies that the one to whom pleasure is expressed is the recipient of good fortune <*congratulate* the groom at his wedding>.

Felicitate, more formal in tone, implies that the recipient of the expression is regarded as happy or is wished happiness <*felicitated* the parents of the new child>.

congregate see GATHER.
congruous see CONSONANT.
conjecture, surmise, guess mean to draw an inference from slight evidence.
Conjecture implies forming an opinion or judgment upon evidence insufficient for definite knowledge <scientists could only *conjecture* about the animal's breeding cycle>.
Surmise implies even slighter evidence and suggests the influence of imagination or suspicion <*surmised* the real reason for the generous gift>.
Guess stresses a hitting upon a conclusion either wholly at random or from very uncertain evidence <you would never *guess* that they were wealthy>.
conjugal see MATRIMONIAL.
connect see JOIN.
connubial see MATRIMONIAL.
conquer, defeat, vanquish, overcome, surmount, subdue, subjugate, reduce, overthrow, rout, beat, lick mean to get the better of by force or strategy.
Conquer implies a major action, all-inclusive effort, and a more or less permanent result <working to *conquer* this pernicious disease>.
Defeat implies merely the fact of getting the better of an adversary at a particular time often with no more than a temporary checking or frustrating <*defeated* her opponent in the tennis match>.
Vanquish suggests a significant action of a certain dignity usually in the defeat of a person rather than a thing <*vanquished* her opponent in the championship match>.
Overcome implies an opposing, often fixed, obstacle that can be dealt with only with difficulty or after a hard struggle <*overcome* a legal obstacle>.
Surmount implies surpassing or exceeding rather than overcoming in a face-to-face confrontation <severe technical problems to be *surmounted*>.
Subdue implies bringing under control by or as if by overpowering <the police *subdued* the unruly man>. ***ant*** awaken, waken
Subjugate stresses bringing into and keeping in subjection and often implies a humbled or servile state in what is subjugated <*subjugated* the minority populations>.
Reduce implies surrender and submission usually as the result of overwhelming by or as if by military action <a city *reduced* by a month-long seige>.
Overthrow stresses the bringing down or destruction of enemy power <a futile attempt to *overthrow* the leader>.
Rout suggests such complete defeat as to cause flight or com-

plete dispersion and disorganization of the adversary <the guerrillas *routed* the attacking force>.

Beat, close to but less formal than *defeat*, is somewhat neutral though it may imply the finality associated with *vanquish* <*beat* an opponent at cards>.

Lick is likely to imply a complete humbling or reduction to ineffectiveness of the one defeated <*lick* a problem>.

conquest see VICTORY.

conscientious see UPRIGHT.

conscious see AWARE.

consecrate see DEVOTE.

consecutive, successive mean following one after the other.

Consecutive stresses immediacy in following, regularity or fixedness of order, and the close connection of the units <named the numbers from one to ten in *consecutive* order>. ***ant*** inconsecutive

Successive is applicable to things that follow regardless of differences in duration, extent, or size or of the length of the interval between the units <weakened progressively by *successive* illnesses>.

consent see ASSENT.

consequence 1. see EFFECT. **2.** see IMPORTANCE.

consequently see THEREFORE.

conserve see SAVE 2.

consider, study, contemplate, weigh mean to think about in order to increase one's knowledge or to arrive at a judgment or decision.

Consider may suggest giving thought to in order to reach a suitable conclusion, opinion, or decision <refused even to *consider* my proposal>.

Study implies sustained purposeful concentration and attention that will reveal details and minutiae <*study* the budget before making sweeping cuts>.

Contemplate stresses the focusing of one's thoughts on something, often without indication of purpose or result <*contemplate* the consequences of such a decision>.

Weigh implies the making of an attempt to reach the truth or arrive at a decision by balancing conflicting claims or evidence <*weigh* the pros and cons of the case>.

considerate see THOUGHTFUL 2.

consign see COMMIT.

consistent see CONSONANT.

console see COMFORT.

consonance see HARMONY.

consonant, consistent, compatible, congruous, congenial, sympathetic mean being in agreement with or agreeable to another.

Consonant implies the absence of elements making for discord or difficulty <a motto *consonant* with the company's philosophy>. ***ant*** inconsonant

Consistent may stress absence of contradiction between things or between details of the same thing <behavior that is not *consistent* with her general character>. ***ant*** inconsistent

Compatible suggests a capacity for existing or functioning together without disagreement, discord, or interference <looking for a *compatible* roommate>. ***ant*** incompatible

Congruous suggests a pleasing effect resulting from fitness or appropriateness of elements <modern furniture is not *congruous* with a colonial house>. ***ant*** incongruous

Congenial implies a generally satisfying harmony between personalities or a fitness to one's personal taste <did not find the atmosphere of the bar *congenial*>. ***ant*** uncongenial, antipathetic *(of persons),* abhorrent *(of tasks or duties)*

Sympathetic suggests a more subtle or quieter kind of harmony <a music critic not very *sympathetic* to rock>.

conspectus see ABRIDGMENT.

conspicuous see NOTICEABLE.

conspiracy see PLOT.

constant **1.** see CONTINUAL. **2.** see FAITHFUL.

constituent see ELEMENT.

constitution see PHYSIQUE.

constrain see FORCE.

constrict see CONTRACT.

consult see CONFER.

consume **1.** see WASTE. **2.** see MONOPOLIZE.

contain, hold, accommodate mean to have or be capable of having within.

Contain implies the actual presence of a specified substance or quantity within something <the can *contains* about a quart of oil>.

Hold implies the capacity of containing or keeping <the container will *hold* a gallon of liquid>.

Accommodate implies holding without crowding or inconvenience <the banquet hall can *accommodate* 500 diners>.

contaminate, taint, pollute, defile mean to make impure or unclean.

Contaminate implies intrusion of or contact with dirt or foulness from an outside source <water *contaminated* by industrial wastes>. ***ant*** purify

Taint stresses the loss of purity or cleanliness that follows contamination <the scandal *tainted* the rest of his political career>.

Pollute, sometimes interchangeable with *contaminate,* may imply that the process which begins with contamination is complete and that what was pure or clean has been made foul, poisoned, or filthy <*polluted* the waters of the lake, so that it became in parts no better than an open cesspool>.

Defile implies befouling of what could or should have been kept clean and pure or held sacred and suggests violation or desecration <*defile* a hero's memory with slanderous innuendo>. ***ant*** cleanse, purify

contemn see DESPISE.

contemplate 1. see CONSIDER. **2.** see SEE 1.

contemplative see THOUGHTFUL 1.

contemporaneous see CONTEMPORARY.

contemporary, contemporaneous, coeval, synchronous, simultaneous, coincident mean existing or occurring at the same time.

Contemporary is likely to apply to people and what relates to them <Abraham Lincoln was *contemporary* with Charles Darwin>.

Contemporaneous applies to events <Victoria's reign was *contemporaneous* with British hegemony>.

Coeval implies contemporaneousness at some remote time or for a long period and refers usually to periods, ages, eras, or eons <the rise of the leisure class was *coeval* with the flowering of the arts>.

Synchronous implies exact correspondence between or during usually brief periods of time, and especially in periodic intervals <the *synchronous* action of a bird's wings in flight>.

Simultaneous implies exact coincidence at a point of time <a *simultaneous* ringing of church bells miles apart>.

Coincident is applied to events that happen at the same time and may be used in order to avoid implication of causal relationship <the end of World War II was *coincident* with a great vintage year>.

contemptible, despicable, pitiable, sorry, scurvy, cheap mean arousing or deserving scorn.

Contemptible may imply any quality provoking scorn or a low standing in any scale of values <a *contemptible* bigot and liar>. ***ant*** admirable, estimable, formidable

Despicable may imply utter worthlessness and usually suggests arousing an attitude of moral indignation <the *despicable* crime of child abuse>. ***ant*** praiseworthy, laudable

Pitiable applies to what inspires mixed contempt and pity and often attributes weakness to the agent <the play is his *pitiable* attempt at tragedy>.

Sorry may stress pitiable or ridiculous inadequacy, wretchedness, or sordidness <the orphanage was a very *sorry* place>.

Scurvy adds to *despicable* an implication of arousing disgust <the offer of help turned out to be a *scurvy* trick>.

Cheap may imply contemptibility resulting from undue familiarity or accessibility <treatment that made her feel *cheap*> but more often implies contempitible pettiness or meanness <critics who condemned the book with *cheap* remarks>. ***ant*** noble

contend see COMPETE.

content see SATISFY 1.

contention see DISCORD.

contentious see BELLIGERENT.

conterminous see ADJACENT.

contest see COMPETE.

contiguous see ADJACENT.

continence see TEMPERANCE.

continent see SOBER.

contingency see JUNCTURE.

contingent see ACCIDENTAL.

continual, continuous, constant, incessant, perpetual, perennial mean characterized by continued occurrence or recurrence.

Continual implies a close or unceasing succession or recurrence <*continual* showers the whole weekend>. ***ant*** intermittent

Continuous usually implies an uninterrupted flow or spatial or temporal extension <the *continuous* roar of the falls>. ***ant*** interrupted

Constant implies uniform or persistent occurrence or recurrence <lived in *constant* pain>. ***ant*** fitful

Incessant implies ceaseless or uninterrupted activity that is viewed as undesirable or distasteful <the *incessant* quarreling frayed her nerves>. ***ant*** intermittent

Perpetual suggests unfailing repetition or lasting duration <the fear of *perpetual* torment after death>. ***ant*** transitory, transient

Perennial implies enduring existence often through constant renewal <a *perennial* source of controversy>.

continue, last, endure, abide, persist mean to exist over a period of time or indefinitely.

Continue applies to a process going on without ending <the stock market will *continue* to rise>.

Last, especially when unqualified, may stress existing beyond what is normal or expected <buy shoes that will *last*>.

Endure adds an implication of resistance to destructive forces or agents <in spite of everything, her faith *endured*>. ***ant*** perish

Abide implies a stable and constant existing, especially as opposed to mutability <through 40 years of marriage, their love *abided*>. ***ant*** pass

Persist suggests outlasting the normal or appointed time and often connotes obstinacy or doggedness <the sense of guilt *persisted*>. ***ant*** desist

continuous see CONTINUAL.

contort see DEFORM.

contour see OUTLINE.

contraband see SMUGGLED.

contract **1.** see INCUR.

2. Contract, shrink, condense, compress, constrict, deflate mean to decrease in bulk or volume.

Contract applies to a drawing together of surfaces or particles or a reduction of area, volume, or length <caused his muscles to *contract*>. ***ant*** expand

Shrink implies a contracting or a loss of material and stresses a falling short of original dimensions <the sweater will *shrink* if washed improperly>. ***ant*** swell

Condense implies a reducing of something homogeneous to greater compactness without significant loss of content <*condense* an essay into a single paragraph>. ***ant*** amplify

Compress implies a pressing into a small compass and definite shape, usually against resistance <*compressed* the comforter to fit the box>. ***ant*** stretch, spread

Constrict implies a narrowing by contraction or squeezing <the throat is *constricted* by too tight a collar>.

Deflate implies a contracting by reducing the internal pressure of a contained substance and stresses the limp or empty state that results <*deflated* his tires to get better traction>. ***ant*** inflate

contradict see DENY.

contradictory see OPPOSITE.

contrary **1.** see OPPOSITE.

2. Contrary, perverse, restive, balky, wayward mean inclined to resist authority, control, or circumstances.

Contrary implies a temperamental unwillingness to accept orders or advice <the most *contrary* child in my class>. ***ant*** complaisant

Perverse may imply wrongheaded, determined, unwholesome, or cranky opposition to what is reasonable or generally accepted <offered the most *perverse* argument for declaring war>.

Restive suggests unwillingness or obstinate refusal to submit to discipline or follow orders and often suggests restlessness or impatience with control <a *restive* horse who refused to stand still>.

Balky suggests a refusal to proceed or acquiesce in a desired direction or course of action <workers became *balky* when asked to accept pay cuts>.

Wayward suggests strong-willed capriciousness and irregularity in behavior <*wayward* inmates isolated from the others>.

contrast see COMPARE.

contravene see DENY.

contribute see CONDUCE.

contrition see PENITENCE.

contrive, devise, invent, frame, concoct mean to find a way of making or doing something or of achieving an end by the exercise of one's mind.

Contrive implies ingenuity or cleverness in planning, designing, or scheming <*contrive* a way of helping them without their knowing it>.

Devise stresses mental effort rather than ingenuity and often implies the reflection and experimentation that precede the bringing of something into being <*devise* new dishes to tempt the palate>.

Invent contains some notion of finding and suggests originating, especially after reflection, as the result of happy accident <the telescope was *invented* by Galileo>.

Frame implies the exact fitting of one thing to another, as of words to thought or of the means to the end <*frame* a proper reply to the letter>.

Concoct suggests a bringing together of ingredients in new or unexpected ways that enhance their effectiveness <*concoct* a plausible excuse for his lateness>.

control *vb* see CONDUCT.

control *n* see POWER 3.

controvert see DISPROVE.

conundrum see MYSTERY.

convene see SUMMON.

convent see CLOISTER.

conventional see CEREMONIAL.

converse see SPEAK.

convert see TRANSFORM.

convey see CARRY.

conviction 1. see CERTAINTY. **2.** see OPINION.

convincing see VALID.

convoke see SUMMON.

convulse see SHAKE.

convulsion see FIT.

convulsive see FITFUL.

cool, composed, collected, unruffled, imperturbable, nonchalant mean actually or apparently free from agitation or excitement.

Cool may imply calmness, deliberateness, or dispassionateness <kept a *cool* head during the emergency>. ***ant*** ardent, agitated

Composed implies freedom from agitation as a result of self-discipline or a sedate disposition <the *composed* pianist gave a flawless concert>. ***ant*** discomposed, anxious

Collected implies a concentration of the mind or spirit that eliminates or overcomes distractions <even in heated debate she remains very *collected*>. ***ant*** distracted, distraught

Unruffled suggests apparent serenity and poise in the face of setbacks or in the midst of excitement <his mother remained *unruffled* during the wedding>. ***ant*** ruffled, excited

Imperturbable implies a temperament that is cool or assured even under severe provocation <a guest speaker who maintained an air of *imperturbable* civility>. ***ant*** choleric, touchy

Nonchalant stresses an easy coolness of manner or casualness that suggests indifference or unconcern <*nonchalant* as ever, she ignored the crying baby>.

copartner see PARTNER.

copious see PLENTIFUL.

copy *vb* **Copy, imitate, mimic, ape, mock** mean to make something so that it resembles an existing thing.

Copy suggests the duplicating of an original as closely as possible <*copied* the painting and sold the fake as an original>. ***ant*** originate

Imitate suggests the following of a model or a pattern but may allow for some variation and may imply inferiority in the product <*imitate* a poet's style>.

Mimic implies a close copying (as of voice or mannerism) often for fun, ridicule, or lifelike simulation <pupils *mimic* their teacher>.

Ape may suggest the presumptuous, slavish, or inept imitating of a superior original <American fashion designers *aped* their European colleagues>.

Mock usually implies imitation, particularly of sounds or movements, with derisive intent <*mocking* a vain man's manner>.

copy *n* see REPRODUCTION.

coquet see TRIFLE.

cordial see GRACIOUS.

corner see MONOPOLY.

corporal see BODILY.

corporeal 1. see BODILY. see MATERIAL.

correct *vb* **1. Correct, rectify, emend, remedy, redress, amend, reform, revise** mean to make right what is wrong.

Correct implies taking action to remove errors, faults, deviations, or defects <*corrected* all her spelling errors>.

Rectify implies a more effective action to make something conform to a rule or standard of what is right, just, or properly controlled or directed <a major error in judgment that should be *rectified* at once>.

Emend specifically implies correction of a text or manuscript <*emend* the text to match the first edition>. ***ant*** corrupt *(a text, passage)*

Remedy implies the removing or making harmless of a cause of trouble, harm, or evil <set out to *remedy* the evils of the world>.

Redress implies making compensation or reparation for an unfairness, injustice, or imbalance <we must *redress* past social injustices>.

Amend implies making corrective changes that are usually slight <a law that needs to be *amended*>. ***ant*** debase, impair

Reform implies corrective changes that are more drastic <plans to *reform* the entire court system>.

Revise suggests a careful examination of something and the making of necessary changes <forced to *revise* the production schedule>.

2. see PUNISH.

correct *adj* **Correct, accurate, exact, precise, nice, right** mean conforming to fact, standard, or truth.

Correct usually implies freedom from fault or error <socially *correct* dress>. ***ant*** incorrect

Accurate implies fidelity to fact or truth attained by exercising care <an *accurate* description of the whole situation>. ***ant*** inacurrate

Exact stresses a very strict agreement with fact, standard, or truth <a suit tailored to *exact* measurements>.

Precise adds to *exact* an emphasis on sharpness of definition or delimitation <the *precise* terms of the contract>. ***ant*** loose

Nice stresses great, sometimes excessive, precision and delicacy of action, adjustment, or discrimination <makes *nice* distinctions between freedom and license>.

Right is close to *correct* but has a stronger positive emphasis on conformity to fact or truth rather than mere absence of error or fault <the *right* thing to do>. ***ant*** wrong

correlate see PARALLEL *n* 2.

correspond see AGREE 3.

corroborate see CONFIRM.

corrupt *vb* see DEBASE.

corrupt *adj* see VICIOUS.

cost see PRICE.

costly, expensive, dear, valuable, precious, invaluable, priceless mean having a high value or valuation, especially in terms of money.

Costly implies high price and may suggest sumptuousness, luxury, or rarity <the *costliest* of delicacies grace her table>. ***ant*** cheap

Expensive may further imply a price beyond the thing's value or the buyer's means <the resort's shops seemed rather *expensive*>. ***ant*** inexpensive

Dear implies a relatively high or exorbitant price or excessive cost usually due to factors other than the thing's intrinsic value <coffee was *dear* during the war>. ***ant*** cheap

Valuable may suggest worth measured in usefulness or enjoyableness as well as in market value <iron ore was a *valuable* commodity>. ***ant*** valueless, worthless

Precious applies to what is of great or even incalculable value because scarce or irreplaceable <our *precious* natural resources>. ***ant*** cheap, worthless

Invaluable implies such great worth as to make valuation all but impossible <a good education is *invaluable*>. ***ant*** worthless

Priceless, used like *invaluable* in a hyperbolical sense, adds a note of even greater intensiveness <a bon mot that was *priceless*>.

coterie see SET *n*.

counsel 1. see ADVICE. **2.** see LAWYER.

counselor see LAWYER.

count see RELY.

countenance see FACE.

counter see ADVERSE.

counteractive see ADVERSE.

counterfeit *vb* see ASSUME.

counterfeit *n* see IMPOSTURE.

counterpart see PARALLEL *n* 2.

countervail see COMPENSATE.

courage, mettle, spirit, resolution, tenacity mean mental or moral strength to resist opposition, danger, or hardship.

Courage implies firmness of mind and will in the face of danger or extreme difficulty <the *courage* to support unpopular causes>. ***ant*** cowardice

Mettle suggests an ingrained capacity for meeting strain or difficulty with fortitude and resilience <a challenge that will test your *mettle*>.

Spirit also suggests a quality of temperament enabling one to hold one's own or keep up one's morale when opposed or threatened <too many failures had broken the *spirit* of the man>.

Resolution stresses firm determination to achieve one's ends <the strong *resolution* of the pioneer women>.

Tenacity adds to *resolution* implications of stubborn persistence and unwillingness to admit defeat <won the argument through sheer *tenacity*>.

courageous see BRAVE.

court see INVITE.

courteous see CIVIL.
cover see SHELTER *n*.
covert see SECRET.
covet see DESIRE.
covetous, greedy, acquisitive, grasping, avaricious mean having or showing a strong desire for possessions and especially material possessions.

Covetous implies inordinate desire, often for what is rightfully another's <*covetous* of his brother's success>.

Greedy stresses lack of restraint and often of discrimination in desire <soldiers *greedy* for glory>.

Acquisitive implies both eagerness to possess and ability to acquire and keep <mansions that were the pride of the *acquisitive* class>. ***ant*** sacrificing, abnegating

Grasping adds an implication of eagerness and selfishness and often suggests use of unfair or ruthless means <*grasping* developers defrauded the homesteaders>.

Avaricious implies obsessive acquisitiveness especially of hoardable wealth and strongly suggests stinginess <*avaricious* thrift that left them morally bankrupt>. ***ant*** generous

cow see INTIMIDATE.
cowardly, pusillanimous, gutless, craven, dastardly mean having or showing a lack of courage.

Cowardly implies a weak or ignoble lack of courage <the *cowardly* retreat of the army>. ***ant*** brave

Pusillanimous suggests a contemptible timidity or lack of courage <*pusillanimous* politicians feared crossing him>.

Craven suggests extreme faintheartedness and lack of resistance <secretly despised the *craven* toadies around her>.

Dastardly implies behavior that is both cowardly and despicably treacherous or outrageous <a *dastardly* attack on unarmed civilians>.

cower see FAWN.
coy see SHY.
cozen see CHEAT.
cozy see COMFORTABLE.
crabbed see SULLEN.
crack see JEST 1.
craft 1. see ART. **2.** see BOAT.
crafty see SLY.
cranky see IRASCIBLE.
crass see STUPID.
crave see DESIRE.
craven see COWARDLY.
crawl see CREEP.
craze see FASHION.
crazed see INSANE.

crazy see INSANE.
create see INVENT.
creator see MAKER.
credence see BELIEF.
credible see PLAUSIBLE.
credit *vb* see ASCRIBE.
credit *n* **1.** see BELIEF. **2.** see INFLUENCE.
creep, crawl mean to move along a surface in a prone or crouching posture.
Creep is more often used of quadrupeds or of human beings who move on all fours and proceed slowly, stealthily, or silently <the cat *crept* up on the mouse>.
Crawl is applied to animals with no legs or many small legs that seem to move by drawing the body along a surface or to human beings who imitate such movement <the injured man tried to *crawl* to the door>.
crime see OFFENSE 2.
cringe see FAWN.
cripple 1. see MAIM. **2.** see WEAKEN.
crisis see JUNCTURE.
crisp 1. see FRAGILE. **2.** see INCISIVE.
criterion see STANDARD.
critical 1. Critical, hypercritical, faultfinding, captious, carping, censorious mean inclined to look for and point out faults and defects.
Critical may imply an effort to see a thing clearly and truly in order to judge or value it fairly <a *critical* essay on modern drama>. ***ant*** uncritical
Hypercritical suggests a tendency to lose objectivity and to judge by unreasonably strict standards <petty, *hypercritical* disparagement of other people's success>.
Faultfinding implies persistent, picayune, often ill-informed criticism and a querulous or exacting temperament <a *faultfinding* theater reviewer>.
Captious suggests a readiness to detect trivial faults or raise objections on trivial grounds <no point is too minute for this *captious* critic to overlook>. ***ant*** appreciative
Carping implies an ill-natured or perverse finding of fault <the *carping* editorial writer soon wearied readers>. ***ant*** fulsome
Censorious implies a disposition to be severely critical and condemnatory <the *censorious* tone of the papal encyclical>. ***ant*** eulogistic
2. see ACUTE.
criticize, reprehend, blame, censure, reprobate, condemn, denounce mean to find fault with openly.
Criticize implies finding fault especially with methods or intentions <*criticized* the police for using violence>. ***ant*** praise

Reprehend implies both criticism and severe rebuke <*reprehends* the self-centeredness of today's students>.

Blame may imply simply the opposite of praise but more often suggests the placing of responsibility or guilt for wrongdoing <*blames* herself for the accident>.

Censure carries a stronger suggestion of authority and of more or less formal reprimand than *blame* <a Senator formally *censured* by his peers>. ***ant*** commend

Reprobate implies strong disapproval or firm refusal to sanction <*reprobated* his son's adulterous adventures>.

Condemn suggests an unqualified and final judgment that is unfavorable and merciless <*condemn* the government's racial policies>.

Denounce adds to *condemn* the implication of a public declaration <stood and *denounced* the war>. ***ant*** eulogize

crooked, devious, oblique mean not straight or straightforward.

Crooked may imply the presence of material curves, bends, or twists <a *crooked* road>, or it may imply departure from a right and proper course and then usually suggests cheating or fraudulence <set up a *crooked* deal to force his partner out of the business>. ***ant*** straight

Devious implies a departure from a direct or usual course <returned home by a *devious* route to avoid the waiting bully>; in application to persons or their acts or practices it is likely to imply unreliability, shiftiness or trickiness, or sometimes obscurity <gained an inheritance by *devious* means>. ***ant*** straightforward

Oblique implies departure from a horizontal or vertical direction <an *oblique* line dividing a rectangle into two equal triangles> and can suggest indirection or lack of straightforwardness <made an *oblique* but damning attack on his character>.

cross see IRASCIBLE.

crotchet see CAPRICE.

crow see BOAST.

crowd, throng, crush, mob, horde mean an assembled multitude of people.

Crowd implies a massing together and often a loss of individuality <a small *crowd* greeted the returning athletes>.

Throng strongly suggests movement and shoving or pushing <a *throng* of reporters followed the President>.

Crush emphasizes the compact concentration of the group, the difficulty of individual movement, and the attendant discomfort <a *crush* of fans waited outside the theater>.

Mob implies a disorderly crowd with the potential or the intent for violence <heard an angry *mob* outside the jail>.

Horde suggests a rushing or tumultuous crowd, often of inferior, rude, or savage character, often linked by common interests or problems <a *horde* of shoppers looking for bargains>.

crucial see ACUTE.

crude see RUDE.

cruel see FIERCE.

crush *vb* **Crush, quell, extinguish, suppress, quash** mean to bring to an end by destroying or defeating.

Crush implies a force that destroys all opposition or brings an operation to a halt <a rebellion that was brutally *crushed*>.

Quell means to overwhelm completely and to reduce to submission, inactivity, or passivity <statements intended to *quell* the fears of the people>. ***ant*** foment

Extinguish suggests ending something as abruptly and completely as putting out a flame <hopes for a promising life *extinguished* by a single bullet>. ***ant*** inflame

Suppress implies a conscious determination to subdue <the government *suppressed* all opposition newspapers>.

Quash implies a sudden and summary extinction <the army *quashed* the rebellion>.

crush *n* see CROWD.

crusty see BLUFF.

cryptic see OBSCURE.

cuddle see CARESS.

cuff see STRIKE.

culmination see SUMMIT.

culpable see BLAMEWORTHY.

cumbersome see HEAVY.

cumbrous see HEAVY.

cumulative, accumulative, additive, summative mean increasing or produced by the addition of new material of the same or similar kind.

Cumulative implies a constant increase (as in amount or power) by successive additions, accretions, or repetitions <the *cumulative* effect of taking a drug for many months>.

Accumulative may distinctively imply that something has reached its maximum or greatest magnitude through many additions <the *accumulative* impact of a well-ordered sales presentation>.

Additive implies that something is capable of assimilation to or incorporation in something else or of growth by additions <as new art forms arise, we develop an *additive* notion of what art is>.

Summative implies that something is capable of association or combination with others so as to create a total effect <the *summative* effect of the show's music, dancing, and staging>.

cunning *n* see ART.

cunning *adj* **1.** see CLEVER. **2.** see SLY.

curb see RESTRAIN.

cure, heal, remedy mean to rectify an unhealthy or undesirable condition.

Cure implies the restoration to health after disease <searched for new medications to *cure* the dread disease>.

Heal may also apply to this but commonly suggests a restoring to soundness of an affected part after a wound or sore <his wounds were slow to *heal*>.

Remedy suggests the correction or relief of a morbid or evil condition through the use of a substance or measure <vainly searched for something to *remedy* her arthritis>.

curious, inquisitive, prying mean interested in what is not one's personal or proper concern.

Curious, a neutral term, connotes an active desire to learn or to know <children are *curious* about everything>. ***ant*** incurious, uninterested

Inquisitive suggests impertinent and habitual curiosity and persistent quizzing and peering after information <dreaded the visits of their *inquisitive* relatives>. ***ant*** incurious

Prying implies busy meddling and officiousness <*prying* neighbors who refuse to mind their own business>.

current *adj* see PREVAILING.

current *n* see TENDENCY.

curse see EXECRATE.

cursory see SUPERFICIAL.

curt see BLUFF.

curtail see SHORTEN.

curve, bend, turn, twist mean to swerve or cause to swerve from a straight line or course.

Curve implies following or producing a line suggesting the arc of a circle or ellipse <the road *curves* sharply to the left>.

Bend suggests a yielding to force and implies a distortion from the anticipated, normal, or desirable straightness <metal rods *bend* under the immense weight>. ***ant*** straighten

Turn implies change of direction essentially by rotation and not usually as a result of force or pressure <the comet will *turn* toward the earth>.

Twist implies the influence of a force having a spiral effect throughout the object or course involved <the *twisted* wreckage of the spacecraft>.

custom see HABIT.

customary see USUAL.

cutting see INCISIVE.

cynical, misanthropic, pessimistic, misogynistic mean deeply distrustful.

Cynical implies having a sneering disbelief in sincerity or in-

tegrity or sometimes a vicious disregard of the rights or concerns of others <always *cynical* about other people's motives>.
Misanthropic suggests a rooted distrust and dislike of human beings and their society <a zoologist who had grown *misanthropic* in recent years>. ***ant*** philanthropic
Pessimistic implies having a gloomy, distrustful view of life and things in general <a philosopher *pessimistic* about the future of the human race>. ***ant*** optimistic
Misogynistic applies to a man having a deep-seated distrust of and aversion to women <a *misogynistic* scientist more at home in his laboratory>.

D

dabbler see AMATEUR.
daily, diurnal, quotidian, circadian mean of each or every day.
Daily is used with reference to the ordinary concerns of the day or daytime and may refer to weekdays as contrasted with holidays and weekends and may also imply an opposition to *nightly* <the *daily* grind>.
Diurnal is used in contrast to *nocturnal* and occurs chiefly in poetic or technical contexts <*diurnal* mammals that are active by day>.
Quotidian emphasizes the quality of daily recurrence and may imply a commonplace, routine, or everyday quality to what it describes <found solace in *quotidian* concerns>.
Circadian, a chiefly technical term, differs from *daily* or *quotidian* in implying only approximate equation with the twenty-four hour day <*circadian* rhythms in insect behavior>.
dainty 1. see CHOICE *adj*. **2.** see NICE.
dally 1. see DELAY 2. **2.** see TRIFLE.
damage see INJURE.
damn see EXECRATE.
damp see WET.
dangerous, hazardous, precarious, perilous, risky mean bringing or involving the chance of loss or injury.
Dangerous applies to whatever may cause harm or loss unless dealt with carefully <soldiers on a *dangerous* mission>. ***ant*** safe, secure
Hazardous implies great and continuous risk of harm or failure and small chance of successfully avoiding disaster <claims that smoking is *hazardous* to your health>.
Precarious suggests insecurity and uncertainty resulting from danger or hazard <has only a *precarious* hold on reality>.
Perilous strongly implies the immediacy of danger <the situation at the foreign embassy has grown *perilous*>.

Risky often applies to a known and voluntarily accepted danger <shy away from *risky* investments>.

dank see WET.

daredevil see ADVENTUROUS.

daring see ADVENTUROUS.

dark 1. Dark, dim, dusky, murky, gloomy mean more or less deficient in light.

Dark, the general term, implies utter or virtual lack of illumination <a *dark* cave>. ***ant*** light

Dim suggests too weak a light for things to be clearly visible <a clandestine meeting in a *dim* bar>. ***ant*** bright, distinct

Dusky suggests deep twilight and a close approach to darkness <trudging through *dusky* woods at day's end>.

Murky implies a heavy obscuring darkness such as that caused by smoke, fog, or dust in air or mud in water <fish cannot live in the river's *murky* waters>.

Gloomy implies serious interference with the normal radiation of light and connotes cheerlessness and pessimism <a *gloomy* room in the basement of the house>. ***ant*** brilliant

2. see OBSCURE.

dastardly see COWARDLY.

daunt see DISMAY.

dauntless see BRAVE.

dawdle see DELAY 2.

dead, defunct, deceased, departed, late mean devoid of life.

Dead is applied literally to what is deprived of vital force but is used figuratively of anything that has lost any attribute of life, such as energy, activity, or radiance <a *dead* engine>. ***ant*** alive

Defunct stresses cessation of active existence or operation <a *defunct* television series>. ***ant*** alive, live

Deceased, departed, and *late* apply to persons who have died recently. *Deceased* occurs especially in legal use <the rights of the *deceased* must be acknowledged>; *departed* usually occurs as a euphemism <pray for our *departed* mother>; and *late* applies especially to a person in a specific relation of status <the *late* president of the company>.

deadly, mortal, fatal, lethal mean causing or capable of causing death.

Deadly applies to whatever is certain or very likely to cause death <a *deadly* disease>.

Mortal appplies to what has caused or is about to cause death <a *mortal* wound>. ***ant*** venial *(especially of a sin)*

Fatal stresses the inevitability of eventual death or destruction <*fatal* consequences>.

Lethal applies to something that is bound to cause death or exists for the destruction of life <*lethal* gas>.

deal 1. see DISTRIBUTE. **2.** see TREAT.
dear see COSTLY.
debar see EXCLUDE.
debase 1. Debase, vitiate, deprave, corrupt, debauch, pervert mean to cause deterioration or lowering in quality or character.
Debase implies a loss of position, worth, value, or dignity <issued a *debased* coinage>. ***ant*** elevate, amend
Vitiate implies the impairment or destruction of purity, validity, or effectiveness by introduction of a fault or defect <partisanship and factionalism *vitiated* our foreign policy>.
Deprave implies moral deterioration by evil thoughts or influences <hoping to banish *depraved* thoughts>.
Corrupt implies loss of soundness, purity, or integrity through the action of debasing or destroying influences <believes that jargon *corrupts* the language>.
Debauch implies a demoralizing or debasing through sensual indulgence <led a *debauched* life after the divorce>.
Pervert implies a twisting or distorting from what is natural or normal so as to debase it completely <*perverted* the original goals of the institute>.
2. see ABASE.
debate see DISCUSS.
debauch see DEBASE.
debilitate see WEAKEN.
decadence see DETERIORATION.
decay, decompose, rot, putrefy, spoil mean to undergo destructive dissolution.
Decay implies a slow and not necessarily complete change from a state of soundness or perfection <a *decaying* Southern mansion>.
Decompose stresses a breaking down by chemical change and often implies a corruption <the body was badly *decomposed*>.
Rot implies decay and decomposition, usually of matter, and often connotes foulness <grain left to *rot* in warehouses>.
Putrefy stresses the offensive quality of what decays or rots <corpses *putrefying* on the battlefield>.
Spoil applies chiefly to the decomposition of foods <be on guard against *spoiled* mayonnaise>.
deceased see DEAD.
deceitful see DISHONEST.
deceive, mislead, delude, beguile mean to lead astray or to frustrate by underhandedness.
Deceive implies imposing a false idea or belief that causes confusion, bewilderment, or helplessness <the salesman tried to *deceive* me about the car>. ***ant*** undeceive, enlighten
Mislead implies a leading astray from the truth that may or may not be intentional <I was *misled* by the confusing sign>.

Delude implies deceiving so thoroughly as to make one a fool or to make one unable to distinguish the false from the true <we were *deluded* into thinking we were safe>. ***ant*** enlighten

Beguile stresses the use of charm and persuasion to deceive <his ingratiating ways *beguiled* us all>.

decency see DECORUM.

decent see CHASTE.

deception, fraud, double-dealing, subterfuge, trickery mean the acts or practices of or the means used by one who deliberately deceives.

Deception may or may not imply blameworthiness, since it may be used of cheating or swindling as well as of arts or games designed merely to mystify <magicians are masters of *deception*>.

Fraud always implies guilt and often criminality in act or practice <indicted for *fraud*>.

Double-dealing suggests duplicity or treachery or action contrary to one's professed attitude <the guerillas accused the go-between of *double-dealing*>.

Subterfuge suggests deception by the adoption of a stratagem or the telling of a lie in order to escape responsibility or duty or to gain an end <obtained the papers by *subterfuge*>.

Trickery implies ingenious or dishonest acts intended to dupe or cheat <will resort to any *trickery* to gain her ends>.

decide, determine, settle, rule, resolve mean to come or cause to come to a conclusion.

Decide implies previous consideration and a cutting off of doubt, wavering, debate, or controversy <will *decide* tonight where to build the school>.

Determine implies a fixing of the identity, character, scope, bounds, or direction of something <*determined* the cause of the problem>.

Settle implies the arrival at a conclusion that brings to an end all doubt, wavering, or dispute <the court's decision *settles* the matter>.

Rule implies a determination by judicial or administrative authority <the judge *ruled* that the evidence was inadmissible>.

Resolve implies an expressed or clear decision or determination to do or refrain from doing something <both nations *resolved* to stop terrorism>.

declare 1. Declare, announce, publish, proclaim, promulgate, advertise mean to make known publicly.

Declare implies explicitness and usually formality in making known <the referee *declared* the contest a draw>.

Announce implies a declaration, especially for the first time, of something that is of interest or is intended to satisfy curiosity <*announced* their engagement at a party>.

Publish implies making public, especially through print <*published* the list of winners in the paper>.
Proclaim implies a clear, forceful, authoritative oral declaring <the president *proclaimed* a national day of mourning>.
Promulgate implies the proclaiming of a dogma, doctrine, or law <*promulgated* an edict of religious toleration>.
Advertise applies to calling public attention to something by widely circulated statements, often marked by extravagance or lack of restraint <*advertised* a new model of vacuum cleaner>.
2. see ASSERT.

decisive see CONCLUSIVE.

deck see ADORN.

decline *vb* **Decline, refuse, reject, repudiate, spurn** mean to turn away by not accepting, receiving, or considering.
Decline implies courteous refusal especially of offers or invitations <*declined* the invitation to dinner>. ***ant*** accept
Refuse suggests more decisiveness or ungraciousness and often implies the denial of something expected or asked for <*refused* them the loan they needed>.
Reject implies a peremptory refusal by or as if by sending away or discarding <*rejected* the plan as unworkable>. ***ant*** accept, choose, select
Repudiate implies a casting off or disowning as untrue, unauthorized, or unworthy of acceptance <*repudiated* the values of their parents>. ***ant*** adopt
Spurn stresses contempt or disdain in rejecting or repudiating <*spurned* his amorous advances>. ***ant*** crave, embrace

decline *n* see DETERIORATION.

decolorize see WHITEN.

decompose see DECAY.

decorate see ADORN.

decorum, decency, propriety, dignity, etiquette mean observance of the rules governing proper conduct.
Decorum suggests conduct that is in accordance with good taste or with a code of rules governing behavior under certain conditions <had failed to exhibit the *decorum* expected of an army officer>. ***ant*** indecorum, license
Decency implies behavior consistent with normal self-respect or humane feeling for others, or with what is fitting to a particular profession or condition in life <maintained a strict *decency* in dress>. ***ant*** indecency
Propriety suggests an artificial standard of what is correct in conduct or speech <regarded the *propriety* expected of a society matron as stifling>. ***ant*** impropriety
Dignity implies reserve or restraint in conduct prompted less by obedience to a code than by a sense of personal integrity or

status <conveyed a quiet *dignity* and sincerity that won him respect>.

Etiquette is the usual term for the detailed rules governing manners and conduct and for the observance of these rules <the *etiquette* peculiar to the U.S. Senate>.

decoy see LURE.

decrease, lessen, diminish, reduce, abate, dwindle mean to grow or make less.

Decrease suggests a progressive decline in size, amount, numbers, or intensity <slowly *decreased* the amount of pressure>. ***ant*** increase

Lessen suggests a decline in amount rather than in number <has been unable to *lessen* her debt at all>.

Diminish emphasizes a perceptible loss and implies its subtraction from a total <his muscular strength has *diminished* with age>.

Reduce implies a bringing down or lowering <*reduce* your caloric intake>.

Abate implies a reducing of something excessive or oppressive in force or amount <voted to *abate* the tax>. ***ant*** augment, intensify *(hopes, fears, a fever)*

Dwindle implies a progressive lessening and is applied to things capable of growing visibly smaller or disappearing <their provisions *dwindled* slowly but surely>.

decree see DICTATE.

decrepit see WEAK.

decry, depreciate, disparage, belittle, minimize mean to express a low opinion of something.

Decry implies open condemnation with intent to discredit <*decried* their do-nothing attitude>. ***ant*** extol

Depreciate implies a representing of something as being of less value than commonly believed <critics *depreciate* his plays for being unabashedly sentimental>. ***ant*** appreciate

Disparage implies depreciation by indirect means such as slighting or invidious comparison <*disparaged* golf as recreation for the middle-aged>. ***ant*** applaud

Belittle suggests a contemptuous attitude and an effort to make something seem small <inclined to *belittle* the achievements of others>. ***ant*** aggrandize, magnify

Minimize connotes an effort to make something seem as small as possible <do not try to *minimize* the danger involved>. ***ant*** magnify

dedicate see DEVOTE.

deduce see INFER.

deep 1. see BROAD.

2. Deep, profound, abysmal mean having great extension downward or inward.

Deep is the more general term, stressing the fact rather than the degree of extension downward from a surface or sometimes backward or inward from a front or outer part <a *deep* river>; when applied to persons or mental processes, it implies the presence of or need for great intellectual activity or emotional conviction <felt *deep* concern for his brother's safety>. ***ant*** shallow

Profound connotes exceedingly great depth <the *profound* depths of the sea> and may imply the need or presence of thoroughness <a *profound* thinker>. ***ant*** shallow

Abysmal carries the idea of *abyss* and implies fathomless distance downward, backward, or inward <on the brink of the *abysmal* precipice> or often of measureless degree, especially with words denoting a lack of something <*abysmal* ignorance>.

deep-rooted see INVETERATE.

deep-seated see INVETERATE.

deface, disfigure mean to mar the appearance of.

Deface, usually applied to inanimate things, implies superficial injuries that impair the surface appearance <*deface* a building with graffiti>.

Disfigure implies deeper or more permanent injury to the surface and permanent impairment of the attractiveness or beauty of a person or thing <a face *disfigured* by scars>. ***ant*** adorn

defame see MALIGN.

defeat see CONQUER.

defect see BLEMISH.

defend 1. Defend, protect, shield, guard, safeguard mean to keep secure from danger or against attack.

Defend denotes warding off or repelling actual or threatened attack <a large army needed to *defend* the country>. ***ant*** combat, attack

Protect implies the use of something as a bar to the admission or impact of what may attack, injure, or destroy <*protect* one's eyes from the sun with dark glasses>.

Shield suggests the intervention of a cover or barrier against imminent danger or actual attack <tried to *shield* her child from the real world>.

Guard implies protecting with vigilance and force against expected danger <all White House entrances are well *guarded*>.

Safeguard implies the taking of precautionary protective measures against merely potential danger <individual rights must be *safeguarded* whatever the cost>.

2. see MAINTAIN.

defer 1. Defer, postpone, suspend, stay mean to delay an action or proceeding.

Defer implies a deliberate putting off to a later date or time <*deferred* payment of the loan>. ***ant*** advance

Postpone implies an intentional deferring usually to a definite time <the game was *postponed* until Saturday>.

Suspend implies a temporary stopping with an added suggestion of waiting until some expressed or implied condition is satisfied <all business has been *suspended* while repairs are being made>.

Stay suggests the stopping or checking by an intervening obstacle, agency, or authority <measures intended to *stay* the rapid rate of inflation>.

2. see YIELD.

deference see HONOR.

defile see CONTAMINATE.

define see PRESCRIBE.

definite see EXPLICIT.

definitive see CONCLUSIVE.

deflate see CONTRACT.

deform, distort, contort, warp mean to mar or spoil by or as if by twisting.

Deform may imply a changing of shape, appearance, character, or nature through stress, injury, or some accident of growth <relentless winds *deformed* the pines into bizarre shapes>.

Distort implies a wrenching from the natural, normal, or true shape, form, or direction <the odd camera angle *distorts* his face in the photograph>.

Contort suggests an extreme distortion that is grotesque or painful <a degenerative bone disease had painfully *contorted* the child's body>.

Warp indicates an uneven shrinking that bends or twists parts out of a flat plane <*warped* floorboards>.

defraud see CHEAT.

deft see DEXTEROUS.

defunct see DEAD.

degenerate see VICIOUS.

degeneration see DETERIORATION.

degrade see ABASE.

deign see STOOP.

dejected see DOWNCAST.

dejection see SADNESS.

delay 1. Delay, retard, slow, slacken, detain mean to cause to be late or behind in movement or progress.

Delay implies a holding back, usually by interference, from completion or arrival <bad weather *delayed* our return>. ***ant*** expedite, hasten

Retard applies chiefly to motion and suggests a slowing, often by interference <language barriers *retarded* their rate of learning>. ***ant*** accelerate, advance, further

Slow, often used with *up* or *down,* also implies a reduction of speed, often with deliberate intention <the engineer *slowed* the train>. ***ant*** speed *up*

Slacken suggests an easing up or relaxing of power or effort <he needs to *slacken* his pace if he intends to finish the race>. ***ant*** quicken

Detain implies a holding back beyond a reasonable or appointed time, often with resulting delay <unexpected business had *detained* her>.

2. Delay, procrastinate, lag, loiter, dawdle, dally mean to move or act slowly so as to fall behind.

Delay usually implies a putting off (as a beginning or departure) <a tight schedule means we cannot *delay* any longer>. ***ant*** hasten, hurry

Procrastinate implies blameworthy delay especially through laziness, hesitation, or apathy <*procrastinates* about making every decision>. ***ant*** hasten, hurry

Lag implies failure to maintain a speed or rate set by others <we *lag* behind other countries in shoe production>.

Loiter implies delay while in progress, especially in walking <*loitered* at several store windows before going to church>.

Dawdle more clearly suggests idleness, aimlessness, or a wandering mind <children *dawdling* on their way home from school>.

Dally suggests delay through trifling or vacillation when promptness is necessary <stop *dallying* and get to work>. ***ant*** hasten

delectation see PLEASURE.

delete see ERASE.

deleterious see PERNICIOUS.

deliberate *vb* see THINK 2.

deliberate *adj* see VOLUNTARY.

delicate see CHOICE *adj*.

delight see PLEASURE.

delirium see MANIA.

deliver see RESCUE.

delude see DECEIVE.

delusion, illusion, hallucination, mirage mean something believed to be or accepted as true or real that is actually false or unreal.

Delusion implies self-deception or deception by others concerning facts or situations and typically suggests a disordered state of mind <suffered from a *delusion* that his family hated him>.

Illusion implies ascribing truth or reality to something that seems to be true or real but in fact is not <clung to the *illusion* of happiness>.

Hallucination implies the perception of visual or other sensory impressions that have no reality but are the product of disordered function <suffered from terrifying *hallucinations*>.

Mirage is comparable with the foregoing words in an extended sense in which it applies to a vision, dream, hope, or aim that is illusory <the dream of peace was but a *mirage*>.

demand, claim, require, exact mean to ask or call for something as due or as necessary or as strongly desired.

Demand implies peremptoriness and insistence and often the claiming of a right to make requests that are to be regarded as commands <the physician *demanded* payment of her bill>.

Claim implies a demand for the delivery or concession of something due as one's own or one's right <*claimed* to be the first to describe the disease>. ***ant*** disclaim, renounce

Require suggests the imperative quality that arises from inner necessity, compulsion of law or regulation, or the exigencies of the situation <the patient *requires* constant attention>.

Exact implies not only demanding but getting what one demands <*exact* a promise from a friend>.

demean see ABASE.

demeanor see BEARING.

demented see INSANE.

demonstrate see SHOW 1.

demur see QUALM.

denounce see CRITICIZE.

dense 1. see CLOSE *adj* 1. **2.** see STUPID.

deny, gainsay, contradict, traverse, impugn, contravene mean to refuse to accept as true or valid.

Deny implies a firm refusal to accept as true, to grant or concede, or to acknowledge the existence or claims of <tried to *deny* the charges>. ***ant*** confirm, concede

Gainsay implies an opposing, usually by disputing, of the truth of what another has said <no one dares *gainsay* the truth of what I've said>. ***ant*** admit

Contradict implies an open or flat denial of the truth of an assertion and usually suggests that the reverse is true <her report *contradicts* every point of his statement to the press>. ***ant*** corroborate

Traverse, chiefly a legal term, implies a formal denial (as of an allegation or the justice of an indictment) <*traversed* the accusation of fraud in his opening remarks>. ***ant*** allege

Impugn suggests a forceful, direct attacking, disputing, or contradicting of something or someone, often by prolonged argument <dared to *impugn* his motives>. ***ant*** authenticate, advocate

Contravene implies not so much an intentional opposition as some inherent incompatibility <laws against whaling that *con-*

travene Eskimo tradition>. ***ant*** uphold *(law, principle)*, allege *(right, claim, privilege)*

depart 1. see GO. **2.** see SWERVE.

departed see DEAD.

depend see RELY.

deplete, drain, exhaust, impoverish, bankrupt mean to deprive of something essential to existence or potency.

Deplete implies a reduction in number or quantity and the actual or potential harm done by such a reduction <we cannot afford to *deplete* our natural resources>. ***ant*** renew, replace

Drain implies a gradual withdrawal and ultimate deprivation of what is necessary to a thing's existence and functioning <a series of personal tragedies *drained* him of hope>.

Exhaust stresses a complete emptying or using up <a theme that can never be *exhausted*>.

Impoverish suggests a deprivation of something essential to vigorous well-being <without the arts we would lead an *impoverished* existence>. ***ant*** enrich

Bankrupt suggests impoverishment to the point of imminent collapse <war had *bankrupted* the nation of manpower and resources>.

deplore, lament, bewail, bemoan mean to express grief or sorrow for something.

Deplore implies strong objection or sorrowful condemnation regarding the loss or impairment of something of value <*deplores* the bad manners of today's young people>.

Lament implies a strong and demonstrative expression of sorrow <never stopped *lamenting* the loss of their only son>. ***ant*** exult, rejoice

Bewail implies sorrow, disappointment, or protest finding outlet in loud words or cries <fans *bewailed* the defeat of their team>. ***ant*** rejoice

Bemoan suggests great lugubriousness in such utterances <purists continually *bemoan* the corruption of the language>. ***ant*** exult

deport 1. see BANISH. **2.** BEHAVE.

deportment see BEARING.

deprave see DEBASE.

depreciate see DECRY.

depreciatory see DEROGATORY.

depressed see DOWNCAST.

depression see SADNESS.

deranged see INSANE.

deride see RIDICULE.

derive see SPRING.

derogatory, depreciatory, disparaging, slighting, pejorative mean designed or tending to belittle.

Derogatory often applies to expressions or modes of expression that are intended to detract or belittle by suggesting something that is discreditable <does not consider the word "politician" a *derogatory* term>. ***ant*** complimentary

Depreciatory is often applied to writing or speech that tends to lower a thing in value or status <her habit of referring to the human body in the most *depreciatory* of ways>. ***ant*** appreciative

Disparaging implies an intent to depreciate by the use of oblique or indirect methods <a *disparaging* look at some popular heroes>.

Slighting may imply mild disparagement, indifference, or even scorn <made brief but *slighting* references to the other candidates in the race>.

Pejorative is applied especially to words whose basic meaning has been given a derogatory twist <"egghead" is a *pejorative* term for an intellectual>.

description see TYPE.

descry see SEE 1.

desecration see PROFANATION.

desert see ABANDON.

design **1.** see INTENTION. **2.** see PLAN.

desire, wish, want, crave, covet mean to have a longing for something.

Desire stresses the strength of feeling and often implies strong intention or fixed aim <*desires* to start a new life in another state>.

Wish often implies a general or transient longing for the unattainable <she *wished* that there were some way she could help>.

Want specifically suggests a longing for something that would fill a felt need <*want* to have a family>.

Crave stresses the force of physical appetite or emotional need <*crave* sweets constantly>. ***ant*** spurn

Covet implies strong envious desire, typically for what belongs to another <one of the most *coveted* honors in the sports world>. ***ant*** renounce *(something desirable)*

desist see STOP.

desolate **1.** see ALONE. **2.** see DISMAL.

despairing see DESPONDENT.

desperate see DESPONDENT.

despicable see CONTEMPTIBLE.

despise, contemn, scorn, disdain, scout mean to regard as unworthy of one's notice or consideration.

Despise may suggest an emotional response ranging from strong dislike to loathing <*despises* those who show any sign of weakness>. ***ant*** appreciate

Contemn, more intellectual, implies a vehement condemnation of a person or thing as low, vile, feeble, or ignominious <*contemns* the image of women promoted by advertisers>.

Scorn implies a ready or indignant and profound contempt <*scorns* the very thought of retirement>. ***ant*** respect

Disdain implies an arrogant aversion to what is regarded as base or unworthy <*disdained* all manner of popular music>. ***ant*** favor, admit

Scout suggests derision or abrupt rejection or dismissal <*scouted* any suggestion that their son was other than angelic>.

despoil see RAVAGE.

despondent, despairing, desperate, hopeless mean having lost all or nearly all hope.

Despondent implies a deep dejection arising from a conviction of the uselessness of further effort <*despondent* over the death of her father>. ***ant*** lighthearted

Despairing suggests the slipping away of all hope and often an accompanying despondency <*despairing* appeals for the return of the kidnapped boy>. ***ant*** hopeful

Desperate implies such despair as prompts reckless action or violence in the face of anticipated defeat or frustration <one last *desperate* attempt to turn the tide of the war>.

Hopeless suggests despair and the cessation of effort or resistance and often implies acceptance or resignation <the situation of the trapped miners is *hopeless*>. ***ant*** hopeful

despotic see ABSOLUTE.

destiny see FATE.

destitution see POVERTY.

destruction see RUIN *n*.

desultory see RANDOM.

detached see INDIFFERENT.

detail see ITEM.

detailed see CIRCUMSTANTIAL.

detain 1. see DELAY 1. **2.** see KEEP 2.

deterioration, degeneration, decadence, decline mean a falling from a higher to a lower level in quality, character, or vitality.

Deterioration implies impairment of such valuable qualities as vigor, resilience, or usefulness <the *deterioration* of her memory in recent years>. ***ant*** improvement, amelioration

Degeneration stresses physical, intellectual, or moral retrogression <the *degeneration* of his youthful idealism>. ***ant*** regeneration

Decadence presupposes a previous attainment of maturity or excellence and implies a turn downward with a consequent loss in vitality or energy <cited rock music as a sign of cultural *decadence*>. ***ant*** rise, flourishing

Decline suggests a more markedly downward direction and greater momentum as well as more obvious evidence of deterioration <the meteoric rise and *decline* of his career>.

determinant see CAUSE.

determinative see CONCLUSIVE.

determine 1. see DECIDE. **2.** see DISCOVER.

detest see HATE.

detestable see HATEFUL.

detrimental see PERNICIOUS.

devastate see RAVAGE.

devastation see RUIN *n*.

develop see MATURE.

deviate see SWERVE.

devious see CROOKED.

devise see CONTRIVE.

devote, dedicate, consecrate, hallow mean to set apart for a particular and often higher end.

Devote is likely to imply a giving up or setting apart because of compelling motives <*devoted* his evenings to study>.

Dedicate implies solemn and exclusive devotion to a sacred or serious use or purpose <*dedicated* her life to medical research>.

Consecrate stresses investment with a solemn or sacred quality <*consecrate* a church to the worship of God>.

Hallow, often differing little from *dedicate* or *consecrate*, may distinctively imply an attribution on intrinsic sanctity <battleground *hallowed* by the blood of patriots>.

devotion see FIDELITY.

devout, pious, religious, pietistic, sanctimonious mean showing fervor in the practice of religion.

Devout stresses genuine feeling and a mental attitude that leads to solemn reverence and fitting observance of rites and practices <a pilgrimage that is the goal of *devout* believers>.

Pious applies to the faithful and dutiful performance of religious duties and maintenance of outwardly religious attitudes <a *pious* family that faithfully observes the Sabbath>. ***ant*** *impious*

Religious may imply devoutness and piety but it emphasizes faith in a deity and adherence to a way of life in keeping with that faith <a basically *religious* man, although not a regular churchgoer>. ***ant*** irreligious

Pietistic stresses the emotional as opposed to the intellectual aspects of religion <regarded religious articles as *pietistic* excess>.

Sanctimonious implies pretentions to holiness or smug appearance of piety <a *sanctimonious* preacher without mercy or human kindness>.

dexterity see READINESS.

dexterous, adroit, deft mean ready and skilled in physical movement or sometimes mental activity.

Dexterous implies expertness with consequent facility and ability in manipulation <a *dexterous* handling of a volatile situation>. ***ant*** clumsy

Adroit implies dexterity but may also stress resourcefulness or artfulness or inventiveness in coping with situations as they arise <the *adroit* host of a radio call-in show>. ***ant*** maladroit

Deft emphasizes lightness, neatness, and sureness of touch or handling <a *deft* interweaving of the novel's several subplots>. ***ant*** awkward

dialect, vernacular, lingo, patois, jargon, cant, argot, slang mean a form of language that is not recognized as standard.

Dialect applies commonly to a form of language found regionally or among the uneducated <the *dialect* of the Cajuns in Louisiana>.

Vernacular applies to the everyday speech of the people in contrast to that of the learned <the doctor used the *vernacular* in describing the disease>.

Lingo is a mildly contemptuous term for any language or form of language not readily understood <foreign tourists speaking some strange *lingo*>.

Patois designates the speech used in a bilingual section or country, especially the mixed English and French spoken in some parts of Canada <children chattering happily in the local *patois*>.

Jargon applies to a technical or esoteric language used by a profession, trade, or cult <educationese is the *jargon* of educational theorists>.

Cant is applied derogatorily to language that is both peculiar to a group or class and marked by hackneyed or unclear expressions <the *cant* of TV sportscasters>.

Argot is applied to a peculiar, often almost secret, language of a clique or other closely knit group <the *argot* of narcotics smugglers>.

Slang designates a class of mostly recently coined and frequently short-lived terms or usages informally preferred to standard language as being forceful, novel, or voguish <the ever-changing *slang* of college students>.

dictate, prescribe, ordain, decree, impose mean to issue something to be followed, observed, obeyed, or accepted.

Dictate implies an authoritative directive given orally or as if orally <in matters of love, do as the heart *dictates*>.

Prescribe implies an authoritative pronouncement that is clear, definite, and incontrovertible <the *prescribed* procedure for requesting new supplies>.

Ordain implies institution, establishment, or enactment by a supreme or unquestioned authority <nature has *ordained* that we humans either swelter or shiver>.

Decree implies a formal pronouncement by one of great or absolute authority <the Pope *decreed* that next year will be a Holy Year>.

Impose implies a subjecting to what must be borne, endured, or submitted to <morality cannot be *imposed* by law>.

dictatorial, magisterial, dogmatic, doctrinaire, oracular mean imposing one's will or opinions on others.

Dictatorial stresses autocratic, high-handed methods and a domineering manner <a *dictatorial* manner that alienates her colleagues>.

Magisterial stresses assumption or use of prerogatives appropriate to a magistrate or schoolmaster in forcing acceptance of one's opinions <the *magisterial* tone of his arguments implies that only a fool would disagree>.

Dogmatic implies being unduly and arrogantly positive in laying down principles and expressing opinions <very *dogmatic* about deciding what is art and what is not>.

Doctrinaire implies a disposition to follow abstract or personal theories and doctrines in teaching, framing laws, or deciding policies affecting people <a *doctrinaire* conservative unable to deal with complex realities>.

Oracular implies the real or implied possession of hidden knowledge and the manner of one who delivers opinions in cryptic phrases or with pompous dogmatism <for three decades she was the *oracular* voice of fashion>.

difference see DISCORD.

different, diverse, divergent, disparate, various mean unlike in kind or character.

Different may imply little more than separateness but it may also imply contrast or contrariness <*different* foods from *different* lands>. ***ant*** identical, alike, same

Diverse implies both distinctness and marked contrast <such *diverse* interests as dancing and football>. ***ant*** identical, self-same

Divergent implies movement away from each other and unlikelihood of ultimate meeting or reconciliation <went on to pursue very *divergent* careers>. ***ant*** convergent

Disparate emphasizes essential incongruity or incompatibility <*disparate* notions of freedom>. ***ant*** comparable, analogous

Various stresses the number of sorts or kinds <*various* methods have been tried>. ***ant*** uniform, cognate

difficult see HARD.

difficulty, hardship, rigor, vicissitude mean something obstructing one's course and demanding effort and endurance if one's end is to be attained.

Difficulty can apply to any condition, situation, experience, or task which presents a problem hard to solve or seemingly beyond one's ability to suffer or surmount <they were determined to succeed; they met and solved each *difficulty* as it arose>.

Hardship stresses extreme suffering, toil, or privation but does not necessarily imply either effort to overcome or patience in enduring <faced many *hardships* that long, hard winter>.

Rigor suggests a hardship necessarily imposed upon one by, for example, an austere religion, a trying climate, or an exacting undertaking <endured the *rigors* of a rite of initiation>. ***ant*** amenity

Vicissitude applies to an inevitable difficulty or hardship that occurs in connection with life or a way of life, a career, or a course of action <the *vicissitudes* of life left them tired, bitter, and alone>.

diffident see SHY.
diffuse see WORDY.
digest see COMPENDIUM.
dignity see DECORUM.
digress see SWERVE.
dilapidate see RUIN *vb*.
dilate see EXPAND.
dilemma see PREDICAMENT.
dilettante see AMATEUR.
diligent see BUSY.
dim see DARK.
diminish see DECREASE.
diminutive see SMALL.

din, uproar, pandemonium, hullabaloo, babel, hubbub, clamor, racket mean a disturbing or confusing welter of sounds or a situation marked by such a welter.

Din suggests prolonged and deafening clangor or insistent ear-splitting metallic sounds <the *din* of a machine shop>. ***ant*** quiet

Uproar suggests tumult or wild disorder or often the sound of a multitude noisily or riotously protesting, arguing, or defying <remarks that threw the crowd into an *uproar*>.

Pandemonium suggests the tumultuous din produced when a crowd or group becomes uncontrollably boisterous <*pandemonium* erupted as soon as the teacher left the room>.

Hullabaloo suggests great excitement, stormy protest, and an interruption of peace and quiet rather than vociferous turmoil <resubmitted his proposal after the *hullabaloo* died down>.

Babel stresses the confusing and seemingly meaningless mass of sound that results from a mingling of languages and vocal qualities <the incomprehensible *babel* of everyone talking at once>.

Hubbub denotes the confusing mixture of sounds characteristic of the incessant movement of activities and business <the *hubbub* of city streets>.

Clamor and ***racket*** stress the psychological effect of a combination of sounds or any excessively noisy scene and imply annoyance and disturbance <the *clamor* of pigs demanding food> <impossible to hear oneself think amid the *racket*>.

diplomatic see SUAVE.

direct *vb* **1.** see COMMAND. **2.** see CONDUCT.

direct *adj* **Direct, immediate** mean uninterrupted.

Direct suggests unbroken connection between one thing and another, for example, between cause and effect, source and issue, or beginning and end <had a *direct* bearing on the case>.

Immediate stresses the absence of any intervening medium or influence <had *immediate* knowledge about the situation>.

directly see PRESENTLY.

dirty, filthy, foul, nasty, squalid mean either physically or morally unclean or impure.

Dirty emphasizes the presence of dirt more than an emotional reaction to it <children *dirty* from play> or stresses meanness or despicableness <a *dirty* little secret>. ***ant*** clean

Filthy carries a strong suggestion of offensiveness and of gradually accumulated dirt that begrimes and besmears <a stained greasy floor, utterly *filthy*> or extreme obscenity <*filthy* language>. ***ant*** neat, spic and span

Foul implies extreme offensiveness and an accumulation of what is rotten or stinking <a *foul*-smelling open sewer> or disgusting obscenity or loathesome behavior <a record of *foul* deeds>. ***ant*** fair, undefiled

Nasty applies to what is actually foul or is repugnant to one used to or expecting freshness, cleanliness, or sweetness <it's a *nasty* job to clean up after a sick cat>, although in practice it is often no more than a synonym of *unpleasant* or *disagreeable* <his answer gave her a *nasty* shock>.

Squalid adds to the idea of dirtiness and filth that of slovenly neglect <living in *squalid* poverty> or sordid baseness and dirtiness <had a series of *squalid* affairs>.

disable see WEAKEN.

disaffect see ESTRANGE.

disallow see DISCLAIM.

disaster, catastrophe, calamity, cataclysm mean an event or situation that is or is regarded as a terrible misfortune.

Disaster implies an unforeseen, ruinous, and often sudden misfortune that happens either through lack of foresight or through some hostile external agency <the war proved to be a *disaster* for the country>.

Catastrophe implies a disastrous conclusion and emphasizes finality <speculation about the *catastrophe* that befell Atlantis>.

Calamity stresses a grievous misfortune involving a great personal or public loss <the father's sudden death was a *calamity* for the family>. ***ant*** boon

Cataclysm, originally a deluge or geological convulsion, applies to any event or situation that produces an upheaval or complete reversal of an existing order <the French Revolution ranks as one of the *cataclysms* of the modern era>.

disavow see DISCLAIM.

disbelief see UNBELIEF.

disburse see SPEND.

discard, cast, shed, slough, scrap, junk mean to get rid of as of no further use, value, or service.

Discard implies the letting go or throwing away of something that has become useless or superfluous though often not intrinsically valueless <*discard* any clothes you are unlikely to wear again>.

Cast, especially when used with *off, away,* and *out,* implies a forceful rejection or repudiation <*cast* off her friends when they grew tiresome>.

Shed refers to the seasonal or periodic casting of natural parts, such as antlers, hair, skin, or leaves, and to the discarding of whatever has become burdensome or uncomfortable <*shed* her tight shoes at the first opportunity>.

Slough implies the shedding of tissue, as from a scar or wound, or the discarding of what has become objectionable or useless <finally *sloughed* off her air of jaded worldliness>.

Scrap suggests a throwing away or breaking up as worthless but implies the possibility of salvage or further utility <all the old ideas of warfare had to be *scrapped*>.

Junk is close to *scrap* but tends to stress finality in disposal <those who would *junk* our entire educational system>.

discern see SEE 1.

discernment, discrimination, perception, penetration, insight, acumen mean a power to see what is not evident to the average mind.

Discernment stresses accuracy, as for example, in reading character or motives or appreciating art <had not the *discernment* to know who her friends really were>.

Discrimination stresses the power to distinguish and select what is true or appropriate or excellent <acquire *discrimination* by looking at a lot of art>.

Perception implies quick and often sympathetic discernment and delicacy of feeling <a novelist of keen *perception*>.

Penetration implies a searching mind that goes beyond what is obvious or superficial <has not the *penetration* to see beneath their deceptive facade>.

Insight suggests depth of discernment coupled with sympathetic understanding <a documentary providing *insight* into the plight of the homeless>. ***ant*** obtuseness

Acumen implies consistent penetration combined with keen practical judgment <a theater director of reliable critical *acumen*>. ***ant*** obtuseness

discharge see PERFORM.

disciple see FOLLOWER.

discipline **1.** see PUNISH. **2.** see TEACH.

disclaim, disavow, repudiate, disown, disallow mean to refuse to admit, accept, or approve.

Disclaim implies a refusal to accept either a rightful claim or an imputation made by another <*disclaimed* in equal measure the virtues and vices attributed to her>. ***ant*** claim

Disavow implies a vigorous denial of personal responsibility, acceptance, or approval <the radical group *disavowed* any responsibility for the bombing>. ***ant*** avow

Repudiate implies a rejection or denial of something that had been previously acknowledged, recognized, or accepted <*repudiated* the socialist views of his college days>. ***ant*** own

Disown implies a vigorous rejection or renunciation of something with which one formerly had a close relationship <*disowned* his allegiance to the country of his birth>. ***ant*** own

Disallow implies the withholding of sanction or approval and sometimes suggests complete rejection or condemnation <IRS auditors *disallowed* that deduction>. ***ant*** allow

disclose see REVEAL.

discomfit see EMBARRASS.

discompose, disquiet, disturb, perturb, agitate, upset, fluster mean to destroy capacity for collected thought or decisive action.

Discompose implies a minor degree of loss of self-control or self-confidence especially through emotional stress <*discomposed* by the heckler's shouts>. ***ant*** compose

Disquiet suggests loss of sense of security or peace of mind and often the resulting uncertainty or fear <the *disquieting* news of a tragic accident>. ***ant*** quiet, tranquilize, soothe

Disturb implies interference with one's mental processes or emotional balance by worry, perplexity, or fear <the puzzling discrepancy *disturbed* me>.

Perturb implies deep disturbance of mind and emotions <*perturbed* by her husband's strange behavior>. ***ant*** compose

Agitate suggests obvious external signs of nervous or emotional excitement <in his *agitated* state he was unfit to go to work>. ***ant*** calm, tranquilize

Upset implies the disturbance of normal or habitual functioning by disappointment, distress, or grief <constant bickering that greatly *upsets* their son>.

Fluster suggests a bewildered agitation caused by unexpected or sudden demands <his amorous advances completely *flustered* her>.

disconcert see EMBARRASS.

disconsolate see DOWNCAST.

discontinue see STOP.

discord, strife, conflict, contention, dissension, difference, variance mean a state or condition marked by a lack of agreement or harmony.

Discord implies an intrinsic or essential lack of harmony that produces quarreling, factiousness, or antagonism between persons or things <years of *discord* had left their mark on the political party>. ***ant*** concord, harmony

Strife emphasizes a struggle for superiority rather than a fundamental disharmony or incompatibility <during his reign the empire was free of *strife*>. ***ant*** peace, accord

Conflict usually stresses the action of forces in opposition but it may also imply an incompatibility or irreconcilability, such as of duties or desires <a *conflict* of professional interests>. ***ant*** harmony

Contention applies to strife or competition that shows itself in quarreling, disputing, or controversy <several points of *contention* between the two sides>.

Dissension implies strife or discord and stresses a division into factions <religious *dissensions* threatened to split the colony>. ***ant*** accord, comity

Difference, often in the plural, suggests actual incompatibility or impossibility of reconciliation because of dissimilarity in opinion, character, or nature <decided to negotiate a reconciliation of their *differences*>.

Variance implies discord or strife between persons or things arising from a difference in nature, opinion, or interest <cultural *variances* delayed the process of national unification>.

discover 1. Discover, ascertain, determine, unearth, learn mean to find out something not previously known to one.

Discover may apply to something requiring exploration or investigation or to a chance encounter and always implies the prior existence of what becomes known <*discovered* the source of the river>.

Ascertain implies an awareness of ignorance or uncertainty and a conscious effort to find the facts or the truth <will try to *ascertain* the population of the region>.

Determine, largely scientific or legal in usage, emphasizes the intent to establish the facts or to decide a dispute or controversy <unable to *determine* the exact cause of the disease>.

Unearth implies a bringing to light of something forgotten or hidden <*unearth* old records>.

Learn implies acquiring knowledge either with little effort or conscious intention <*learned* the truth by chance> or by study and practice <spent years *learning* Greek>.

2. see INVENT.

3. see REVEAL.

discrete see DISTINCT.

discrimination see DISCERNMENT.

discuss, argue, debate, dispute mean to discourse about something in order to reach conclusions or to convince others of the validity of one's position.

Discuss implies a sifting of possibilities by presenting considerations pro and con <*discussed* the need for widening the expressway>.

Argue implies the often heated offering of reasons or evidence in support of convictions already held <*argued* that the project would be too costly>.

Debate suggests formal or public argument between opposing parties <*debated* the merits of the proposed constitutional amendment>; it may also apply to deliberation with oneself <I'm *debating* whether I should go>.

Dispute implies contentious or heated argument <scientists *dispute* the reasons for the extinction of the dinosaurs>. ***ant*** concede

disdain see DESPISE.

disdainful see PROUD.

disembarrass see EXTRICATE.

disencumber see EXTRICATE.

disentangle see EXTRICATE.

disfigure see DEFACE.

disgrace, dishonor, disrepute, shame, infamy, ignominy, opprobrium mean the loss of esteem and good repute and the enduring of reproach and contempt.

Disgrace often implies loss of favor or complete humiliation and sometimes ostracism <his conviction for bribery brought *disgrace* upon his family>. ***ant*** respect, esteem

Dishonor emphasizes the loss of honor that one has previously enjoyed or the loss of self-esteem <prefer death to life with *dishonor*>. ***ant*** honor

Disrepute stresses loss of one's good name or the acquiring of a bad reputation <a once-proud name now fallen into *disrepute*>. ***ant*** repute

Shame implies particularly humiliating disgrace or disrepute and is likely to stress the strong emotional reaction of the one affected <could hardly live with the *shame*>. ***ant*** glory, pride

Infamy implies notoriety as well as exceeding shame <a gangster whose name retains an enduring *infamy*>.

Ignominy stresses the almost unendurable contemptibility or despicableness of the disgrace <suffered the *ignominy* of being brought back in irons>.

Opprobrium adds to *disgrace* the notion of being severely reproached or condemned <bring *opprobrium* on oneself by expulsion from school>.

disguise, cloak, mask, dissemble mean to alter the dress or appearance so as to conceal the identity, intention, or true feeling.

Disguise implies a deceptive changing of appearance or behavior that serves to conceal an identity, a motive, or an attitude <*disguised* himself as a peasant to escape detection>.

Cloak suggests the assumption of something that covers and conceals identity or intention completely <*cloaks* her greed and self-interest in the rhetoric of philosophy>. ***ant*** uncloak

Mask suggests the prevention of recognition of a thing's true character usually by some obvious means and does not always imply deception or pretense <a smiling front that *masks* a will of iron>.

Dissemble stresses simulation for the purpose of deceiving and disguising especially feelings and opinions <*dissembled* madness to survive the intrigues at court>. ***ant*** betray

dishonest, deceitful, mendacious, lying, untruthful mean unworthy of trust or belief.

Dishonest implies a willful perversion of truth in order to deceive, cheat, or defraud <a swindle usually involves *dishonest* people>. ***ant*** honest

Deceitful usually implies an intent to mislead and commonly suggests a false appearance or duplicitous behavior <learned of the secret of his *deceitful* partner>. ***ant*** trustworthy

Mendacious, less forthright than *lying*, may suggest bland or even harmless mischievous deceit and often suggests a habit of telling untruths <his sea stories became increasingly *mendacious*>. ***ant*** veracious

Lying implies a specific act or instance rather than a habit or tendency and suggests guilt <a conviction based upon testimony of a *lying* witness>. ***ant*** truthtelling

Untruthful is a less harsh term than *lying* and stresses a discrepancy between what is said or represented and the facts or reality of the situation rather than an intent to deceive <the

version given in her memoirs is *untruthful* in several respects>. ***ant*** truthful

dishonor see DISGRACE.

disillusioned see SOPHISTICATED.

disinclined, hesitant, reluctant, loath, averse mean lacking the will or desire to do something indicated.

Disinclined implies lack of taste for or inclination toward something and may imply disapproval <*disinclined* to go out in bad weather>. ***ant*** inclined

Hesitant implies a holding back through fear, uncertainty, or disinclination <*hesitant* about asking her for a date>.

Reluctant implies a holding back through resistance or unwillingness <I'm *reluctant* to blame anyone just now>.

Loath implies lack of harmony between what one anticipates doing and one's opinions, predilections, or liking <*loath* to believe that he could do anything right>. ***ant*** anxious

Averse implies a turning away from what is distasteful or unwelcome <seems *averse* to anything requiring work>. ***ant*** avid *(of or for),* athirst *(for)*

disinterested see INDIFFERENT.

disloyal see FAITHLESS.

dismal, dreary, cheerless, dispiriting, bleak, desolate mean devoid of all that is cheerful and comfortable.

Dismal may imply extreme gloominess or somberness that is utterly depressing <a *dismal* day of unrelenting rain>.

Dreary implies a sustained gloom, dullness, or tiresomeness that discourages or enervates <spent her days alone in a *dreary* apartment>.

Cheerless stresses a pervasive, disheartening joylessness or hopelessness <faced a *cheerless* life as a drudge>. ***ant*** cheerful

Dispiriting implies a disheartening or lessening of morale or determination <problems that made for a *dispiriting* start for their new venture>. ***ant*** inspiriting

Bleak implies a chilly, dull barrenness that disheartens and lacks any notions of cheer, shelter, or comfort <a *bleak,* windswept landscape offering no refuge for the wayward traveler>.

Desolate implies that something disheartens by being utterly barren, lifeless, uninhabitable, or abandoned <the long trek into the country's *desolate* interior>.

dismay, appall, horrify, daunt mean to unnerve or deter by arousing fear, apprehension, or aversion.

Dismay implies a loss of power to proceed because of a sudden fear or anxiety or because one does not know how to deal with a situation <*dismayed* to find herself the center of attention>. ***ant*** cheer

Appall implies that one is faced with that which perturbs, confounds, or shocks <*appalled* by your utter lack of concern>. ***ant*** nerve, embolden

Horrify stresses a reaction of horror or revulsion from what is ghastly or hideously offensive <the scope of the famine is quite *horrifying*>.

Daunt suggests a cowing, subduing, disheartening, or frightening in a venture requiring courage <problems that would *daunt* even the most intrepid of reformers>. ***ant*** enhearten

dismiss see EJECT.

disown see DISCLAIM.

disparage see DECRY.

disparaging see DEROGATORY.

disparate see DIFFERENT.

dispassionate see FAIR.

dispatch *n* see HASTE.

dispatch *vb* see KILL.

dispel see SCATTER.

dispense see DISTRIBUTE.

disperse see SCATTER.

dispirited see DOWNCAST.

dispiriting see DISMAL.

displace see REPLACE.

display see SHOW 2.

dispose see INCLINE.

disposition, temperament, temper, complexion, character, personality mean the dominant quality or qualities distinguishing a person or group.

Disposition implies customary moods and attitudes toward the life around one <a boy of cheerful *disposition*>.

Temperament implies a pattern of innate characteristics that result from one's specific physical, emotional, and mental makeup <an artistic *temperament* inherited from his mother>.

Temper implies the qualities acquired through experience that determines how a person or group meets difficulties or handles situations <the national *temper* has always been one of optimism>.

Complexion implies some distinctive quality of mood, attitude, and way of thinking that determines the impression produced on others <a leader of severe and authoritarian *complexion*>.

Character applies to the aggregate of moral qualities by which a person is judged apart from his intelligence, competence, or special talents <a woman of resolute *character*>.

Personality applies to an aggregate of qualities that distinguish one as an individual <a somber *personality* not to everyone's liking>.

disprove, refute, confute, rebut, controvert mean to show or try to show by presenting evidence that something is not true.

Disprove implies the successful demonstration by any method of the falsity or invalidity of a claim or argument <the view that one can neither prove nor *disprove* the existence of God>. ***ant*** prove, demonstrate

Refute stresses a logical method of disproving and suggests adducing of evidence, bringing forward of witnesses or authorities, and close reasoning <*refuted* every piece of his argument>.

Confute implies reducing an opponent to silence by an overwhelming refutation or by such methods as raillery, denunciation, or sarcasm <a triumphal flight that *confuted* all of the doubters>.

Rebut suggests formality of method but not assurance of success in answering an opponent's argument, evidence, or testimony <give the opposing side time to *rebut*>.

Controvert stresses both the denial of and the attempt to disprove what is put forward without necessarily implying success in refutation <a thesis that withstood every attempt to *controvert* it>. ***ant*** assert

dispute see DISCUSS.

disquiet see DISCOMPOSE.

disregard see NEGLECT.

disrepute see DISGRACE.

dissect see ANALYZE.

dissemble see DISGUISE.

dissension see DISCORD.

dissipate **1.** see SCATTER. **2.** see WASTE.

dissolve see ADJOURN.

distant, far, far-off, faraway, remote, removed mean not close in space, time, or relationship.

Distant stresses separation and implies an obvious interval whether long or short <went to live in a *distant* city>.

Far in most of its uses applies to what is a long way off <retreat to the *far* reaches of the wilderness>. ***ant*** near, nigh

Far-off stresses distance and is often preferred when distance in time is specifically implied <some *far-off* day>. ***ant*** near-at-hand

Faraway differs little from *far-off* but may sometimes connote a hazy remoteness or even obscurity <began to have a *faraway* look in her eyes>. ***ant*** near, nigh

Remote suggests a far removal from one's point of view, time, or location and is likely to connote a consequent lessening of importance to oneself <spent her life on a *remote* island>. ***ant*** close, adjacent

Removed carries a stronger implication of separateness and may suggest a contrast not only in time and space but in character or quality <sought a quiet retreat, *removed* from the everyday world and its tensions>. ***ant*** adjoining

distasteful see REPUGNANT.

distend see EXPAND.

distinct 1. Distinct, separate, several, discrete mean not being each and every one the same.

Distinct indicates that something is distinguished by the mind or eye as being apart or different from others <each and every bowl is hand-decorated and *distinct*>. ***ant*** indistinguishable

Separate often stresses lack of connection in space or time or a difference in identity between the things in question <the two schools are *separate* and unequal>.

Several indicates distinctness, difference, or separation from similar items <a survey of the *several* opinions of the new building>.

Discrete strongly emphasizes individuality and lack of material connection despite apparent similarity or continuity <two *discrete* issues are being confused here>.

2. see EVIDENT.

distinctive see CHARACTERISTIC.

distinguished see FAMOUS.

distort see DEFORM.

distract see PUZZLE.

distress *n* **Distress, suffering, misery, agony** mean the state of being in great trouble or in pain of body or mind.

Distress implies an external cause of great physical or mental strain and stress and is likely to connote the possibility of or the need for relief <news of the hurricane put everyone in great *distress*>.

Suffering implies conscious endurance of pain or distress and often a stoical acceptance <the *suffering* of earthquake victims>.

Misery stresses the unhappiness attending distress or suffering and often connotes sordidness, abjectness, or dull passivity <the poor live with *misery* every day>. ***ant*** felicity, blessedness

Agony suggests pain too intense to be borne by body or mind <in *agony* over their daughter's suicide>.

distress *vb* see TROUBLE.

distribute, dispense, divide, deal, dole mean to give out, usually in shares, to each member of a group.

Distribute implies an apportioning by separation of something into parts, units, or amounts and a spreading out of those parts equally, systematically, or at random <*distributed* the work to all employees>. ***ant*** collect, amass

Dispense suggests the giving of a carefully weighed or measured portion to each of a group according to need or as a right or as due <*dispensed* medicine during the epidemic>.

Divide stresses the separation of a whole into parts before giving out or delivering and implies that the parts are equal <three charitable groups *divided* the proceeds>.

Deal emphasizes the allotment of something piece by piece in turn to each of the members of a group <*deal* out equipment and supplies to each soldier>.

Dole implies a scantiness or niggardliness in the amount dispensed <*doled* out the little food there was>.

disturb see DISCOMPOSE.
dither see SHAKE 1.
diurnal see DAILY.
dive see PLUNGE.
diverge see SWERVE.
divergent see DIFFERENT.
diverse see DIFFERENT.
divert see AMUSE.
divide 1. see DISTRIBUTE. **2.** see SEPARATE.
divine see FORESEE.
division see PART.
divorce see SEPARATE.
divulge see REVEAL.
docile see OBEDIENT.
doctrinaire see DICTATORIAL.
doctrine, dogma, tenet mean a principle accepted as valid and authoritative.

Doctrine may imply authoritative teaching backed by acceptance by a body of believers or adherents <a catechism of religious *doctrines*> but *doctrine* can be used more broadly to denote a formulated theory that is supported by evidence, backed by authority, and proposed for acceptance <the *doctrine* of organic evolution>.

Dogma implies a doctrine that is laid down as true and beyond dispute <in 1870 Pope Pius IX defined the *dogma* of papal infallibility> and may connote arbitrary or even arrogant insistence on authority or imposition by authority <the *dogma* that the king can do no wrong>.

Tenet stresses acceptance and belief rather than teaching and applies to a principle held or adhered to and implies a body of adherents <the *tenets* of socialism>.

dogged see OBSTINATE.
dogma see DOCTRINE.
dogmatic see DICTATORIAL.
doldrums see TEDIUM.
dole *n* see RATION.
dole *vb* see DISTRIBUTE.

dominant, predominant, paramount, preponderant, sovereign mean superior to all others in power, influence, or importance.

Dominant applies to something that is uppermost because it rules or controls <a *dominant* wolf>. ***ant*** subordinate

Predominant applies to something that exerts, often temporarily, the most marked influence on a person or a situation <at the time fear was my *predominant* emotion>. ***ant*** subordinate

Paramount implies supremacy in importance, rank, or jurisdiction <inflation was the *paramount* issue in the campaign>.

Preponderant applies to an element or factor that outweighs all others with which it may come into comparison in influence, power, number, or effect <*preponderant* evidence in his favor>.

Sovereign indicates quality or rank to which everything else is clearly subordinate or inferior <the *sovereign* power resides in the people>.

domineering see MASTERFUL.

dominion see POWER 3.

donate see GIVE.

doom see FATE.

dormant see LATENT.

double-dealing see DECEPTION.

double entendre see AMBIGUITY.

doubt see UNCERTAINTY.

doubtful, dubious, problematic, questionable mean not affording assurance of the worth, soundness, or certainty of something or someone.

Doubtful is likely to impute worthlessness, unsoundness, failure, or uncertainty <still *doubtful* about the cause of the explosion>. ***ant*** positive

Dubious stresses suspicion, mistrust, or hesitation <*dubious* about the practicality of the scheme>. ***ant*** cocksure, reliable, trustworthy

Problematic applies especially to things or situations whose existence, meaning, or realization is highly uncertain <whether the project will ever be finished is *problematic*>. ***ant*** unproblematic

Questionable may imply no more than the existence of doubt but usually suggests doubt about propriety or well-grounded suspicions <a real estate agent of *questionable* honesty>. ***ant*** authoritative, unquestioned

dour see SULLEN.

dowdy see SLATTERNLY.

downcast, dispirited, dejected, depressed, disconsolate, woebegone mean affected by or showing very low spirits.

Downcast implies being overcome by shame, mortification, or loss of hope or confidence and an utter lack of cheerfulness <negative reviews left the actors feeling *downcast*>. ***ant*** elated

Dispirited implies extreme low-spiritedness and discouragement resulting from failure to accomplish what one wants or to achieve one's goal <*dispirited,* the doomed explorers resigned themselves to failure>. ***ant*** high-spirited, inspirited

Dejected implies a sudden but often temporary severe loss of hope, courage, or vigor <a crushing defeat that left the team in a *dejected* mood>. ***ant*** animated

Depressed may imply either a temporary or a chronic low-spiritedness and may indicate a serious inability to be normally happy and active <*depressed* by his failures to the point of suicide>. ***ant*** exhilarated, animated

Disconsolate implies being inconsolable or very uncomfortable <*disconsolate* motorists leaning against their disabled car>. ***ant*** cheerful

Woebegone suggests a defeated, spiritless condition and emphasizes the impression of dejection and discouragement produced by facial expression, posture, and surroundings <a rundown, *woebegone* motel on an empty back road>.

drag see PULL.

drain see DEPLETE.

dramatic, theatrical, melodramatic, histrionic mean having a character or effects typical of acted plays.

Dramatic applies to a speech, action, gesture, or situation capable of stirring the imagination and emotions deeply <a *dramatic* meeting of world leaders>.

Theatrical implies a crude appeal to the emotions through artificiality or exaggeration in gesture, action, or vocal expression <a *theatrical* oration>.

Melodramatic suggests an exaggerated emotionalism or an inappropriate theatricalism <making a *melodramatic* scene in public>.

Histrionic applies to tones, gestures, and motions and suggests a deliberate affectation or staginess <a *histrionic* show of grief>.

draw see PULL.

dread see FEAR.

dreadful see FEARFUL 2.

dreary see DISMAL.

drench see SOAK.

drift see TENDENCY.

drill see PRACTICE.

drive see MOVE.

droll see LAUGHABLE.

drowsy see SLEEPY.

drudgery see WORK 1.

drunk, drunken, intoxicated, inebriated, tipsy, tight, plastered mean considerably and conspicuously affected by alcohol.

Drunk and ***drunken*** are the plainspoken, direct, and inclusive terms <arrived at the party already *drunk*> <a *drunken* man stumbled out of the bar> but *drunken* may imply habitual excess in drinking and also applies to whatever proceeds from intoxication <a *drunken* brawl>. ***ant*** sober

Intoxicated is a more formal, less derogatory term and likely to be used in legal or medical contexts <arrested for driving while *intoxicated*>. ***ant*** sober

Inebriated implies such a state of intoxication that exhilaration, noise, or undue excitement results <the *inebriated* revelers bellowed out songs>.

Tipsy may imply only slight drunkenness and the consequent lessening of muscular and mental control <a *tipsy* patron began making unwelcome amorous advances>.

Tight usually suggests obvious drunkenness <at midnight he returned, *tight* as a drum>.

Plastered refers to one who has become wholly incompetent through intoxication <so *plastered* they could not stand up>.

drunken see DRUNK.

dry, arid mean lacking or deficient in moisture.

Dry may suggest freedom from noticeable moisture either as a characteristic or a desirable state <a *dry* climate> or it may suggest deficiency of moisture or the lack or loss of normal or needed moisture <the spring has gone *dry*> or lack of those qualities in anything that compel interest or attention or in a person indicate vitality, warmth, or responsiveness <possessed a *dry* manner and a droning voice>. ***ant*** wet

Arid implies destitution or deprivation of moisture and extreme dryness; in its typical applications to regions or territory it suggests waste or desert lands <a bare *arid* stretch of country>; it may also suggest absence of those qualities that mark a thing as worthwhile, fruitful, or significant <presented an *arid* paper devoid of intellectual content>. ***ant*** moist, verdant

dubiety see UNCERTAINTY.

dubious see DOUBTFUL.

ductile see PLASTIC.

dudgeon see OFFENSE 1.

dulcet see SWEET.

dull 1. Dull, blunt, obtuse mean not sharp, keen, or acute.

Dull suggests a lack or loss of keenness, zest, or pungency <a *dull* pain>. ***ant*** sharp, poignant, lively

Blunt suggests an inherent lack of sharpness or quickness of feeling or perception <even a person of his *blunt* sensibility was moved>. ***ant*** keen, sharp

Obtuse implies such bluntness as makes one insensitive in perception, speech, or imagination <too *obtuse* to realize that she had deeply hurt us>. ***ant*** acute

2. see STUPID.

dumb see STUPID.

dumbfound see PUZZLE.

dumpy see STOCKY.

dupe, gull, trick, hoax mean to deceive by underhanded means for one's own ends.

Dupe suggests unwariness in the person deluded <*duped* us into buying a lemon of a car>.

Gull stresses credulousness or readiness to be imposed on or made a fool of <you are so easily *gulled* by these contest promoters>.

Trick implies an intent, not always vicious, to delude by means of a ruse or fraud <special effects can *trick* moviegoers into believing anything>.

Hoax implies the contriving of an elaborate or adroit imposture in order to deceive <*hoaxed* the public by broadcasting news of a Martian invasion>.

duplicate see REPRODUCTION.

durable see LASTING.

dusky see DARK.

duty 1. see FUNCTION. **2.** see TASK.

dwell see RESIDE.

dwindle see DECREASE.

E

eager, avid, keen, anxious, athirst mean moved by a strong and urgent desire or interest.

Eager implies ardor and enthusiasm and sometimes impatience at delay or restraint <*eager* to get started on the trip>. ***ant*** listless

Avid adds to *eager* the implication of insatiability or greed <young pleasure-seekers *avid* for the next thrill>. ***ant*** indifferent, averse

Keen suggests intensity of interest and quick responsiveness in action <very *keen* on the latest styles and fashions>.

Anxious suggests earnest desire but emphasizes fear of frustration, failure, or disappointment <*anxious* to know that they got home safely>. ***ant*** loath

Athirst stresses yearning or longing but not necessarily readiness for action <*athirst* for adventure on her first trip to India>.

earn see GET.

earnest see SERIOUS.

earsplitting see LOUD.

earthly, mundane, worldly mean belonging to or characteristic of the earth.

Earthly often implies a contrast with what is heavenly or spiritual <abandoned *earthly* concerns and entered a convent>.

Mundane implies a relation to the immediate concerns and activities of human beings and stresses what is transitory and impermanent or practical and ordinary <a *mundane* discussion of finances>. ***ant*** eternal

Worldly implies indifference to spiritual matters and preoccupation with the mundane and the satisfaction of the appetites <nightclub habitués with a *worldly* air>. ***ant*** otherworldly

ease see READINESS.

easy 1. Easy, facile, simple, light, effortless, smooth mean not demanding undue effort or involving difficulty.

Easy is applicable either to persons or things imposing tasks or making demands or to activities required by such tasks or demands <an *easy* college course requiring little work>. ***ant*** hard

Facile chiefly applies to something that is achieved or gains its ends apparently without effort and implies lack of restraint, undue haste, or shallowness <offers only *facile* solutions to complex problems>. ***ant*** arduous *(referring to the thing accomplished)*, constrained, clumsy *(referring to the agent or the method)*

Simple stresses ease in understanding or apprehending because free from complication, intricacy, or elaboration <a *simple* problem in arithmetic>. ***ant*** complicated, difficult

Light stresses freedom from what is burdensome or difficult and exacting, and often suggests quickness of movement <her novels are pretty *light* stuff>. ***ant*** heavy, arduous, burdensome

Effortless stresses the appearance of ease and implies the prior attainment of artistry or expertness <a champion figure skater moving with *effortless* grace>. ***ant*** painstaking

Smooth stresses the absence or removal of all difficulties, hardships, or obstacles from a course or career <made *smooth,* swift progress up the corporate ladder>. ***ant*** labored

2. see COMFORTABLE.

ebb see ABATE.

eccentric see STRANGE.

eccentricity, idiosyncrasy mean singularity in behavior or an instance of this.

Eccentricity retains its basic notion of being off center and in this use stresses divergence from the usual or customary <led a life of charming *eccentricities*>.

Idiosyncrasy stresses a strongly individual and independent quality and is likely to imply a following of one's peculiar bent or temperament <a style marked by *idiosyncrasy*>.

economical see SPARING.

ecstasy, rapture, transport mean intense exaltation of mind and feelings.

Ecstasy may apply to any strong emotion (such as joy, fear, rage, or adoration) that can entrance <the sculptor was in *ecstasy* when his work was unveiled>. ***ant*** depression

Rapture implies intense bliss or utter delight <in speechless *rapture* during the entire wedding>.

Transport applies to any powerful emotion that lifts one out of oneself and provokes vehement expression or frenzied action <in a *transport* of rage after reading the article>.

edge see BORDER.

educate see TEACH.

educe, evoke, elicit, extract, extort mean to draw out something hidden, latent, or reserved.

Educe implies the development and bringing out of something potential or latent <*educe* from common sense the best solution to the problem>.

Evoke implies a strong stimulus that arouses an emotion or an interest or recalls an image or memory from the past <a song that *evokes* many memories>.

Elicit implies some effort or skill in drawing forth a response and often implies resistance in the object of effort <unable to *elicit* a straight answer from the candidate>.

Extract implies the use of force or pressure in obtaining answers or information <*extract* testimony from a hostile witness>.

Extort suggests a wringing or wresting of something from one who resists strongly <*extorted* the money from his father-in-law>.

eerie see WEIRD.

efface see ERASE.

effect *n* **Effect, consequence, result, issue, outcome** mean a condition or occurrence traceable to a cause.

Effect designates something that necessarily and directly follows upon or occurs by reason of a cause <the *effects* of radiation on the body>. ***ant*** cause

Consequence implies a direct but looser or remoter connection with a cause and usually implies that the cause is no longer operating <a single act that had far-reaching *consequences*>. ***ant*** antecedent

Result applies often to the last in a series of effects <the end *result* was a growth in business>.

Issue applies to a result that ends or solves a problem, a difficulty, or a conflict <a successful *issue* that rendered all the controversy moot>.

Outcome suggests the final result of complex or conflicting causes or forces <the *outcome* of generations of controlled breeding>.

effect *vb* see PERFORM.

effective, effectual, efficient, efficacious mean producing or capable of producing a result.

Effective stresses the actual production of or the power to produce an effect <an *effective* rebuttal>. ***ant*** ineffective, futile

Effectual suggests the accomplishment of a desired result or the fulfillment of a purpose especially as viewed after the fact <the measures to halt crime proved *effectual*>. ***ant*** ineffectual, fruitless

Efficient suggests an acting or a potential for action or use in such a way as to avoid loss or waste of energy in effecting, producing, or functioning <an *efficient* small car>. ***ant*** inefficient

Efficacious suggests possession of a special quality or virtue that gives effective power <a detergent that is *efficacious* in removing grease>. ***ant*** inefficacious, powerless

effectual see EFFECTIVE.

effeminate see FEMALE.

efficacious see EFFECTIVE.

efficient see EFFECTIVE.

effort, exertion, pains, trouble mean the active use of energy in producing a result.

Effort often suggests a single action or attempt or persistent activity and implies the calling up or directing of energy by the conscious will <made the supreme *effort* and crossed the finish line first>. ***ant*** ease

Exertion may describe the bringing into effect of any power of mind or body or it may suggest laborious and exhausting effort <a job not requiring much physical *exertion*>.

Pains implies toilsome or solicitous effort by a conscientious agent <take *pains* to do the job well>.

Trouble implies effort that inconveniences or wastes time and patience <went to a lot of *trouble* to get the right equipment>.

effortless see EASY.

effrontery see TEMERITY.

egregious see FLAGRANT.

eject, expel, oust, evict, dismiss mean to drive or force out.

Eject carries an especially strong implication of throwing or thrusting out from within <*ejected* the obnoxious patron from the bar>. ***ant*** admit

Expel stresses a voluntary, often permanent thrusting out or driving away <a student *expelled* from college>. ***ant*** admit

Oust implies removal or dispossession by power of the law, by force, or by compulsion of necessity <issued a general order *ousting* all foreigners>.

Evict chiefly applies to a turning out of house and home by a legal or comparable process <*evicted* for nonpayment of rent>.

Dismiss implies a getting rid of something unpleasant or troublesome by refusing to consider it further <simply *dismissed* the quarrel from her mind>.

elastic, resilient, springy, flexible, supple mean able to endure strain without being permanently altered or injured.

Elastic implies the property of resisting deformation by stretching <slacks that come with an *elastic* waistband>. ***ant*** rigid

Resilient implies the ability to recover shape quickly when the deforming force or pressure is removed <a good running shoe has a *resilient* innersole>.

Springy stresses both the ease with which something yields to pressure and the quickness of its return to original shape <the cake is done when the top is *springy*>. ***ant*** rigid, springless

Flexible applies to something which may or may not be resilient or elastic but which can be bent or folded without breaking <*flexible* plastic tubing>. ***ant*** inflexible

Supple applies to something that can be readily bent, twisted, or folded without any sign of injury <shoes made of luxurious, *supple* leather>. ***ant*** stiff

elect see SELECT.

election see CHOICE *n*.

electrify see THRILL.

elegant see CHOICE *adj*.

element, component, constituent, ingredient, factor mean one of the parts, substances, or principles of a compound or complex whole.

Element applies to any such part and often connotes irreducible simplicity <the basic *elements* of the gothic novel>. ***ant*** compound, composite

Component stresses the separate identity or distinguishable character of the elements <able to identify every *component* of his firearm>. ***ant*** composite, complex

Constituent stresses the essential and formative relationship of the elements, substances, or qualities to the whole <analyzed the *constituents* of the compound>. ***ant*** aggregate, whole

Ingredient applies to any of the substances which can be combined to form a mixture that has qualities that may be different from those of the constituents <the *ingredients* of a cocktail>.

Factor applies to any constituent or element whose presence actively helps to perform a certain kind of work or produce a particular result <price was a *factor* in her decision to buy>.

elevate see LIFT.
elevation see HEIGHT.
elicit see EDUCE.
eliminate see EXCLUDE.
elite see ARISTOCRACY.
elongate see EXTEND.
eloquent see VOCAL 2.
elucidate see EXPLAIN.
elude see ESCAPE.
emanate see SPRING.
emancipate see FREE *vb*.
emasculate see UNNERVE.
embarrass, discomfit, abash, disconcert, rattle, faze mean to distress by confusing or confounding.

Embarrass implies some influence that impedes thought, speech, or action <*embarrassed* to admit that she liked the movie>.

Discomfit implies a hampering or frustrating accompanied by confusion <persistent heckling *discomfited* the speaker>.

Abash presupposes some initial self-confidence that receives a sudden check by something that produces shyness, shame, or a conviction of inferiority <completely *abashed* by her swift and cutting retort>. ***ant*** embolden, reassure

Disconcert implies an upsetting of equanimity or assurance producing uncertainty or hesitancy <*disconcerted* by the sight of the large audience>.

Rattle implies a disorganizing agitation that impairs thought and judgment and undermines normal poise and composure <a tennis player not at all *rattled* by television cameras>.

Faze, found chiefly in negative phrases, suggests a loss of assurance or equanimity, often sudden and thorough <a veteran teacher *fazed* by nothing>.

embellish see ADORN.
emblem see SYMBOL.
embolden see ENCOURAGE.
embrace 1. see ADOPT. **2.** see INCLUDE.
emend see CORRECT *vb*.
emergency see JUNCTURE.
eminent see FAMOUS.
emotion see FEELING.
empathy see SYMPATHY.
employ see USE *vb*.
employment see WORK 2.

empower see ENABLE.

empty 1. Empty, vacant, blank, void, vacuous mean lacking contents which could or should be present.

Empty suggests a complete absence of contents <an *empty* bucket>. ***ant*** full

Vacant suggests an absence of appropriate contents or occupants <a *vacant* apartment>. ***ant*** occupied

Blank stresses the absence of any significant, relieving, or intelligible features on a surface <a *blank* wall>.

Void suggests absolute emptiness as far as the mind or senses can determine <a statement *void* of meaning>.

Vacuous suggests the emptiness of a vacuum and especially the lack of intelligence or significance <a *vacuous* facial expression>.

2. see VAIN.

emulate see RIVAL 1.

enable, empower mean to make one able to do something.

Enable implies provision of the means or opportunity to do something <a job that *enables* them to live with dignity>.

Empower refers to the provision of the power or the delegation of the authority to do something <a law which *empowers* the courts to try such cases>.

enchant see ATTRACT.

encomium. eulogy, panegyric, tribute, citation mean a formal expression of praise.

Encomium implies warm enthusiasm in praise of a person or a thing <the subject of several spirited *encomiums* at the banquet>.

Eulogy applies to a prepared speech, especially a funeral oration or an essay extolling the virtues and services of a person <delivered the *eulogy* at the funeral>. ***ant*** calumny, tirade

Panegyric suggests an elaborate often rhetorical or poetic compliment <coronations once inspired *panegyrics*>.

Tribute implies deeply felt praise conveyed either through words or through a significant act <a book of *tributes* marking his fifty years of service>.

Citation applies to the formal praise accompanying the mention of a person in a military dispatch or in awarding an honor <a *citation* noting her lasting contribution to biology>.

encourage, inspirit, hearten, embolden mean to fill with courage or strength of purpose.

Encourage suggests the raising of one's confidence especially by an external agency <the teacher's praise *encouraged* the student to try even harder>. ***ant*** discourage

Inspirit implies the instilling of life, energy, courage, or vigor into something <pioneers *inspirited* by the stirring accounts of the explorers>. ***ant*** dispirit

Hearten implies the lifting of a dispiritedness or despondency by an infusion of fresh courage or zeal <a hospital patient *heartened* by the display of moral support>. ***ant*** dishearten

Embolden implies the giving of courage sufficient to overcome timidity or reluctance <a successful climb *emboldened* her to try more difficult ones>. ***ant*** abash

encroach see TRESPASS.

end *n* **1. End, termination, ending, terminus** mean the point or line beyond which something does not or cannot go.

End is the inclusive term, implying the final limit in time or space, in extent of influence, or in range of possibility <the report put an *end* to all speculation>. ***ant*** beginning

Termination applies to the end of something having predetermined limits or being complete or finished <the *termination* of a lease>. ***ant*** inception, source

Ending often includes the portion leading to the actual final point <a film marred by a contrived *ending*>. ***ant*** beginning

Terminus applies commonly to a point toward which one moves or progresses <Chicago is the *terminus* for many air routes>. ***ant*** starting point

2. see INTENTION.

end *vb* see CLOSE *vb*.

endeavor see ATTEMPT.

endemic see NATIVE.

ending see END.

endorse see APPROVE.

endure 1. see BEAR. **2.** see CONTINUE.

enemy, foe mean an individual or a group who shows hostility or ill will to another.

Enemy stresses antagonism that may range from a deep hatred or a will to harm and destroy to no more than active or evident dislike or a habit of preying upon <a man with many friends and no *enemies*>.

Foe, preferred in rhetorical or poetic use, stresses active fighting or struggle rather than emotional reaction <a *foe* of all injustice>. ***ant*** friend

energetic see VIGOROUS.

energize see VITALIZE.

energy see POWER 1.

enervate see UNNERVE.

enfeeble see WEAKEN.

engagement see BATTLE.

engaging see SWEET.

engineer see GUIDE.

engross see MONOPOLIZE.

enhance see INTENSIFY.

enigma see MYSTERY.
enigmatic see OBSCURE.
enjoin see COMMAND.
enjoy see HAVE.
enjoyment see PLEASURE.
enlarge see INCREASE.
enliven see QUICKEN.
enmity, hostility, antipathy, antagonism, animosity, rancor, animus mean deep-seated dislike or ill will or a manifestation of such a feeling.

Enmity suggests positive hatred which may be open or concealed <an unspoken *enmity* seethed between the two>. ***ant*** amity

Hostility suggests a strong, open enmity showing itself in attacks or aggression <a history of *hostility* between the two nations>.

Antipathy implies a natural or logical basis for one's hatred or dislike, suggesting repugnance or a desire to avoid or reject <a natural *antipathy* for self-important upstarts>. ***ant*** taste *(for),* affection *(for)*

Antagonism suggests a clash of temperaments leading readily to hostility <a long-standing *antagonism* between the banker and his prodigal son>. ***ant*** accord, comity

Animosity suggests anger, intense ill will, and vindictiveness that threaten to hurt or destroy < *animosity* that eventually led to revenge>. ***ant*** good will

Rancor stresses bitter brooding or the nursing of a grudge or grievance <*rancor* filled every line of his letters>.

Animus implies strong prejudice and often malevolent or spiteful ill will <my objections are devoid of any personal *animus*>. ***ant*** favor

ennui see TEDIUM.
enormous, immense, huge, vast, gigantic, colossal, mammoth mean exceedingly or excessively large.

Enormous suggests an exceeding of all ordinary bounds in size or amount or degree and often adds an implication of abnormality or monstrousness <the *enormous* expense of the program>. ***ant*** tiny

Immense implies size far in excess of ordinary measurements or accustomed concepts <the *immense* size of the new shopping mall>.

Huge commonly suggests an immensity of size, bulk, or capacity <quickly incurred a *huge* debt>.

Vast suggests extreme largeness or broadness and immensity of extent <the *vast* Russian steppes>.

Gigantic stresses the contrast with the size of others of the same kind <a *gigantic* sports stadium>.

Colossal applies especially to something of stupendous or incredible dimensions <a *colossal* statue of Lincoln>.

Mammoth suggests both hugeness and ponderousness of bulk <a *mammoth* boulder>.

enough see SUFFICIENT.

enrapture see TRANSPORT 2.

ensnare see CATCH.

ensue see FOLLOW.

ensure, insure, assure, secure mean to make a thing or person sure.

Ensure implies a virtual guarantee <the government has *ensured* the safety of the foreign minister>.

Insure sometimes stresses the taking of necessary measures beforehand to make a result certain or to provide for any probable contingency <careful planning should *insure* the success of the party>.

Assure distinctively implies the removal of doubt, worry, or uncertainty from the mind <I *assure* you that no one will be harmed>. ***ant*** alarm

Secure implies the taking of action to ensure safety, protection, or certainty against adverse contingencies <*secure* their cooperation by payment of a large fee>.

enter, penetrate, pierce, probe mean to make way into something.

Enter, the most general of these, may imply either going in or forcing a way in <*entered* the city in triumph>. ***ant*** issue *(from)*

Penetrate carries a strong implication of an impelling force or compelling power that achieves entrance <no bullet has ever *penetrated* a vest of that material>.

Pierce adds to *penetrate* a clear implication of an entering point or wedge <a fracture in which the bone *pierces* the skin>.

Probe implies a penetration to investigate or explore something hidden from easy observation or knowledge <*probed* the depths of the sea>.

entertain 1. see AMUSE. **2.** see HARBOR.

enthuse see THRILL.

enthusiasm see PASSION.

entice see LURE.

entire 1. see PERFECT. **2.** see WHOLE.

entrance see TRANSPORT 2.

entrap see CATCH.

entreat see BEG.

entrench see TRESPASS.

entrust see COMMIT.

envious, jealous mean begrudging another possession of something desirable.

Envious stresses a coveting of something such as riches or attainments which belongs to another or of something such as success or good luck which has come to another and may imply an urgent, even malicious desire to see the other person dispossessed of what gives gratification, or it may imply no more than a mild coveting without desire to injure <we are all *envious* of your new dress>.

Jealous is likely to stress intolerance of a rival for the possession of what one regards as peculiarly one's own possession or due, but sometimes it implies no more than intensely zealous efforts to keep or maintain what one possesses; it often carries a strong implication of distrust, suspicion, enviousness, or sometimes anger <stabbed by a *jealous* lover>.

environment see BACKGROUND.

envisage see THINK 1.

envision see THINK 1.

ephemeral see TRANSIENT.

epicure, gourmet, gastronome, gourmand, bon vivant mean one who takes pleasure in eating and drinking.

Epicure implies fastidiousness and voluptuousness of taste <a delicacy that only an *epicure* would appreciate>.

Gourmet applies to a connoisseur in food and drink and suggests discriminating enjoyment <*gourmets* rate the restaurant highly>.

Gastronome stresses the possession of expert knowledge and appreciation of fine food and wine and of the rituals of preparation and serving them <an annual banquet that attracts *gastronomes* from all over>.

Gourmand implies a less fastidious or discerning appreciation of food and wine, but a hearty interest in an enjoyment of them <a robust dinner fit for an eager *gourmand*>.

Bon vivant stresses liveliness and spirit in the enjoyment of fine food and drink in company <*bon vivants* rang in the New Year in style>.

epicurean see SENSUOUS.

episode see OCCURRENCE.

epitome see ABRIDGMENT.

epoch see PERIOD.

equable see STEADY.

equal *adj* see SAME

equal *vb* see MATCH.

equanimity, composure, sangfroid, phlegm mean the quality of one who is self-possessed and not easily disturbed or perturbed.

Equanimity suggests a habit of mind that is disturbed rarely or only under great strain <accepted fortune's slings and arrows with great *equanimity*>.

Composure implies great controlling of emotional or mental agitation by an effort of will or as a matter of habit <maintained his *composure* even under hostile questioning>. ***ant*** discomposure, perturbation

Sangfroid implies great coolness and steadiness under strain perhaps stemming from a constitutional coldness <an Olympian diver of remarkable *sangfroid*>.

Phlegm implies insensitiveness and suggests apathy or sluggishness rather than self-control <possessed of a temperamental *phlegm* unaffected by good news and bad news alike>.

equip see FURNISH.

equitable see FAIR.

equity see JUSTICE.

equivalent see SAME.

equivocal see OBSCURE.

equivocate see LIE.

equivocation see AMBIGUITY.

era see PERIOD.

eradicate see EXTERMINATE.

erase, expunge, cancel, efface, obliterate, blot out, delete mean to strike out or remove something so that it no longer has any effect or existence.

Erase implies the act of rubbing or wiping out, as of letters or impressions, often in preparation for correction or replacement by new matter <*erase* what you wrote and start over>.

Expunge stresses a removal or destruction that leaves no trace <*expunged* all references to the deposed leader>.

Cancel implies an action, as marking, revoking, or neutralizing, that nullifies or invalidates a thing <a crime that *cancelled* all her good deeds>.

Efface implies the removal of an impression, imprint, or image by damage to or elimination of the surface on which it appears or removal of every visible sign of its existence <coins with dates *effaced* by wear>.

Obliterate implies a covering up or smearing over or utter destruction that removes all traces of a thing's existence <an outdoor mural almost *obliterated* by graffiti>.

Blot out, like *obliterate,* suggests a rendering of something indecipherable or nonexistent by smearing over or hiding completely <*blotted out* the offensive passage with black ink>.

Delete implies a deliberate exclusion, or a marking to direct exclusion, of written matter <his editor *deleted* all unflattering references to others>.

erratic see STRANGE.

error, mistake, blunder, slip, lapse, faux pas mean a departure from what is true, right, or proper.

Error suggests the existence of a standard or guide and implies a straying from the right course through failure to make effective use of this <one *error* in planning lost the battle>.

Mistake implies misconception or inadvertence and usually expresses less criticism than *error* <dialed the wrong number by *mistake*>.

Blunder regularly imputes stupidity or ignorance as a cause and connotes some degree of blame <a political campaign noted mostly for its series of *blunders*>.

Slip stresses inadvertence or accident and applies especially to trivial but embarrassing mistakes <during the speech I made several *slips*>.

Lapse stresses forgetfulness, weakness, or inattention as a cause <apart from a few grammatical *lapses,* the paper is good>.

Faux pas is applied to a mistake in etiquette <committed a grievous *faux pas* by drinking from the finger bowl>.

ersatz see ARTIFICIAL.

erudite see LEARNED.

erudition see KNOWLEDGE.

escape, avoid, evade, elude, shun, eschew mean to get away or keep away from something.

Escape stresses the fact of getting away or being passed by not necessarily through effort or by conscious intent <nothing *escapes* her sharp eyes>.

Avoid stresses forethought and caution in keeping clear of danger or difficulty <with careful planning we can *avoid* the fate of previous expeditions>. ***ant*** face, meet

Evade implies adroitness, ingenuity, or lack of scruple in escaping or avoiding <*evaded* the question by changing the subject>.

Elude implies a slippery or baffling quality in the person or thing that gets away <what she sees in him *eludes* me>.

Shun often implies an avoiding as a matter of habitual practice or policy and may imply repugnance or abhorrence <you have *shunned* their company>.

Eschew implies an avoiding or abstaining from as unwise or distasteful or immoral <a playwright who *eschews* melodrama and claptrap>. ***ant*** choose

eschew see ESCAPE.

escort see ACCOMPANY.

especial see SPECIAL.

espy see SEE 1.

espouse see ADOPT.

essay see ATTEMPT.

essential, fundamental, vital, cardinal mean so important as to be indispensable.

Essential implies belonging to the very nature of a thing and therefore being incapable of removal without destroying the thing itself or altering its character <conflict is an *essential* element in drama>.

Fundamental applies to something that forms a foundation without which an entire system or complex whole would collapse <the *fundamental* principles of democracy>.

Vital suggests something that is necessary to a thing's continued existence or operation <air bases that are *vital* to our national security>.

Cardinal suggests something on which an outcome turns or actively depends <one of the *cardinal* events of the Civil War>. ***ant*** negligible

establish see SET *vb*.

esteem see REGARD.

estimate 1. Estimate, appraise, evaluate, value, rate, assess mean to judge something with respect to its worth or significance.

Estimate implies a judgment, considered or casual, that precedes or takes the place of actual measuring or counting or testing out <*estimated* that there were a hundred people there>.

Appraise commonly implies the fixing by an expert of the monetary worth of a thing, but it may be used of any intent to give a critical judgment <a real estate agent *appraised* the house>.

Evaluate suggests an attempt to determine either the relative or intrinsic worth of something in terms other than monetary <instructors will *evaluate* all students' work>.

Value comes close to *appraise* but does imply expertness of judgment <a watercolor *valued* by the donor at $500>.

Rate adds to *estimate* the notion of placing a thing in a scale of value <an actress who is *rated* highly by her peers>.

Assess implies a rendering of a critical appraisal for the purpose of assigning a taxable value or for understanding or interpreting or as a guide to action <officials are still trying to *assess* the damage>.

2. see CALCULATE.

estrange, alienate, disaffect, wean mean to cause one to break a bond of affection or loyalty.

Estrange implies the development of indifference or hostility with consequent loss of sympathy or divorcement <had become *estranged* from their family after years of neglect>. ***ant*** reconcile

Alienate may or may not suggest separation but always implies loss of affection or interest <managed to *alienate* all her co-workers with her arrogance>. ***ant*** unite, reunite

Disaffect refers to those from whom loyalty is expected or demanded and stresses the effects, such as rebellion or discontent, of alienation without actual separation <a coup led by *disaffected* party members>. ***ant*** win *(over)*

Wean implies a commendable separation from something on which one is weakly or immaturely dependent < *wean* yourself from a bad habit>. ***ant*** addict

ether see AIR.

ethical see MORAL.

etiolate see WHITEN.

etiquette see DECORUM.

eulogy see ENCOMIUM.

evade see ESCAPE.

evaluate see ESTIMATE.

evanescent see TRANSIENT.

even **1.** see LEVEL. **2.** see STEADY.

event see OCCURRENCE.

eventual see LAST.

evict see EJECT.

evidence see SHOW 1.

evident, manifest, patent, distinct, obvious, apparent, plain, clear mean readily perceived or apprehended.

Evident implies the presence of visible signs which point to a definite conclusion <an *evident* fondness for the company of friends>. ***ant*** inevident

Manifest implies an external display so evident that little or no inference is required <her *manifest* joy upon receiving the award>. ***ant*** latent

Patent applies to a cause, effect, or significant feature that is clear and unmistakable once attention has been drawn to it <*patent* defects in the item when sold>. ***ant*** latent

Distinct implies such sharpness of outline or definition that no unusual effort to see or hear or comprehend is required <my offer met with a *distinct* refusal>. ***ant*** indistinct, nebulous

Obvious implies such ease in discovering or accounting for that it often suggests conspicuousness in the thing or little need for perspicacity in the observer <the motives are *obvious* to all but the most obtuse>. ***ant*** obscure, abstruse

Apparent may imply conscious exercise of elaborate reasoning as well as inference from evidence <the absurdity of the charge is *apparent* to all who know him>. ***ant*** unintelligible

Clear implies an absence of anything that confuses the mind or obscures the issues <it's *clear* now what's been going on>. ***ant*** obscure

evil see BAD.

evince see SHOW 1.
evoke see EDUCE.
exact *adj* see CORRECT *adj*.
exact *vb* see DEMAND.
exacting see ONEROUS.
exaggeration, overstatement, hyperbole mean an overstepping of the bounds of truth, especially in describing the extent, size, kind, or amount of something.

Exaggeration implies an unwillingness to be held down by the facts, or a bias so great that one cannot clearly see or accurately estimate the exact situation <unable to tell the story without *exaggeration*>. ***ant*** understatement

Overstatement suggests a simple exceeding of the truth <a style that avoids *overstatement*>. ***ant*** understatement

Hyperbole suggests a desire, often literary, to create a planned impression or effect through extravagance in statement <sang her praises through poetic *hyperbole*>. ***ant*** litotes

examine see SCRUTINIZE.
example 1. see INSTANCE. **2.** see MODEL.
exasperate see IRRITATE.
exceed, surpass, transcend, excel, outdo, outstrip mean to go or be beyond a stated or implied limit, measure, or degree.

Exceed implies going beyond a limit set by authority or established by custom or by prior achievement <*exceed* the speed limit>.

Surpass suggests superiority in quality, merit, or skill <the book *surpassed* our expectations>.

Transcend implies a rising or extending notably above or beyond ordinary limits <*transcended* the values of their peers>.

Excel implies an attaining of preeminence in achievement, accomplishment, or quality and may suggest superiority to all others <*excels* in mathematics>.

Outdo applies to a bettering or exceeding of what has been done before <*outdid* herself this time>.

Outstrip suggests a succeeding or surpassing in a race or competition <*outstripped* other firms in selling the new plastic>.

excel see EXCEED.
excessive, immoderate, inordinate, extravagant, exorbitant, extreme mean going beyond a normal or acceptable limit.

Excessive implies an amount or degree too great to be reasonable or endurable <punishment that was deemed *excessive*>. ***ant*** deficient

Immoderate implies lack of desirable or necessary restraint <an *immoderate* amount of time spent on grooming>. ***ant*** moderate

Inordinate implies an exceeding of limits dictated by reason or good judgment <an *inordinate* portion of their budget goes to entertainment>. ***ant*** temperate

Extravagant implies a wild, lawless, prodigal, or foolish wandering from proper and accustomed limits <*extravagant* claims for the product>. ***ant*** restrained

Exorbitant implies a departure from accepted standards regarding amount or degree <a menu with *exorbitant* prices>. ***ant*** just *(price, charge)*

Extreme may imply an approach to the farthest limit possible or conceivable but commonly means only to a notably high degree <views concerning marriage that are a bit *extreme*>.

excite see PROVOKE.

exclude, debar, eliminate, suspend mean to shut or put out.

Exclude implies a keeping out of what is already outside by or as if by closing some barrier <children under 17 are *excluded* from the movie>. ***ant*** admit, include

Debar stresses the effectiveness of an existent barrier in excluding a person or class from what is open or accessible to others <arbitrary standards that effectively *debar* most female candidates>. ***ant*** admit

Eliminate implies the getting rid of what is already within, typically as a constituent part or element <a company's plans to *eliminate* a fourth of its work force>.

Suspend implies temporary and usually disciplinary removal, as from a membership in an organization, or restraining, as from functioning or expression <a student *suspended* for possession of drugs>.

exclusive see SELECT.

exculpate, absolve, exonerate, acquit, vindicate mean to free from a charge or burden.

Exculpate implies a clearing from blame or burden <I cannot *exculpate* myself of the charge of overenthusiasm>. ***ant*** accuse

Absolve implies a release either from an obligation that binds the conscience or from the consequences of its violation <*absolved* the subject from his oath of allegiance>. ***ant*** hold *(to)*, charge *(with)*

Exonerate implies a complete clearance from an accusation or charge and from any attendant suspicion of blame or guilt <a committee *exonerated* the governor from charges of bribery>. ***ant*** incriminate

Acquit implies a decision in one's favor with respect to a definite charge <*acquitted* of murder by a jury>. ***ant*** convict

Vindicate may refer to things as well as persons that have been subjected to critical attack of imputation of guilt, weakness, or folly, and implies a clearing through proof of the injustice or unfairness of such criticism or blame <an investigation *vindicated* the senator on all counts>. ***ant*** calumniate

excuse *vb* **Excuse, condone, pardon, forgive** mean to exact neither punishment nor redress.

Excuse may refer to the overlooking of specific acts especially in social or conventional situations or to the person responsible for these <*excuse* an interruption>. ***ant*** punish

Condone implies that one passes over without censure or punishment a kind of behavior, such as dishonesty or violence, that involves a serious breach of a moral, ethical, or legal code <a society that *condones* alcohol but not drugs>.

Pardon implies that one remits a penalty due for an admitted or established offense or refrains from exacting punishment <*pardon* a criminal>. ***ant*** punish

Forgive implies that one gives up all claim to requital and all resentment or desire for revenge <*forgave* their previous lapses>.

excuse *n* see APOLOGY.

execrate, curse, damn, anathematize mean to denounce violently and indignantly.

Execrate implies intense loathing and usually passionate fury <*execrated* the men who had molested his family>. ***ant*** eulogize

Curse implies angry denunciation by blasphemous oaths or profane imprecations <*cursed* the fate that had brought them to this pass>. ***ant*** bless

Damn, like *curse,* suggests the invoking of divine vengeance with fervor but is more informal <*damns* the city council for not anticipating the problem>.

Anathematize implies solemn denunciation of an evil or an injustice <preachers *anathematizing* pornography>.

execute, administer mean to carry out the declared intent of another.

Execute stresses the enforcing of the specific provisions of a law, will, commission, or command <charged with failing to *execute* the order>.

Administer implies the continuing exercise of delegated authority in pursuance of only generally indicated goals rather than specifically prescribed means of attaining them <the agency in charge of *administering* Indian affairs>.

2. see KILL.

3. see PERFORM.

exemplar see MODEL.

exercise see PRACTICE.

exertion see EFFORT.

exhaust **1.** see DEPLETE. **2.** see TIRE.

exhibit see SHOW 2.

exigency **1.** see JUNCTURE. **2.** see NEED.

exiguous see MEAGER.

exile see BANISH.
exonerate see EXCULPATE.
exorbitant see EXCESSIVE.
expand, amplify, swell, distend, inflate, dilate mean to increase in size or volume.

Expand may apply whether the increase comes from within or without and regardless of manner, whether by growth, unfolding, or addition of parts <our business has *expanded* with every passing year>. ***ant*** contract, abridge

Amplify implies the extension or enlargement of something that is inadequate <*amplify* the statement with some details>. ***ant*** abridge, condense

Swell implies gradual expansion beyond a thing's original or normal limits <the bureaucracy *swelled* to unmanageable proportions>. ***ant*** shrink

Distend implies outward expansion caused by pressure from within <a stomach *distended* by gas>. ***ant*** constrict

Inflate implies distension by or as if by the introduction of a gas or something insubstantial and suggests a resulting instability and liability to sudden change <an *inflated* ego>. ***ant*** deflate

Dilate applies especially to the expansion of diameter and suggests a widening of something circular <dim light causes the pupils of the eyes to *dilate*>. ***ant*** constrict, circumscribe, attenuate

expect, hope, look, await mean to anticipate in the mind some occurrence or outcome.

Expect implies a high degree of certainty and involves the idea of preparing or envisioning <I *expect* to be finished by Tuesday>. ***ant*** despair *(of)*

Hope implies little certainty but suggests confidence or assurance in the possibility that what one desires or longs for will happen <she *hopes* to find a job soon>. ***ant*** despair *(of)*, despond

Look, followed by *for,* suggests a degree of expectancy and watchfulness rather than confidence or certainty <we *look* for great things in the new year>; followed by *to,* it suggests strongly a counting on or a freedom from doubt <*looked* to their children to care for them in old age>. ***ant*** despair *(of)*

Await often adds to *look for* the implication of being ready, mentally or physically <we *await* your decision>. ***ant*** despair

expedient *adj* **Expedient, politic, advisable** mean dictated by practical or prudent motives.

Expedient usually implies a choice that is immediately advantageous without regard for ethics or consistent principles <a truce was the *expedient* answer>. ***ant*** inexpedient

Politic stresses practicality, judiciousness, and tactical value but usually implies material or self-centered motives <converted to Catholicism when it was *politic* to do so>.

Advisable applies to what is practical, prudent, or advantageous, without the derogatory connotations of *expedient* and *politic* <it's *advisable* to say nothing at all>. ***ant*** inadvisable

expedient *n* see RESOURCE.

expedition see HASTE.

expeditious see FAST.

expel see EJECT.

expend see SPEND.

expense see PRICE.

expensive see COSTLY.

expert see PROFICIENT.

explain, expound, explicate, elucidate, interpret mean to make something clear or understandable.

Explain implies making plain or intelligible what is not immediately obvious or clearly known <the doctor *explained* what the operation would entail>. ***ant*** obfuscate

Expound implies a careful often elaborate or learned explanation <a professor *expounding* the theory of relativity>.

Explicate adds to *expound* the idea of a developed or detailed analysis of a topic <a passage that critics have been inspired to *explicate* at length>.

Elucidate stresses the throwing of light upon as explanation, exposition, or illustration <a newspaper report that *elucidated* the reason for the crime>.

Interpret adds to *explain* the implication of the need for imagination or sympathy or special knowledge to make something clear <*interprets* the play as an allegory about good and evil>.

explicate see EXPLAIN.

explicit, express, specific, definite mean perfectly clear in meaning.

Explicit implies such verbal plainness and distinctness that there is no need for inference and no reason for ambiguity or difficulty in understanding <the dress code is *explicit*>. ***ant*** ambiguous

Express implies both explicitness and direct and forceful utterance <her *express* wish was to be cremated>.

Specific applies to what is precisely and fully referred to or treated in detail or particular <two *specific* criticisms of the proposal>. ***ant*** vague

Definite stresses precise, clear statement or arrangement that leaves no uncertainty or indecision <the law is *definite* regarding such cases>. ***ant*** indefinite, equivocal

exploit see FEAT.

expose see SHOW 2.

exposed see LIABLE.

expostulate see OBJECT.

expound see EXPLAIN.

express *vb* **Express, vent, utter, voice, broach, air** mean to let out or make known what one thinks or feels.

Express suggests an impulse to reveal in words, gestures, or actions, or through what one creates or produces <paintings that *express* the artist's loneliness>.

Vent stresses a strong inner compulsion to express something such as a pent-up emotion, especially in a highly emotional manner <her stories *vent* the frustrations of women>. ***ant*** bridle

Utter implies the use of the voice not necessarily in articulate speech <would occasionally *utter* words of encouragement>.

Voice implies expression or formulation in words but not necessarily by vocal utterance <an editorial *voicing* the concerns of many>.

Broach suggests the disclosing for the first time of something long thought over or reserved for a suitable occasion <*broached* the subject of a divorce>.

Air implies an exposing or parading of one's views often in order to gain relief or sympathy or attention <cabinet members publicly *airing* their differences>.

express *adj* see EXPLICIT.

expression see PHRASE.

expunge see ERASE.

exquisite see CHOICE *adj*.

extemporaneous, improvised, impromptu, offhand, unpremeditated mean composed, done, or devised at the moment and not beforehand.

Extemporaneous stresses the demands imposed by the occasion or situation and may imply a certain sketchiness or roughness <an *extemporaneous* shelter prompted by the sudden storm>.

Improvised implies the constructing or devising of something without advance knowledge, thought, or preparation and often without the necessary or proper equipment <*improvised* a barbecue pit at the campground>.

Impromptu stresses the immediacy and the spontaneity of the thing composed or devised <an *impromptu* speech at an awards ceremony>.

Offhand strongly implies casualness, carelessness, or indifference <his *offhand* remarks often got him into trouble>.

Unpremeditated suggests some strong, often suddenly provoked emotion that impels one to action <*unpremeditated* murder>. ***ant*** premeditated

extend, lengthen, elongate, prolong, protract mean to draw out or add to so as to increase in length.

Extend implies a drawing out of extent in space or time and may also imply increase in width, scope, area, influence or range <*extend* welfare services>. ***ant*** abridge, shorten

Lengthen suggests an increase of length in either time or space <*lengthen* the school year>. ***ant*** shorten

Elongate usually implies increase in spatial length and frequently suggests stretching <the dancer's ability to *elongate* her body>. ***ant*** abbreviate, shorten

Prolong suggests chiefly increase in duration especially beyond usual, normal, or pleasing limits <*prolonged* illness>. ***ant*** curtail

Protract adds to *prolong* implications of needlessness, vexation, or indefiniteness <*protracted* litigation>. ***ant*** curtail

exterior see OUTER.

exterminate, extirpate, eradicate, uproot, wipe out mean to effect the destruction or abolition of something.

Exterminate implies complete and immediate extinction by killing off <failed attempts to *exterminate* the mosquitoes>.

Extirpate implies extinction of a race, family, species, kind, or sometimes an idea or doctrine by destruction or by removal of its means of propagation <having *extirpated* the last vestiges of the religion>.

Eradicate implies the driving out or elimination of something that has taken root or established itself firmly <polio had virtually been *eradicated*>.

Uproot implies a forcible or violent removal and stresses displacement or dislodgment rather than immediate destruction <the war had *uprooted* thousands>. ***ant*** establish

Wipe out can imply extermination or suggest a canceling or obliterating <*wipe out* the entire population>.

external see OUTER.

extinguish 1. see CRUSH. **2.** see ABOLISH.

extirpate see EXTERMINATE.

extort see EDUCE.

extract see EDUCE.

extraneous see EXTRINSIC.

extravagant see EXCESSIVE.

extreme see EXCESSIVE.

extricate, disentangle, untangle, disencumber, disembarrass mean to free from what binds or holds back.

Extricate implies the use of force or ingenuity in freeing from a difficult position or situation <a knack for *extricating* himself from damaging political rows>.

Disentangle suggests a painstaking separation of something from what enmeshes or entangles <a biography that *disentangles* the myth from the man>. ***ant*** entangle

Untangle is sometimes used in place of *disentangle* <*untangled* a web of deceit>. ***ant*** entangle, tangle

Disencumber implies a release from something that clogs or weighs down or imposes a heavy burden <a science article *disencumbered* of scientific jargon>. ***ant*** encumber

Disembarrass suggests a release from something that embarrasses by impeding or hindering <*disembarrassed* herself of her frivolous companions>.

extrinsic, extraneous, foreign, alien mean external to a thing, its essential nature, or its original character.

Extrinsic applies to what is distinctly outside the thing in question or is not contained in or derived from its essential nature <sentimental attachment that is *extrinsic* to the house's market value>. ***ant*** intrinsic

Extraneous applies to what is on or comes from the outside and may or may not be capable of becoming an essential part <*extraneous* arguments that obscure the real issue>. ***ant*** relevant

Foreign applies to what is so different as to be rejected or repelled or, if admitted, to be incapable of becoming identified or assimilated by the thing in question <inflammation resulting from a *foreign* body in the eye>. ***ant*** germane

Alien is stronger than *foreign* in suggesting such strangeness as leads to opposition, repugnance, or incompatibility <a practice that is totally *alien* to our democratic principles>. ***ant*** akin, assimilable

exuberant see PROFUSE.

eyewitness see SPECTATOR.

F

fabricate see MAKE.

fabulous see FICTITIOUS.

face, countenance, visage, physiognomy mean the front part of the head from forehead to chin.

Face is the simple, direct, and also the inclusive term <a strikingly handsome *face*>.

Countenance applies to a face as seen and as revealing a mood, character, or attitude <the benign *countenance* of my grandmother>.

Visage suggests attention to shape and proportions of the face and sometimes to the impression it gives or the changes in moods it reflects <a penetrating gaze and an aquiline nose gave him a birdlike *visage*>.

Physiognomy suggests attention to the contours and characteristic expression as indicative of race, temperament, disease, or qualities of mind or character <a youth with the *physiognomy* of a warrior>.

facet see PHASE.

facetious see WITTY.

facile see EASY.

facility see READINESS.

facsimile see REPRODUCTION.

factitious see ARTIFICIAL.

factor see ELEMENT.

faculty 1.see GIFT. **2.** see POWER 2.

fad see FASHION.

fag see TIRE.

failing see FAULT.

fair 1. Fair, equitable, impartial, unbiased, dispassionate, objective mean free from favor toward either or any side.

Fair implies an elimination of one's own feelings, prejudices, and interests so as to achieve a proper balance of conflicting interests <a *fair* decision by a judge>. ***ant*** unfair

Just implies an exact following of a standard of what is right and proper <a *just* settlement of territorial claims>. ***ant*** unjust

Equitable implies a freer and less rigorous standard than *just* and suggests fair and equal treatment of all concerned <provides for the *equitable* distribution of his property>. ***ant*** inequitable, unfair

Impartial stresses an absence of favor or prejudice in making a judgment <arbitration by an *impartial* third party>. ***ant*** partial

Unbiased implies even more strongly an absence of all prejudice and implies the firm intent to be fair to all <your *unbiased* opinion of the whole affair>. ***ant*** biased

Dispassionate suggests freedom from emotional involvement or from the influence of strong feeling and often implies cool or even cold judgment <a *dispassionate* summation of the facts>. ***ant*** passionate, intemperate

Objective stresses a tendency to view events or persons as apart from oneself and one's own interest or feelings <it's impossible for me to be *objective* about my own child>. ***ant*** subjective

2. see BEAUTIFUL.

faith see BELIEF.

faithful, loyal, constant, staunch, steadfast, resolute mean firm in adherence to whatever one owes allegiance.

Faithful implies unswerving adherence to a person or thing or to the oath or promise by which a tie was contracted <*faithful* to her marriage vows>. ***ant*** faithless

Loyal implies firm resistance to any temptation to desert or betray <the army remained *loyal* to the czar>. ***ant*** disloyal

Constant stresses continuing firmness of emotional attachment without necessarily implying strict obedience to promises or vows <*constant* lovers>. ***ant*** inconstant, fickle

Staunch suggests fortitude and resolution in adherence and imperviousness to influences that would weaken it <a *staunch* defender of free speech>.

Steadfast implies a steady and unwavering course in love, allegiance, or conviction <*steadfast* in their support of democratic principles>. ***ant*** capricious

Resolute emphasizes firm determination to adhere to a cause or purpose <*resolute* in his determination to see justice done>.

faithless, false, disloyal, traitorous, treacherous, perfidious mean untrue to someone or something that has a right to expect one's fidelity or allegiance.

Faithless applies to any failure to keep a promise or pledge or to any breach or betrayal of obligation, allegiance, or loyalty <*faithless* allies refused to support the sanctions>. ***ant*** faithful

False stresses the fact of failing to be true in any manner or degree ranging from fickleness to cold treachery <betrayed by *false* friends>. ***ant*** true

Disloyal implies a lack of complete faithfulness in thought or words or actions to a friend, cause, leader, or country <accused the hostages of being *disloyal* to their country>. ***ant*** loyal

Traitorous implies either actual treason or a serious betrayal of trust <*traitorous* acts punishable by death>.

Treacherous implies readiness to betray trust or confidence <the victim of *treacherous* allies>.

Perfidious adds to *treacherous* the implication of an incapacity for fidelity or reliability and of baseness or vileness <repeated and *perfidious* violations of the treaty>.

fake see IMPOSTURE.

false see FAITHLESS.

falsify see MISREPRESENT.

falter see HESITATE.

familiar 1. Familiar, intimate mean closely acquainted.

Familiar suggests the ease, informality, and absence of reserve or constraint natural among members of a family or acquaintances of long standing <resent being addressed by strangers in a *familiar* tone>. ***ant*** aloof

Intimate stresses the closeness and intensity rather than the mere frequency or continuity of personal association and suggests either deep mutual understanding or the sharing of deeply personal thoughts and feelings <their love letters became increasingly *intimate*>.

2. see COMMON.

famous, renowned, celebrated, noted, notorious, distinguished, eminent, illustrious mean known far and wide.

Famous implies little more than the fact of being, sometimes briefly, widely and popularly known <a *famous* television actress>. ***ant*** obscure

Renowned implies more glory and acclamation <one of the most *renowned* figures in sports history>.

Celebrated implies popular notice and attention especially in print <the most *celebrated* beauty of her day>. ***ant*** obscure

Noted suggests well-deserved public attention <the *noted* mystery writer>. ***ant*** unnoted

Notorious frequently adds to *famous* pejorative implications of questionableness or evil <a *notorious* gangster>.

Distinguished implies acknowledged excellence or superiority <a *distinguished* scientist who recently won the Nobel Prize>. ***ant*** undistinguished

Eminent implies conspicuousness for outstanding quality or character and is applicable to one rising above others of the same class <a conference of the country's most *eminent* writers>.

Illustrious stresses enduring and merited honor and glory attached to a deed or person <the *illustrious* deeds of national heroes>. ***ant*** infamous

fanciful see IMAGINARY.

fancy see THINK 1.

fantastic 1. Fantastic, bizarre, grotesque mean conceived, made, or carried out without evident reference or adherence to truth or reality.

Fantastic may connote unrestrained extravagance in conception or remoteness from reality or merely ingenuity of decorative invention <*fantastic* theories about the origins of life>.

Bizarre applies to the sensationally odd or strange and implies violence of contrast or incongruity of combination <a *bizarre* pseudo-medieval castle>. ***ant*** chaste, subdued

Grotesque may apply to what is conventionally ugly but artistically effective, or it may connote ludicrous awkwardness or incongruity, often with sinister or tragic overtones <*grotesque* statues adorn the cathedral>.

2. see IMAGINARY.

far see DISTANT.

faraway see DISTANT.

far-off see DISTANT.

fascinate see ATTRACT.

fashion *n* **1. Fashion, style, mode, vogue, fad, rage, craze** mean the usage, as in dressing, decorating, or living, that is accepted by those who want to be up-to-date.

Fashion is the most general term and applies to any way of dressing, behaving, writing, or performing that is favored at any one time or place or by any group <the current *fashion* for Russian ballet dancers>.

Style often implies a distinctive fashion adopted by people of wealth or taste <a media mogul used to traveling in *style*>.

Mode suggests the fashion of the moment among those anxious to appear elegant and sophisticated <sleek, tanned bodies are the *mode* at such resorts>.

Vogue stresses the prevalence or wide acceptance of a fashion <a novelist who is no longer much in *vogue*>.

Fad suggests caprice in taking up or in dropping a fashion <nothing is more dated than last year's *fad*>.

Rage stresses intense enthusiasm in adopting a fad <Cajun food was quite the *rage*>.

Craze, like *rage,* emphasizes senseless enthusiasm in pursuing a fad <a sport that is more than a passing *craze*>.

2. see METHOD.

fashion *vb* see MAKE.

fast, rapid, swift, fleet, quick, speedy, hasty, expeditious mean moving, proceeding, or acting quickly.

Fast applies particularly to a moving object <a *fast* horse>. ***ant*** slow

Rapid emphasizes the movement itself <a *rapid* current>. ***ant*** deliberate, leisurely

Swift suggests great rapidity coupled with ease of movement <returned the ball with one *swift* stroke>. ***ant*** sluggish

Fleet adds the implication of lightness and nimbleness <*fleet* runners>.

Quick suggests promptness and the taking of little time <a *quick* wit>. ***ant*** sluggish

Speedy implies quickness of successful accomplishment and may also suggest unusual velocity <a *speedy* recovery>. ***ant*** dilatory

Hasty suggests hurry and precipitousness and often connotes carelessness and resultant confusion or inefficiency <a *hasty* inspection>.

Expeditious suggests efficiency together with rapidity of accomplishment <an *expeditious* processing of a merchandise order>. ***ant*** sluggish

fasten, fix, attach, affix mean to make something stay firmly in place.

Fasten implies an action such as tying, buttoning, nailing, locking, or otherwise securing <*fastened* the horse to a post>. ***ant*** unfasten, loosen, loose

Fix usually implies a driving in, implanting, or embedding in an attempt to secure something <*fix* the stake in the earth>.

Attach suggests a connecting or uniting by or as if by a bond, link, or tie in order to keep things together <*attach* the W-2 form here>. ***ant*** detach

Affix implies an imposing of one thing on another by such means as gluing, impressing, or nailing <*affix* your address label here>. ***ant*** detach

fastidious see NICE.

fatal see DEADLY.

fate, destiny, lot, portion, doom mean a predetermined state or end.

Fate implies an inevitable and sometimes an adverse outcome <the *fate* of the mariners remains unknown>.

Destiny implies something foreordained and often suggests a great or noble course or end <our country's *destiny*>.

Lot suggests a distribution by fate or destiny <it was her *lot* to die childless>.

Portion implies the apportioning of good and evil <the *portion* that has been meted out to me>.

Doom distinctly stresses finality and implies a grim or calamitous fate <if the rebellion fails, our *doom* is certain>.

fateful see OMINOUS.

fatigue see TIRE.

fatuous see SIMPLE.

fault, failing, frailty, foible, vice mean an imperfection or weakness of character.

Fault implies a failure, not necessarily culpable, to reach some standard of perfection in disposition, action, or habit <a woman of many virtues and few *faults*>. ***ant*** merit

Failing suggests a minor shortcoming in character of which one may be unaware <procrastination is one of my *failings*>. ***ant*** perfection

Frailty implies a general or chronic proneness to yield to temptation <a fondness for chocolate is the most human of *frailties*>.

Foible applies to a harmless or endearing weakness or idiosyncrasy <*foibles* that make him all the more lovable>.

Vice can be a general term for any imperfection or weakness, but it often suggests violation of a moral code or the giving of offense to the moral sensibilities of others <gambling and drunkenness were the least of his *vices*>.

faultfinding see CRITICAL.

faux pas see ERROR.

favor see OBLIGE.

favorable, auspicious, propitious mean pointing toward a happy outcome.

Favorable implies that the persons involved are approving or helpful or that the circumstances are advantageous <*favorable* weather conditions for a rocket launch>. ***ant*** unfavorable, antagonistic

Auspicious suggests the presence of signs and omens promising success <an *auspicious* beginning for a great partnership>. ***ant*** inauspicious, ill-omened

Propitious, milder than *auspicious,* describes events or conditions that constitute favorable indications and implies a continuing favorable condition <the time was not *propitious* for starting a new business>. ***ant*** unpropitious, adverse

fawn, toady, truckle, cringe, cower mean to act or behave abjectly before a superior.

Fawn implies seeking favor by servile flattery or exaggerated attention and submissiveness <waiters *fawning* over a celebrity>. ***ant*** domineer

Toady suggests the attempt to ingratiate oneself by an abjectly menial or subservient attitude <never misses an opportunity to *toady* to his boss>.

Truckle implies the subordination of oneself and one's desires, opinions, or judgment to those of a superior <the rich are used to seeing others *truckle*>.

Cringe suggests a bowing or shrinking in physical or mental distress or in fear or servility <*cringing* before a blow>.

Cower suggests a display of abject fear before someone who threatens or domineers <as an adult he still *cowered* before his father>.

faze see EMBARRASS.

fealty see FIDELITY.

fear 1. Fear, dread, fright, alarm, panic, terror, horror, trepidation mean painful agitation in the presence or anticipation of danger.

Fear, often the most general term, implies anxiety and loss of courage <*fear* of the unknown>. ***ant*** fearlessness

Dread usually adds the idea of intense reluctance to face or meet a person or situation and suggests aversion as well as anxiety <the *dread* of having to face her mother>.

Fright implies the shock of sudden, startling fear <imagine our *fright* at being awakened by screams>.

Alarm suggests a sudden and intense apprehension produced by newly perceived awareness of immediate danger <view the situation with *alarm*>. ***ant*** assurance, composure

Panic implies unreasoning and overmastering fear causing hysterical, disordered, and useless activity <news of the invasion caused great *panic*>.

Terror implies the most extreme degree of consternation or fear <immobilized with *terror*>.

Horror adds the implication of shuddering abhorrence or aversion before a sight, activity, or demand that causes fear <harbored a secret *horror* of dark, close places>. ***ant*** fascination

Trepidation adds to *dread* the implications of timidity, trembling, and hesitation <raised the subject of marriage with some *trepidation*>.

2. see REVERENCE.

fearful 1. Fearful, apprehensive, afraid mean disturbed by fear.

Fearful implies a timorous or worrying temperament more often than a real cause for fear <the child is *fearful* of loud noises>. ***ant*** fearless, intrepid

Apprehensive suggests having good reasons for fear and implies a premonition of evil or danger <*apprehensive* that war would break out>. ***ant*** confident

Afraid often suggests weakness or cowardice and regularly implies inhibition of action or utterance <*afraid* to speak the truth>. ***ant*** unafraid, sanguine

2. Fearful, awful, dreadful, frightful, terrible, terrific, horrible, horrific, shocking, appalling mean of a kind to cause grave distress of mind. Additionally, all these words have a lighter, chiefly conversational value in which they mean little more than *extreme*.

Fearful applies to what produces fear, agitation, loss of courage, or mere disquiet <a *fearful* predicament>. ***ant*** reassuring

Awful implies the creating of an awareness of transcendent or overpowering force, might, or significance <waited in the *awful* dark for their rescuers to come>.

Dreadful applies to what fills one with shuddering fear or loathing and strikes one as at least disagreeable or extremely unpleasant <cancer is a *dreadful* disease>.

Frightful implies such a startling or outrageous quality as produces utter consternation or a paralysis of fear <a *frightful* tornado>.

Terrible suggests painfulness too great to be endured or a capacity to produce and prolong extreme and agitating fear <caught in the grip of the *terrible* maelstrom>.

Terrific applies to something intended or fitted to inspire terror as by its size, appearance, or potency <a *terrific* outburst of fury>.

Appalling describes what strikes one with dismay as well as with terror or horror <had to perform the operation under *appalling* conditions>. ***ant*** reassuring

Horrible applies to something the sight of which induces fear or terror combined with loathing or aversion and suggests hatefulness or hideousness <the *horrible* carnage of war>.

Horrific suggests qualities or properties intended or suited to produce a horrible effect <a *horrific* account of the tragedy>.

Shocking implies characteristics which startle because they are contrary to expectations, standards of good taste, rational thought, or moral sense <fond of *shocking* stories>.

fearless see BRAVE.

feasible see POSSIBLE.

feat, exploit, achievement mean a remarkable deed.

Feat applies to an act involving strength or dexterity or daring <the *feat* of crossing the Atlantic in a balloon>.

Exploit suggests an adventurous, brilliant, or heroic act <his celebrated *exploits* as a spy>.

Achievement implies hard-won success in the face of difficulty or opposition <honored for her *achievements* as a chemist>. ***ant*** failure

fecund see FERTILE.

federation see ALLIANCE.

fee see WAGE.

feeble see WEAK.

feel see TOUCH.

feeling 1. Feeling, emotion, affection, sentiment, passion mean a subjective reaction or response to a person, thing, or situation.

Feeling denotes any response marked by such qualities as pleasure, pain, attraction, or repulsion and may imply nothing about the nature or intensity of the response <whatever *feelings* I had for him are gone>.

Emotion carries a strong implication of excitement or agitation and, like *feeling,* encompasses both positive and negative responses <a play in which the *emotions* are real>.

Affection applies to feelings that are also inclinations or likings <memoirs filled with *affection* and understanding>. ***ant*** antipathy

Sentiment implies refined, perhaps romantic, and sometimes artificial or affected emotion with an intellectual component <her feminist *sentiments* are well known>.

Passion suggests a powerful or controlling emotion marked by urgency of desire <revenge became his ruling *passion*>.

2. see SENSATION.

3. see ATMOSPHERE.

feign see ASSUME.

feint see TRICK.

felicitate see CONGRATULATE.

felicitous see FIT *adj.*

female, feminine, womanly, womanlike, womanish, effeminate, ladylike mean of, characteristic of, or like a female, especially of the human species.

Female (opposed to *male*) applies to plants and animals as well as persons and stresses the fact of sex <the more numerous *female* births as compared to male>. ***ant*** male

Feminine applies to qualities or attributes or attitudes characteristic of women and not shared by men <a *feminine* approach to a problem>. ***ant*** masculine

Womanly suggests the qualities of the mature woman, especially those qualities that make her effective as wife and mother or indicate the absence of mannish qualities <possessed all the *womanly* virtues>. ***ant*** unwomanly, manly

Womanlike is more likely to suggest characteristically feminine faults and foibles <displayed *womanlike* rage at the slight>.

Womanish is often used derogatorily in situations in which manliness might naturally be expected <shed *womanish* tears at his loss>. ***ant*** mannish

Effeminate emphasizes the softer and more delicate aspects of womanly nature and in its usual application to men implies lack of virility or masculinity <a country grown weak and *effeminate* on its wealth>. ***ant*** virile

Ladylike suggests decorous propriety <all three were *ladylike* and well brought-up girls>.

feminine see FEMALE.

ferocious see FIERCE.

fertile, fecund, fruitful, prolific mean producing or capable of producing offspring or fruit.

Fertile implies the power to reproduce in kind or to assist in reproduction and growth <*fertile* soil>, or it may suggest readiness of invention and development <a most *fertile* imagination>. ***ant*** infertile, sterile

Fecund emphasizes abundance or rapidity in bearing fruits or offspring or projects, inventions, or works of art <came from a remarkably *fecund* family>. ***ant*** barren

Fruitful adds to *fertile* and *fecund* the implication of desirable or useful results <undertook *fruitful* research in virology>. ***ant*** unfruitful, fruitless

Prolific stresses rapidity of spreading or multiplying by or as if by natural reproduction <one of the most *prolific* writers of science fiction>. ***ant*** barren, unfruitful

fervent see IMPASSIONED.

fervid see IMPASSIONED.

fervor see PASSION.

fetid see MALODOROUS.

fetish, talisman, charm, amulet mean an object believed to have the power to avert evil or attract good.

Fetish is applied to an object that is regarded as sacred or magical or to something that is cherished unreasonably or obsessively <make a *fetish* of the Bill of Rights>.

Talisman, primarily applicable to an astrological figure or image held to have magical power, such as to heal or protect, can also denote something that seems to exert a magical, extraordinary, and usually happy influence <wore the ring as a *talisman*>.

Charm applies to an object or a formula of words believed to repel evil spirits or malign influences or to attract their opposites <a *charm* against the evil eye>; it may also apply to some quality that is appealing or attractive <captivated by the *charm* of the old inn>.

Amulet applies especially to something worn or carried on the person as a protection against evil, danger, or disease <protected by an *amulet* of jaguar teeth>.

fetter see HAMPER.

fib see LIE.

fickle see INCONSTANT.

fictitious, fabulous, legendary, mythical, apocryphal mean having the nature of something imagined or mentally invented.

Fictitious implies fabrication and suggests artificiality or contrivance more than deliberate falsification or deception <all names used in the broadcast are *fictitious*>. ***ant*** historical

Fabulous stresses the marvelous or incredible character of something without necessarily implying impossibility or actual nonexistence <a land of *fabulous* riches>.

Legendary suggests the elaboration of invented details and distortion of historical facts produced by popular tradition <the *legendary* courtship of Miles Standish>.

Mythical implies a fanciful, often symbolic explanation of facts or the creation of beings and events <*mythical* creatures such as centaurs>. ***ant*** historical

Apocryphal implies an unknown or dubious source or origin or may imply that the thing itself is dubious or inaccurate <a book that repeats many *apocryphal* stories>.

fidelity, allegiance, fealty, loyalty, devotion, piety mean faithfulness to something to which one is bound by pledge or duty or by a sense of what is right or appropriate.

Fidelity implies strict and continuing faithfulness to an obligation, trust, or duty <*fidelity* in the performance of one's duties>. ***ant*** faithlessness, perfidy

Allegiance suggests an adherence like that of a citizen to his country and implies an unswerving fidelity maintained despite conflicting obligations or claims <a politician who owes *allegiance* to no special interest>. ***ant*** treachery, treason

Fealty implies a fidelity acknowledged by the individual and as compelling as a sworn vow <a critic's only *fealty* is to truth>. ***ant*** perfidy

Loyalty implies a personal and emotional faithfulness that is steadfast in the face of any temptation to renounce, desert, or betray <valued the *loyalty* of his friends>. ***ant*** disloyalty

Devotion stresses zeal and service amounting to self-dedication <a painter's *devotion* to her artistic vision>.

Piety stresses fidelity to obligations regarded as natural and fundamental and the observance of duties required by such fidelity <filial *piety* demands that I visit my parents>. ***ant*** impiety

fierce, ferocious, barbarous, savage, cruel mean showing fury or malignity in looks or actions.

Fierce applies to humans and animals that inspire terror because of their wild and menacing appearance or fury in attack or to qualities, expressions, or events characteristic of these <a battle marked by *fierce* fighting>. ***ant*** tame, mild

Ferocious implies extreme fierceness and unrestrained violence and brutality <signs warned of a *ferocious* dog>. ***ant*** tender

Barbarous implies a ferocity or mercilessness regarded as unworthy of civilized people <the *barbarous* treatment of prisoners>. ***ant*** clement

Savage implies the absence of inhibitions restraining civilized people filled with rage, lust, hate, fear, or other violent passions <*savage* reviews of the new play>.

Cruel implies indifference to suffering or even positive pleasure in witnessing or inflicting it <the *cruel* jokes of young children>.

figure see FORM.

filch see STEAL.

filthy see DIRTY.

final see LAST.

financial, monetary, pecuniary, fiscal mean of or relating to money.

Financial implies money matters conducted on a large scale or involving some degree of complexity <a business deal secured through a complex *financial* arrangement>.

Monetary refers to money as coined, distributed, or circulating <the country's basic *monetary* unit is the peso>.

Pecuniary implies reference to practical money matters as they affect the individual <a struggling single mother constantly in *pecuniary* difficulties>.

Fiscal refers to money as providing public revenue or to the financial affairs of an institution or corporation <the *fiscal* year of the United States ends on June 30>.

fine see PENALIZE.

finicky see NICE.

finish see CLOSE *vb*.

fire see LIGHT.

firm, hard, solid mean having a texture or consistency that resists deformation.

Firm implies such compactness and coherence and often elasticity of substance as to resist pulling, distorting, or pressing <a *firm* mattress with good back support>. ***ant*** loose, flabby

Hard implies impenetrability and nearly complete but inelastic resistance to pressure or tension <a diamond is one of the *hardest* substances known>. ***ant*** soft

Solid implies a texture of uniform density so as to be not only firm but also resistant to external deforming forces <*solid* furniture that will last>.

fiscal see FINANCIAL.

fit *adj* **Fit, suitable, meet, proper, appropriate, fitting, apt, happy, felicitous** mean right with respect to some end, need, use, or circumstance.

Fit stresses adaptability and sometimes special readiness for use or action <the vessel is now *fit* for service>. ***ant*** unfit

Suitable implies an answering to requirements or demands <shopped for clothes *suitable* for camping>. ***ant*** unbecoming, unsuitable

Meet suggests a rightness or just proportioning and suitability <a tip that was *meet* for the services rendered>. ***ant*** unmeet

Proper suggests a suitability through essential nature or accordance with custom <the *proper* role of the First Lady>. ***ant*** improper

Appropriate implies eminent or distinctive fitness <a golf bag is an *appropriate* gift for a golfer>. ***ant*** inappropriate

Fitting implies harmony of mood or tone or purpose <*fitting* subjects for dinner table conversation>.

Apt connotes a fitness marked by nicety and discrimination <a speech laced with some *apt* quotations>. ***ant*** inapt, inept

Happy suggests what is effectively or successfully appropriate <a *happy* choice of words>. ***ant*** unhappy

Felicitous suggests an aptness that is opportune, telling, or graceful <a *felicitous* note of apology>. ***ant*** infelicitous

fit *n* **Fit, attack, access, accession, paroxysm, spasm, convulsion** mean a sudden seizure or spell resulting from an abnormal condition of body or mind.

Fit sometimes designates a sudden seizure or period of increased activity characteristic of a disease <fell unconscious in a *fit*> or sometimes refers to a temporary sudden or violent mood or period of activity <works by *fits* and starts>.

Attack implies a sudden and often violent onslaught but connotes nothing about length or duration <an *attack* of melancholy>.

Access and ***accession*** distinctively imply the initiation of an attack or fit <an *access* of sudden rage> or the intensification of a mood or state of mind to the point where control is lost or nearly lost <driven mad by an *accession* of guilt>.

Paroxysm refers to the sudden occurrence or intensification of a symptom or a state and to its recurrence <*paroxysms* of fear>.

Spasm connotes sudden involuntary muscular contractions <suffered from *spasms* of his back muscles> or possession by some emotion or state that momentarily grips and paralyzes <seized by *spasms* of fear>.

Convulsion suggests repeated spasms that alternately contract and relax the muscles and produce violent contortions and distortions <a face distorted by *convulsions* of unsuppressed anger>.

fit *vb* see PREPARE.

fitful, spasmodic, convulsive mean lacking steadiness or regularity in movement.

Fitful implies intermittence and a succession of starts and stops or risings and fallings <the *fitful* beginnings of a new enterprise>. ***ant*** constant

Spasmodic adds to *fitful* the implication of violent intensity of activity, effort, or zeal alternating with lack of intensity <*spasmodic* trading on the stock exchange>.

Convulsive suggests the breaking of regularity or quiet by uncontrolled movement and usually connotes distress of body, mind, or spirit <the *convulsive* shocks of the earthquake>.

fitting see FIT *adj*.

fix *n* see PREDICAMENT.

fix *vb* **1.** see FASTEN. **2.** see SET *vb*.

flabbergast see SURPRISE 2.

flabby see LIMP.

flaccid see LIMP.

flagrant, glaring, egregious, gross, rank mean conspicuously bad or objectionable.

Flagrant applies usually to offenses or errors so bad that they can neither escape notice nor be condoned <*flagrant* abuse of the office of president>.

Glaring implies painful or damaging obtrusiveness of something that is conspicuously wrong, faulty, or improper <*glaring* errors in judgment>. ***ant*** unnoticeable

Egregious is applicable to something that stands out by reason of its bad quality or because it is in poor taste <made an *egregious* error>.

Gross implies the exceeding of reasonable or excusable limits of badness as applied to attitudes, qualities, or faults <*gross* carelessness on your part>. ***ant*** petty

Rank applies to what is openly and extremely objectionable and utterly condemned <it's *rank* heresy to say that>.

flair see LEANING.
flame see BLAZE.
flare see BLAZE.
flash, gleam, glance, glint, sparkle, glitter, glisten, glimmer, shimmer mean to send forth light.

Flash implies a sudden and transient burst of bright light <lightning *flashed*>.

Gleam suggests a steady light seen through an obscuring medium or against a dark background <the lights of the town *gleamed* in the valley below>.

Glance suggests a bright darting light reflected from a moving surface <sunlight *glanced* off the hull of the boat>.

Glint implies a quickly glancing or gleaming light <steel bars *glinted* in the moonlight>.

Sparkle suggests innumerable moving points of bright light <the *sparkling* waters of the gulf>.

Glitter connotes a brilliant sparkling or gleaming <*glittering* diamonds>.

Glisten applies to the soft, persistent sparkle from or as if from a wet or oily surface <rain-drenched sidewalks *glistened* under the street lamps>.

Glimmer suggests a faint, obscured, or wavering gleam <a lone light *glimmered* in the distance>.

Shimmer implies a soft tremulous gleaming or a blurred reflection <a *shimmering* satin dress>.

flashy see GAUDY.
flat 1. see INSIPID. **2.** see LEVEL.
flatulent see INFLATED.
flaunt see SHOW 2.
flavor see TASTE 1.
flaw see BLEMISH.
fleer see SCOFF.
fleet see FAST.
fleeting see TRANSIENT.
fleshly see CARNAL.
flexible see ELASTIC.
flightiness see LIGHTNESS.
flimsy see LIMP.
flinch see RECOIL.
fling see THROW.
flippancy see LIGHTNESS.
flirt see TRIFLE.
floppy see LIMP.
flourish 1. see SUCCEED. **2.** see SWING 1.
flout see SCOFF.
flow see SPRING.
fluctuate see SWING 2.

fluent see VOCAL 2.
fluid see LIQUID.
flurry see STIR *n*.
flush see LEVEL.
fluster see DISCOMPOSE.
foe see ENEMY.
fog see HAZE.
foible see FAULT.
foil see FRUSTRATE.
follow 1. Follow, succeed, ensue, supervene mean to come after something or someone.
Follow may apply to a coming after in time, position, understanding, or logical sequence <speeches *followed* the dinner>. ***ant*** precede
Succeed implies a coming after immediately in a sequence determined by some rational cause or rule, such as natural order, inheritance, election, or laws of rank <she *succeeded* her father as head of the business>.
Ensue commonly suggests a logical consequence or naturally expected development <after the lecture, a general discussion *ensued*>.
Supervene suggests the following by something added or conjoined and often unforeseen or unpredictable <events *supervened* that brought tragedy into his life>.
2. Follow, chase, pursue, trail mean to go after or on the track of someone or something.
Follow is the comprehensive term and usually implies the lead or guidance of one going before, but, in itself, gives no clue as to the purpose of the one that follows <*follow* a path to town>. ***ant*** precede
Chase implies speed in following, sometimes in order to catch what flees and sometimes to turn or drive away what advances <*chasing* the boys out of the orchard>.
Pursue usually suggests an attempt to overtake, reach, or attain often with eagerness or persistence, sometimes with hostile intent <*pursued* the bandits on foot>.
Trail implies a following in the tracks of one gone before <*trail* along behind the leader>.
follower, adherent, disciple, partisan mean one who attaches himself to another.
Follower denotes a person who attaches himself either to the person or beliefs of another <an evangelist and his *followers*>. ***ant*** leader
Adherent suggests a close and persistent attachment <*adherents* to the cause>. ***ant*** renegade
Disciple implies a devoted allegiance to the teachings of one chosen or accepted as a master <*disciples* of Gandhi>.

Partisan suggests a zealous often prejudiced attachment <*partisans* of the President>.

foment see INCITE.

fondle see CARESS.

foolhardy see ADVENTUROUS.

foolish see SIMPLE.

forbear see REFRAIN.

forbearing, tolerant, lenient, indulgent mean not inclined by nature, disposition, or circumstances to be severe or rigorous.

Forbearing implies patience under provocation and deliberate abstention from harsh judgment, punishment, or vengeance <the most *forbearing* of music teachers>. ***ant*** unrelenting

Tolerant implies a freedom from bias or dogmatism and a reluctance to judge or restrict others harshly who hold opinions or doctrines different from one's own <a very *tolerant* attitude towards dissenters>. ***ant*** intolerant

Lenient implies softness of temper and a relaxation of discipline or rigor <*lenient* parents pay for it later>. ***ant*** stern, exacting

Indulgent implies compliancy, mercifulness, and a willingness to make concessions out of charity or clemency <an aunt *indulgent* of her nephews' and nieces' shortcomings>. ***ant*** strict

forbid, prohibit, interdict, inhibit, ban mean to debar one from using or doing something or to order that something not be used or done.

Forbid implies absolute proscription and expected obedience of an order from one in authority <smoking is *forbidden* in the building>. ***ant*** permit

Prohibit suggests the issuing of laws, statutes, or regulations <*prohibited* the manufacture and sale of firearms>. ***ant*** permit

Interdict implies prohibition by civil or ecclesiastical authority for a given time or a declared purpose <*interdicted* trade with belligerent nations>. ***ant*** sanction

Inhibit implies the imposition of restraints or restrictions that amount to prohibitions, not only by authority but also by the requirements of a situation or by voluntary self-restraint <laws that *inhibit* the growth of free trade>. ***ant*** allow

Ban suggests prohibition stemming from legal or social pressure and strongly connotes condemnation or disapproval <*banned* the new music video>.

force *vb* **Force, compel, coerce, constrain, oblige** mean to make someone or something yield.

Force is the general term and implies the overcoming of resistance by the exertion of strength, power, weight, stress, or duress <*forced* the prisoner to sign the confession>.

Compel typically requires a personal or personalized object and suggests the working of authority or of an irresistible force <all workers are *compelled* to pay taxes>.

Coerce suggests the overcoming of resistance or unwillingness by actual or threatened severe violence or intimidation <*coerced* by gangsters into selling his business>.

Constrain suggests a forcing by constricting, confining, or binding action or choice <*constrained* by my conscience to see that justice was done>.

Oblige implies the constraint of necessity, law, reason, or duty <I am *obliged* to inform you of your rights>.

force *n* see POWER 1.

foreboding see APPREHENSION.

forecast see FORETELL.

foregoing see PRECEDING.

foreign see EXTRINSIC.

foreknow see FORESEE.

forerunner, precursor, harbinger, herald mean one who goes before or announces the coming of another.

Forerunner is applicable to anything that serves as a sign, omen, or warning of something to come <the international incident was a *forerunner* to war>.

Precursor applies to a person or thing that paves the way for the success or accomplishment of another <18th century poets who were *precursors* of the Romantics>.

Harbinger and ***herald*** both apply, chiefly figuratively, to one that proclaims or announces the coming or arrival of a notable event or person <robins, the *harbingers* of spring> <the *herald* of a new age in medical science>.

foresee, foreknow, divine, apprehend, anticipate mean to know or prophesy beforehand.

Foresee implies nothing about how the knowledge is derived and may apply to ordinary reasoning and experience <no one could *foresee* the economic crisis>.

Foreknow stresses prior knowledge and implies supernatural assistance, as through revelation <if only we could *foreknow* our own destinies>.

Divine adds to *foresee* the suggestion of exceptional wisdom or discernment <a European traveler who *divined* the course of American destiny>.

Apprehend implies foresight mingled with uncertainty, anxiety, or dread <*apprehended* that his odd behavior was a sign of a troubled soul>.

Anticipate implies such foreknowledge as leads or allows one to take action about or respond emotionally to something before it happens <the servants *anticipated* our every need>.

forestall see PREVENT 1.

foretaste see PROSPECT.

foretell, predict, forecast, prophesy, prognosticate mean to tell beforehand.

Foretell applies to the telling of a future event by any procedure or from any source of information <seers *foretold* of calamitous events>.

Predict commonly implies inference from facts or from accepted laws of nature <astronomers *predicted* the return of the comet>.

Forecast adds the implication of anticipating eventualities and differs from *predict* in being usually concerned with probabilities rather than certainties <*forecast* a snowfall of six inches>.

Prophesy connotes inspired or mystic knowledge of the future, especially as the fulfilling of divine threats or promises, or implies great assurance in predicting <preachers *prophesying* a day of divine retribution>.

Prognosticate suggests prediction based on the learned or skilled interpretation of signs or symptoms <economists are *prognosticating* a slow recovery>.

forewarn see WARN.

forge see MAKE.

forget see NEGLECT.

forgetful, oblivious, unmindful mean losing from one's mind something once known or learned.

Forgetful implies a heedless or negligent habit of or propensity for failing to remember <*forgetful* of my duties as host>.

Oblivious suggests a failure to notice or remember as a result of external causes or conditions or of a determination to ignore <lost in thought, *oblivious* to the rushing crowd around her>.

Unmindful may suggest inattention and heedlessness or a deliberate disregard <a crusading reformer who was *unmindful* of his family's needs>. ***ant*** mindful, solicitous

forgive see EXCUSE.

forlorn see ALONE.

form *n* **Form, figure, shape, conformation, configuration** mean outward appearance.

Form usually suggests reference to both internal structure and external outline and often the principle that gives unity to the whole <an architect who appreciates the interplay of *forms*>.

Figure applies chiefly to the form as determined by bounding or enclosing outlines <cutting doll *figures* out of paper>.

Shape, like *figure,* suggests an outline but carries a stronger implication of the enclosed body or mass <the *shape* of the monument was pyramidal>.

Conformation implies a complicated structure composed of harmoniously related parts <a *conformation* that is well-proportioned and symmetrical>.

Configuration refers to the pattern formed by the disposition and arrangement of component parts <modular furniture allows for a number of *configurations*>.

form *vb* see MAKE.

formal see CEREMONIAL.

former see PRECEDING.

fornication see ADULTERY.

forsake see ABANDON.

forswear **1.** see ABJURE. **2.** see PERJURE.

forth see ONWARD.

forthright see STRAIGHTFORWARD.

fortitude, grit, backbone, pluck, guts mean courage and staying power.

Fortitude stresses firmness in enduring physical or mental hardships and suffering <a trip that tested their *fortitude*>. ***ant*** pusillanimity

Grit stresses unyielding resolution and indomitableness in the face of hardship or danger <*grit* beyond her years>. ***ant*** faintheartedness

Backbone emphasizes resoluteness of character and implies either ability to stand firm in the face of opposition or such determination and independence as requires no support from without <held their own as long as they kept their *backbone*>. ***ant*** spinelessness

Pluck implies a willingness to fight or continue against odds <fought on with *pluck* and courage>.

Guts, considered by some to be not entirely polite, stresses fortitude and stamina and implies effectiveness and determination in facing and coping with what alarms or repels or discourages <lacked the *guts* to pull it off>. ***ant*** gutlessness

fortuitous see ACCIDENTAL.

fortunate see LUCKY.

fortune see CHANCE.

forward *adv* see ONWARD.

forward *vb* see ADVANCE.

foul see DIRTY.

foundation see BASE *n*.

foxy see SLY.

fragile **1. Fragile, frangible, brittle, crisp, friable** mean easily broken.

Fragile implies extreme delicacy of material or construction and need for careful handling <a *fragile* antique chair>. ***ant*** durable

Frangible implies an inherent susceptibility to being broken without implying weakness or delicacy <*frangible* stone used as paving material>.

Brittle implies hardness together with lack of elasticity or flexibility or toughness <elderly patients with *brittle* bones>. ***ant*** supple

Crisp implies a firmness and brittleness desirable especially in some foods <*crisp* lettuce>.

Friable applies to substances that are easily crumbled or pulverized <*friable* soil>.

2. see WEAK.

fragment see PART.

fragrance, perfume, bouquet, scent, incense, redolence mean a sweet or pleasant odor.

Fragrance suggests the pleasant odors of flowers or other growing things <household cleansers with the *fragrance* of pine>. ***ant*** stench, stink

Perfume may suggest a stronger or heavier odor and applies especially to a prepared or synthetic liquid <the *perfume* of lilacs filled the room>.

Bouquet, often used of wine, implies a delicate, complex odor that suggests the distinctive, savory quality of its source <the *bouquet* of ripe apples>.

Scent is very close to *perfume* but more neutral in connotation <furniture polish with a fresh lemon *scent*>.

Incense applies to the smoke from burning spices and gums and suggests a pleasing odor <the exotic *incense* of a Middle Eastern bazaar>.

Redolence implies a mixture of fragrant or pungent odors <the *redolence* of a forest after a rain>.

fragrant see ODOROUS.

frail see WEAK.

frailty see FAULT.

frame see CONTRIVE.

framework see STRUCTURE.

frangible see FRAGILE.

frank, candid, open, plain mean showing willingness to tell what one feels or thinks.

Frank stresses lack of reticence in expressing oneself and connotes freedom from shyness, secretiveness, or considerations of tact or expedience <*frank* discussions on arms control>. ***ant*** reticent

Candid suggests expression marked by sincerity and honesty especially in offering unwelcome criticism or opinion <a *candid* appraisal of her singing ability>. ***ant*** evasive

Open implies frankness and candor but suggests more artlessness than *frank* and less earnestness than *candid* <young children are *open* and artless in saying what they think>. ***ant*** close, clandestine

Plain suggests outspokenness and freedom from affectation or subtlety in expression <was very *plain* about telling them to leave>.

fraud 1. see DECEPTION. **2.** see IMPOSTURE.

freak see CAPRICE.

free *adj* **Free, independent, autonomous, sovereign** mean not subject to the rule or control of another.

Free stresses the complete absence of external control and the full right to make all of one's own decisions <you're *free* to do as you like>.

Independent implies a standing alone; applied to a state it implies lack of connection with any other having power to interfere with its citizens, laws, or policies <the struggle for Ireland to become *independent*>. ***ant*** dependent

Autonomous stresses independence combined with freedom; or, applied politically, independence in matters pertaining to self-government <the establishment of *autonomous* school districts>.

Sovereign stresses the absence of a superior or dominant power and implies supremacy within one's own domain or sphere <a *sovereign* nation not subject to the laws of another>.

free *vb* **Free, release, liberate, emancipate, manumit** mean to set loose from restraint or constraint.

Free implies a usually permanent removal from whatever binds, confines, entangles, or oppresses <*freed* the animals from their cages>.

Release suggests a setting loose from confinement, restraint, or a state of pressure or tension <*released* his anger by exercising>. ***ant*** detain

Liberate stresses particularly the resulting state of freedom <*liberated* the novel from Victorian inhibitions>.

Emancipate implies the liberation of a person from subjection or domination <labor-saving devices that *emancipated* women from housework>. ***ant*** enslave

Manumit implies emancipation from slavery <the proclamation *manumitted* the slaves>. ***ant*** enslave

freedom, liberty, license mean the power or condition of acting without compulsion.

Freedom has a broad range of application and may imply anything from total absence of restraint to merely a sense of not being unduly hampered or frustrated <*freedom* of the press>. ***ant*** necessity

Liberty suggests the power to choose or the release from former restraint or compulsion <the prisoners were willing to fight for their *liberty*>. ***ant*** restraint

License implies unusual freedom granted because of special circumstances <poetic *license*> or may connote an abuse of freedom by willfully following one's own course without regard for propriety or the rights of others <the editorial takes considerable *license* with the facts>. ***ant*** decorum

frenzy see MANIA 2.

frequently see OFTEN.

fresh see NEW.

friable see FRAGILE.

friendly see AMICABLE.

fright see FEAR.

frightful see FEARFUL 2.

fritter see WASTE.

frivolity see LIGHTNESS.

frown, scowl, glower, lower mean to put on a dark or threatening countenance or appearance.

Frown implies a stern face and contracted brows that express concentration, bewilderment, anger, displeasure, or contempt <the teachers *frowned* on my boyish pranks>. ***ant*** smile

Scowl suggests a similar facial expression that conveys bad humor, sullenness, or resentful puzzlement <a grumpy old man who *scowled* habitually>.

Glower implies a direct defiant brooding stare or glare as in contempt or defiance <the natives merely *glowered* at the invading tourists>.

Lower suggests a menacing darkness or gloomy anger and refers either to persons or to skies that promise bad weather <*lowered* as he went about his work, never uttering a word>.

frowzy see SLATTERNLY.

frugal see SPARING.

fruitful see FERTILE.

fruitless see FUTILE.

frustrate, thwart, foil, baffle, balk, circumvent, outwit mean to check or defeat another's desire, plan, or goal.

Frustrate implies making vain or ineffectual all efforts, however vigorous or persistent <*frustrated* all attempts at government reform>. ***ant*** fulfill

Thwart suggests a frustrating or checking by deliberately crossing or opposing one making headway <the park department is *thwarted* by public indifference to littering>.

Foil implies a checking or defeating so as to discourage further effort <her parents *foiled* my efforts to see her>.

Baffle implies a frustrating by confusing or puzzling <*baffled* by the maze of rules and regulations>.

Balk suggests the interposing of obstacles or hindrances <legal restrictions *balked* police efforts to control crime>. ***ant*** forward

Circumvent implies a frustrating by means of a particular stratagem <*circumvented* the law by finding loopholes>. ***ant*** conform *(to laws, orders)*, cooperate *(with persons)*

Outwit suggests craft and cunning in frustrating or circumventing <the rebels *outwitted* the army repeatedly>.

fugitive see TRANSIENT.

fufill 1. see PERFORM. **2.** see SATISFY 3.

full, complete, plenary, replete mean containing all that is wanted or needed or possible.

Full implies the presence or inclusion of everything that is wanted or required by something or that can be held, contained, or attained by it <a *full* schedule of appointments>. ***ant*** empty

Complete applies when all that is needed or wanted is present <the report does not give a *complete* picture of the situation>. ***ant*** incomplete

Plenary adds to *complete* the implication of fullness without qualification and strongly suggests absoluteness <given *plenary* power as commander in chief>. ***ant*** limited

Replete stresses abundance of supply and implies being filled to the brim or to satiety <a speech *replete* with innuendos and half-truths>.

fulsome, oily, unctuous, oleaginous, slick mean too obviously extravagant or ingratiating to be accepted as genuine or sincere.

Fulsome implies that something which is essentially good has been carried to an excessive and offensive degree <the *fulsome* flattery of a celebrity interviewer>.

Oily implies an offensively ingratiating quality and sometimes suggests a suavity or benevolence or kindliness that masks a sinister or dubious intent <*oily* land developers trying to persuade older residents to sell>.

Unctuous implies the hypocritical adoption of a grave, devout, or spiritual manner <the *unctuous* pleading of the First Amendment by pornographers>.

Oleaginous may be used in place of *oily* to suggest pomposity or to convey a mocking note <an *oleaginous* host fawning over the female guests>.

fun, jest, sport, game, play mean action or speech that provides amusement or arouses laughter.

Fun usually implies laughter or gaiety but may imply merely a lack of serious or ulterior purpose <played cards just for *fun*>. ***ant*** earnestness, seriousness

Jest implies lack of earnestness in what is said or done and may suggest a hoaxing or teasing <took seriously remarks said only in *jest*>. ***ant*** earnest

Sport applies especially to the arousing of laughter against someone by raillery or ridicule <teasing begun in *sport* ended in an ugly brawl>.

Game is close to *sport* and often stresses mischievous or malicious fun but may also apply to any activity carried on in a spirit of fun <habitually made *game* of their poor relations>.

Play stresses the opposition to *earnest* or *serious* and connotes the absence of any element of malice or mischief <pretended to strangle his brother in *play*>. ***ant*** work

function 1. Function, office, duty, province mean the acts or operations expected of a person or thing.

Function, applicable to anything living, natural, or constructed, implies a definite end or purpose that the thing in question serves or a particular kind of work it is intended to perform <the *function* of the stomach is to digest food>.

Office is typically applied to the function or service expected of a person by reason of his or her trade, profession, or special relationship to others <exercised the *offices* of both attorney and friend>.

Duty applies to a task or responsibility imposed by one's occupation, rank, status, or calling <the lieutenant governor had a few official *duties*>.

Province applies to a function, office, or duty that naturally or logically falls within one's range of jurisdiction or competence <it is not the governor's *province* to set foreign policy>.

2. see POWER 2.

fundamental see ESSENTIAL.

funny see LAUGHABLE.

furnish, equip, outfit, appoint, accoutre, arm mean to supply one with what is needed.

Furnish implies the provision of any or all essentials for performing a function or serving an end <a sparsely *furnished* apartment>.

Equip suggests the provision of something making for efficiency in action or use <a fully *equipped* kitchen with every modern appliance>.

Outfit implies provision of a complete list or set of articles as for a journey, an expedition, or a special occupation <*outfitted* the whole family for a ski trip>.

Appoint implies provision of complete and usually elegant or elaborate equipment or furnishings <a lavishly *appointed* penthouse apartment>.

Accoutre suggests the supplying of personal dress or equipment for a special activity <the fully *accoutred* members of a polar expedition>.

Arm implies provision for effective action or operation especially in war <*armed* to the teeth>.

2. see PROVIDE.

further see ADVANCE.

furtive see SECRET.

fury see ANGER.

fuse see MIX.
fuss see STIR *n*.
fussy see NICE.
fustian see BOMBAST.
fusty see MALODOROUS.
futile, vain, fruitless, bootless, abortive mean barren of or producing no result.

Futile may connote completeness of the failure or unwisdom of the undertaking <a *futile* search for survivors of the crash>. ***ant*** effective

Vain usually implies simple failure to achieve a desired result <a *vain* attempt to get the car started>.

Fruitless comes close to *vain* but often suggests long and arduous effort or severe disappointment <*fruitless* efforts to obtain a lasting peace>. ***ant*** fruitful

Bootless, chiefly literary, applies to petitions or efforts to obtain relief <a *bootless* request for aid>.

Abortive suggests failure before plans are matured or activities begun <an *abortive* attempt to escape>. ***ant*** consummated

G

gag see JEST.
gain 1. see GET. **2.** see REACH.
gainsay see DENY.
gall see TEMERITY.
gallant see CIVIL.
gallantry see HEROISM.
gambit see TRICK *n*.
game see FUN.
games see ATHLETICS.
gamut see RANGE.
gape see GAZE.
garble see MISREPRESENT.
garish see GAUDY.
garner see REAP.
garnish see ADORN.
garrulous see TALKATIVE.
gastronome see EPICURE.
gather 1. Gather, collect, assemble, congregate mean to come or bring together into a group, mass, or unit.

Gather, the most general term, is usually neutral in connotation or may suggest plucking and culling or harvesting <a crowd *gathers* whenever there is excitement>. ***ant*** scatter

Collect often implies careful selection or orderly arrangement with a definite end in view <*collected* books on gardening>. ***ant*** disperse, distribute

Assemble implies an ordered union or organization of persons or things and a conscious or definite end for their coming or being brought together <the country's leading experts on aeronautics *assembled* under one roof>. ***ant*** disperse

Congregate implies a spontaneous flocking together into a crowd or huddle, usually of similar types <persons were forbidden to *congregate* under martial law>. ***ant*** disperse

2. see REAP.

3. see INFER.

gauche see AWKWARD.

gaudy, tawdry, garish, flashy, meretricious mean vulgarly or cheaply showy.

Gaudy implies a tasteless use of overly bright, often clashing colors or excessive ornamentation <circus performers in *gaudy* costumes>. ***ant*** quiet

Tawdry applies to what is at once gaudy and cheap and sleazy <*tawdry* saloons along the waterfront>.

Garish describes what is distressingly or offensively bright <*garish* signs on the casinos>. ***ant*** somber

Flashy implies an effect of brilliance quickly and easily revealed to be shallow or vulgar <a *flashy* nightclub act with leggy chorus girls>.

Meretricious stresses falsity and may describe a tawdry show that beckons with a false allure or promise <a *meretricious* wasteland of nightclubs and bars>.

gauge see STANDARD.

gaunt see LEAN.

gay see LIVELY.

gaze, gape, stare, glare, peer, gloat mean to look attentively.

Gaze implies fixed and prolonged attention, as in wonder, admiration, or abstractedness <*gazing* at the waves breaking along the shore>.

Gape suggests an openmouthed and often stupid wonder <a crowd *gaped* at the man threatening to jump>.

Stare implies a direct open-eyed gazing denoting curiosity, disbelief, or insolence <kept *staring* at them as they tried to eat>.

Glare suggests a fierce or angry staring <silently *glared* back at her accusers>.

Peer suggests a straining to see more closely or fully, often with narrowed eyes and as if through a small opening <*peered* at the bird through his binoculars>.

Gloat implies prolonged or frequent gazing, often in secret and with deep or malignant satisfaction <*gloated* over the treasure>.

general see UNIVERSAL.

generic see UNIVERSAL.
generous see LIBERAL 1.
genial see GRACIOUS.
genius see GIFT.
gentle see SOFT.
gentry see ARISTOCRACY.
genuine see AUTHENTIC.
germane see RELEVANT.
get 1. Get, obtain, procure, secure, acquire, gain, win, earn mean to come into possession of.

Get is a very general term and may or may not imply effort or initiative <*got* a car for my birthday>.

Obtain suggests the attainment of something sought for with some expenditure of time and effort <*obtained* statements from all of the witnesses>.

Procure implies effort in obtaining something for oneself or for another <in charge of *procuring* supplies for the office>.

Secure implies difficulty in obtaining or keeping safely in one's possession or under one's control <an ad agency that *secured* many top accounts>.

Acquire often suggests an adding to what is already possessed <*acquired* a greater appreciation of music>. ***ant*** forfeit

Gain suggests struggle or competition and usually a material value in the thing obtained <gradually *gained* a reputation as a skilled musician>. ***ant*** lose

Win suggests that favoring qualities or circumstances played a part in the gaining <*won* the admiration of his fellow actors>. ***ant*** lose

Earn implies a correspondence between one's effort and what one gets by it <a compelling performance that *earned* her many awards>.

2. see INDUCE.

ghastly, grisly, gruesome, macabre, grim, lurid mean horrifying and repellent in appearance or aspect.

Ghastly suggests the terrifying aspects of bloodshed, death, corpses, and ghosts <a *ghastly* portrait of life after a nuclear war>.

Grisly and ***gruesome*** suggest additionally the results of extreme violence or cruelty and an appearance that inspires shuddering or horror <the case of an unusually *grisly* murder> <the *gruesome* history of the Nazi death camps>.

Macabre implies a marked or excessive preoccupation with the horrible aspects especially of death <a *macabre* tale of premature burial>.

Grim suggests a fierce and forbidding aspect <the *grim* face of the executioner>.

Lurid suggests shuddering fascination with violent death and especially with murder <the tabloids wallowed in the crime's *lurid* details>.

gibe see SCOFF.

gift, faculty, aptitude, bent, talent, genius, knack mean a special ability or unusual capacity for doing something.

Gift often implies special favor by God, nature, or fortune <the *gift* of a beautiful singing voice>.

Faculty applies to an innate or acquired ability for a particular accomplishment or function <a rare *faculty* for remembering people's names>.

Aptitude implies an innate capacity as well as a natural liking for some activity <a boy with a definite mechanical *aptitude*>.

Bent is nearly equal to *aptitude* but it stresses inclination perhaps more than ability <a family that has always had an artistic *bent*>.

Talent suggests a marked natural ability that needs to be developed <allowed her dancing *talent* to go to waste>.

Genius suggests impressive inborn creative ability and often the inner drive that forces its possessor to achieve <the *genius* of Mozart>.

Knack implies a comparatively minor but special ability making for ease and dexterity in performance <has the *knack* for making swift, cutting retorts>.

gigantic see ENORMOUS.

give, present, donate, bestow, confer, afford mean to convey to another.

Give, the general term, is applicable to any passing over of anything by any means <*give* alms> <*give* a boy a ride on a pony> <*give* my love to your mother>.

Present carries a note of formality and ceremony <*presented* him with the keys to the city>.

Donate is likely to imply a publicized giving such as to charity <*donate* a piano to the orphanage>.

Bestow implies the conveying of something as a gift and may suggest condescension on the part of the giver <*bestow* unwanted advice>.

Confer implies a gracious giving, such as a favor or honor <the Pope *conferred* the rank of cardinal on three bishops>.

Afford implies a giving or bestowing usually as a natural or legitimate consequence of the character of the giver <the trees *afforded* us a welcome shade>.

glad, happy, cheerful, lighthearted, joyful, joyous mean characterized by or expressing the mood of one who is pleased or delighted.

Glad may convey polite conventional expressions of pleasure <we are so *glad* you could come> or it may convey the idea of an actual lifting of spirits, delight, or even elation <a face that makes me *glad*>. ***ant*** sad

Happy implies a sense of well-being and complete content <nothing made him so *happy* as to be at home with his family>. ***ant*** unhappy, disconsolate

Cheerful suggests a strong spontaneous flow of good spirits <broke into a *cheerful* song as he strode along>. ***ant*** cheerless

Lighthearted stresses freedom from worry, care, and discontent <went off to school, *lighthearted* and gay>. ***ant*** despondent

Joyful usually suggests an emotional reaction to a situation that calls forth rejoicing of happiness or elation <heard the news with a *joyful* heart>. ***ant*** joyless

Joyous is more likely to apply to something that is by its nature filled with joy or a source of joy <sang song after *joyous* song>. ***ant*** lugubrious

glance see FLASH.

glare 1. see GAZE. **2.** SEE BLAZE.

glaring see FLAGRANT.

gleam see FLASH.

glean see REAP.

glee see MIRTH.

glib see VOCAL 2.

glimmer see FLASH.

glint see FLASH.

glisten see FLASH.

glitter see FLASH.

gloat see GAZE.

gloom see SADNESS.

gloomy 1. see DARK. **2.** see SULLEN.

glorious see SPLENDID.

glossy see SLEEK.

glow see BLAZE.

glower see FROWN.

glum see SULLEN.

glut see SATIATE.

gluttonous see VORACIOUS.

go 1. Go, leave, depart, quit, withdraw, retire mean to move out of or away from the place where one is.

Go is the general term and is commonly used as the simple opposite of *come* <*go* away for the day>. ***ant*** come

Leave stresses the fact of separation from someone or something <*leave* one's hometown to take a new job>.

Depart carries a stronger implication of separation than *leave* and is likely to suggest formality <a plane that *departs* this evening>. ***ant*** arrive, abide, remain

Quit may add to *leave* the notion of freeing, ridding, or disentangling from something that burdens or tries <*quit* a dull job>.

Withdraw suggests a deliberate removal for good reason <the visitors *withdrew* when the doctor came into the room>.

Retire implies distinctively renunciation, retreat, or recession <*retire* from the world to a monastery>. ***ant*** advance

2. see RESORT.

goad see MOTIVE.

goal see INTENTION.

good-natured see AMIABLE.

gorge see SATIATE.

gorgeous see SPLENDID.

gory see BLOODY.

gossip see REPORT.

gourmand see EPICURE.

gourmet see EPICURE.

govern, rule mean to exercise power or authority in controlling others.

Govern implies a keeping in a straight course or smooth operation for the good of the individual or the whole <the British monarch reigns, but the prime minister *governs*>.

Rule may imply no more than a possessing of the power to lay down laws or issue commands that must be obeyed but often suggests the exercising of despotic or arbitrary power <the emperor *ruled* with an iron hand>.

grab see TAKE.

grace see MERCY.

gracious, cordial, affable, genial, sociable mean markedly pleasant and easy in social intercourse.

Gracious implies courtesy and kindly consideration <her *gracious* acceptance of the award>. ***ant*** ungracious

Cordial stresses warmth and heartiness <our *cordial* host greeted us at the door>.

Affable implies easy approachability and readiness to respond pleasantly to conversation or requests or proposals <the dean of students was surprisingly *affable*>. ***ant*** reserved

Genial stresses cheerfulness and even joviality <the emcee must be a *genial* extrovert>. ***ant*** caustic, saturnine

Sociable suggests a genuine liking and need for the companionship of others and a readiness to engage in social intercourse <*sociable* people enjoying an ocean cruise>. **ant** unsociable

grand, magnificent, imposing, stately, majestic, grandiose mean large and impressive.

Grand adds to greatness of size or conception the implications of handsomeness and dignity <a mansion with a *grand* staircase>.

Magnificent implies an impressive largeness proportionate to

scale without sacrifice of dignity or good taste <*magnificent* paintings and tapestries>. ***ant*** modest
Imposing implies great size and dignity but stresses impressiveness <large, *imposing* buildings line the avenue>. ***ant*** unimposing
Stately may suggest impressive size combined with poised dignity, erect bearing, handsome proportions, and ceremonious deliberation of movement <the *stately* procession proceeded into the cathedral>.
Majestic combines the implications of *imposing* and *stately* and adds a suggestion of solemn grandeur <a *majestic* waterfall>.
Grandiose implies a size or scope exceeding ordinary experience but is most commonly applied derogatorily to inflated pretension or absurd exaggeration <*grandiose* schemes of world conquest>.

grandiose see GRAND.

grant, concede, vouchsafe, accord, award mean to give as a favor or a right.
Grant implies the giving to a claimant or petitioner, often a subordinate, of something that could be withheld <*granted* them another month to finish the work>.
Concede implies requested or demanded yielding of something reluctantly in response to a rightful or compelling claim <even her critics *concede* she can be charming>. **ant** deny
Vouchsafe implies the granting of something as a courtesy or an act of gracious condescension <the star refused to *vouchsafe* an interview>.
Accord implies the giving to another of what is due or proper or in keeping with the other's character or status <*accorded* all the honors befitting a head of state>. ***ant*** withhold
Award implies the giving of what is deserved or merited after a careful weighing of pertinent factors <*awarded* the company a huge defense contract>.

graphic, vivid, picturesque, pictorial mean giving a clear visual impression especially in words.
Graphic stresses the evoking of a clear lifelike image <a *graphic* account of his combat experiences>.
Vivid stresses the intense vital quality of either the description or the response to it <a *vivid* re-creation of an exciting history>.
Picturesque suggests the presence of features notable for qualities such as distinctness, unfamiliarity, sharp contrast, and charm <Dickens is famous for his *picturesque* characters>.
Pictorial implies representation of a vivid picture with emphasis on colors, shapes, and spatial relations <a *pictorial* style of poetry marked by precise, developed imagery>.

grasp 1. see TAKE. **2.** see HOLD.

grasping see COVETOUS.

grateful 1. Grateful, thankful mean feeling or expressing gratitude.

Grateful is employed to express a proper sense of favors received from another person or persons <*grateful* for the company>. ***ant*** ungrateful

Thankful is often preferred to express one's acknowledgment of divine favor or of what is vaguely felt to be providential <be *thankful* that you were not badly hurt>. ***ant*** thankless, unthankful

2. see PLEASANT.

gratifying see PLEASANT.

gratuitous see SUPEREROGATORY.

grave see SERIOUS.

great see LARGE.

greedy see COVETOUS.

green see RUDE.

grief see SORROW.

grievance see INJUSTICE.

grieve, mourn, sorrow mean to feel or express sorrow or grief.

Grieve implies actual mental suffering, whether it is shown outwardly or not and connotes the concentration of one's mind on one's loss, trouble, or cause of distress <still *grieves* for her dead child>. ***ant*** rejoice

Mourn stresses the outward expressions of grief, sincere or conventional, and usually suggests a specific cause such as the death of someone loved or respected <a nation *mourns* the loss of its hero>.

Sorrow, interchangeable with either *grieve* or *mourn* when sincere mental distress is implied, stresses the sense of regret or loss and of deep sadness and suggests an inner distress rather than outward expressions of grief <*sorrowed* with great dignity>.

grim see GHASTLY.

grind see WORK 1.

grip see HOLD.

grisly see GHASTLY.

grit see FORTITUDE.

gross 1. see COARSE. **2.** see FLAGRANT.

grotesque see FANTASTIC.

ground see BASE *n.*

groundwork see BASE *n.*

group, cluster, bunch, parcel, lot mean a collection or assemblage of separate units.

Group implies some unifying relationship and ordinarily a degree of physical closeness <a *group* of people waiting for a bus>.

Cluster basically refers to a group of things growing together <a *cluster* of grapes> but it is often extended to persons or things that form small groups especially within larger masses <cataloging *clusters* of stars>.

Bunch is likely to imply a natural or homogeneous association of similar things or persons <a *bunch* of bananas>.

Parcel is likely to convey an impression of disapproval <the whole story was a *parcel* of lies>.

Lot applies to persons or things that are associated or that have to be dealt with as a whole <the books were sold in *lots*>.

grovel see WALLOW.

grown-up see MATURE *adj.*

grudge see MALICE.

gruesome see GHASTLY.

gruff see BLUFF.

guard see DEFEND 1.

guess see CONJECTURE.

guide, lead, steer, pilot, engineer mean to direct in a course or show the way to be followed.

Guide implies intimate knowledge of the way and of all its difficulties and dangers <*guided* the other scouts through the darkened cave>. ***ant*** misguide

Lead implies a going ahead to show the way and often to keep those that follow under control and in order <the flagship *led* the fleet>. ***ant*** follow

Steer implies an ability to keep to a chosen course and stresses the capacity for maneuvering correctly <*steered* the ship through the narrow channel>.

Pilot suggests special skill or knowledge used in guiding over a dangerous, intricate, or complicated course <successfully *piloted* the bill through the Senate>.

Engineer implies guidance by one who finds ways to avoid or overcome difficulties in achieving an end or carrying out a plan <*engineered* his son's election to the governorship>.

guilty see BLAMEWORTHY.

gull see DUPE.

gumption see SENSE.

gush see POUR.

gusto see TASTE 2.

guts see FORTITUDE.

H

habit 1. Habit, habitude, practice, usage, custom, use, wont mean a way of acting that has become fixed through repetition.

Habit implies a doing unconsciously or without premeditation and often compulsively <the *habit* of constantly tapping his fingers>.

Habitude suggests a fixed attitude or usual state of mind <greeted her friends warmly from *habitude*>.

Practice suggests an act or method followed with regularity and usually through choice <our *practice* is to honor all major credit cards>.

Usage suggests a customary action so generally followed that it has become a social norm <western-style dress is now common *usage* in international business>.

Custom applies to a practice or usage so steadily associated with an individual or group as to have almost the force of unwritten law <the *custom* of mourners wearing black at funerals>.

Use stresses the fact of customary usage and its distinctive quality <conform to the *uses* of polite society>.

Wont applies to an habitual manner, method, or practice distinguishing an individual or group <as was her *wont,* she slept until noon>.

2. see PHYSIQUE.

habitual see USUAL.

habitude see HABIT 1.

hackneyed see TRITE.

hale see HEALTHY.

hallow see DEVOTE.

hallucination see DELUSION.

hamper, trammel, clog, fetter, shackle, manacle mean to hinder or impede in moving, progressing, or acting.

Hamper implies the encumbering or embarrassing effect of any impeding or restraining influence <*hampered* the investigation by refusing to cooperate>. ***ant*** assist *(as a person),* expedite *(as work)*

Trammel suggests hindering by or as if by or confining within a net <rules that serve only to *trammel* the artist's creativity>.

Clog usually implies a slowing by something extraneous or encumbering <feels that free enterprise is *clogged* by government regulation>.

Fetter suggests a restraining so severe that freedom to move or progress is almost lost <a nation that is *fettered* by an antiquated class system>.

Shackle and ***manacle*** are stronger than *fetter* and suggest total loss of the power to move, to progress, or to act <a mind *shackled* by stubborn pride and prejudice> <hatred can *manacle* the soul>.

handle 1. Handle, manipulate, wield mean to manage dexterously or efficiently.

Handle implies directing an acquired skill to the accomplishment of immediate ends <*handled* the crisis with cool efficiency>.

Manipulate implies adroit handling and often suggests the use of craft or fraud to attain one's ends <brutally *manipulates* other people for his own selfish ends>.

Wield implies mastery and vigor in handling a tool or a weapon or in exerting influence, authority, or power <the news media *wield* a tremendous influence on the electorate>.

2. see TOUCH.

3. see TREAT.

handsome see BEAUTIFUL.

hanger-on see PARASITE.

hanker see LONG.

hap see CHANCE.

haphazard see RANDOM.

happen, chance, occur, transpire mean to come about.

Happen is the ordinary and general term applying to whatever comes about with or without obvious causation or intention <remembering an incident that *happened* in his childhood>.

Chance regularly implies absence of design or apparent lack of causation <a man he *chanced* to know>.

Occur stresses presentation to sight or attention <such events, when they *occur*, fascinate the public>.

Transpire implies a leaking out so as to become known or apparent <the meeting *transpired* as planned>.

happy **1.** see FIT *adj*. **2.** see GLAD. **3.** see LUCKY.

harass see WORRY.

harbinger see FORERUNNER.

harbor, shelter, entertain, lodge, house, board mean to provide a place, such as one's home, quarters, or confines, where someone or something may stay or be kept for a time.

Harbor implies provision of a place of refuge especially for an evil, hunted, or harmful person or animal <*harbor* thieves> or suggests the holding in the mind of thoughts, wishes, or designs, especially evil or harmful ones <*harbored* thoughts of suicide>.

Shelter suggests the place or thing that affords protection or a retreat, especially from such things as the elements, attackers, or a bombardment <*sheltered* themselves from the posse in the hayloft>.

Entertain implies the giving of hospitality, often with special efforts to insure pleasure and comfort, to a guest <*entertained* lavishly most nights> or suggests consideration of ideas, notions, or fears <privately *entertained* a theory about the education of children>.

Lodge implies the supplying of a place to stay, often temporary <*lodged* the wanderers for the night> or the reception into the mind or any place in which a thing may be deposited or imbedded <a series of events that are *lodged* in her memory>.

House implies shelter like that of a building with a roof and walls that offers protection from the weather <found a nest *housed* in a tree>.

Board implies the provision of meals or of room and meals for compensation <*boarded* with the Smiths>.

hard 1. Hard, difficult, arduous mean demanding great exertion or effort.

Hard implies the opposite of all that is easy <farming is *hard* work>. ***ant*** easy

Difficult implies the presence of obstacles to be surmounted or complications resolved and suggests the need of skill, patience, endurance, or courage <a *difficult* decision requiring much thought>. ***ant*** simple

Arduous stresses the need for laborious and persevering exertion <the *arduous* task of rebuilding the town>. ***ant*** light, facile

2. see FIRM.

hardihood see TEMERITY.

hardship see DIFFICULTY.

harm see INJURE.

harmonize see AGREE 3.

harmony 1. Harmony, consonance, accord, concord mean the state resulting when different things come together without clashing or disagreement.

Harmony implies a beautiful effect achieved by the agreeable interrelation, blending, or arrangement of parts in a complex whole <a resort in splendid *harmony* with its natural setting>. ***ant*** conflict

Consonance implies the fact or means by which harmony is achieved through coincidence and concurrence <immediate *consonance* of action and custom>. ***ant*** dissonance *(in music)*, discord

Accord may imply personal agreement or goodwill or the absence of friction or ill will <parents and teachers are in *accord* on this issue>. ***ant*** dissension, strife, antagonism

Concord adds to *accord* implications of peace and amity <a planned utopian community in which all would live in *concord*>. ***ant*** discord

2. see SYMMETRY.

harry see WORRY.

harsh see ROUGH.

harvest see REAP.

haste, hurry, speed, expedition, dispatch mean quickness in movement or action.

Haste implies urgency, undue hastiness, and often rashness in persons <why this headlong *haste* to get married?>. ***ant*** deliberation

Hurry often has a strong suggestion of agitated bustle or confusion <in the *hurry* of departure she forgot her toothbrush>.

Speed suggests swift efficiency in movement or action <exercises to increase your reading *speed*>.

Expedition stresses ease or efficiency of performance <made plans with *expedition*>. ***ant*** procrastination

Dispatch carries a suggestion of promptness in bringing matters to a conclusion <regularly paid her bills with the greatest possible *dispatch*>. ***ant*** delay

hasty see FAST.

hate, detest, abhor, abominate, loathe mean to feel strong aversion or intense dislike for.

Hate implies an emotional aversion often coupled with enmity or malice <*hated* his former friend with a passion>. ***ant*** love

Detest suggests violent antipathy or dislike, but without active hostility or malevolence <I *detest* moral cowards>. ***ant*** adore

Abhor implies a deep, often shuddering repugnance from or as if from fear or horror <child abuse is a crime *abhorred* by all>. ***ant*** admire

Abominate suggests strong detestation and often moral condemnation <virtually every society *abominates* incest>. ***ant*** esteem, enjoy

Loathe implies utter disgust and intolerance <*loathed* self-appointed moral guardians>. ***ant*** dote on

hateful, odious, abhorrent, detestable, abominable mean deserving of or arousing intense dislike.

Hateful applies to something or someone that arouses active hatred and hostility <the *hateful* prospect of another war>. ***ant*** lovable, sympathetic

Odious applies to that which is disagreeable or offensive or arouses repugnance <you apparently find the plain truth *odious*>.

Abhorrent characterizes that which outrages a sense of what is right, decent, just, or honorable <the *abhorrent* practice of stereotyping minority groups>. ***ant*** admirable

Detestable suggests something deserving extreme contempt <his *detestable* habit of passing the blame to subordinates>. ***ant*** adorable

Abominable suggests something fiercely condemned as vile or unnatural <the *abominable* living conditions of the plantation slaves>. ***ant*** laudable, delightful, enjoyable

haughty see PROUD.

haul see PULL.

have, hold, own, possess, enjoy mean to keep, control, retain, or experience as one's own.

Have is a general term carrying no specific implication of a cause or reason for regarding the thing had as one's own <they *have* plenty of money>.

Hold suggests stronger control, grasp, or retention and suggests continuity or actual occupation <*held* absolute power over the whole country>.

Own implies a natural or legal right to regard as one's property and under one's full control <*own* property in several states>.

Possess is often the preferred term when referring to an intangible such as a characteristic, a power, or a quality <*possesses* a first-rate intellect>.

Enjoy implies the having of something as one's own or for one's use <a company that *enjoyed* a fine reputation>.

havoc see RUIN *n.*

hazard see CHANCE.

hazardous see DANGEROUS.

haze, mist, fog, smog mean an atmospheric condition that deprives the air of its transparency.

Haze implies a diffusion of smoke or dust or light vapor sufficient to blur vision but not to obstruct it <mountains rendered blue by the *haze*>.

Mist implies a suspension of water droplets, floating and slowly falling through the air, that impairs but does not cut off vision <hair damp from the *mist*>.

Fog implies a denser suspension than a mist, with power to enshroud and to cut off vision more or less completely <visibility reduced to inches by the *fog*>.

Smog applies to a haze, mist, or fog made thicker and darker by the smoke and fumes of an industrial area <cast a pall of *smog* over the city>.

headlong see PRECIPITATE.

headstrong see UNRULY.

heal see CURE.

healthful, healthy, wholesome, salubrious, salutary mean conducive or favorable to the health or soundness of mind or body.

Healthful implies a beneficial contribution to a healthy condition <*healthful* diet will provide more energy>. ***ant*** unhealthful

Healthy, like *healthful,* applies to what promotes good health and vigor <a *healthy* climate>. ***ant*** unhealthful

Wholesome applies to what benefits, builds up, or sustains physically, mentally, or spiritually or to what is not detrimental to health or well-being <*wholesome* foods> <the movie is *wholesome* family entertainment>. ***ant*** noxious, unwholesome

Salubrious applies chiefly to the helpful effects of climate or air that is devoid of harshness or extremes <the *salubrious* climate of the American Southwest>. ***ant*** insalubrious

Salutary describes something corrective or beneficially effective, even though it may in itself be unpleasant <a *salutary* warning that resulted in increased production>. ***ant*** deleterious, unsalutary

healthy 1. Healthy, sound, wholesome, robust, hale, well mean enjoying or indicative of good health.

Healthy implies the possession of full strength and vigor or freedom from signs of disease or may apply to what manifests or indicates these conditions <the doctor pronounced the whole family *healthy*>. ***ant*** unhealthy

Sound emphasizes the absence of disease, weakness, or malfunction <an examination showed his heart to be *sound*>.

Wholesome implies appearance and behavior indicating soundness and balance or equilibrium <she looks especially *wholesome* in her tennis togs>.

Robust implies the opposite of all that is delicate or sickly and connotes vigor and health shown by muscularity, fresh color, a strong voice, and an ability to work long and hard <a lively, *robust* little boy>. ***ant*** frail, feeble

Hale applies particularly to robustness in old age <still *hale* at the age of eighty>. ***ant*** infirm

Well implies merely freedom from disease or illness <she has never been a *well* person>. ***ant*** ill, unwell

2. see HEALTHFUL.

hearsay see REPORT.

hearten see ENCOURAGE.

heartfelt see SINCERE.

hearty see SINCERE.

heave see LIFT.

heavy, weighty, ponderous, cumbrous, cumbersome mean having great weight.

Heavy implies that something has greater density or thickness or sometimes power than the average of its kind or class <a *heavy* child for his age>. ***ant*** light

Weighty suggests actual as well as relative heaviness <really *weighty* parcels are shipped by freight> or implies a momentous or highly important character <pondered *weighty* matters late into the night>. ***ant*** weightless

Ponderous implies having great weight because of size and massiveness with resulting great inertia and clumsiness <*ponderous* galleons were outmaneuvered by smaller vessels>.

Cumbrous and ***cumbersome*** imply heaviness and massive bulkiness that make a thing difficult to grasp, move, carry, or manipulate <abandoned the *cumbrous* furniture rather than

move it> <the old cameras were *cumbersome* and inconvenient>.

heckle see BAIT.

hector see BAIT.

height, altitude, elevation mean vertical distance either between the top and bottom of something or between a base and something above it.

Height refers to any vertical distance whether great or small <a wall two meters in *height*>. ***ant*** depth

Altitude refers to vertical distance above the surface of the earth or above sea level or to the vertical distance above the horizon in angular measurement <fly at an *altitude* of 10,000 meters>.

Elevation is used especially in reference to vertical height above sea level on land <Denver is a city with a high *elevation*>.

heighten see INTENSIFY.

heinous see OUTRAGEOUS.

help 1. Help, aid, assist mean to supply what is needed to accomplish an end.

Help carries a strong implication of advance toward an objective <*helped* to find a cure for the disease>. ***ant*** hinder

Aid suggests the need of help or relief and so imputes weakness to the one aided and strength to the one aiding <an army of volunteers *aided* the flood victims>.

Assist suggests a secondary role in the assistant or a subordinate character in the assistance <*assisted* the chief surgeon during the operation>.

2. see IMPROVE.

helper see ASSISTANT.

hence see THEREFORE.

herald see FORERUNNER.

hereditary see INNATE.

heritage, inheritance, patrimony, birthright mean something which one receives or is entitled to receive by succession, as from a parent or predecessor.

Heritage may apply to anything that is passed on not only to an heir or heirs but to the succeeding generation or generations <want, the *heritage* of waste>.

Inheritance refers to what passes from parents to children, such as money, property, or character traits, or to the fact or means of inheriting <brown eyes, her *inheritance* from her father>.

Patrimony applies to the money or property inherited from one's father, but also generally to one's ancestral inheritance <the intellectual *patrimony* of the Renaissance>.

Birthright generally implies the rights to which one is entitled by nativity, as by being a native-born citizen or a descendant of a particular family <honor that was their *birthright*>.

heroism, valor, prowess, gallantry mean conspicuously courageous behavior.

Heroism implies superlative courage especially in fulfilling a high purpose against odds <the boy's outstanding act of *heroism* during the fire>. ***ant*** pusillanimity

Valor implies illustrious bravery and vigorous audacity in fighting <awarded the army's highest honor for *valor* in battle>. ***ant*** pusillanimity, pusillanimousness

Prowess stresses skill as well as bravery in both arms and other pursuits <demonstrated her *prowess* with a bow and arrow>.

Gallantry implies dash and spirit as well as courage and an indifference to danger or hardship <special forces with a proud tradition of *gallantry*>. ***ant*** dastardliness

hesitant see DISINCLINED.

hesitate, waver, vacillate, falter mean to show irresolution or uncertainty.

Hesitate implies pausing before deciding or acting or choosing <*hesitated* before answering the question>.

Waver implies hesitation after seeming to reach a decision and so connotes weakness or a retreat <*wavered* in his support of the rebels>.

Vacillate implies prolonged hesitation from inability to reach a firm decision and suggests the play of opposing factors that results in indecision <*vacillated* until it was too late and events were out of control>.

Falter implies a wavering or stumbling and often connotes nervousness, lack of courage, or outright fear <never once *faltered* during her testimony>.

heterogeneous see MISCELLANEOUS.

hide, conceal, screen, secrete, bury mean to withhold or withdraw from sight or observation.

Hide may or may not suggest intent <a house *hidden* by trees>.

Conceal usually implies intent and often specifically implies a refusal to divulge <*concealed* the weapon in a pocket>. ***ant*** reveal

Screen implies an interposing of something that shelters and hides or merely obscures <*screened* her true identity from her colleagues>.

Secrete suggests a depositing, often by stealth, in a place screened from view or unknown to others <*secreted* the cocaine in the hold of the ship>.

Bury implies a covering with or submerging in something that hides completely <*buried* the note in a pile of papers>.

hideous see UGLY.

high, tall, lofty mean above the average in height.

High implies marked extension upward and is applied chiefly to things which rise from a base or foundation <a *high* hill> or are placed at a conspicuous height above a lower level <a *high* ceiling>. ***ant*** low

Tall applies to what grows or rises high by comparison with others of its kind and usually implies relative narrowness <a *tall* thin man>.

Lofty suggests great or imposing altitude <*lofty* mountain peaks>.

hilarity see MIRTH.

hinder, impede, obstruct, block mean to interfere with the activity or progress of.

Hinder stresses harmful or annoying delay or interference with progress <the rain *hindered* our climbing>. ***ant*** further

Impede implies making forward progress difficult by clogging, hampering, or fettering <tight clothing *impeded* my movement>. ***ant*** assist, promote

Obstruct implies interfering with something in motion or in progress by the often intentional placing of obstacles in the way <the view was *obstructed* by billboards>.

Block implies the complete obstructing of passage or progress <boulders *blocked* the road>.

hint see SUGGEST.

hire, let, lease, rent, charter mean to engage or grant for use at a price.

Hire implies the act of engaging or taking for use <we *hired* a car for the summer>.

Let suggests the granting of use <decided to *let* the cottage to a young couple>.

Lease strictly implies a letting under the terms of a contract but is often applied to the act of hiring on a lease <the diplomat *leased* an apartment for a year>.

Rent stresses the payment of money for the full use of property and may imply either hiring or letting <instead of buying a house, they decided to *rent*>.

Charter applies to the hiring or letting of a public vessel or vehicle usually for exclusive use <*charter* a bus to go to the game>.

history, chronicle, annals mean a written record of events.

History implies more than a mere recital of occurrences and regularly entails order and purpose in narration and usually a degree of interpretation of the events recorded <studied American *history*>.

Chronicle applies strictly to any recital of events in chronological order without interpretation <recited a lengthy *chronicle* of their disastrous trip>.

Annals tends to emphasize the progress or succession of events from year to year and need not imply a discursive treatment or a continued narrative <kept meticulous *annals* of the senate's activities>.

histrionic see DRAMATIC.

hit see STRIKE.

hoax see DUPE.

hoist see LIFT.

hold *vb* **1.** see CONTAIN. **2.** see HAVE.

hold *n* **Hold, grip, grasp, clutch** mean the power of getting or keeping in possession or control.

Hold is widely applicable and may imply mere possession or control, or possession or control firmly maintained <tried to keep a *hold* on his temper>.

Grip regularly suggests a firm or tenacious hold <had a firm *grip* on the reins of power>.

Grasp differs from *grip* chiefly in suggesting a power to reach out and get possession or control of something <success was almost within his *grasp*>.

Clutch implies a seizing and holding with or as if with the avidity or rapacity of a bird of prey <stayed out of the extortioner's *clutches*>.

hollow see VAIN.

homage see HONOR.

homely see PLAIN.

homogeneous see SIMILAR.

honest see UPRIGHT.

honesty, honor, integrity, probity mean uprightness of character or action.

Honesty implies refusal to lie, steal, or deceive in any way <a politician of scrupulous *honesty*>. ***ant*** dishonesty

Honor suggests an active or anxious regard for the standards of one's profession, calling, or position <a keen sense of *honor* in business matters>. ***ant*** dishonor, dishonorableness

Integrity implies trustworthiness and incorruptibility to a degree that one is incapable of being false to a trust, responsibility, or pledge <her unimpeachable *integrity* as a journalist>. ***ant*** duplicity

Probity implies tried and proven honesty or integrity <a judge with a reputation for *probity*>.

honor **1. Honor, homage, reverence, deference** mean respect and esteem shown to another.

Honor may apply to the recognition of one's right to great respect or to any expression of such recognition <an *honor* just to be nominated>. ***ant*** dishonor

Homage adds the implication of accompanying praise or tributes or esteem from those who owe allegiance <for centuries dramatists have paid *homage* to Shakespeare>.

Reverence implies profound respect mingled with love, devotion, or awe <have the greatest *reverence* for my father>.

Deference implies a yielding or submitting to another's judgment or preference out of respect or reverence <refused to show any *deference* to senior staffers>. ***ant*** disrespect

2. see HONESTY

honorable see UPRIGHT.

hope see EXPECT.

hopeless see DESPONDENT.

horde see CROWD.

horrible see FEARFUL 2.

horrific see FEARFUL 2.

horrify see DISMAY.

horror see FEAR.

hostility see ENMITY.

hound see BAIT.

house see HARBOR.

hubbub see DIN.

hue see COLOR.

huff see OFFENSE 1.

huge see ENORMOUS.

hullabaloo see DIN.

humble *adj* **Humble, meek, modest, lowly** mean lacking all signs of pride, aggressiveness, or self-assertiveness.

Humble may suggest a virtuous absence of pride or vanity or it may suggest undue self-depreciation or humiliation <a quiet life as a simple, *humble* parish priest>. ***ant*** conceited

Meek may suggest mildness or gentleness of temper or it may connote undue submissiveness <the refugees were *meek* and grateful for whatever they got>. ***ant*** arrogant

Modest implies a lack of boastfulness or conceit, without any implication of abjectness <sincerely *modest* about her singing talents>. ***ant*** ambitious

Lowly stresses lack of pretentiousness <a volunteer willing to accept the *lowliest* hospital duties>. ***ant*** pompous

humble *vb* see ABASE.

humbug see IMPOSTURE.

humid see WET.

humiliate see ABASE.

humor *vb* see INDULGE.

humor *n* **1.** see WIT. **2.** see MOOD.

humorous see WITTY.

hunger see LONG.

hurl see THROW.

hurry see HASTE.

hurt see INJURE.

hyperbole see EXAGGERATION.

hypercritical see CRITICAL.

hypocritical, sanctimonious, pharisaical, canting mean affecting more virtue or religious devotion than one actually possesses.

Hypocritical implies an appearance of goodness, sincerity, or piety by one who is deficient in these qualities or who is corrupt, dishonest, or irreligious <had no use for such *hypocritical* gestures>. ***ant*** sincere

Sanctimonious implies an affectation or merely outward show of holiness or piety <made a *sanctimonious* appearance in church every week>. ***ant*** unsanctimonious

Pharisaical stresses close adherence to outward forms and a censorious attitude toward others' defects in these respects, coupled with little real concern for spiritual matters <always under the gaze of *pharisaical* neighbors>.

Canting implies the use of religious or pietistic language without evidence of underlying religious feeling <a *canting* moralist>.

hypothesis, theory, law mean a formulation of a general or abstract principle that is derived from observed data and that explains that data.

Hypothesis implies insufficiency of evidence to provide more than a tentative explanation <an *hypothesis* regarding the extinction of the dinosaurs>.

Theory implies a greater range of evidence and greater likelihood of truth than *hypothesis* <the *theory* of evolution>.

Law emphasizes certainty and truth and implies a statement about order and relationships that has been found to be invariable under a particular set of conditions <the *law* of gravitation>.

hysteria see MANIA.

I

idea, concept, conception, thought, notion, impression mean what exists in the mind as a representation or as a formulation.

Idea may apply to a mental image or formulation of something seen or known or imagined, to a pure abstraction, or to something assumed or vaguely sensed <a mind filled with innovative *ideas*>.

Concept may apply to the idea formed after consideration of instances of a category or, more broadly, to any widely accepted idea of what a thing ought to be <a society with no *concept* of private property>.

Conception, often interchangeable with *concept*, stresses the process of imagining or formulating and often applies to a peculiar or individual idea rather than to a widely held one <the writer's *conception* of such a situation>.

Thought is likely to suggest the result of reflecting, reasoning, or meditating rather than of imagining <commit your *thoughts* to paper>.

Notion suggests an idea not much resolved by analysis or reflection and may suggest the tentative, capricious, or accidental <the oddest *notions* fly in and out of her head>.

Impression applies to an idea or notion resulting immediately from some external stimulation <the first *impression* is of soaring height>.

ideal see MODEL.

identical see SAME.

identification see RECOGNITION.

idiom see PHRASE.

idiosyncrasy see ECCENTRICITY.

idle 1. see INACTIVE. **2.** see VAIN.

ignite see LIGHT.

ignoble see MEAN.

ignominy see DISGRACE.

ignorant, illiterate, unlettered, untutored, unlearned mean not having knowledge.

Ignorant may imply a general condition <an *ignorant* fool> or it may apply to lack of knowledge or awareness of a particular thing <he's *ignorant* of nuclear physics>. ***ant*** cognizant, conversant, informed

Illiterate applies to either an absolute or a relative inability to read and write <much of that country's population is still *illiterate*>. ***ant*** literate

Unlettered implies ignorance of the knowledge gained by being educated or by reading <a literary reference that is meaningless to the *unlettered*>. ***ant*** educated, lettered

Untutored may imply lack of schooling in the arts and ways of civilization <strange megalithic monuments left by an *untutored* people>.

Unlearned suggests ignorance of advanced or scholarly subjects <a poet who speaks to the *unlearned*>. ***ant*** erudite, learned

ignore see NEGLECT.

ilk see TYPE.

ill see BAD.

illegal see UNLAWFUL.

illegitimate see UNLAWFUL.

ill-favored see UGLY.

illicit see UNLAWFUL.

illiterate see IGNORANT.

illusion see DELUSION.
illusory see APPARENT.
illustration see INSTANCE.
illustrious see FAMOUS.
ill will see MALICE.
imaginary, fanciful, visionary, fantastic, chimerical, quixotic mean unreal or unbelievable.

Imaginary applies to something which is fictitious and purely the product of one's imagination <a chronic sufferer of several *imaginary* illnesses>. ***ant*** actual, real

Fanciful suggests something affected or created by the free play of the imagination <the *fanciful* characters created by Lewis Carroll>. ***ant*** realistic

Visionary applies to something that seems real and practical to its conceiver but is impractical or incapable of realization <*visionary* schemes for creating a rural utopia>.

Fantastic implies fanciful incredibility or strangeness beyond belief <a *fantastic* world inhabited by prehistoric monsters>.

Chimerical applies to what is wildly or fantastically visionary or improbable <*chimerical* plans for restoring the British Empire>. ***ant*** feasible

Quixotic implies a devotion to romantic or chivalrous ideals unrestrained by ordinary prudence and common sense <the *quixotic* notion that absolute equality is attainable>.

imagine see THINK 1.
imbibe see ABSORB.
imbue see INFUSE.
imitate see COPY.
immediate see DIRECT *adj.*
immense see ENORMOUS.
immoderate see EXCESSIVE.
immoral, unmoral, nonmoral, amoral mean not moral.

Immoral implies a positive and active opposition to what is moral and may designate whatever is counter to accepted ethical principles or the dictates of conscience <*immoral* ideas and conduct>. ***ant*** moral

Unmoral implies a lack of ethical perception and moral awareness or a disregard of moral principles <possessed the *unmoral* conscience of a newborn baby>.

Nonmoral implies that the thing described is patently outside the sphere where moral judgments are applicable <whether your car runs or not is a *nonmoral* issue>.

Amoral is often applied to something that is not customarily exempted from moral judgment <a review that called the film *amoral*>.

impair see INJURE.
impartial see FAIR.

impassioned, passionate, ardent, fervent, fervid, perfervid mean showing intense feeling.

Impassioned implies warmth and intensity without violence and suggests fluent verbal or artistic expression <an *impassioned* plea for international understanding>. ***ant*** unimpassioned

Passionate implies great vehemence and often violence and wasteful diffusion of emotion <*passionate* denunciations of American arrogance>. ***ant*** dispassionate

Ardent implies an intense degree of zeal, devotion, or enthusiasm <an *ardent* admirer of the novels of Jane Austen>. ***ant*** cool

Fervent stresses sincerity and steadiness of emotional warmth or zeal <*fervent* Christians on a pilgrimage>.

Fervid suggests warmly spontaneous and often feverishly urgent emotion <*fervid* love letters that suggested mental unbalance>.

Perfervid implies the expression of exaggerated, insincere, or overwrought feelings <wary of such *perfervid* expresssions of selfless patriotism>.

impassive, stoic, phlegmatic, apathetic, stolid mean unresponsive to something that might normally excite interest or emotion.

Impassive stresses the absence of any external sign of emotion in action or facial expression <just sat there with an *impassive* look>. ***ant*** responsive

Stoic implies an apparent indifference to pleasure or especially to pain, often as a matter of principle or self-discipline <remained resolutely *stoic* even in the face of adversity>.

Phlegmatic implies a temperament or constitution hard to arouse <a *phlegmatic* person immune to amorous advances>.

Apathetic may imply a puzzling or deplorable indifference or inertness <charitable appeals met an *apathetic* response>. ***ant*** alert

Stolid implies an habitual absence of interest, responsiveness, or curiosity about anything beyond an accustomed routine <a *stolid* woman, wedded to routine>.

impeach see ACCUSE.

impede see HINDER.

impel see MOVE.

imperative see MASTERFUL.

imperious see MASTERFUL.

impertinent, officious, meddlesome, intrusive, obtrusive mean given to thrusting oneself into the affairs of another.

Impertinent implies exceeding the bounds of propriety in showing interest or curiosity or in offering advice <a little brat asking *impertinent* questions>.

Officious implies the offering of services or attentions that are unwelcome or annoying <an *officious* salesman followed me outside>.

Meddlesome stresses an annoying and usually prying interference in others' affairs <*meddlesome* old gossips with nothing to do>.

Intrusive implies a tactless or otherwise objectionable curiosity about or a thrusting of oneself into the company or affairs of others <an *intrusive* interruption in our conversation>. ***ant*** retiring, unintrusive

Obtrusive stresses improper or offensive conspicuousness of interfering actions <*obtrusive* relatives monopolizing the wedding photographs>. ***ant*** unobtrusive, shy

imperturbable see COOL.

impetuous see PRECIPITATE.

implant, inculcate, instill, inseminate, infix mean to introduce into the mind.

Implant implies teaching that makes for permanence of what is taught <*implanted* an enthusiasm for reading in her students>.

Inculcate implies persistent or repeated efforts to impress on the mind <*inculcated* in him high moral standards>.

Instill stresses gradual, gentle imparting of knowledge over a long period of time <*instill* traditional values in your children>.

Inseminate applies to a sowing of ideas in many minds so that they spread through a class or nation <*inseminated* an unquestioning faith in technology>.

Infix stresses firmly inculcating a habit of thought <*infixed* a chronic cynicism>.

implement, tool, instrument, appliance, utensil mean a relatively simple device for performing work.

Implement may apply to anything necessary to perform a task <lawn and gardening *implements*>.

Tool suggests an implement adapted to facilitate a definite kind of stage of work and suggests the need of skill <a carpenter's *tools*>.

Instrument suggests a tool or device capable of performing delicate or precise work or one precisely adapted to the end it serves <the surgeon's *instruments*>.

Appliance refers to a tool or instrument utilizing a power source and often adapted to a special purpose <modern *appliances* that take the drudgery out of housework>.

Utensil applies to a device, tool, or vessel, usually with a particular function, used in domestic work or some routine unskilled activity <knives, graters, and other kitchen *utensils*>.

implore see BEG.

imply 1. see SUGGEST. **2.** see INCLUDE.
import 1. see MEANING. **2.** see IMPORTANCE.
importance, consequence, moment, weight, significance, import mean a quality or aspect that is felt to be of great worth, value, or influence.

Importance implies a judgment by which superior worth or influence is ascribed to something or someone <there are no cities of *importance* in this area>. ***ant*** unimportance

Consequence may imply importance in social rank but more generally implies importance because of probable or possible effects <whatever style you choose is of little *consequence*>.

Moment implies conspicuous or self-evident consequence <a decision of very great *moment*>.

Weight implies a judgment of the immediate relevant importance of something that must be taken into account or that may seriously affect an outcome <idle chitchat of no particular *weight*>.

Significance implies a quality or character that should mark a thing as important or of consequence but that may or may not be self-evident or recognized <time would reveal the *significance* of that casual act>. ***ant*** insignificance

Import is essentially interchangeable with *significance* <a speech of enormous *import*>.

importune see BEG.
impose see DICTATE.
imposing see GRAND.
imposture, fraud, sham, fake, humbug, counterfeit mean a thing which pretends to be one thing in nature, character, or quality but is really another.

Imposture applies to any situation in which a spurious object or performance is passed off as genuine <the movie's claim of social concern is an *imposture*>.

Fraud usually implies a deliberate perversion of truth but, applied to a person, may imply no more than pretense and hypocrisy <a diary that was exposed as a *fraud*>.

Sham applies to a fraudulent but close imitation of a real thing or action <condemned the election as a *sham* and a travesty of democracy>.

Fake implies an imitation of or substitution for the genuine but does not necessarily imply dishonesty as a motive <these are *fakes*, the real jewels being in the vault>.

Humbug suggests elaborate pretense that may be deliberate or may result from self-deceit <the diet business is populated with *humbugs*>.

Counterfeit applies especially to the close imitation of something valuable <20-dollar bills that were *counterfeits*>.

impotent 1. see POWERLESS. **2.** see STERILE.

impoverish see DEPLETE.
impregnate see SOAK.
impress see AFFECT.
impression see IDEA.
impressive see MOVING.
impromptu see EXTEMPORANEOUS.
improper see INDECOROUS.
improve, better, help, ameliorate mean to make more acceptable or bring nearer some standard.

Improve, the general term, applies to what is capable of being made better whether it is good or bad <measures to *improve* the quality of medical care>. ***ant*** impair, worsen

Better, more vigorous and homely than *improve,* differs little from it in meaning <immigrants hoping to *better* their lot in life>. ***ant*** worsen

Help implies a bettering that still leaves room for improvement <a coat of paint would *help* that house>.

Ameliorate implies making more tolerable or acceptable conditions that are hard to endure <a cancerous condition that cannot be *ameliorated* by chemotherapy>. ***ant*** worsen, deteriorate

improvised see EXTEMPORANEOUS.
impudent see SHAMELESS.
impugn see DENY.
impulse see MOTIVE.
impulsive see SPONTANEOUS.
impute see ASCRIBE.
inactive, idle, inert, passive, supine mean not engaged in work or activity.

Inactive applies to anyone or anything not in action or in use or at work <a playwright who's been *inactive* for several years>. ***ant*** active, live

Idle applies to persons, their powers, or their implements that are not busy or occupied <tractors were *idle* in the fields>. ***ant*** busy

Inert as applied to things implies powerlessness to move or to affect other things <*inert* ingredients in drugs>; as applied to persons it suggests an inherent or habitual indisposition to activity <an *inert* citizenry uninterested in social change>. ***ant*** dynamic, animated

Passive implies immobility or lack of normally expected response to an external force or influence and often suggests deliberate submissiveness or self-control <a *passive* individual incapable of strong emotion>. ***ant*** active

Supine applies only to persons and commonly implies abject or cowardly inertia or passivity as a result of apathy or indolence <remained *supine* in the face of verbal abuse>. ***ant*** alert

inane see INSIPID.
inaugurate see BEGIN.
inborn see INNATE.
inbred see INNATE.
incense see FRAGRANCE.
incentive see MOTIVE.
inception see ORIGIN.
incessant see CONTINUAL.
incest see ADULTERY.
incident see OCCURRENCE.
incidental see ACCIDENTAL 2.

incisive, trenchant, clear-cut, cutting, biting, crisp mean having or showing or suggesting a keen alertness of mind.

Incisive implies a power to impress the mind by directness and decisiveness <an *incisive* command that left no room for doubt>.

Trenchant implies an energetic cutting or probing that defines differences sharply and clearly or reveals what is hidden <a *trenchant* critic of political pretensions>.

Clear-cut suggests the absence of any blurring, ambiguity, or uncertainty of statement or analysis <made a *clear-cut* distinction between the two military actions>.

Cutting implies a ruthless accuracy or directness that is wounding to the feelings and may suggest sarcasm, harshness, or asperity <makes the most *cutting* remarks with that quiet voice>.

Biting adds a greater implication of harsh vehemence or ironic force and suggests a power to impress deeply the mind or memory <a *biting* commentary on the election>.

Crisp suggests both incisiveness and vigorous terseness <jurors were impressed by the witness's *crisp* answers>.

incite, instigate, abet, foment mean to spur to action or to exite into activity.

Incite stresses a stirring up and urging on and may or may not imply active prompting <charged with *inciting* a riot>. ***ant*** restrain

Instigate definitely implies responsibility for the initiating of another's action and often connotes underhandedness or evil intention <*instigated* a conspiracy against the commander>.

Abet implies both the assisting and encouraging of some action already begun <accused of aiding and *abetting* the enemy>. ***ant*** deter

Foment implies a persistence in goading in regard to something already in seething activity <years of *fomenting* kept the flame of rebellion burning>. ***ant*** quell

incline 1. see SLANT.

2. Incline, bias, dispose, predispose mean to influence one to have or take an attitude toward something.

Incline implies a tendency to favor one of two or more actions or conclusions <*inclined* to do nothing for the moment>. ***ant*** disincline, indispose

Bias suggests a settled and predictable leaning in one direction and connotes unfair prejudice <*biased* against young urban professionals>.

Dispose suggests an affecting of one's mood or temper so as to incline one toward something or someone <the sunny day *disposed* her to think more positively>. ***ant*** indispose

Predispose implies the operation of a disposing influence well in advance of the opportunity to manifest itself <fictional violence *predisposes* them to accept violence in real life>.

include, comprehend, embrace, involve, imply mean to contain within as a part or portion of the whole.

Include suggests that the thing contained forms a constituent, component, or subordinate part of a larger whole <the price of dinner *includes* dessert>. ***ant*** exclude

Comprehend implies that something comes within the scope or range of a statement, definition, or concept <his notion of manners *comprehends* more than just table etiquette>.

Embrace implies a reaching out and gathering of separate items into or within a whole <her faith *embraces* both Christian and non-Christian beliefs>.

Involve suggests an entangling of a thing with a whole, often as a natural or inevitable cause or consequence <a procedural change that will *involve* more work for everyone>.

Imply, otherwise close to *involve,* suggests that something's presence can be inferred with more or less certainty from a hint <smoke often *implies* fire>.

inconstant, fickle, capricious, mercurial, unstable mean lacking firmness or steadiness in such things as purpose or devotion.

Inconstant implies an incapacity for steadiness and an inherent tendency to change <the supply of materials was too *inconstant* to depend on>. ***ant*** constant

Fickle suggests unreliability because of perverse changeability and incapacity for steadfastness <performers discover how *fickle* the public can be>. ***ant*** constant, true

Capricious suggests motivation by sudden whim or fancy and stresses unpredictability <an utterly *capricious* manner of selecting candidates>. ***ant*** steadfast

Mercurial implies a rapid changeability in mood, especially between depression and elation <so *mercurial* in temperament that no one knew what to expect>. ***ant*** saturnine

Unstable implies an incapacity for remaining in a fixed position or on a steady course and, when applied to persons, suggests a lack of emotional balance <in love she was impulsive and *unstable*>. ***ant*** stable

increase, enlarge, augment, multiply mean to make or become greater or more numerous.

Increase used intransitively implies progressive growth in size, amount, or intensity <his waistline *increased* with age>; used transitively it may imply simple not necessarily progressive addition <*increased* her land holdings>. ***ant*** decrease

Enlarge implies an expanding or extending that makes something greater in size or capacity <*enlarged* the restaurant to its present capacity>.

Augment implies an addition in size, extent, number, or intensity to what is already well grown or well developed <an inheritance that only *augmented* his fortune>. ***ant*** abate

Multiply implies increase in number by natural generation, by splitting, or by indefinite repetition of a process <with each tampering the problems *multiplied*>.

incredulity see UNBELIEF.

inculcate see IMPLANT.

incur, contract, catch mean to bring something, usually unwanted, upon oneself.

Incur usually implies responsibility for the acts that bring about what is incurred <a couple who adopts a child *incurs* a great responsibility>.

Contract more strongly implies effective acquisition but often no definite responsibility for the act of acquiring; it also suggests a meeting between two things that permits transmission of something from one to the other <*contract* a disease>.

Catch implies the acquiring of infection and in its broader use implies an acquiring through personal contact or association <*caught* their interest>.

incurious see INDIFFERENT.

indecent see INDECOROUS.

indecorous, improper, unseemly, indecent, unbecoming, indelicate mean not conforming to what is accepted as right, fitting, or in good taste.

Indecorous suggests a violation of accepted standards of good manners <your *indecorous* manners marred the wedding reception>. ***ant*** decorous

Improper applies to a broader range of transgressions of rules not only of social behavior but of ethical practice or logical procedure or prescribed method <the *improper* use of campaign contributions>. ***ant*** proper

Unseemly adds a suggestion of special inappropriateness to a situation or an offensiveness to good taste <married again with *unseemly* haste>. ***ant*** seemly

Indecent implies great unseemliness or gross offensiveness especially in referring to sexual matters <a scene judged *indecent* by the censors>. ***ant*** decent

Unbecoming suggests behavior or language that is felt to be beneath or unsuited to one's character or status <conduct *unbecoming* an officer>. ***ant*** becoming, seemly

Indelicate implies a lack of modesty or of tact or of refined perception of feeling <*indelicate* expressions for bodily functions>. ***ant*** delicate, refined

indefatigable, tireless, untiring, unwearied, unflagging mean capable of prolonged and strenuous effort.

Indefatigable implies persistent and unremitting activity or effort <an *indefatigable* champion of women's rights>. ***ant*** fatigable

Tireless implies a remarkable energy or stamina <honored as a teacher of *tireless* industry and limitless patience>.

Untiring implies the extraordinary ability to go on continuously and without interruption <*untiring* researchers who fight against the disease>.

Unwearied stresses the apparent absence of any sign of fatigue in the person or thing concerned <detectives remain *unwearied* in their search for the killer>.

Unflagging stresses the absence of any diminution or relaxation in one's efforts or powers <an *unflagging* attention to detail>. ***ant*** flagging

indelicate see INDECOROUS.

indemnify see PAY.

independent see FREE.

indict see ACCUSE.

indifferent 1. Indifferent, unconcerned, incurious, aloof, detached, disinterested mean not showing or feeling interest.

Indifferent implies neutrality of attitude from lack of inclination, preference, or prejudice <*indifferent* to the dictates of fashion>. ***ant*** avid

Unconcerned suggests such indifference as arises from unconsciousness or from a lack of sensitivity or regard for others' needs or troubles <*unconcerned* about the problems of the homeless>. ***ant*** concerned

Incurious implies an inability to take a normal interest due to dullness of mind or to self-centeredness <*incurious* about the world beyond their village>. ***ant*** curious, inquisitive

Aloof suggests a cool reserve arising from a sense of superiority or disdain for inferiors or from shyness or suspicion <remained *aloof* from the other club members>. ***ant*** familiar, outgoing

Detached implies an objective aloofness achieved through absence of prejudice or selfishness <observed family gatherings with *detached* amusement>. ***ant*** interested, selfish

Disinterested implies a circumstantial freedom from concern for personal or especially financial advantage that enables one to judge or advise without bias <a panel of *disinterested* observers to act as judges>. ***ant*** interested, prejudiced, biased **2.** see NEUTRAL.

indigence see POVERTY.

indigenous see NATIVE.

indignation see ANGER.

indiscriminate, wholesale, sweeping mean including all or nearly all within the range of choice, operation, or effectiveness.

Indiscriminate implies lack of consideration of individual merit or worth in giving, treating, selecting, or including <*indiscriminate* praise>. ***ant*** selective, discriminating

Wholesale stresses extensiveness and action upon all within range of choice, operation, or effectiveness <*wholesale* vaccination of a population>.

Sweeping suggests a reaching out to draw everyone or everything into one mass and usually carries a strong implication of indiscriminateness <*sweeping* generalizations>.

individual 1. see CHARACTERISTIC. **2.** see SPECIAL.

indolent see LAZY.

induce, persuade, prevail, get mean to move one to act or decide in a certain way.

Induce implies an influencing of the reason or judgment often by pointing out the advantages or gains that depend upon the desired decision <*induced* them to vote for his proposal>.

Persuade implies appealing as much to the emotions as to reason by such things as pleas, entreaty, or expostulation in attempting to win over <*persuaded* them to obey the cease-fire>. ***ant*** dissuade *(from)*

Prevail, usually used with *on* or *upon,* carries a strong implication of overcoming opposition or reluctance with sustained argument or pressure or cogent appeals <*prevailed* upon them to stay for the night>.

Get, the most neutral of these terms, can replace any of them, especially when the method by which a decision is brought about is irrelevant or is deliberately not stressed <finally *got* the boy to do his homework>.

inducement see MOTIVE.

indulge, pamper, humor, spoil, mollycoddle mean to show undue favor or attention to a person's desires and feelings.

Indulge implies excessive compliance and weakness in gratifying another's or one's own wishes or desires <*indulged* herself with food at the slightest excuse>. ***ant*** discipline

Pamper implies inordinate gratification of an appetite or desire for luxury and comfort <*pampered* by the conveniences of modern living>. ***ant*** chasten

Humor stresses a yielding to a person's moods or whims <*humored* him by letting him tell the story>.

Spoil stresses the injurious effects of indulging or pampering on character <fond but foolish parents *spoil* their children>.

Baby suggests excessive and often inappropriate care, attention, or solicitude <*babying* students by not holding them accountable>.

Mollycoddle suggests an excessive degree of care and attention to another's health or welfare <refused to *mollycoddle* her teenaged patients>.

indulgent see FORBEARING.

industrious see BUSY.

industry see BUSINESS.

inebriated see DRUNK.

inept see AWKWARD.

inerrable see INFALLIBLE.

inerrant see INFALLIBLE.

inert see INACTIVE.

inexorable see INFLEXIBLE.

infallible, inerrable, inerrant, unerring mean having or showing the inability to make errors.

Infallible may imply that one's freedom from error is divinely bestowed <fundamentalists believe in an *infallible* Bible>. ***ant*** fallible

Inerrable may be preferable when one wishes to avoid any association with religious or papal infallibility <no reference source should be considered *inerrable*>. ***ant*** errable

Inerrant stresses the fact that no mistakes were made <an *inerrant* interpretation of the most demanding role in drama>. ***ant*** errant

Unerring stresses reliability, sureness, exactness, or accuracy <a photographer with an *unnerring* eye for beauty>.

infamous see VICIOUS.

infamy see DISGRACE.

infer, deduce, conclude, judge, gather mean to arrive at a mental conclusion.

Infer implies the formulating of an opinion, a principle, a decision, or a conclusion by reasoning from evidence <from that remark, I *inferred* that they knew each other>.

Deduce adds to *infer* the special implication of drawing a particular inference from a generalization <from that we can *deduce* that man is a mammal>.

Conclude implies an arriving at a logically necessary inference at the end of a chain of reasoning <*concluded* that only he could have committed the crime>.

Judge stresses a critical testing of the premises or examination of the evidence on which a conclusion is based <*judge* people by their actions, not words>.

Gather suggests a direct or intuitive forming of a conclusion from hints or implications <*gathered* that the couple wanted to be alone>.

infertile see STERILE.

infirm see WEAK.

infix see IMPLANT.

inflate see EXPAND.

inflated, flatulent, tumescent, tumid, turgid mean swollen by or as if by fluid beyond normal size.

Inflated implies expansion by or as if by introduction of gas <an *inflated* balloon> or a stretching or extending often by artificial or questionable means <*inflated* currency with little real buying power>. ***ant*** pithy

Flatulent applies basically to distension of the belly by internally generated gases or suggests something seemingly full but actually without substance <read a series of bombastic, *flatulent* poems>.

Tumescent suggests the process of becoming swollen or bloated or the result of this process <politicians enraptured with their own *tumescent* rhetoric>.

Tumid implies swelling or bloating usually beyond what is normal or wholesome or desirable <took a sharp blow to his *tumid* pride>.

Turgid is likely to be preferred when normal swelling rather than bloating is described <a *turgid* plant stem>; it can also suggest an unrestrained, undisciplined manner accompanied by such faults as overemotionalism or bombast <an author known for her *turgid* prose>.

inflexible 1. Inflexible, inexorable, obdurate, adamant mean unwilling to alter a predetermined course or purpose.

Inflexible implies rigid adherence or even slavish conformity to established principle <*inflexible* in her demands>. ***ant*** flexible

Inexorable implies relentlessness of purpose or ruthlessness or finality or, especially when applied to things, inevitableness <the *inexorable* path of progress>. ***ant*** exorable

Obdurate stresses hardness of heart and insensitivity to appeals for mercy or the influence of divine grace <an *obdurate* governor who refused to grant clemency>.

Adamant suggests extraordinary strength of will and implies utter immovability in the face of all temptation or entreaty <was *adamant* that the project be completed on time>. ***ant*** yielding

2. see STIFF.

influence *n* **Influence, authority, prestige, weight, credit** mean power exerted over the minds or behavior of others.

Influence may apply to a force or power exercised consciously or unconsciously to guide or determine a course of action or an effect <used all of her *influence* to get the bill passed>.

Authority implies power from a source such as personal merit or learning to compel devotion or allegiance or acceptance <a policy that has the *authority* of the school board behind it>.

Prestige implies the ascendancy given by conspicuous excellence or recognized superiority <the *prestige* of the newspaper>.

Weight implies measurable or decisive influence in determining acts or choices <the wishes of the President obviously had much *weight*>.

Credit suggests influence that arises from proven merit or reputation for inspiring confidence and admiration <the *credit* that he had built up in the town>. ***ant*** discredit

influence *vb* see AFFECT.

inform, acquaint, apprise, notify mean to make one aware of something.

Inform implies the imparting of knowledge especially of facts or occurrences necessary for an understanding of a matter or as a basis for action <*informed* us of the crisis>.

Acquaint lays stress on introducing to or familiarizing with <*acquainted* myself with the basics of the game>.

Apprise implies the communicating of something of special interest or importance to the recipient <*apprise* me of any rallies in the stock market>.

Notify implies the formal communication of something requiring attention or demanding action <*notified* them that their mortgage payment was due>.

infraction see BREACH.

infrequent, uncommon, scarce, rare, sporadic mean not common or abundant.

Infrequent implies occurrence at wide intervals in space or time <family visits that were *infrequent* and brief>. ***ant*** frequent

Uncommon suggests something that occurs or is found so infrequently as to be exceptional or extraordinary <smallpox is now *uncommon* in many countries>. ***ant*** common

Scarce implies a falling short of a standard or required abundance <jobs were *scarce* during the Depression>. ***ant*** abundant

Rare suggests extreme scarcity or infrequency and often implies consequent high value <*rare* first editions of classics fetch high prices>.

Sporadic implies occurrence in scattered instances or isolated outbursts <*sporadic* cases of the genetic disorder>. ***ant*** frequent

infringe see TRESPASS.

infringement see BREACH.

infuse, suffuse, imbue, ingrain, inoculate, leaven mean to introduce one thing into another so as to affect it throughout.

Infuse implies a pouring in and permeating of something that gives new life or vigor or significance <new members *infused* the club with new enthusiasm>.

Suffuse implies a spreading through or over of something that gives a distinctive color or quality <a room *suffused* with light and cheerfulness>.

Imbue implies a permeating so deep and so complete that the very substance and nature of the thing affected are altered <*imbued* her students with intellectual curiosity>.

Ingrain suggests the indelible stamping or deep implanting of a quality, idea, or trait <clung to *ingrained* habits and beliefs>.

Inoculate implies an imbuing or implanting with a germinal idea and often suggests surreptitiousness or subtlety <tried to *inoculate* the child with a taste for opera>.

Leaven implies introducing something that enlivens, tempers, or alters the total quality <a serious play *leavened* with comic moments>.

ingenious see CLEVER.

ingenuous see NATURAL.

ingrain see INFUSE.

ingredient see ELEMENT.

inheritance see HERITAGE.

inhibit see FORBID.

iniquitous see VICIOUS.

initiate see BEGIN.

injure, harm, hurt, damage, impair, mar mean to affect someone or something so as to rob it of soundness or strength or to reduce its value, usefulness, or effectiveness.

Injure implies the inflicting of anything detrimental to one's looks, comfort, health, or success <an accident that *injured* him physically and emotionally>. ***ant*** aid

Harm often stresses the inflicting of pain, suffering, or loss <careful not to *harm* the animals>. ***ant*** benefit

Hurt implies the inflicting of a wound to the body or to the feelings <*hurt* by her callous remarks>. ***ant*** benefit

Damage suggests the inflicting of an injury that lowers value or impairs usefulness <a table that was *damaged* in shipping>. ***ant*** repair

Impair suggests a making less complete or efficient by deterioration or diminution <years of smoking had *impaired* his health>. ***ant*** improve, repair

Mar applies to disfigurement or maiming that spoils perfection or well-being <the text is *marred* by numerous typos>.

injury see INJUSTICE.

injustice, injury, wrong, grievance mean an act that inflicts undeserved damage, loss, or hardship on a person.

Injustice applies to any act that involves unfairness to another or violation of rights <the *injustices* inflicted by society>.

Injury applies specifically to an injustice for which there is a legal remedy <a libeled reputation is legally considered an *injury*>.

Wrong applies in law to any act punishable according to the criminal code and connotes a flagrant injustice <a crusading reporter determined to right society's *wrongs*>.

Grievance applies to any circumstance or condition that, in the opinion of the one affected, constitutes an injustice or gives just grounds for complaint <a committee for investigating employee *grievances*>.

innate, inborn, inbred, congenital, hereditary mean not acquired after birth.

Innate applies to qualities or characteristics that are part of one's inner essential nature <a person with an *innate* sense of his own superiority>. ***ant*** acquired

Inborn suggests a quality or tendency either actually present at birth or so marked and deep-seated as to seem so <her *inborn* love of the rugged, outdoorsy life>. ***ant*** acquired

Inbred suggests something acquired from parents, either by heredity or nurture, or deeply rooted and ingrained <a person with *inbred* extremist political views>.

Congenital applies to things acquired before or at birth during fetal development <a *congenital* heart murmur>.

Hereditary applies to things acquired before or at birth and transmitted from one's ancestors <eye color is *hereditary*>.

inoculate see INFUSE.

inordinate see EXCESSIVE.

inquire see ASK 1.

inquisitive see CURIOUS.

insane, mad, crazy, crazed, demented, deranged, lunatic, maniac mean having or showing an unsound mind or being unable to control one's rational processes.

Insane implies that one is unable to function safely and competently in everyday life and is not responsible for one's actions <adjudged *insane* after a period of observation>. ***ant*** sane

Mad strongly suggests wildness, rabidness, raving, or complete loss of self-control <drove her husband *mad* with jealousy>.

Crazy may suggest such mental breakdown as comes from old age or may suggest a distraught or wild state of mind induced by intense emotion <*crazy* with grief>; when applied to a scheme, project, or notion, it usually suggests the product of a disordered mind <got those *crazy* ideas into her head>. ***ant*** sane

Crazed, often used instead of *crazy,* implies the existence of a temporary disorder, usually with a specific cause <stampeding cattle *crazed* with fear>.

Demented suggests mental unsoundness that manifests itself by apathy or incoherence in thought, speech, or action <years of solitary confinement had left him *demented*>.

Deranged stresses a clear loss of mental balance or order resulting in a functional disorder <assassinated by a *deranged* anarchist>.

Lunatic may be the equivalent of *insane* or may imply no more than extreme folly <invested in one *lunatic* scheme after another>.

Maniac is close to *mad* and often suggests violence, fury, or raving <once behind the wheel, she turns into a *maniac* driver>.

inscrutable see MYSTERIOUS.

inseminate see IMPLANT.

insert see INTRODUCE.

insight see DISCERNMENT.

insinuate 1. see INTRODUCE. **2.** see SUGGEST.

insipid, vapid, flat, jejune, banal, wishy-washy, inane mean devoid of qualities that make for spirit and character.

Insipid implies a lack of sufficient taste or savor to please or interest <*insipid* art and dull prose>. ***ant*** sapid, zestful

Vapid suggests a lack of liveliness, freshness, sparkle, force, or spirit <a potentially exciting story given a *vapid* treatment>.

Flat applies to things that have lost their sparkle or zest and become dull and lifeless <although well-regarded in its day, this novel now seems *flat*>.

Jejune suggests a lack of rewarding or satisfying substance and connotes barrenness, aridity, or meagerness <on close reading the poem comes across as *jejune*>.

Banal stresses the presence of trite and commonplace elements and the complete absence of freshness, novelty, or immediacy <a *banal* tale of unrequited love>. ***ant*** original

Wishy-washy implies that essential or striking qualities are so weak or diluted as to seem utterly insipid or vapid <a set of *wishy-washy* opinions on national issues>.

Inane implies a lack of any significant or convincing quality or of any sense or point <an *inane* interpretation of the play>. ***ant*** deep, profound

insolent see PROUD.

inspect see SCRUTINIZE.
inspirit see ENCOURAGE.
instance *n* **Instance, case, illustration, example, sample, specimen** mean something that exhibits the distinguishing characteristics of the category to which it belongs.
Instance applies to any individual person, act, or thing that may be offered to illustrate or explain, or prove or disprove a general statement <an *instance* of history repeating itself>.
Case applies to an instance that directs attention to a real or assumed occurrence or situation that is to be considered, studied, or dealt with <a *case* of mistaken identity>.
Illustration applies to an instance offered as a means of clarifying or illuminating a general statement <an *illustration* of Murphy's law>.
Example applies to a typical, representative, or illustrative instance or case <a typical *example* of bureaucratic waste>.
Sample implies a random part or unit taken as representative of the larger whole to which it belongs <show us a *sample* of your work>.
Specimen applies to any example or sample of a whole or to an example or sample carefully selected to illustrate important or typical qualities <one of the finest *specimens* of the jeweler's art>.
instance *vb* see MENTION.
instigate see INCITE.
instill see IMPLANT.
instinctive **1. Instinctive, intuitive** mean not based on ordinary processes of reasoning.
Instinctive implies a relation to instinct and stresses the automatic quality of the reaction or the fact that it occurs below the level of conscious thought and volition <an *instinctive* response to an emergency>. ***ant*** reasoned
Intuitive implies a relation to intuition and suggests activity above and beyond the level of conscious reasoning <an *intuitive* understanding of the complexities of the situation>. ***ant*** ratiocinative
2. see SPONTANEOUS.
instruct **1.** see COMMAND. **2.** see TEACH.
instrument **1.** see IMPLEMENT. **2.** see MEAN *n* 2.
insult see OFFEND.
insure see ENSURE.
insurrection see REBELLION.
intact see PERFECT.
integrity **1.** see HONESTY. **2.** see UNITY.
intelligent, clever, alert, quick-witted, bright, smart, knowing, brilliant mean mentally keen or quick.
Intelligent stresses superiority of mind and success in coping

with new situations or in solving problems <an *intelligent* person could assemble it in 10 minutes>. ***ant*** unintelligent

Clever implies native ability or aptness and sometimes suggests a lack of more substantial qualities <a hack writer who was somewhat *clever* with words>. ***ant*** dull

Alert stresses quickness in perceiving and understanding <*alert* to new developments in technology>.

Quick-witted implies promptness in finding answers or in devising expedients in moments of danger or challenge <no match for her *quick-witted* opponent>.

Bright suggests cleverness, especially in liveliness of mind or talk or manner <a press secretary who was very young but very *bright*>. ***ant*** dense, dull

Smart implies cleverness combined with an alertness or quick-wittedness that allows one to get ahead <a *smart* girl with her eye out for the right opportunity>. ***ant*** stupid

Knowing suggests the possession of information or knowledge that is necessary or useful and can also suggest sophistication or secretiveness <difficult to deceive a *knowing* consumer>.

Brilliant implies such unusual, and outstanding keenness of intellect as to excite admiration <a *brilliant* scientist>. ***ant*** dense, dull

intensify, aggravate, heighten, enhance mean to increase markedly in measure or degree.

Intensify implies a deepening or strengthening of a thing or of its characteristic quality <police *intensified* their investigation>. ***ant*** temper, mitigate, allay, abate

Aggravate implies an increasing in gravity or seriousness of something already bad or undesirable <the problem has been *aggravated* by neglect>. ***ant*** alleviate

Heighten suggests a lifting above the ordinary or accustomed <special effects *heightened* the sense of terror>.

Enhance implies a raising or strengthening above the normal of such qualities as desirability, value, or attractiveness <shrubbery *enhanced* the grounds of the estate>.

intent see INTENTION.

intention, intent, purpose, design, aim, end, object, objective, goal mean what one intends to accomplish or attain.

Intention implies little more than what one has in mind to do or bring about <announced his *intention* to marry>.

Intent suggests clearer formulation or greater deliberateness <the clear *intent* of the law>. ***ant*** accident

Purpose suggests a more settled determination or more resolution <she stopped for a *purpose*, not for an idle chat>.

Design implies a more carefully calculated plan and carefully ordered details and sometimes scheming <the order of events was by *design*, not by accident>.

Aim adds implications of effort clearly directed toward attaining or accomplishing <pursued her *aims* with great courage>.

End stresses the intended effect of action often in distinction or contrast to the action or means as such <will use any means to achieve his *end*>.

Object may equal *end* but more often applies to a more individually determined wish or need <the *object* of the research study>.

Objective implies something tangible and immediately attainable <their *objective* is to seize the oil fields>.

Goal suggests something attained only by prolonged effort and hardship <worked years to achieve her *goal*>.

intentional see VOLUNTARY.

intercalate see INTRODUCE.

intercede see INTERPOSE.

interdict see FORBID.

interfere 1. see INTERPOSE. **2.** see MEDDLE.

interject see INTRODUCE.

interlope see INTRUDE.

intermeddle see MEDDLE.

intermission see PAUSE.

intermittent, recurrent, periodic, alternate mean occurring or appearing in interrupted sequence.

Intermittent stresses breaks in continuity <an *intermittent* correspondence with a distant relative>. ***ant*** incessant, continual

Recurrent stresses repetition and reappearance <the boy suffered from *recurrent* illness>.

Periodic implies recurrence at essentially regular intervals <*periodic* appearances of a comet>.

Alternate may apply to two contrasting things appearing repeatedly one after the other or to every second member of a series <club meetings on *alternate* Tuesdays>.

interpolate see INTRODUCE.

interpose 1. Interpose, interfere, intervene, mediate, intercede mean to come or go between.

Interpose implies no more than this <a road *interposed* between the house and the beach>.

Interfere implies a getting in the way or otherwise hindering <noise *interfered* with my concentration>.

Intervene may imply a coming between two things in space or time or a stepping in to halt or settle a quarrel or conflict <family duties *intervened*, and the work came to a halt>.

Mediate implies an intervening between hostile factions or conflicting ideas or principles <chosen to *mediate* between union and management>.

Intercede implies an acting in behalf of another, often an of-

fender, to seek mercy or forgiveness <asked to *intercede* on the daughter's behalf>.
2. see INTRODUCE.

interpret see EXPLAIN.

interrogate see ASK 1.

interstice see APERTURE.

intervene see INTERPOSE.

intimate *adj* see FAMILIAR.

intimate *vb* see SUGGEST.

intimidate, cow, bulldoze, bully, browbeat mean to frighten into submission.
Intimidate implies an inducing of fear or a sense of inferiority in another <*intimidated* by all the other bright young freshmen>.
Cow implies a reduction to a state where the spirit is broken or all courage is lost <not at all *cowed* by the odds against making it in show business>.
Bulldoze implies an intimidating or an overcoming of resistance usually by urgings, demands, or threats <*bulldozed* the city council into approving the plan>.
Bully implies an intimidation through swaggering threats or insults <tourists being *bullied* by taxi drivers>. ***ant*** coax
Browbeat implies a cowing through arrogant, scornful, contemptuous, or insolent treatment <inmates were routinely *browbeaten* by the staff>.

intoxicated see DRUNK.

intractable see UNRULY.

intrepid see BRAVE.

intricate see COMPLEX.

intrigue 1. see PLOT. **2.** see AMOUR.

introduce, insert, insinuate, interpolate, intercalate, interpose, interject mean to put between or among others.
Introduce is a general term for bringing or placing a thing or person into a group or body already in existence <*introduced* a new topic into the conversation>. ***ant*** withdraw, abstract
Insert implies a putting into a fixed or open space between or among other things <*insert* a clause in the contract>. ***ant*** abstract, extract
Insinuate implies a slow, careful, sometimes artful introduction <slyly *insinuated* himself into their confidence>.
Interpolate applies to the inserting of something extraneous or spurious <*interpolated* her own comments into the report>.
Intercalate suggests an intrusive inserting of something into an existing series or sequence <a book in which new material is *intercalated* with old>.
Interpose suggests the inserting of an obstruction or cause of

delay <rules that *interpose* barriers between children and creativity>.

Interject implies an abrupt or forced introduction of something that breaks in or interrupts <quickly *interjected* a question>.

introductory see PRELIMINARY.

intrude, obtrude, interlope, butt in mean to thrust oneself or something in without invitation or authorization.

Intrude suggests rudeness or officiousness in invading another's property, time, or privacy <didn't mean to *intrude* upon the family's private gathering>.

Obtrude may imply the mere fact of pushing something into view, or it may stress the impropriety or offensiveness of the intrusion <hesitant about *obtruding* her opinions when they were not welcome>.

Interlope implies placing oneself in a position that has injurious or adverse consequences <*interloping* nouveaux riches who didn't belong in the club>.

Butt in implies an abrupt or offensive intrusion lacking in ceremony, propriety, or decent restraint <in-laws who *butt in* and tell newlyweds what to do>.

intrusive see IMPERTINENT.

intuition see REASON.

invade see TRESPASS.

invalidate see NULLIFY.

invaluable see COSTLY.

invective see ABUSE.

inveigle see LURE.

invent 1. Invent, create, discover mean to bring something new into existence.

Invent implies fabricating something useful usually as a result of the use of the imagination or ingenious thinking or experiment <*invented* numerous energy-saving devices>.

Create implies an evoking or causing of life out of or as if out of nothing <*created* few lasting works of art>.

Discover presupposes preexistence of something and implies a finding of what is hidden or an exploring of the unknown rather than a making <attempts to *discover* the source of the Nile>.

2. see CONTRIVE.

invert 1. see TRANSPOSE. **2.** see REVERSE.

inveterate, confirmed, chronic, deep-seated, deep-rooted mean firmly established.

Inveterate applies to something, such as a habit, attitude, or feeling, of such long existence as to be almost ineradicable or unalterable <an *inveterate* smoker>.

Confirmed implies a growing stronger and firmer with the passage of time so as to resist change or reform <a *confirmed* bachelor>.

Chronic suggests the long duration of something usually undesirable that resists attempts to alleviate or cure <sick and tired of his *chronic* complaining>.

Deep-seated applies to qualities or attitudes so firmly established as to become part of the very structure <a *deep-seated* fear of heights>. ***ant*** skin-deep

Deep-rooted applies to something deeply established and of lasting endurance <the causes of the problem are *deep-rooted* and cannot be eliminated overnight>.

invidious see REPUGNANT.

inviolable see SACRED.

inviolate see SACRED.

invite, bid, solicit, court mean to request or encourage someone or something to respond or to act.

Invite commonly implies a formal or courteous requesting of one's presence or participation but may also apply to a tacit or unintended attracting or tempting <a movie remake that *invites* comparison with the original>.

Bid implies the making of an effort or appeal to win or attract or the offering of a tempting opening for something <*bidding* for their sympathy>.

Solicit suggests urgency rather than courtesy in encouraging or asking <continually *solicited* our advice>.

Court suggests an endeavoring to win something, such as favor, or to gain something, such as love, by suitable acts or words <a candidate *courting* the votes of young urban professionals>.

involve see INCLUDE.

involved see COMPLEX.

iota see PARTICLE.

irascible, choleric, splenetic, testy, touchy, cranky, cross mean easily angered or enraged.

Irascible implies a tendency to be angered on slight provocation <teenagers got a rise out of the *irascible* old man>.

Choleric may suggest impatient excitability and unreasonableness in addition to an irritable frame of mind <a *choleric* invalid who tried the nurses' patience>. ***ant*** placid, imperturbable

Splenetic suggests moroseness, and a bad rather than a hot temper <the *splenetic* type that habored a grudge>.

Testy suggests irascibility over small annoyances <everyone grew *testy* under the emotional strain>.

Touchy implies readiness to take offense and undue irritability or sensitiveness <*touchy* about references to her weight>. ***ant*** imperturbable

Cranky suggests an habitual fretful irritability with those who fail to conform to one's set notions, fixed ideas, or unvarying standards <*cranky* neighbors much given to complaining>.

Cross suggests a temporary irascibility or grumpy irritability as from disappointment or discomfort <a squabble that left her feeling *cross* all day>.

ire see ANGER.

irenic see PACIFIC.

irk see ANNOY.

ironic see SARCASTIC.

irony see WIT.

irrational, unreasonable mean not governed or guided by reason or not having the power to reason.

Irrational can imply mental derangement but it more often suggests lack of control by or open conflict with reason <our world which often seems *irrational*>. ***ant*** rational

Unreasonable is likely to suggest guidance by some force other than reason such as ambition, greed, or stubbornness that makes or shows one deficient in good sense <make *unreasonable* demands on a friend>. ***ant*** reasonable

irregular, anomalous, unnatural mean not conforming to, in accordance with, or explainable by rule, law, or custom.

Irregular implies a lack of accord with a law or regulation imposed for the sake of uniformity in methods, practice, or conduct <concerned about her *irregular* behavior>. ***ant*** regular

Anomalous implies not conforming to what might be expected because of the class or type to which the thing in question belongs or the laws that govern its existence <an *anomalous* example of 18th century domestic architecture>.

Unnatural suggests what is contrary to nature or to principles or standards felt to be essential to the well-being of civilized society and often suggests reprehensible abnormality <treated their prisoners of war with *unnatural* cruelty>. ***ant*** natural

irritate, exasperate, nettle, provoke, aggravate, rile, peeve mean to excite a feeling of angry annoyance.

Irritate implies an often gradual arousing of angry feelings that may range from impatience to rage <her constant nagging *irritated* him to no end>.

Exasperate suggests galling annoyance or vexation and the arousing of extreme impatience <his *exasperating* habit of putting off every decision>. ***ant*** appease, mollify

Nettle suggests a light and sharp but transitory stinging or piquing <your high-handed attitude *nettled* several people>.

Provoke implies an arousing of strong annoyance or vexation that may excite to action <remarks that were made solely to *provoke* him>. ***ant*** gratify

Aggravate implies persistent, often petty, goading that leads to displeasure, impatience, or anger <the *aggravating* drone of self-important politicians>. ***ant*** appease

Rile implies the inducing of an angry or resentful agitation <the new rules *riled* the employees>.

Peeve suggests the arousing of fretful, often petty, or querulous irritation <she is easily *peeved* after a sleepless night>.

isolation see SOLITUDE.

issue *n* see EFFECT.

issue *vb* see SPRING.

item, detail, particular mean one of the distinct parts of a whole.

Item applies to each thing that is specified separately in a list or in a group of things that might be separately listed or enumerated <ordered every *item* on the list>.

Detail applies to one of the small component parts of a larger whole, and may specifically denote one of the minutiae that lends finish or character to the whole <leave the petty *details* to others>.

Particular stresses the smallness, singleness, and especially the concreteness of a detail or item <a verbal attack that included few *particulars*>.

iterate see REPEAT.

J

jade see TIRE.

jam see PREDICAMENT.

jargon see DIALECT.

jealous see ENVIOUS

jeer see SCOFF.

jejune see INSIPID.

jerk, snap, twitch, yank mean to make a sudden sharp quick movement.

Jerk stresses suddenness and abruptness and is likely to imply a movement both graceless and forceful <gave the dog's leash a quick *jerk*>.

Snap implies a sharp quick action abruptly terminated, as in biting, seizing, locking, or breaking suddenly <the crocodile *snapped* at the child but missed>.

Twitch applies to a light, sudden, and sometimes spasmodic movement that usually combines tugging and jerking <the sleeping cat, its body *twitching* as it dreamt>.

Yank implies a quick and heavy tugging and pulling <*yank* the bedclothes over one's head>.

jest **1. Jest, joke, quip, witticism, wisecrack, crack, gag** mean something said or done for the purpose of evoking laughter.

Jest applies to any utterance not seriously intended, whether sarcastic, ironic, witty, or merely playful <wry *jests* that were lost on her unsophisticated friends>.

Joke may apply to an act intended to fool or deceive someone, or to a story or remark designed to promote good humor <he's very good at taking a *joke*>.

Quip suggests a quick, neatly turned, witty remark <whatever the topic, she's ready with a quick *quip*>.

Witticism implies a clever and often biting or ironic remark <many felt the sting of that critic's *witticisms*>.

Wisecrack suggests a sophisticated or knowing witticism and may suggest flippancy or unfeelingness <a comic known for abrasive *wisecracks*>.

Crack implies a sharp, witty, often sarcastic remark or retort <responded to the challenge with a series of biting *cracks*>.

Gag applies especially to a brief, laughter-provoking, foolish remark or act <a frivolous person, given to *gags*>.

2. see FUN.

jibe see AGREE 3.

job 1. see TASK. **2.** see POSITION 2.

jocose see WITTY.

jocular see WITTY.

jocund see MERRY.

join, combine, unite, connect, link, associate, relate mean to bring or come together into some manner of union.

Join implies a bringing into some degree of contact or conjunction of clearly discrete things <*joined* forces in an effort to win>. ***ant*** disjoin, part

Combine implies a merging or mingling that obscures the identity of each unit <*combine* the ingredients for a cake>. ***ant*** separate

Unite stresses the bond by which two or more individual entities are joined and implies somewhat greater loss of separate identity <the colonies *united* to form a republic>. ***ant*** alienate, disunite, divide

Connect suggests a loose or external attachment with little or no loss of identity <a bridge *connects* the island to the mainland>. ***ant*** disconnect

Link may imply strong attachment or inseparability of elements <a name forever *linked* with liberty>. ***ant*** sunder

Associate stresses the mere fact of occurrence or existence together in space or in logical sequence <opera is popularly *associated* with high society>.

Relate suggests the existence of a real or presumed natural or logical connection <the two events were not *related*>.

joint, articulation, suture mean the place where or the mechanism by which two things are united.

Joint is the most inclusive term and is freely applicable to either a natural or a man-made structure <the complicated flexible *joint* of the elbow>.

Articulation, chiefly an anatomical term in this sense, can apply to any joint, with particular emphasis on the fitting together of the parts involved, and is likely to be used when the mechanism of a joint or the elements entering into its construction are under consideration <the ball-and-socket structure of highly movable *articulations*> or when the process or method of joining is involved <the finely-crafted *articulation* of the parts>.

Suture is used of a joint that suggests a seam in linear form or lack of mobility or that has been formed by sewing <the joints between the two parts of a bean or pea pod called *sutures*>

joke see JEST.

jollity see MIRTH.

jolly see MERRY.

jot see PARTICLE.

jovial see MERRY.

joy see PLEASURE.

joyful see GLAD.

joyous see GLAD.

judge see INFER.

judgment see SENSE.

judicious see WISE.

junction, confluence, concourse mean an act, state, or place of meeting or uniting.

Junction is likely to apply to the meeting or uniting of material things such as roads, rivers, or railroads <a town grew up at the *junction* of the two rivers>.

Confluence suggests a flowing movement by which things or persons seem to merge and mingle <the turbulent *confluence* of two cultures>.

Concourse places emphasis on a rushing or hurrying together of persons or things to form a great crowd <a fortuitous *concourse* of atoms> and it may apply to a place where people throng to and fro <hurried across the *concourse* to the gate where the train was waiting>.

juncture, pass, exigency, emergency, contingency, pinch, straits, crisis mean a critical or crucial time or state of affairs.

Juncture stresses the significant concurrence or convergence of events that is likely to lead to a turning point <at an important *juncture* in our country's history>.

Pass implies a bad or distressing state or situation brought about by a combination of causes <things have come to a sorry *pass* when it's not safe to be on the streets>.

Exigency stresses the pressure of necessity or the urgency of demands created by a juncture or pass <made no effort to provide for *exigencies*>.

Emergency applies to a sudden or unforeseen situation requiring prompt action to avoid disaster <the presence of mind needed to deal with *emergencies*>.

Contingency implies an emergency or exigency that is regarded as possible or even probable but uncertain of occurrence <*contingency* plans prepared by the Pentagon>.

Pinch implies a juncture, especially in personal affairs, that exerts pressure and demands vigorous counteractive action, but to a less intense degree than *exigency* or *emergency* <this will do in a *pinch*>.

Straits applies to a troublesome or dangerous situation from which escape is difficult <in dire *straits* since the death of their father>.

Crisis applies to a juncture whose outcome will make a decisive difference <the fever broke and the *crisis* passed>.

junk see DISCARD.

jurisdiction see POWER.

just 1. see FAIR. **2.** see UPRIGHT.

justice, equity mean the art, practice, or obligation of rendering to another what is his, her, or its due.

Justice may apply to an ideal abstraction, to a quality of mind reflecting this, to a quality of inherent truth and fairness, or to the treatment due one who has transgressed a law or who seeks relief when wronged or threatened <refused to allow such travesties of *justice* while she was judge>. ***ant*** injustice

Equity stresses the notions of fairness and impartiality and implies a justice that transcends the strict letter of the law and is in keeping with what is reasonable rather than with what is merely legal <divided the pie with absolute *equity* among the greedy children>. ***ant*** inequity

justify 1. see MAINTAIN.

2. Justify, warrant mean to be what constitutes sufficient grounds for doing, using, saying, or preferring something.

Justify may be preferred when the stress is on providing grounds that satisfy conscience as well as reason <an end that surely did not *justify* such harsh means>.

Warrant is especially appropriate when the emphasis is on something that requires an explanation or reason rather than an excuse and is likely to suggest support by the authority of precedent, experience, or logic <the deposits have shown enough ore to *warrant* further testing>.

juxtaposed see ADJACENT.

K

keen 1. see EAGER. **2.** see SHARP.

keep 1. Keep, observe, celebrate, commemorate mean to notice or honor a day, occasion, or deed.

Keep suggests a customary or wonted noticing without anything untoward or inappropriate <*keep* the Sabbath>. ***ant*** break

Observe suggests marking the occasion by ceremonious performance of required acts or rituals <not all holidays are *observed* nationally>. ***ant*** break, violate

Celebrate suggests the acknowledging of an occasion by festivity or indulgence <traditionally *celebrates* Thanksgiving with a huge dinner>.

Commemorate suggests the marking of an occasion by observances that remind one of origin and significance <*commemorate* Memorial Day with the laying of wreaths>.

2. Keep, retain, detain, withhold, reserve mean to hold in one's possession or under one's control.

Keep may suggest a holding securely of something tangible or intangible in one's possession, custody, or control <*keep* this while I'm gone>. ***ant*** relinquish

Retain implies continued keeping, especially against threatened seizure or forced loss <managed to *retain* their dignity even in poverty>.

Detain suggests a keeping through a delay in letting go <*detained* them for questioning>.

Withhold implies a restraint in letting go or a refusal to let go, often for good reason <*withheld* information from the authorities>. ***ant*** accord

Reserve suggests a keeping in store for other or future use <*reserve* some of your energy for the last mile>.

kibitzer see SPECTATOR.

kick see OBJECT.

kill, slay, murder, assassinate, dispatch, execute mean to deprive of life.

Kill merely states the fact of death by an agency of some sort in some manner <frost *killed* the plants>.

Slay is a chiefly literary term implying a killing marked by deliberateness and violence <*slew* thousands of the enemy>.

Murder specifically implies a killing with stealth and motive and premeditation and therefore full moral responsibility <convicted of *murdering* his parents>.

Assassinate applies to a deliberate killing openly or secretly often for impersonal or political motives <terrorists *assassinated* the Senator>.

Dispatch stresses quickness and directness in putting to death <*dispatched* the sentry with a single stab>.

Execute stresses a putting to death as a legal penalty <to be *executed* by firing squad at dawn>.

kind *adj* **Kind, kindly, benign, benignant** mean showing or having a gentle, considerate nature.

Kind stresses a disposition to be sympathetic and helpful <a *kind* heart beneath a gruff exterior>. ***ant*** unkind

Kindly stresses more the expression of a sympathetic nature, mood, or impulse <take a *kindly* interest in the poor of the community>. ***ant*** unkindly, acrid

Benign implies mildness and mercifulness and applies more often to gracious or gentle acts or utterances of a superior rather than an equal <the belief that a *benign* supreme being controls destiny>. ***ant*** malign

Benignant implies serene mildness and kindliness that produce a favorable or beneficial effect <cultural exchange programs have a *benignant* influence in world affairs>. ***ant*** malignant

kind *n* see TYPE.

kindle see LIGHT.

kindly see KIND *adj*.

kindred see RELATED.

knack see GIFT.

knock see TAP.

knotty see COMPLEX.

know, believe, think mean to hold something in one's mind as true or as being what it purports to be.

Know stresses assurance and implies sound logical or factual information as its basis <what we don't *know*, we can find out>.

Believe, too, stresses assurance but implies trust and faith rather than evidence as its basis <no longer *believed* in the Tooth Fairy>.

Think suggests probability rather than firm assurance and implies mental appraisal of pertinent circumstances as its basis <*thinks* she will do well on the test>.

knowing see INTELLIGENT.

knowledge, learning, erudition, scholarship mean what is or can be known by an individual or by mankind.

Knowledge applies to facts or ideas acquired by study, investigation, observation, or experience <rich in the *knowledge* gained from life>. ***ant*** ignorance

Learning applies to knowledge acquired especially through formal, often advanced, schooling and close application <a book that is evidence of the author's vast *learning*>.

Erudition strongly implies the acquiring or possession of profound, recondite, or bookish learning <an *erudition* unusual even for a classicist>. ***ant*** illiteracy

Scholarship implies the possession of learning characteristic of the advanced scholar in a specialized field of study or investigation <a work of first-rate literary *scholarship*>.

L

labor see WORK 1.

lack, want, need, require mean to be without something essential or greatly desired.

Lack may imply either an absence or a shortage in supply <a club that *lacked* a room to meet in>.

Want adds to *lack* the implication of needing or desiring urgently <you may have whatever you *want*>.

Need stresses urgent necessity more than absence or shortage <everyone *needs* a friend>.

Require is often interchangeable with *need* but it may heighten the implication of urgent necessity <a situation that *required* drastic measures>.

laconic see CONCISE.

ladylike see FEMALE.

lag see DELAY.

lament see DEPLORE.

languor see LETHARGY.

lank see LEAN.

lanky see LEAN.

lapse *n* see ERROR.

lapse *vb* **Lapse, relapse, backslide** mean to fall back from a higher or better state or condition into a lower or poorer one.

Lapse usually presupposes attainment of a high level of something such as of morals, manners, or habits and implies an abrupt departure from this level or standard; it may reflect culpability or grave weakness or, sometimes, mere absent-mindedness <suffered a momentary *lapse* of manners>.

Relapse presupposes definite improvement or an advance, toward, for example, health or a higher state, and implies a severe, often dangerous reversal of direction <a young person *relapsing* into childishness>.

Backslide, similar in presuppositions and implications to *relapse,* is restricted almost entirely to moral and religious lapses, and tends more than the other words to suggest unfaithfulness to duty or to allegiance or to principles once professed <kept a constant vigil lest he *backslide*>.

larceny see THEFT.

large, big, great mean above average in magnitude, especially physical magnitude.
Large may be preferred when dimensions or extent or capacity or quantity or amount are being considered <a *large* meal>, or when breadth, comprehensiveness, or generosity are stressed <tried to respond to some *large* issues>. ***ant*** small
Big emphasizes bulk or mass or weight or volume <a *big* book> or impressiveness or importance <yearned mainly to be a *big* man on campus>. ***ant*** little
Great may sometimes imply physical magnitude, usually with connotations of wonder, surprise, or awe <the *great* canyon cut by the Colorado River>, but it more often implies eminence, distinction, or supremacy <possessed a very *great* talent>. ***ant*** little

lassitude see LETHARGY.

last *adj* **Last, final, terminal, eventual, ultimate** mean following all others in time, order, or importance.
Last applies to something that comes at the end of a series but does not always imply that the series is completed or has stopped <the *last* news we had of him>. ***ant*** first
Final applies to that which definitely closes a series, process, or progress <the *final* day of school>. ***ant*** initial
Terminal may indicate a limit of extension, growth, or development <the *terminal* phase of a disease>. ***ant*** initial
Eventual applies to something that is bound to follow sooner or later as the final effect of causes already in operation and implies a definite ending of a sequence of preliminary events <the *eventual* defeat of the enemy>.
Ultimate implies the last degree or stage of a long process or a stage beyond which further progress or change is impossible <the *ultimate* collapse of civilization>.

last *vb* see CONTINUE.

lasting, permanent, durable, stable mean enduring for so long as to seem fixed or established.
Lasting implies a capacity to continue indefinitely <a book that left a *lasting* impression on me>. ***ant*** fleeting
Permanent adds the implication of being designed or planned or expected to stand or continue indefinitely <a *permanent* living arrangement>. ***ant*** temporary, ad interim *(of persons)*
Durable implies power of resistance to destructive agencies that exceeds that of others of the same kind or sort <*durable* fabrics>.
Stable implies lastingness or durability because deep-rooted or balanced or established and therefore resistant to being overturned or displaced <a *stable* government>. ***ant*** unstable, changeable

late 1. see TARDY. **2.** see DEAD. **3.** see MODERN.

latent, dormant, quiescent, potential, abeyant mean not now manifest or showing signs of activity or existence.

Latent applies to a concealed power or quality that is not yet in sight or action but may emerge and develop in the future <a *latent* sadism that emerged during the war>. ***ant*** patent

Dormant suggests the inactivity of something, such as a feeling or power, as though it were sleeping and capable of renewed activity <a *dormant* passion existed between them>. ***ant*** active, live

Quiescent suggests a usually temporary cessation of activity <political tensions were *quiescent* for the moment>.

Potential applies to what does not yet have existence, nature, or effect but has the capacity for having it and is likely soon to do so <a toxic waste dump that is a *potential* disaster>. ***ant*** active, actual

Abeyant applies to what is for the time being held off or suppressed <an *abeyant* distrust of the neighbors>. ***ant*** active, operative

laughable, ludicrous, ridiculous, comic, comical, risible, droll, funny mean provoking laughter or mirth.

Laughable applies to anything that occasions laughter whether intentionally or unintentionally <her attempts at roller-skating were *laughable*>.

Ludicrous suggests absurdity or preposterousness that excites both laughter and scorn and sometimes pity <a spy thriller with a *ludicrous* plot>.

Ridiculous suggests extreme absurdity, foolishness, or contemptibility <a *ridiculous* portrayal of wartime combat>.

Comic applies especially to that which arouses thoughtful or wry amusement <Falstaff is one of Shakespeare's great *comic* characters>. ***ant*** tragic

Comical applies to that which arouses unrestrained spontaneous hilarity <his *comical* appearance would have tested a saint>. ***ant*** pathetic

Risible connotes that which causes laughter or is funny <a *risible* account of their mishap>.

Droll suggests laughable qualities arising from oddness, quaintness, or deliberate waggishness <amused us with *droll* stories of questionable veracity>.

Funny, interchangeable with any of the other terms, may suggest curiousness or strangeness as the basis of a laughable quality <had a *funny* feeling about the whole encounter>. ***ant*** unfunny

lavish see PROFUSE.

law 1. Law, rule, regulation, precept, statute, ordinance, canon mean a principle governing action or procedure.

Law implies imposition by a sovereign authority and the obligation of obedience on the part of all who are subject to that authority <obey the *law*>. ***ant*** chance

Rule suggests closer relation to individual conduct and may imply restriction, usually in regard to a specific situation, for the sake of an immediate end <the *rules* of a game>.

Regulation implies prescription by authority in order to control an organization, situation, or system <*regulations* affecting nuclear power plants>.

Precept commonly suggests something advisory and authoritative but not obligatory that is communicated typically through teaching <the *precepts* of effective writing>. ***ant*** practice, counsel

Statute implies a law enacted by a legislative body <a *statute* requiring the use of seat belts>.

Ordinance applies to an order governing some detail of procedure or conduct enforced by a limited authority such as a municipality <a city *ordinance*>.

Canon in religious use applies to a law of a church; in nonreligious use it suggests a principle or rule of behavior or procedure commonly accepted as a valid guide <a house that violates all the *canons* of good taste>.

2. see HYPOTHESIS.

lawful, legal, legitimate, licit mean being in accordance with law.

Lawful may apply to conformity with law of any sort, such as natural, divine, common, or canon <the *lawful* sovereign>. ***ant*** unlawful

Legal applies to what is sanctioned by law or in conformity with the law, especially as it is written or administered by the courts <*legal* residents of the state>. ***ant*** illegal

Legitimate may apply to a legal right or status but also, in extended use, to a right or status supported by tradition, custom, or accepted standards <a perfectly *legitimate* question about finances>. ***ant*** illegitimate, arbitrary *(powers, means)*

Licit applies to a strict conformity to the provisions of the law and applies especially to what is regulated by law <the *licit* use of the drug by hospitals>. ***ant*** illicit

lawyer, counselor, barrister, counsel, advocate, attorney, solicitor mean one authorized to practice law.

Lawyer applies to anyone versed in the principles of law and authorized to practice law in the courts or to act as legal agent or advisor <the best defense *lawyer* in town>.

Counselor applies to one who accepts court cases and gives advice on legal problems <met with their legal *counselor*>.

Barrister, the British equivalent of *counselor,* emphasizes court pleading which in English practice is permitted in higher courts only to barristers <*barristers* before the bench in wigs and robes>.

Counsel can be equivalent to *counselor* but is typically used collectively to designate a group of lawyers acting for a legal cause in court <*counsel* for the prosecution>.

Advocate is similar in implication to *counselor* and *barrister,* but it is used chiefly in countries such as Scotland where the legal system is based on Roman law <acted as *advocate* in the trial>.

Attorney is often used interchangeably with *lawyer,* but in precise use it denotes a lawyer who acts as a legal agent for a client in such matters as conveying property, settling wills, or defending or prosecuting a civil law case <*attorney* for the deceased>.

Solicitor is the British term corresponding to *attorney* with, however, emphasis on the transaction of legal business for a client as distinct from actual court pleading <sent his *solicitor* to negotiate on his behalf>.

lax 1. see LOOSE. **2.** see NEGLIGENT.

lazy, indolent, slothful mean not easily aroused to action or activity.

Lazy suggests a disinclination to work or to take trouble and is likely to imply idleness or dawdling even when at work <his habitually *lazy* son>. ***ant*** industrious

Indolent suggests a love of ease and a settled dislike of movement or activity <the summer's heat made us all *indolent*>. ***ant*** industrious

Slothful implies a temperamental inability to act promptly or speedily when promptness or speed is called for <the agency is usually *slothful* about fulfilling requests>. ***ant*** industrious

lead see GUIDE.

league see ALLIANCE.

lean *n* **Lean, spare, lank, lanky, gaunt, rawboned, scrawny, skinny** mean thin because of an absence of excess flesh.

Lean stresses lack of fat and of curving contours <a *lean* racehorse>. ***ant*** fleshy

Spare suggests leanness from abstemious living or constant exercise <the *spare* form of a long-distance runner>. ***ant*** corpulent

Lank implies tallness as well as leanness <the pale, *lank* limbs of a prisoner of war>.

Lanky suggests awkwardness and loose-jointedness as well as thinness <a *lanky* youth, all arms and legs>. ***ant*** burly

Gaunt implies marked thinness or emaciation as from overwork, undernourishment, or suffering <her *gaunt* face showed the strain of poverty>.

Rawboned suggests a large ungainly build without implying undernourishment <*rawboned* lumberjacks squeezed into the booth>.

Scrawny suggests extreme thinness and slightness or shrunkenness <*scrawny* kitten>. ***ant*** brawny, fleshy, obese

Skinny implies leanness that suggests deficient strength and vitality <*skinny* fashion models>. ***ant*** fleshy

lean *vb* see SLANT.

leaning, propensity, proclivity, penchant, flair mean a strong instinct or liking for something.

Leaning suggests a liking or attraction not strong enough to be decisive or uncontrollable <accused of having socialist *leanings*>. ***ant*** distaste

Propensity implies a deeply ingrained or innate and usually irresistible longing <the natural *propensity* of in-laws to offer advice>. ***ant*** antipathy

Proclivity suggests a strong natural or habitual proneness usually to something objectionable or evil <movies that reinforce viewers' *proclivities* for violence>.

Penchant implies a strongly marked taste for something or an irresistible attraction by something <has a *penchant* for overdramatizing his troubles>.

Flair implies an instinctive attraction that leads someone to something <a woman with a real *flair* for business>.

learn see DISCOVER.

learned, scholarly, erudite mean possessing or manifesting unusually wide and deep knowledge.

Learned implies academic knowledge gained by long study and research and is applicable to persons, their associations, or their writings and professional publications <members of a *learned* society>.

Scholarly implies learning and applies particularly to persons who have attained mastery of a field of knowledge or to their utterances, ideas, or writings <a *scholarly* study of the causes of war>.

Erudite, sometimes interchangeable with *learned* and *scholarly,* can imply a love of learning for its own sake, a taste for out-of-the-way knowledge, or even mere pedanticism <a mind filled with *erudite* and arcane lore>.

learning see KNOWLEDGE.

lease see HIRE.

leave *vb* **1.** see GO. **2.** see LET.

leave *n* see PERMISSION.

leaven see INFUSE.

leech see PARASITE.

legal see LAWFUL.

legend see MYTH.

legendary see FICTITIOUS.

legitimate see LAWFUL.
lengthen see EXTEND.
lenient 1. see FORBEARING. **2.** see SOFT.
lenity see MERCY.
lessen see DECREASE.
let 1. Let, allow, permit, suffer, leave mean not to forbid or prevent.

Let may imply a positive giving of permission but more often implies failure to prevent either through inadvertence and negligence or through lack of power or effective authority <the goalie *let* the ball get by her>.

Allow implies little more than a forbearing to prohibit or to exert this power <a teacher who *allows* her pupils to do as they like>. ***ant*** inhibit

Permit implies express willingness or acquiescence <the park *permits* powerboats on the lake>. ***ant*** prohibit, forbid

Suffer can be close to *allow* or may distinctively imply indifference or reluctance <*suffered* themselves to be photographed>.

Leave stresses the implication of noninterference in letting or allowing or permitting and can suggest the departure of the person who might interfere <*left* them to resolve the matter among themselves>.

2. see HIRE.

lethal see DEADLY.
lethargy, languor, lassitude, stupor, torpor mean physical or mental inertness.

Lethargy implies a drowsiness or aversion to activity such as is induced by disease, injury, or drugs <months of *lethargy* followed my skiing accident>. ***ant*** vigor

Languor suggests inertia induced by an enervating climate or illness or soft living or love <*languor* induced by a tropical vacation>. ***ant*** alacrity

Lassitude stresses listlessness or indifference resulting from fatigue or poor health <a deepening depression marked by *lassitude*>. ***ant*** vigor

Stupor implies a deadening of the mind and senses by or as if by shock, narcotics, or intoxicants <lapsed into a *stupor* following a night of drinking>.

Torpor implies a state of suspended animation as of hibernating animals but may suggest merely extreme sluggishness <a once-alert mind now in a state of *torpor*>. ***ant*** animation

level, flat, plane, even, smooth, flush mean having a surface without bends, curves, or irregularities, and with no part higher than any other.

Level applies to a horizontal surface that lies on a line parallel with the horizon <the vast prairies are nearly *level*>.

Flat applies to any surface devoid of noticeable curvatures, prominences, or depressions <the work surface must be totally *flat*>.

Plane applies to any real or imaginary flat surface in which a straight line between any two points on it lies wholly and continuously within that surface <the *plane* sides of a crystal>.

Even applies to a surface that is noticeably flat or level or to a line that is observably straight <trim the hedge so that it is *even*>. ***ant*** uneven

Smooth applies to a flat or even surface especially free of irregularities <a *smooth* dance floor>. ***ant*** rough

Flush applies to a surface or line that forms a continuous surface or line with another surface or line <the river's surface is now *flush* with the top of the banks>.

levity see LIGHTNESS.

liable 1. Liable, open, exposed, subject, prone, susceptible, sensitive mean being by nature or through circumstances likely to experience something adverse.

Liable implies a possibility or probability of incurring something because of position, nature, or the action of forces beyond one's control <unless you're careful, you're *liable* to fall>. ***ant*** exempt, immune

Open stresses ease of access and a lack of protective barriers <a claim that is *open* to question>. ***ant*** closed

Exposed suggests lack of protection or powers of resistance against something actually present or threatening <the town's *exposed* position makes it impossible to defend>.

Subject implies an openness for any reason to something that must be suffered or undergone <all reports are *subject* to editorial revision>. ***ant*** exempt

Prone stresses natural tendency or propensity to incur something <a person who is *prone* to accidents>.

Susceptible implies conditions existing in one's nature or individual constitution that make one unusually open to something, especially something deleterious <young children are *susceptible* to colds>. ***ant*** immune

Sensitive implies a readiness to respond to or be influenced by forces or stimuli <her eyes are *sensitive* to light>. ***ant*** insensitive

2. see RESPONSIBLE.

liaison see AMOUR.

libel see MALIGN *vb*.

liberal 1. Liberal, generous, bountiful, munificent mean giving freely and unstintingly.

Liberal suggests openhandedness in the giver and largeness in the thing or amount given <a teacher *liberal* in bestowing praise>. ***ant*** close

Generous stresses warmhearted readiness to give more than the size or importance of the gift <a friend's *generous* offer of assistance>. ***ant*** stingy

Bountiful suggests lavish, unremitting generosity in giving or providing <*bountiful* grandparents spoiling the children>.

Munificent suggests splendid or princely lavishness in giving <the Queen was especially *munificent* to her favorite>.

2. Liberal, progressive, advanced, radical mean freed from or opposed to what is orthodox, established, or conservative.

Liberal implies a greater or less degree of emancipation from convention, tradition, or dogma and may suggest either pragmatism and tolerance or unorthodoxy, extremism, and laxness <a politician's *liberal* tendencies>. ***ant*** authoritarian

Progressive is likely to imply a comparison with what is backward or reactionary and a readiness to forsake old methods and beliefs for new ones that hold more promise <went to the most *progressive* school her parents could find>. ***ant*** reactionary

Advanced applies to what is or seems to be ahead of its proper time and can connote liberalism and mental daring or extreme foolhardiness and experimental impracticality <a man with *advanced* ideas>. ***ant*** conservative

Radical is likely to imply willingness to destroy the institutions which conserve the ideas or policies condemned and comes close to *revolutionary* in meaning <an idea conceived by a group of *radical* reformers>. ***ant*** conservative

liberate see FREE *vb.*

liberty see FREEDOM.

license see FREEDOM.

licit see LAWFUL.

lick see CONQUER.

lie, prevaricate, equivocate, palter, fib mean to tell an untruth.

Lie is the blunt term, imputing dishonesty to the speaker <to *lie* under oath is a serious crime>.

Prevaricate softens the bluntness of *lie* by implying a quibbling or an evading or confusing of the issue <during the hearings the witness did his best to *prevaricate*>.

Equivocate implies the using of ambiguous words in an attempt to mislead or deceive <*equivocated,* dodged questions, and generally misled her inquisitors>.

Palter implies the making of unreliable statements of fact or intention or insincere promises <a cad *paltering* with a naive, young girl>.

Fib applies to the telling of a trivial untruth <*fibbed* about the price of the suit>.

lift, raise, rear, elevate, hoist, heave, boost mean to move from a lower to a higher place or position.

Lift usually implies exerting effort to overcome the resistance of weight <*lift* the chair while I vacuum>. ***ant*** lower

Raise carries an implication of bringing up to the vertical or to a high position <soldiers *raising* a flagpole>.

Rear can be used in place of *raise* but can also be used meaning to raise itself <a steeple *rearing* into the sky>.

Elevate may replace *lift* or *raise* especially when exalting or enhancing is implied <*elevated* the musical tastes of the public>. ***ant*** lower

Hoist implies the lifting of something heavy, especially by mechanical means <*hoisted* the cargo on board>.

Heave implies lifting with a great effort or strain <struggled to *heave* the heavy crate>.

Boost suggests assisting to climb or advance by a push <*boosted* his brother over the fence>.

light *adj* see EASY.

light *vb* **Light, kindle, ignite, fire** mean to start something to burn.

Light is likely to imply an action for a specific end, such as illuminating, heating, or smoking <*light* a fire in the stove>. ***ant*** extinguish

Kindle may connote difficulty in setting combustible materials alight and is appropriate when special preparations are needed <we *kindled* the bonfire just after dark> or may connote an exciting, arousing, or stimulating <a look that *kindled* a responsive spark>. ***ant*** smother

Ignite, like *kindle,* stresses successful lighting but is more likely to apply to highly flammable materials <*ignite* a firecracker>, or it may imply a stirring into activity <a love of learning *ignited* by her first-grade teacher>.

Fire suggests blazing and rapid combustion and is usually used with respect to something that ignites readily and burns fiercely <*fire* a haystack> or may imply an inspiring, as with passion, zeal, or desire, to energetic activity <an imagination *fired* with a thousand new ideas>.

lighten see RELIEVE.

lighthearted see GLAD.

lightness, levity, frivolity, flippancy, volatility, flightiness mean gaiety or indifference when seriousness is called for.

Lightness implies a lack of weight and seriousness and sometimes an instability or careless heedlessness in character, mood, or conduct <the only bit of *lightness* in a dreary, ponderous drama>. ***ant*** seriousness

Levity suggests trifling or unseasonable gaiety <injected a moment of *levity* in the solemn proceedings>. ***ant*** gravity

Frivolity suggests irresponsible indulgence in gaieties or in idle speech or conduct <a playgirl living a life of uninterrupted *frivolity*>. ***ant*** seriousness, staidness

Flippancy implies an unbecoming levity especially in speaking of grave or sacred matters <spoke of the bombing with annoying *flippancy*>. ***ant*** seriousness

Volatility implies such lightness or fickleness of disposition as prevents long attention to any one thing <the *volatility* of the public interest in foreign aid>.

Flightiness implies extreme volatility that may approach loss of mental balance <the *flightiness* of my grandmother in her old age>. ***ant*** steadiness, steadfastness

like see SIMILAR,

likely see PROBABLE.

likeness, similarity, resemblance, similitude, analogy, affinity mean agreement or correspondence in details.

Likeness implies a close correspondence <a remarkable *likeness* to his late father>. ***ant*** unlikeness

Similarity often implies that things are merely somewhat alike <some *similarity* between the two cases>. ***ant*** dissimilarity

Resemblance implies similarity chiefly in appearance or in external or superficial qualities <statements that bear no *resemblance* to the truth>. ***ant*** difference, distinction

Similitude applies chiefly when the abstract idea of likeness is under consideration <the *similitude* of environments was rigidly maintained>. ***ant*** dissimilitude, dissimilarity

Analogy implies comparison of things that are basically unlike and is more apt to draw attention to likeness or parallelism in relations rather than in appearance or qualities <pointed out the *analogies* to past situations>.

Affinity suggests a cause such as kinship or sympathetic experience or historical influence in common that is responsible for the similarity <a writer with a striking *affinity* for American Indian culture>.

limb see SHOOT.

limber see SUPPLE.

limit, restrict, circumscribe, confine mean to set bounds for.

Limit implies the setting of a point or line, as in time, space, speed, or degree, beyond which something cannot or is not permitted to go <visits are *limited* to 30 minutes>. ***ant*** widen

Restrict suggests a narrowing or tightening or restraining within or as if within an encircling boundary <laws intended to *restrict* the freedom of the press>.

Circumscribe stresses a restriction in every direction and by clearly defined boundaries <the work of the investigating committee was carefully *circumscribed*>. ***ant*** dilate, expand

Confine suggests severe restraint within bounds that cannot or must not be passed and a resulting cramping, fettering, or hampering <our freedom of choice was *confined* by finances>.

limp, floppy, flaccid, flabby, flimsy, sleazy mean deficient in firmness of texture, substance, or structure.

Limp implies a lack or loss of stiffness or body and a resulting tendency to droop <a faded flower on a *limp* stem>.

Floppy applies to something that sags or hangs limply and is likely to suggest flexibility and a natural or intended lack of stiffness <wore a large *floppy* garden hat that shaded her eyes>.

Flaccid applies primarily to living tissues and implies a loss of normal and especially youthful firmness or a lack of force or energy or substance <a *flaccid* resolve that easily gave way>. ***ant*** resilient

Flabby in its application to material things is very close to *flaccid*, but it also suggests spinelessness, spiritlessness, or lethargy <a *flabby* substitute for a hero>. ***ant*** firm

Flimsy applies to something of such looseness of structure or insubstantiality of texture as to be unable to stand up under strain; it may also stress a lack of real worth or of capacity for endurance <a *flimsy* excuse>.

Sleazy implies a flimsiness due to cheap or careless workmanship and may stress a lack or inferiority of standards <a *sleazy* tale of second-rate intrigue>.

limpid see CLEAR 1.

line, align, range, array mean to arrange in a line or lines.

Line implies a setting in single file or parallel rows <*line* up prisoners for identification>.

Align stresses the bringing of points or parts that should be in a straight line into correct adjustment or into correspondence <*align* the front and rear wheels of an automobile>.

Range stresses orderly disposition, sometimes by aligning but often by separating into classes according to some plan <students *ranged* in groups by age and gender>.

Array applies especially to a setting in battle order and therefore suggests readiness for action or use as well as ordered arrangement <a splendid collection of legal talent *arrayed* against the prosecution>. ***ant*** disarray

linger see STAY.

lingo see DIALECT.

link see JOIN.

liquid, fluid mean composed of particles that move easily and flowingly and change their relative position without perceptible break in continuity.

Liquid applies to substances that, like water, are only slightly compressible and are capable of conversion, under suitable conditions of pressure and temperature, into gases <watched as

a *liquid* tear rolled down the child's cheek>, or it implies a softness or transparency <heard with joy the *liquid* song of the hermit thrush>. ***ant*** solid, vaporous

Fluid is applicable to both liquids and gases or it can be opposed to *rigid, fixed, unchangeable* and apply to whatever is essentially unstable or to what tends to flow easily or freely <the *fluid* nature of international relations>. ***ant*** solid

lissome see SUPPLE.

lithe see SUPPLE.

lithesome see SUPPLE.

little see SMALL.

live see RESIDE.

lively, animated, vivacious, sprightly, gay mean keenly alive and spirited.

Lively suggests briskness, alertness, or energy <a *lively* hour of news and information>. ***ant*** dull

Animated applies to what is spirited, active, and sparkling <an *animated* discussion of current events>. ***ant*** depressed, dejected

Vivacious suggests an activeness of gesture and wit, often playful or alluring <a *vivacious* party hostess>. ***ant*** languid

Sprightly suggests lightness and spirited vigor of manner or of wit <a tuneful, *sprightly* musical revue>.

Gay stresses complete freedom from care and exuberantly overflowing spirits <the *gay* spirit of Paris in the 1920s>. ***ant*** grave, sober

livid see PALE 1.

living, alive, animate, animated, vital mean having or showing life.

Living applies to organic bodies having life as opposed to those from which life has gone <*living* artists>. ***ant*** lifeless

Alive, opposed to *dead*, is like *living*, but follows the word it modifies <toss the lobster into the pot while it's still *alive*>. ***ant*** dead, defunct

Animate is used chiefly in direct opposition to *inanimate* to denote things alive or capable of life <a child seemingly afraid of every *animate* object>. ***ant*** inanimate

Animated is applied to that which becomes alive and active or is given motion simulating life <an *animated* cartoon>. ***ant*** inert

Vital implies the energy and especially the power to grow and reproduce that are characteristic of life <all of his *vital* functions seemed normal>.

loath see DISINCLINED.

loathe see HATE.

location see PLACE.

locution see PHRASE.

lodge 1. see HARBOR. **2.** see RESIDE.
lofty see HIGH.
logical, analytic, analytical, subtle mean having or showing skill in thinking or reasoning.

Logical may imply a capacity for orderly thinking or, more especially, the power to impress others that clearness of thought and freedom from bias underlie the products of one's thinking <an infuriatingly *logical* mind, utterly devoid of emotion>. ***ant*** illogical

Analytic, often as the variant ***analytical,*** stresses the power to simplify what is complicated or complex or what is chaotic or confused by separating and recombining elements in a logical manner <proceeded by precise *analytic* processes to find the hidden cause>.

Subtle basically implies a capacity to penetrate below the surface and perceive fine distinctions and minute relations, and it usually connotes exceptional skill in reasoning and analysis <saw the heart of the crisis through *subtle* logic>. ***ant*** dense *(in mind),* blunt *(in speech)*

logistics see STRATEGY.
loiter see DELAY 2.
lone see ALONE.
lonely see ALONE.
lonesome see ALONE.
long, yearn, hanker, pine, hunger, thirst mean to have a strong desire for something.

Long implies a wishing with one's whole heart for something remote or not easily attainable <*longed* for some peace and quiet>.

Yearn suggests an eager, restless, or painful longing <*yearned* for a career on the stage>. ***ant*** dread

Hanker suggests the uneasy promptings of unsatisfied appetite or desire <always *hankering* for more money>.

Pine implies a languishing or a fruitless longing for what is impossible of attainment <*pined* for a long-lost love>.

Hunger implies an insistent or impatient craving or a compelling need like that for food <*hungered* for a business of his own>.

Thirst suggests a compelling need like that for liquid <*thirsted* for absolute power>.

look 1. see EXPECT. **2.** see SEE 2. **3.** see SEEM.
looker-on see SPECTATOR.
loose, relaxed, slack, lax mean not tightly bound, held, restrained, or stretched.

Loose is widely referable to persons or things free from a usual or former restraint <a book with a *loose* page> or to something not firmly or tightly held or connected between points of contact <drive with *loose* reins> or to a substance or fabric with particles or filaments in open arrangement <a *loose*-woven woolen>. ***ant*** strict, tight

Relaxed implies a loss of some tightness, tension, strictness, or rigidity; it may also imply an easing of rather than a freeing from what restrains <the *relaxed* discipline of the last few days of school>. ***ant*** stiff

Slack, otherwise close to *relaxed,* may stress lack of firmness and steadiness <an overweight body, pudgy and *slack*>. ***ant*** taut, tight

Lax stresses lack of steadiness, firmness, and tone or, in respect to immaterial things, may stress lack of needed or proper steadiness and firmness <a *lax* administration>. ***ant*** rigid

loot see SPOIL.

loquacious see TALKATIVE.

lordly see PROUD.

lot 1. see FATE. **2.** see GROUP.

loud, stentorian, earsplitting, raucous, strident mean marked by intensity or volume of sound.

Loud applies to any volume above normal and may suggest undue vehemence or obtrusiveness <a *loud* obnoxious person>. ***ant*** low, soft

Stentorian, chiefly used of voices, implies great power and range <an actor with a *stentorian* voice>.

Earsplitting implies loudness that is physically oppressive and shrilly discomforting <the *earsplitting* sound of a siren>.

Raucous implies a loud harsh grating tone, especially of voice, and may suggest rowdiness <a barroom filled with the *raucous* shouts of drunken revelers>.

Strident implies a rasping discordant but insistent quality, especially of voice <the *strident* voices of hecklers>.

loutish see BOORISH.

lovely see BEAUTIFUL.

low see BASE *adj.*

lower see FROWN.

lowly see HUMBLE.

loyal see FAITHFUL.

loyalty see FIDELITY.

lucid see CLEAR 2.

luck see CHANCE.

lucky, fortunate, happy, providential mean meeting with or producing unforeseen success.

Lucky stresses the agency of chance in bringing about a favorable result <the *lucky* day I met my future wife>. ***ant*** luckless, unlucky

Fortunate suggests being rewarded beyond one's deserts or expectations <have been *fortunate* in my business investments>. ***ant*** unfortunate

Happy combines the implications of *lucky* and *fortunate* with its more common meaning of being blessed <a life that has been a series of *happy* accidents>. ***ant*** unhappy

Providential more definitely implies the help or intervention of a higher power in the coming of good or the averting of evil fortune <it was *providential* that rescuers arrived in the nick of time>.

ludicrous see LAUGHABLE.

lull see PAUSE.

luminous see BRIGHT.

lunatic see INSANE.

lure, entice, inveigle, decoy, tempt, seduce mean to draw one from a usual, desirable, or proper course or situation into one considered unusual, undesirable, or wrong.

Lure implies a drawing into danger, evil, or difficulty through attracting and deceiving <*lured* naive investors with get-rich-quick schemes>. ***ant*** revolt, repel

Entice suggests a drawing by artful or adroit means <advertising designed to *entice* new customers>. ***ant*** scare *(off)*

Inveigle implies an enticing by cajoling or flattering <*inveigled* her suitor into proposing marriage>.

Decoy implies a luring away or into entrapment by artifice and false appearances <the female bird attempted to *decoy* us away from her nest>.

Tempt implies the exerting of an attraction so strong that it overcomes the restraints of conscience or better judgment <*tempted* him to abandon his diet>.

Seduce implies a leading astray by persuasion or false promises <*seduced* young runaways into the criminal life>.

lurid see GHASTLY.

lurk, skulk, slink, sneak mean to behave furtively so as to escape attention.

Lurk implies a lying in wait in a place of concealment and often suggests an evil intent <suspicious men *lurking* in alleyways>.

Skulk suggests furtive movement and cowardice or fear or sinister intent <spied something *skulking* in the shadows>.

Slink implies a stealthiness in moving to escape attention and may connote sly caution <during the festivities, I *slunk* away>.

Sneak may add an implication of entering or leaving a place or evading a difficulty by furtive, indirect, or underhanded methods <he *sneaked* out after the others had fallen asleep>.

lush see PROFUSE.

lustrous see BRIGHT.

lusty see VIGOROUS.
luxuriant see PROFUSE.
luxurious 1. Luxurious, sumptuous, opulent mean ostentatiously rich or magnificent.
Luxurious applies to what is choice and costly and suggests gratification of the senses and desire for comfort <a millionaire's *luxurious* penthouse apartment>.
Sumptuous applies to what is overwhelmingly or extravagantly rich, splendid, or luxurious <an old-fashioned grand hotel with a *sumptuous* lobby>.
Opulent suggests a flaunting of luxuriousness, luxuriance, or costliness <an *opulent* wedding intended to impress the guests>.
2. see SENSUOUS.
lying see DISHONEST.

M

macabre see GHASTLY.
machination see PLOT.
mad see INSANE.
magisterial see DICTATORIAL.
magnificent see GRAND.
maim, cripple, mutilate, batter, mangle mean to injure so severely as to cause lasting damage.
Maim implies the loss or injury of a limb or member usually through violence <a swimmer *maimed* by a shark>.
Cripple implies the loss or serious impairment of an arm or leg <the fall *crippled* her for life>.
Mutilate implies the cutting off or removal of an essential part of a person or thing thereby impairing its completeness, beauty, or function <a poignant drama *mutilated* by inept acting>.
Batter implies a pounding with series of blows that bruises deeply, deforms, or mutilates <a ship *battered* by fierce storms at sea>.
Mangle implies a tearing or crushing that leaves deep extensive wounds or lacerations <thousands are *mangled* every year by auto accidents>.
maintain, assert, defend, vindicate, justify mean to uphold as true, right, just, or reasonable.
Maintain stresses firmness of conviction, and is likely to suggest persistent or insistent upholding of a cause and may suggest aggressiveness or obtrusiveness <steadfastly *maintained* his client's innocence>.
Assert suggests a determination to make others accept one's

claim of one's position <fiercely *asserted* that credit for the discovery belonged to her>.

Defend implies maintaining one's claim in the face of attack or criticism <I need not *defend* my wartime record>.

Vindicate implies a successful defending <his success *vindicated* our faith in him>.

Justify implies a showing to be true, right, acceptable, or valid by appeal to a standard or to precedent <threats to public safety *justified* such drastic steps>.

majestic see GRAND.

majority, plurality mean a number or quantity or part larger than some other expressed or implied, particularly in reference to an election.

Majority implies that the winning candidate or opinion has received more votes than the other candidates or opinions combined; that is, the winning vote is in excess of half the votes cast <elected to the senate by a very slim *majority*>.

Plurality merely implies that the winner has more votes than any other candidate or opinion, whether a majority of the total or not <a *plurality* of the voters defeated the referendum>.

make, form. shape, fashion, fabricate, manufacture, forge mean to cause to come into being.

Make applies to any action of producing or creating whether by an intelligent agency or blind forces and whether the product has material or immaterial existence <the factory *makes* furniture>.

Form implies the generating of a definite outline, structure, or design in the thing produced <*form* a plan>.

Shape suggests the impressing of a form upon some material by some external agent <*shaped* shrubbery into animal figures>.

Fashion suggests the use of inventive power or ingenuity <*fashioned* a bicycle out of spare parts>.

Fabricate suggests a uniting of many parts into a whole and often implies an ingenious inventing of something false <*fabricated* an exotic background for her biography>.

Manufacture implies a making repeatedly by a fixed process and usually by machinery <*manufacture* shoes>.

Forge implies a making or devising or concocting by great physical or mental effort <*forged* an agreement after months of negotiating>.

make-believe see PRETENSE.

maker, creator, author mean one who brings something new into being or existence. (When written with an initial capital letter all three terms are used to designate God or the Supreme Being.)

Maker is likely to imply a close and immediate relationship between the one who makes and the thing that is made and an ensuing responsibility for what is turned out <thought of herself as a *maker* of tales>.

Creator stresses a bringing into existence of what the mind conceives and is likely to suggest originality and delving into the unknown <a robot, ultimately destructive of his *creator*>.

Author applies to one who originates something and who is the source of its being and as such wholly responsible for its existence <the *author* of several books>.

makeshift see RESOURCE.

maladroit see AWKWARD.

male see MASCULINE.

malevolence see MALICE.

malice, malevolence, ill will, spite, malignity, malignancy, spleen, grudge mean the desire or wish to see another experience pain, injury, or distress.

Malice implies a deep-seated often unexplainable desire to see another suffer <felt no *malice* for their former enemies>, or it may suggest a causeless passing mischievous impulse <a rascal full of *malice*>. ***ant*** charity

Malevolence suggests a bitter persistent hatred and may suggest inherent evil that is likely to be expressed in malicious conduct <deep *malevolence* governed his every act>. ***ant*** benevolence

Ill will implies a feeling of antipathy that is of limited duration and usually lacks any element of mental turmoil <a directive that provoked *ill will* among the employees>. ***ant*** goodwill, charity

Spite implies a petty feeling of envy and resentment that is often expressed in small harassments and meanness <petty insults inspired only by *spite*>.

Malignity implies deep passion and relentless driving force <never viewed her daughter-in-law with anything but *malignity*>. ***ant*** benignity

Malignancy suggests aggressive maliciousness that comes from a basically evil or injurious nature <proceeded to treat the employees with insupportable *malignancy*>. ***ant*** benignity

Spleen suggests the wrathful release of latent spite or persistent malice <quick to vent his *spleen* at incompetent subordinates>.

Grudge implies a harbored or cherished feeling of resentment or ill will that seeks satisfaction <never one to harbor a *grudge*>.

malign *adj* see SINISTER.

malign *vb* **Malign, traduce, asperse, vilify, calumniate, defame, slander, libel** mean to injure by speaking ill of.

Malign suggests a specific and often subtle misrepresentation but may not always imply deliberate lying <the most *maligned* monarch in British history>. ***ant*** defend

Traduce stresses the resulting ignominy and distress to the victim <so *traduced* the governor that he was driven from office>.

Asperse implies a continued attack on a reputation often by indirect or insinuated detraction <each candidate *aspersed* the other's motives>.

Vilify implies an attempting to destroy a reputation by open and direct abuse <no President was more *vilified* by the press>. ***ant*** eulogize

Calumniate imputes malice to the speaker and falsity to his or her assertion <threatened with a lawsuit for publicly *calumniating* the company>. ***ant*** eulogize, vindicate

Defame stresses the actual loss of or injury to one's good name <forced to pay a substantial sum for *defaming* her reputation>. ***ant*** laud, puff

Slander stresses the suffering of the victim from oral or written calumniation <town gossips carelessly *slandered* their good name>.

Libel implies the printing or writing and publication or circulation of something that defames a person or his or her reputation <sued the magazine for *libel*>.

malignancy 1. see MALICE. **2.** see TUMOR.

malignity see MALICE.

malleable see PLASTIC.

malodorous, stinking, fetid, noisome, putrid, rancid, rank, fusty, musty mean having a bad or unpleasant smell.

Malodorous may range from the unpleasant to the strongly offensive <*malodorous* unidentifiable substances in the refrigerator>.

Stinking suggests the foul or disgusting <prisoners were held in *stinking* cells>.

Fetid implies an odor which is peculiarly offensive <skunk cabbage is a *fetid* weed>. ***ant*** fragrant

Noisome adds a suggestion of being harmful or unwholesome as well as offensive <a *noisome* toxic waste dump>. ***ant*** balmy

Putrid implies particularly the sickening odor of decaying organic matter <the typically *putrid* smell of a fish pier>.

Rancid suggests foulness of both taste and smell, usually of fatty substances that have spoiled <the unmistakable stink of *rancid* butter>.

Rank suggests a strong, unpleasant, but not necessarily foul smell <rooms filled with the *rank* smoke of cigars>. ***ant*** balmy

Fusty suggets lack of fresh air and sunlight and implies prolonged uncleanliness <the *fusty* rooms of a bus station>.

Musty implies staleness marked by dampness, darkness, and moldiness <the *musty* odor of a damp cellar>.

mammoth see ENORMOUS.

manacle see HAMPER.

manage see CONDUCT.

maneuver see TRICK.

manful see MASCULINE.

mangle see MAIM.

mania, delirium, frenzy, hysteria mean a state marked by exaggerated reactions and a loss of emotional, mental, or nervous control.

Mania usually implies excessive or unreasonable enthusiasm <a society with a *mania* for football>.

Delirium adds the notion of extreme emotional excitement <in a *delirium* of ecstasy at the thought of seeing her again>. ***ant*** apathy

Frenzy suggests loss of self-control and violent agitation often manifested in action <shoppers driven to a *frenzy* during the annual sale>.

Hysteria implies emotional instability that is often marked by swift transitions of mood <the *hysteria* of the fans>.

maniac see INSANE.

manifest *adj* see EVIDENT.

manifest *vb* see SHOW 1.

manipulate see HANDLE.

manlike see MASCULINE.

manly see MASCULINE.

manner 1. see BEARING. **2.** see METHOD.

mannerism see POSE.

mannish see MASCULINE.

manufacture see MAKE.

manumit see FREE *vb*.

many-sided see VERSATILE.

mar see INJURE.

margin see BORDER.

marital see MATRIMONIAL.

mark see SIGN.

marshal see ORDER.

martial, warlike, military mean of or characteristic of war.

Martial suggests especially the pomp and circumstance of war <standing in *martial* array>.

Warlike is more likely to imply the spirit or temper or acts that lead to or accompany war <spouting *warlike* rhetoric>. ***ant*** unwarlike

Military may imply reference to war, to arms, or to armed

forces <a *military* expedition> and may be specifically opposed to *civil* or *civilian* <*military* law> or restricted to land, or land and air, forces as opposed to *naval* <*military* and naval attachés>. ***ant*** unmilitary

masculine, male, manly, manlike, mannish, manful, virile mean of, characteristic of, or like a male, especially of the human species.

Masculine applies to qualities or attributes or attitudes characteristic of men and not shared by women <a *masculine* physique>. ***ant*** feminine

Male is broadly applicable to plants, animals, and persons and stresses the fact of sex <a *male* tiger>. ***ant*** female

Manly suggests the qualities of the mature man, especially the finer qualities of a man or the powers and skills that come with maturity <wounded his *manly* pride>. ***ant*** unmanly, womanly

Manlike is more likely to suggest characteristically masculine faults and foibles <exhibited a thoroughly *manlike* disregard for details>, but sometimes its reference is to human beings in general and then it suggests resemblance to the human kind <an early hominid, vaguely *manlike* in appearance>.

Mannish is often used derogatorily in situations in which womanliness might naturally be expected or wanted <adopted an aggressively *mannish* stance> but in more neutral use, especially as applied to styles and dress, it carries little more than a suggestion of actual masculinity <dressed nattily in a *mannish* suit of tweed>. ***ant*** womanish

Manful stresses sturdiness and resolution <a *manful* effort to achieve success>.

Virile suggests the qualities of fully developed manhood but is at once stronger in emphasis and more specific in many of its applications than *manly* or *masculine* <a man of eighty yet still strong and *virile*> and in more general applications is likely to imply manful vigor <walked with a *virile* stride>. ***ant*** effeminate, impotent

mask see DISGUISE.

mass see BULK.

massacre, slaughter, butchery, carnage, pogrom mean a great and usually wanton killing of human beings.

Massacre implies promiscuous and wholesale slaying, especially of those not in a position to defend themselves <arrived in time to view the aftermath of the *massacre*>.

Slaughter implies extensive and ruthless killing as in a battle or a massacre<went meekly, like lambs to the *slaughter*>.

Butchery adds to *slaughter* the implication of exceeding cruelty and complete disregard of the sufferings of the victims <barbarians engaged in savage *butchery* of the conquered people>.

Carnage stresses bloodshed and great loss of life <saw scenes of the crash and attendant *carnage*>.

Pogrom describes an organized massacre and looting of defenseless people, carried on usually with official connivance <a governmentally sanctioned *pogrom* against other ethnic groups>.

masterful, domineering, imperious, peremptory, imperative mean tending to impose one's will on others.

Masterful implies a strong personality and ability to act authoritatively <her *masterful* personality soon dominated the movement>.

Domineering suggests an overbearing or tyrannical manner and an obstinate determination to enforce one's will <*domineering* older siblings, ordering the younger ones about>. ***ant*** subservient

Imperious implies a commanding nature or manner and often suggests arrogant assurance <an *imperious* executive used to getting his own way>. ***ant*** abject

Peremptory implies an abrupt dictatorial manner coupled with an unwillingness to tolerate disobedience or dissent <a *peremptory* style that does not allow for compromise>.

Imperative implies peremptoriness arising more from the urgency of the situation than from an inherent will to dominate <an *imperative* appeal for assistance>.

match, rival, equal, approach, touch mean to come up to or nearly up to the standard of something else.

Match implies that one thing is the mate rather than the duplicate of another, as in power, strength, beauty, or interest <feels that no language can *match* French for clarity and exactness>.

Rival suggests a close competition, as for superiority or in excellence <a voice which none could *rival*>.

Equal implies such close equivalence, as in quantity, worth, or degree, that no question concerning a difference or deficiency can arise <a love of glory *equaled* only by a fear of shame>.

Approach implies such closeness in matching or equaling that the difference, though detectable, scarcely matters <a beauty *approaching* perfection>.

Touch suggests close equivalence, as in quality or value, and is typically used in negative constructions <as for durability, no current product can *touch* the new product>.

material 1. Material, physical, corporeal, phenomenal, sensible, objective mean of or belonging to the world of actuality or to things apparent to the senses.

Material implies formation out of tangible matter, but may imply a contrast to *spiritual, ideal,* or *intangible* <*material* possessions>. ***ant*** immaterial

Physical applies to what is perceived directly by the senses or can be measured or calculated and may contrast with *mental, spiritual,* or *imaginary* <the benefits of *physical* exercise>. ***ant*** spiritual

Corporeal implies having the tangible qualities of a body, such as shape, size, or resistance to force <artists have portrayed angels as *corporeal* beings>. ***ant*** incorporeal

Phenomenal applies to what is known or perceived through the senses and experience rather than by intuition or rational deduction <scientists concerned only with the *phenomenal* world>. ***ant*** noumenal

Sensible stresses the capability of being readily or forcibly known through the senses <the earth's rotation is not *sensible* to us>. ***ant*** insensible

Objective may stress material existence apart from a subject perceiving it <tears are the *objective* manifestation of grief>. ***ant*** subjective

2. see RELEVANT.

matrimonial, marital, conjugal, connubial, nuptial mean of, relating to, or characteristic of marriage.

Matrimonial and ***marital*** apply to whatever has to do with marriage and the married state <enjoyed 40 years of *matrimonial* bliss> <a *marital* relationship built upon mutual trust and understanding>.

Conjugal specifically applies to married persons and their relations <inmates of the prison now have *conjugal* rights>.

Connubial refers to the married state <a *connubial* contract of no legal standing>.

Nuptial usually refers to marriage or to the marriage ceremony <busy all week with the *nuptial* preparations>.

matter see AFFAIR.

matter-of-fact see PROSAIC.

mature *adj* **Mature, ripe, adult, grown-up** mean fully developed.

Mature stresses completion of development; when applied to persons it implies attainment of the prime of life and powers <a writer with a deft, *mature* style>, whereas in application to things it is more likely to imply completion of a course, process, or period <reinvested the *matured* bonds>. ***ant*** immature

Ripe stresses readiness, as for use, enjoyment, or action <a people *ripe* for democracy>. ***ant*** unripe, green

Adult is very close to *mature*, especially when applied to living things; in extended use it is likely to imply successful surmounting of the weaknesses of immaturity <an *adult* approach to a problem>. ***ant*** juvenile, puerile

Grown-up may be preferred to *adult* when an antithesis to *childish* is desired <adults incapable of *grown-up* behavior>. ***ant*** childish, callow

mature *vb* **Mature, develop, ripen, age** mean to come or cause to come to be fit for use or enjoyment.

Mature, in its basic application to living things, stresses fullness of growth and attainment of adult characteristics <*matured* nicely during her college years>.

Develop stresses the unfolding of what is latent and the attainment of what is possible to the species and potential to the individual <a child who had not yet *developed* a cynical outlook>.

Ripen emphasizes the approach to or attainment of the peak of perfection <bided his time, waiting for his hatred to *ripen*>.

Age may equal *mature* when applied to the young but more often it implies approach to the period of decline or decay <wine and cheese improve as they *age*>.

meager, scanty, scant, skimpy, exiguous, spare, sparse mean falling short of what is normal, necessary, or desirable.

Meager implies the absence of elements, qualities, or numbers necessary to a thing's richness, substance, or potency <a *meager* portion of meat>. ***ant*** ample, copious

Scanty stresses insufficiency in amount, quantity, or extent <supplies too *scanty* to last the winter>. ***ant*** ample, plentiful, profuse

Scant suggests a falling short of what is desired or desirable rather than of what is essential <accorded the guests *scant* welcome>. ***ant*** plentiful, profuse

Skimpy usually suggests niggardliness or penury as the cause of the deficiency <tacky housing developments on *skimpy* lots>.

Exiguous implies a marked deficiency in number or measure that makes the thing described compare unfavorably with others of its kind <trying to function and thrive despite *exiguous* resources>. ***ant*** capacious, ample

Spare may suggest a slight falling short of adequacy or merely an absence of superfluity <a *spare,* concise style of writing>. ***ant*** profuse

Sparse implies a thin scattering of units <a *sparse* population>. ***ant*** dense

mean *adj* **Mean, ignoble, abject, sordid** mean below the normal standards of human decency and dignity.

Mean suggests having repellent characteristics, such as small-mindedness, ill temper, or cupidity, or it may stress inferiority and suggest poverty or penury <a *mean,* rundown neighborhood>.

Ignoble suggests a loss or lack of some essential high quality of mind or spirit <*ignoble* collectors who view artworks merely as investments>. ***ant*** noble, magnanimous

Abject may imply degradation, debasement, or servility <the *abject* poverty of her youth>. ***ant*** exalted *(as in rank)*, imperious *(as in manner)*

Sordid is stronger than all of these in stressing dirtiness and physical or spiritual degradation and abjectness <a *sordid* story of murder and revenge>.

mean *n* **1.** see AVERAGE.

2. Mean, instrument, agent, medium mean something or someone necessary or useful in effecting an end.

Mean, now usually in the plural *means*, is very general and may apply to anything or anyone that serves an end <had no *means* of traveling but his own two feet>.

Instrument, as applied to persons, implies a secondary role, sometimes as a tool, sometimes as a dupe <used him as the *instrument* of her ambitions> and, as applied to things, is likely to suggest a degree of fitness or adaptation for use as a tool <politics, a powerful *instrument* for change>.

Agent applies to a person who acts to achieve an end conceived by another <dealt with a real estate *agent*> or to a thing that produces an immediate effect or definite result <salt, an *agent* in the melting of ice>.

Medium applies to a usually intangible means of conveying, transmitting, or communicating <resorted to sign language as a *medium* of communication>.

meander see WANDER.

meaning, sense, acceptation, signification, significance, import mean an idea which is conveyed to the mind.

Meaning is the general term used of anything, such as a word, sign, poem, or action, requiring or allowing of interpretation <the poem's *meaning* has been fiercely debated>.

Sense denotes the meaning or a particular meaning of a word or phrase <used "nighthawk" in its figurative *sense*>.

Acceptation is used of a sense of a word or phrase as regularly understood by most people <the writer isn't using "sane" in its common *acceptation*>.

Signification denotes the established meaning of a term, symbol, or character <any Christian would immediately know the *signification* of "INRI">.

Significance applies to a covert as distinguished from the ostensible meaning of an utterance, act, or work of art <an agreement that seemed to have little *significance* at the time>.

Import suggests momentousness and denotes the meaning or impression a speaker conveyed through language <failed at first to appreciate the *import* of the news>.

mechanical see SPONTANEOUS.

meddle, interfere, intermeddle, tamper mean to concern oneself with someone or something officiously, impertinently, or indiscreetly.

Meddle suggests officiousness and an acting without right or permission of those properly concerned <they will tolerate no *meddling* in their affairs>.

Interfere implies a meddling in such a way as to hinder, interrupt, frustrate, disorder, or defeat, although not necessarily with conscious intent <the rain *interfered* with their game>.

Intermeddle suggests a meddling impertinently and officiously and in such a way as to interfere <government agencies *intermeddling* in their business>.

Tamper implies a seeking to make unwarranted alterations, to perform meddlesome experiments, or to exert an improper influence, and may but need not suggest corruption or clandestine operation <obvious signs that the lock had been *tampered* with>.

meddlesome see IMPERTINENT.

median see AVERAGE.

mediate see INTERPOSE.

meditate see PONDER.

meditative see THOUGHTFUL 1.

medium see MEAN *n*.

meek see HUMBLE.

meet *adj* see FIT *adj*.

meet *vb* see SATISFY 3.

melancholia see SADNESS.

melancholy see SADNESS.

melodramatic see DRAMATIC.

melody, air, tune mean a clearly distinguishable succession of rhythmically ordered tones.

Melody stresses the sweetness and beauty of the sound produced and often suggests the expressiveness or moving power of a carefully wrought pattern <a poignant *melody*>.

Air is likely to apply to an easily remembered succession of tones which identifies a simple musical composition, such as a ballad or waltz, but in technical use it applies to the dominating melody, usually carried by the upper voices, of a piece of vocal music <hummed a lovely Celtic *air*>.

Tune can denote a usually simple musical composition or the air that gives it its character <can you remember the *tune* of "America"?>.

member see PART.

memorable see NOTEWORTHY.

memory, remembrance, recollection, reminiscence mean the capacity for or the act of remembering, or the thing remembered.

Memory applies both to the capacity to bring back what one has once experienced or known and to what is remembered <no *memory* of that incident>. ***ant*** oblivion

Remembrance applies to the act of remembering or the fact of being remembered <any *remembrance* of his deceased wife was painful>. ***ant*** forgetfulness

Recollection suggests the act of consciously bringing back to mind often with some effort or the thing brought back <after a moment's *recollection* he produced the name>.

Reminiscence suggests the act of recalling incidents, experiences, or feelings from a remote past or things so recalled <recorded my grandmother's *reminiscenses* of her Iowa girlhood>.

menace see THREATEN.

mend, repair, patch, rebuild mean to put into good order something that is injured, damaged, or defective.

Mend implies the making whole or sound of something that is broken, torn, or injured <the wound *mended* slowly>.

Repair applies to the mending of more extensive damage or dilapidation requiring professional skill or special equipment <the car needs to be *repaired* by a mechanic>.

Patch implies an often temporary or hasty mending of a rent or breach with new material <*patch* potholes with asphalt>.

Rebuild suggests the making like new of something without completely replacing it <a *rebuilt* television is cheaper than a brand-new one>.

mendacious see DISHONEST.

menial see SUBSERVIENT.

mention, name, instance, specify mean to make clear or specific by referring to something explicitly.

Mention indicates a calling attention to, either by name or by clear but incidental reference <failed to *mention* the incident>.

Name implies the clear mentioning of a name and therefore may suggest greater explicitness <*named* three people as participants in the crime>.

Instance may indicate a clear specific reference or citation as a typical example or special case <failed in her attempt to *instance* a clear example>.

Specify implies the making of a statement so precise, explicit, and detailed that misunderstanding is impossible <use only ingredients and amounts *specified*>.

mercurial see INCONSTANT.

mercy, charity, clemency, grace, lenity mean a showing of or a disposition to show kindness or compassion.

Mercy implies compassion that forbears punishing even when justice demands it or that extends help even to the lowliest or most undeserving <admitted his guilt and then begged for *mercy*>.

Charity stresses benevolence and goodwill as shown in generosity and in broad understanding and tolerance of others <show a little *charity* for the weak-willed>. ***ant*** ill will, malice

Clemency implies a mild and merciful disposition in one having the power or duty of judging and punishing <a judge little inclined to show *clemency*>. ***ant*** harshness

Grace implies a benign attitude and a willingness to grant favors or make concessions <the victor's *grace* in treating the vanquished>.

Lenity implies extreme, even undue, lack of severity in punishing and may suggest a weak softness <criticized the courts for excessive *lenity*>. ***ant*** severity

meretricious see GAUDY.

merge see MIX.

merry, blithe, jocund, jovial, jolly mean showing high spirits or lightheartedness.

Merry suggests cheerful, joyous, uninhibited enjoyment of frolic or festivity <a *merry* group of holiday revelers>.

Blithe suggests carefree, innocent, or even heedless gaiety <arrived late in her usual *blithe* way>. ***ant*** atrabilious, morose

Jocund stresses gladness marked by liveliness, elation and exhilaration of spirits <good news had left him in a *jocund* mood>.

Jovial suggests the stimulation of conviviality and good fellowship or the capacity for these <grew increasingly *jovial* with every drink>.

Jolly suggests high spirits expressed in laughing, bantering, and jesting and a determination to keep one's companions easy and laughing <our *jolly* host enlivened the party>. ***ant*** somber

metamorphose see TRANSFORM.

meter see RHYTHM.

method, mode, manner, way, fashion, system mean the means or procedure followed in achieving an end.

Method implies an orderly, logical, and effective arrangement usually in steps <effective *methods* of birth control>.

Mode implies an order or course followed by custom, tradition, or personal preference <the preferred *mode* of transportation>.

Manner is close to *mode* but may imply a procedure or method that is individual or distinctive <a highly distinctive *manner* of conducting>.

Way is very general and may be used in place of any of the preceding words <her usual slapdash *way* of doing things>.

Fashion may suggest a peculiar or characteristic but perhaps

superficial or ephemeral way of doing something <rushing about, in typical New Yorker *fashion*>.
System suggests a fully developed or carefully formulated method often emphasizing the idea of rational orderliness <follows no *system* in playing the horses>.

methodize see ORDER.
meticulous see CAREFUL.
métier see WORK 2.
mettle see COURAGE.
microscopic see SMALL.
mien see BEARING.
might see POWER 1.
mild see SOFT.
milieu see BACKGROUND.
militant see AGGRESSIVE.
military see MARTIAL.
mimic see COPY.
mind 1. see OBEY. **2.** see TEND.
mingle see MIX.
miniature see SMALL.
minimize see DECRY.
minute 1. see CIRCUMSTANTIAL. **2.** see SMALL.
mirage see DELUSION.
mirth, glee, jollity, hilarity mean a mood or temper of joy and high spirits that is expressed in laughter, play, or merrymaking.
Mirth implies lightness of heart, love of gaiety, and ready laughter <family gatherings that were the occasions of much *mirth*>. ***ant*** melancholy
Glee stresses exultation shown in laughter, cries of joy, or sometimes malicious delight <cackled with *glee* at their misfortune>. ***ant*** gloom
Jollity suggests exuberance or lack of restraint in mirth or glee <his endless flow of jokes added to the *jollity*>. ***ant*** somberness
Hilarity suggests loud or irrepressible laughter or high-spirited boisterousness <a dull comedy not likely to inspire much *hilarity*>.

misanthropic see CYNICAL.
miscellaneous, assorted, heterogeneous, motley, promiscuous mean a group, collection, or mass, or the things that make up a group, collection, or mass, marked by diversity or variety.
Miscellaneous implies a mixture of many kinds showing few signs of selection and often suggesting dependence on chance <a *miscellaneous* assortment of jars and bottles>.
Assorted implies a selection that includes various kinds or involves considerations of tastes or needs <a box of *assorted* cookies>.

Heterogeneous applies to masses or groups in which diverse or varied individuals or elements are in proximity or relationship by chance <the *heterogeneous* structure of granite>. ***ant*** homogeneous

Motley adds the suggestion of discordance in the individuals or elements or their striking contrast to each other and carries a depreciative connotation <a *motley* aggregation of curs and mongrels>.

Promiscuous usually implies selection that is completely devoid of discrimination or restriction and that results in disorderly confusion <gave all the money away in *promiscuous* acts of charity>.

mischance see MISFORTUNE.

mise-en-scène see BACKGROUND.

miserable, wretched mean deplorably or contemptibly bad or mean.

Miserable implies that a person is in a state of misery that may arise in extreme distress of body or mind or in pitiable poverty or degradation <looked *miserable*, with eyes red and swollen from crying>; in reference to things, it suggests such meanness or inferiority or unpleasantness that it arouses utter dislike or disgust in an observer <what *miserable* weather>. ***ant*** comfortable

Wretched stresses the unhappiness or despondency of a person exposed to a grave distress, such as want, grief, oppression, affliction, or anxiety <wretched survivors of the terrible flood>; applied to things, it stresses extreme or deplorable badness <made a life as best they could in their *wretched* hovel>.

miserly see STINGY.

misery see DISTRESS.

misfortune, mischance, mishap, adversity mean adverse fortune or an instance of this.

Misfortune may apply either to the incident or conjunction of events that is the cause of an unhappy change of fortune or to the ensuing state of distress <never lost hope even in the depths of *misfortune*>. ***ant*** happiness, prosperity

Mischance applies especially to a situation involving no more than slight inconvenience or minor annoyance <took the wrong road by *mischance*>.

Mishap applies to a trivial instance of bad luck <the usual *mishaps* that are part of a family vacation>.

Adversity applies to a state of grave or persistent misfortune <had never experienced much *adversity* in life>. ***ant*** prosperity

misgiving see APPREHENSION.

mishap see MISFORTUNE.

mislay see MISPLACE.
mislead see DECEIVE.
misogynistic see CYNICAL.
misplace, mislay mean to put in a wrong place so as to be as unavailable as if lost.

Misplace implies a putting of something in other than its customary or usual place, but often it suggests a setting or fixing of something where it should not be <her confidence in him was *misplaced*>.

Mislay usually implies a misplacing in the basic sense but stresses a forgetting of the place in which the thing has been put and therefore often means to lose, usually temporarily <I have *mislaid* my glasses>.

misrepresent, falsify, belie, garble mean to present or represent in a manner contrary to the truth.

Misrepresent usually implies an intent to deceive and may suggest deliberate lying and often bias, prejudice, or a will to be unfair <*misrepresent* the value of property offered for sale>.

Falsify implies a tampering with or distorting of facts or reality that is usually, but not necessarily, deliberate and intended to deceive <*falsify* the records of a business to conceal embezzlement>.

Belie implies an impression given that is at variance with fact; it stresses contrast but does not ordinarily suggest intent <an agility that *belies* her age>. ***ant*** attest

Garble implies mutilation or distortion of such things as reports, testimony, or translations that may or may not be intentional but that regularly creates a wrong impression of the original <the victims of badly *garbled* accounts>.

mist see HAZE.
mistake *n* see ERROR.
mistake *vb* **Mistake, confuse, confound** mean to mix things up or take one thing to be another.

Mistake implies that one fails to recognize a thing or to grasp its real nature and therefore identifies it with something not itself <*mistake* synthetic fur for real>. ***ant*** recognize

Confuse suggests that one fails to distinguish two things that have similarities or common characteristics <*confuse* moral and political issues>. ***ant*** differentiate

Confound implies that one mixes things up so hopelessly as to be unable to detect their differences or distinctions and usually connotes mental bewilderment or a muddled mind <hopelessly *confounded* by the wealth of choices available>. ***ant*** distinguish, discriminate

mistrust see UNCERTAINTY.
mite see PARTICLE.
mitigate see RELIEVE.

mix, mingle, commingle, blend, merge, coalesce, amalgamate, fuse mean to combine or to be combined into a more or less uniform whole.

Mix implies a homogeneous product, but may or may not imply loss of each element's identity <*mix* the salad greens>.

Mingle usually suggests that the elements are still somewhat distinguishable or separately active <fear *mingled* with anticipation in my mind>.

Commingle implies a closer or more thorough unity and harmoniousness <a sense of duty *commingled* with a fierce pride>.

Blend implies that the elements as such disappear in the resulting mixture <*blended* several teas to create a balanced brew>.

Merge suggests a combining in which one or more elements are lost in the whole <in her mind reality and fantasy *merged*>.

Coalesce implies an affinity in the merging elements and usually a resulting organic unity <telling details that *coalesce* into a striking portrait>.

Amalgamate suggests the forming of a close union rather than a loss of individual identities <immigrants that were readily *amalgamated* into the population>.

Fuse stresses oneness and indissolubility of the resulting product <a building in which modernism and classicism are *fused*>.

mixture, admixture, blend, compound, composite, amalgam mean a product formed by the combination of two or more things.

Mixture, the most general term, often implies miscellaneousness <planted a *mixture* of seeds to get a colorful bed of flowers>.

Admixture suggests that one or more elements has an alien character <an *admixture* of coffee and roasted nuts>.

Blend implies the thorough mingling of similar elements or ingredients <an expression that was a *blend* of pity and fear>.

Compound suggests the union of two or more distinguishable or analyzable parts, elements, or ingredients <a *compound* of elegance and frivolity>.

Composite implies that the constituent elements have been artificially or fortuitously combined <a population that is the *composite* of many races>.

Amalgam suggests a complex mixture or the final form into which it hardens <a beneficent attitude that was an *amalgam* of generosity and disdain>.

mob see CROWD.

mobile see MOVABLE.

mock 1. see COPY. **2.** see RIDICULE.

mode 1. see FASHION. **2.** see METHOD.

model, example, pattern, exemplar, ideal mean someone or something set or held before one for guidance or imitation.

Model applies to something taken or proposed as worthy of imitation <a performance that is a *model* of charm and intelligence>.

Example applies to something, especially a person, to be imitated or, in some contexts, on no account to be imitated but to be regarded as a warning <for better or worse, children follow the *example* of their parents>.

Pattern suggests a clear and detailed archetype or prototype <American industry set a *pattern* for others to follow>.

Exemplar suggests either a faultless example to be emulated or a perfect typification <cited Hitler as the *exemplar* of power-mad egomania>.

Ideal implies the best possible exemplification either in reality or in conception <never found a suitor who matched her *ideal*>.

moderate *adj* **Moderate, temperate** mean not excessive in degree, amount, or intensity.

Moderate is likely to connote absence or avoidance of excess <proceeded at a *moderate* rate of speed>. ***ant*** immoderate

Temperate connotes deliberate restraint or restriction and is opposed to *inordinate* and *intemperate* <a person of modest, *temperate* virtues>. ***ant*** intemperate, inordinate

moderate *vb* **Moderate, qualify, temper** mean to modify so as to avoid an extreme or to keep within bounds.

Moderate stresses reduction of what is excessive without necessarily reaching an optimum <the sun *moderated* the chill>.

Qualify emphasizes a restricting that more precisely defines and limits <*qualified* her praise with some doubts about the project>.

Temper strongly implies an accommodating to a special need or requirement and is likely to suggest a counterbalancing or mitigating addition <*temper* justice with mercy>. ***ant*** intensify

modern 1. Modern, recent, late mean having taken place, come into existence, or developed in times close to the present.

Modern may apply to anything that is not ancient or medieval <a *modern* ship set next to an ancient trireme> or anything that bears the marks of a period nearer in time than another <*modern* methods of harvesting replaced the scythe> or to whatever is felt to be new, fresh, or up-to-date <wearing the very latest *modern* hairstyle>. ***ant*** antique, ancient

Recent usually lacks such implications and applies to a date that approximates the immediate past more or less precisely according to the nature of the thing qualified <a *recent* change of plans>.

Late usually implies a series or succession of which the one described is the most recent in time <the *late* war>, but it can sometimes be less indefinite and equivalent to "not long ago being" <the firm's new director of research was the *late* professor of chemistry at the state university>.

2. see NEW.

modest 1. see CHASTE. **2.** see HUMBLE. **3.** see SHY.

modify see CHANGE.

moist see WET.

mollify see PACIFY.

mollycoddle see INDULGE.

moment see IMPORTANCE.

momentary see TRANSIENT.

monastery see CLOISTER.

monetary see FINANCIAL.

monopolize, engross, absorb, consume mean to take up completely.

Monopolize, the most general term, means to possess or control completely <*monopolized* their attention>.

Engross sometimes implies getting a material control of <*engross* a market by buying up available supplies>, but more often it implies an unprotested monopolizing of time, attention, or interest <*engrossed* with a new magazine>.

Absorb is often interchangeable with *engross* but it tends to carry a hint of submission to pressure rather than ready acceptance <grinding tasks that *absorbed* her efforts>.

Consume implies a monopolization of one's time, interest, or attention <*consumed* with a desire to climb every mountain in the range>.

monopoly, corner, pool, syndicate, trust, cartel mean a method of or system for controlling prices.

Monopoly implies exclusive control of a public service or exclusive power to buy or sell a commodity in a particular market <our modern electric utilities are controlled and regulated *monopolies*>.

Corner applies to a temporary effective monopoly of something sold on an exchange so that buyers are forced to pay the price asked <maintained his *corner* on wheat for three days>.

Pool applies to a combining of interests and joint undertaking by apparently competing companies to regulate output and manipulate prices <refused to join the commodities *pool*>.

Syndicate, in financial circles, refers to a temporary association of individuals or firms to effect a particular piece of business; in more general terms, it applies to a combination of things, such as newspapers, business firms, or criminals, interested in a common project or enterprise and often carries suggestions of monopoly <own a horse through the *syndicate*>.

Trust historically applies to a merger of companies in which control is vested in trustees and stockholders exchange their stock for trust certificates in the new company, but it is often extended to any large or complex combination of business interests especially when felt to represent a threat to healthy competition <prosecuted for violation of *trust* laws>.

Cartel commonly implies an international combination for controlling production and sale of one or more products <carried on delicate negotiations with the oil *cartel*>.

monstrous 1. Monstrous, prodigious, tremendous, stupendous mean extremely impressive.

Monstrous implies a departure from the normal in such qualities as size, form, or character and often carries suggestions of deformity, ugliness, or fabulousness <the *monstrous* waste of the project>.

Prodigious suggests a marvelousness exceeding belief, usually in something felt as going far beyond a previous maximum of goodness, greatness, intensity, or size <made a *prodigious* effort and rolled the stone aside>.

Tremendous may imply a power to terrify or inspire awe <the *tremendous* roar of the cataract>, but in more general use it means little more than very large or great or intense <success gave him *tremendous* satisfaction>.

Stupendous implies a power to stun or astound, usually because of size, numbers, complexity, or greatness beyond one's power to describe <a *stupendous* volcanic eruption that destroyed the city>.

2. see OUTRAGEOUS.

mood, humor, temper, vein mean a state of mind in which an emotion or set of emotions gains ascendancy.

Mood, the most general term, imputes pervasiveness and compelling quality to the principal emotion and may apply not only to the frame of mind but to its expression <the melancholy *mood* of the poem>.

Humor implies a mood that is imposed on one by one's special temperament or one's physical or mental condition at the moment <in ill *humor* and out of sorts through fatigue>.

Temper applies to a mood dominated by a single strong emotion, often that of anger <gave vent to his bad *temper* in a series of angry yowls>.

Vein suggests a transitory mood or humor usually without any profound temperamental or physical basis <spoke in the same humorous *vein*>.

moral, ethical, virtuous, righteous, noble mean conforming to a standard of what is right and good.

Moral implies conformity to established codes or accepted notions of right and wrong <the basic *moral* values of a community>.

Ethical may suggest the involvement of more difficult or subtle questions of rightness, fairness, or equity and usually implies the existence of or conformance to an elevated code of standards <his strict *ethical* code would not tolerate it>. ***ant*** unethical

Virtuous implies the possession or manifestation of moral excellence in character <a person not conventionally religious, but *virtuous* in all other respects>. ***ant*** vicious

Righteous stresses guiltlessness or blamelessness and often suggests sanctimoniousness <responded to the charge with *righteous* indignation>. ***ant*** iniquitous

Noble implies moral eminence and freedom from anything petty, mean, or dubious in conduct and character <had only the *noblest* of reasons for pursuing the case>. ***ant*** base *(of actions),* atrocious *(of acts, deeds)*

morally see VIRTUALLY.

mordant see CAUSTIC.

morose see SULLEN.

mortal see DEADLY.

motive *adj* see MOVABLE.

motive *n* **Motive, impulse, incentive, inducement, spur, goad** mean a stimulus to action.

Motive implies an emotion or desire operating on the will and causing it to act <a crime without apparent *motive*>.

Impulse suggests a driving power arising from personal temperament or constitution <my first *impulse* was to hit him>.

Incentive applies to an external influence, such as an expected reward or a hope, that incites to action <a bonus was offered as an *incentive* for meeting the deadline>.

Inducement suggests a motive prompted by the deliberate enticements or allurements of another <offered a watch as an *inducement* to subscribe>.

Spur applies to a motive that stimulates the faculties or increases energy or ardor <fear was the *spur* that kept me going>.

Goad suggests a motive that keeps one going against one's will or desire <the need to earn a living is the daily *goad*>. ***ant*** curb

motley see MISCELLANEOUS.

mount 1. see ASCEND. **2.** see RISE.

mourn see GRIEVE.

movable, mobile, motive mean capable of moving or of being moved.

Movable applies to what can be moved or to what is not fixed in position or date <an engine with just a few *movable* parts>. ***ant*** immovable, stationary

Mobile stresses facility and ease in moving or, occasionally, in being moved <a *mobile* radio-transmitting unit>. ***ant*** immobile

Motive applies to an agent capable of causing movement or impelling to action <diesel engines supply the *motive* power for the ship>.

move, actuate, drive, impel mean to set or keep in motion.

Move is very general and implies no more than the fact of changing position <the force that *moves* the moon around the earth>.

Actuate stresses transmission of power so as to work or set in motion <turbines are *actuated* by the force of a current of water>.

Drive implies imparting forward and continuous motion and often stresses the effect rather than the impetus <a ship *driven* aground by hurricane winds>.

Impel suggests a greater impetus producing more headlong action <burning ambition *impelled* her to the seat of power>.

moving, impressive, poignant, affecting, touching, pathetic mean having the power to produce deep and usually somber emotion.

Moving may apply to any stirring that produces a strong emotional effect including thrilling, agitating, saddening, or evoking pity or sympathy <a *moving* appeal for charitable contributions>.

Impressive implies such forcefulness as compels attention, admiration, wonder, or conviction <an *impressive* list of achievements>. ***ant*** unimpressive

Poignant applies to what keenly or sharply affects one's sensibilities <a *poignant* documentary on the plight of the homeless>.

Affecting is close to *moving* but often suggests pathos <an *affecting* reunion of a mother and her child>.

Touching implies a capacity to arouse tenderness or compassion <the *touching* innocence in a child's eyes>.

Pathetic implies a capacity to move to pity or sometimes contempt <*pathetic* attempts to justify gross negligence>.

mulct see PENALIZE.

mulish see OBSTINATE.

multiply see INCREASE.

mundane see EARTHLY.

munificent see LIBERAL 1.

murder see KILL.
murky see DARK.
muse see PONDER.
muster see SUMMON.
musty see MALODOROUS.
mutilate see MAIM.
mutiny see REBELLION.
mutual see RECIPROCAL.

mysterious, inscrutable, arcane mean beyond one's powers to discover, understand, or explain.
Mysterious suggests a quality that excites wonder, curiosity, or surmise yet baffles attempts to explain it <couldn't account for the *mysterious* noise upstairs>.
Inscrutable applies to something that defies one's efforts to examine or investigate it or to interpret its significance or meaning <sat calmly with an *inscrutable* look on her face>.
Arcane implies a quality that is beyond comprehension because known or knowable only to the possessor of a restricted body of knowledge <a book filled with spells and *arcane* lore>.

mystery, problem, enigma, riddle, puzzle, conundrum mean something which baffles or perplexes.
Mystery applies to what cannot be fully understood by human reason or less strictly to whatever resists or defies explanation <the *mystery* of the stone monoliths on Easter Island>.
Problem applies to any question or difficulty calling for a solution or causing concern <the *problems* created by high technology>. ***ant*** solution
Enigma applies to an utterance or behavior that is difficult to interpret <his suicide was an *enigma* his family never understood>.
Riddle suggests an enigma or problem involving paradox or apparent contradiction <the *riddle* of the reclusive billionaire>.
Puzzle applies to an enigma or problem involving paradox or apparent contradiction that challenges ingenuity for its solution <the mechanisms of heredity were long a *puzzle* for scientists>.
Conundrum applies to a riddle or puzzle whose answer involves a pun or less often to a problem whose solution can only be speculative <posed *conundrums* to which there are no practical solutions>.

myth, legend, saga mean a traditional story of ostensibly historical content whose origin has been lost or forgotten.
Myth is varied in application and connotation and can apply to a fanciful explanation as of a natural phenomenon, social practice, or belief <*myths* of ancient Greece> or a story, belief, or

notion commonly held to be true but utterly without fact <the *myth* that money buys happiness>.

Legend typically applies to a story, incident, or notion attached to a particular person or place that purports to be historical though in fact unverifiable or incredible <the *legend* of Paul Bunyan>.

Saga may refer to a long, continued, heroic story that deals with a person or a group and is historical or legendary or a mixture of both <the building of the railroad was part of the great *saga* of the West>.

mythical see FICTITIOUS.

N

naive see NATURAL.

naked see BARE.

name see MENTION.

narcotic see ANODYNE 2.

narrative see STORY.

nasty see DIRTY.

national see CITIZEN.

native, indigenous, endemic, aboriginal mean belonging to a locality.

Native implies birth or origin in a place or region and may suggest compatibility with it <a *native* New Yorker>. ***ant*** alien, foreign

Indigenous applies to species or races and adds to *native* the implication of not having been introduced from elsewhere <maize is *indigenous* to America>. ***ant*** naturalized, exotic

Endemic implies being *indigenous* and peculiar to or restricted to a region <edelweiss is *endemic* in the Alps>. ***ant*** exotic, pandemic

Aboriginal implies having no known race preceding in occupancy of the region <the *aboriginal* peoples of Australia>.

natural 1. Natural, ingenuous, naive, unsophisticated, artless mean free from pretension or calculation.

Natural implies lacking artificiality and self-consciousness and having a spontaneousness suggesting the natural rather than the man-made <her unaffected, *natural* quality comes across on film>.

Ingenuous implies inability to disguise or conceal one's feelings or intentions and usually implies candid frankness and lack of reserve <the *ingenuous*, spontaneous utterances of children>. ***ant*** disingenuous, cunning

Naive suggests lack of worldly wisdom often connoting credulousness and unchecked innocence <in money matters she was distressingly *naive*>.

Unsophisticated implies a lack of experience and training necessary for social ease and adroitness <the store intimidates *unsophisticated* customers>. ***ant*** sophisticated

Artless suggests a naturalness resulting from unawareness of the effect one is producing on others <gave an *artless* impromptu speech at the dinner>. ***ant*** artful, affected

2. see REGULAR.

nature see TYPE.

naughty see BAD.

nearest, next mean closest in time, place, or degree.

Nearest indicates the highest degree of propinquity, as in space, time, or kinship <named the baby after their *nearest* relative>.

Next usually implies immediate succession or precedence in an order, a series, or a sequence <the *next* day> but in legal usage defines the closest degree of kinship <notified the victim's *next* of kin>.

nearly, almost, approximately, well-nigh mean within a little of being, becoming, reaching, or sufficing.

Nearly implies mere proximity <we were *nearly* home when the accident happened>.

Almost stresses a falling short or deficiency <*almost* out of her mind with grief>.

Approximately suggests that the difference is of no practical importance and that there is a reasonable approach to accuracy <weather forecasts cannot be more than *approximately* accurate>.

Well-nigh implies the closest approach short of identity <they found him *well-nigh* dead from cold>.

neat, tidy, trim mean manifesting care and orderliness.

Neat implies clearness, be it manifested in freedom from dirt and soil <her house is as *neat* as a pin> or in freedom from clutter, complication, or confusion <*neat* workmanship> or in freedom from any admixture <took whiskey *neat*>. ***ant*** filthy

Tidy suggests pleasing neatness and order diligently maintained <a *tidy* desk with everything in its proper place>. ***ant*** untidy

Trim implies both neatness and tidiness, but it stresses the smartness and spruceness of appearance that is given by clean lines and excellent proportions <a *trim* yacht>. ***ant*** frowsy

necessity see NEED.

need *n* **Need, necessity, exigency** mean a pressing lack of something essential.

Need implies pressure and urgency <children have a *need* for affection> and may suggest distress or indispensability <the *need* for a new water supply>.

Necessity is likely to stress imperative demand or compelling cause <call me only in case of *necessity*>.

Exigency adds the implication of unusual difficulty or restriction imposed by special circumstances <coped as best they could with the *exigencies* of the famine>.

need *vb* see LACK.

nefarious see VICIOUS.

negate see NULLIFY.

negative see NEUTRAL.

neglect, omit, disregard, ignore, overlook, slight, forget mean to pass over without giving due attention.

Neglect implies giving insufficient attention to something that has a claim to one's care or attention <habitually *neglected* his studies>. ***ant*** cherish

Omit implies a leaving out of a part of a whole <*omit* a verse of a song> or a neglecting entirely <*omitted* ro remove the telltale fingerprints>.

Disregard suggests voluntary inattention <*disregarded* the wishes of the other members>. ***ant*** regard

Ignore implies a failure, sometimes deliberate, to regard something obvious <*ignored* the snide remarks of passersby>. ***ant*** heed, acknowledge

Overlook suggests a disregarding or ignoring through haste or lack of care <in my rush I *overlooked* some relevant examples>.

Slight implies a contemptuous or disdainful disregarding or omitting <*slighted* several worthy authors in her survey>.

Forget may suggest either a willful ignoring or a failure to impress something on one's mind <*forget* what others say and listen to your conscience>. ***ant*** remember

neglectful see NEGLIGENT.

negligent, neglectful, lax, slack, remiss mean culpably careless or indicative of such carelessness.

Negligent implies culpable inattention to one's duty or business <I had been *negligent* in my letter-writing>. ***ant*** attentive

Neglectful adds an implication of laziness or deliberate inattention <a society callously *neglectful* of the poor>. ***ant*** attentive

Lax implies a blameworthy lack of needed strictness, severity, or precision <a reporter who is *lax* about getting the facts straight>. ***ant*** strict, stringent

Slack implies want of due or necessary diligence or care through indolence, sluggishness, or indifference <the *slack* workmanship and slipshod construction>.

Remiss implies blameworthy carelessness shown in slackness, forgetfulness, or negligence <had been *remiss* in her domestic duties>. ***ant*** scrupulous

negotiate 1. see CONFER.

2. Negotiate, arrange mean to bring about through an exchange of views and wishes and agreement reached by bargaining and compromise.

Negotiate suggests that the dealings are carried on by diplomatic, business, or legal agencies <*negotiate* a new contract>.

Arrange implies dealings intended for the restoration or establishment of order or those carried out between private persons or their representatives <*arrange* a marriage, as they did long ago>.

neighborly see AMICABLE.

neophyte see NOVICE.

neoplasm see TUMOR.

nepenthe see ANODYNE 2.

nerve see TEMERITY.

nervous see VIGOROUS.

nettle see IRRITATE.

neutral, negative, indifferent mean lacking decisiveness or distinctness.

Neutral implies a quality, an appearance, or a reaction that belongs to neither of two opposites or extremes and often connotes vagueness, indefiniteness, indecisiveness, or ineffectualness <maintained a *neutral* position in the argument>.

Negative carries a stronger implication of absence of positive or affirmative qualities and commonly implies lack of effect, activity, or definite and concrete form <won't accomplish anything with such a *negative* attitude>. ***ant*** affirmative

Indifferent implies a quality, a character, or an appearance that is not readily categorized, especially as good or bad, right or wrong, and that, therefore, is unlikely to stir up strong feeling or elicit firm opinions <she was a hard worker but an *indifferent* student>.

new, novel, modern, original, fresh mean having recently come into existence or use or into a particular state or condition.

New may apply to what is freshly made and unused <*new* brick> or has not been known or experienced before <starts his *new* job>. ***ant*** old

Novel applies to what is not only new but strange or unprecedented <a *novel* approach to the problem>.

Modern applies to what belongs to or is characteristic of the present time or the present era <the life-style of the *modern* woman>. ***ant*** ancient, antique

Original applies to what is or produces the first of its kind to exist <a man without one *original* idea>. ***ant*** dependent, banal, trite

Fresh applies to what is or seems new or has not lost its qualities of newness, such as liveliness, energy, or brightness <a *fresh* start>. ***ant*** stale

next see NEAREST.

nice 1. Nice, dainty, fastidious, finicky, particular, fussy, squeamish mean having or showing exacting standards.

Nice implies fine discrimination in perception and evaluation <makes a *nice* distinction between an artist and a craftsman>.

Dainty suggests a tendency to reject what does not conform to one's delicate taste or sensibility <when camping, one cannot afford to be *dainty* about food>.

Fastidious implies having very high and often capricious ethical, artistic, or social standards <a woman too *fastidious* to tolerate messy little boys>.

Finicky implies an affected, often exasperating, fastidiousness <small children are usually *finicky* eaters>.

Particular implies an insistence that one's exacting standards be met <a customer who is very *particular* about his fried eggs>.

Fussy adds a connotation of querulousness to *finicky* and *particular* <very *fussy* about the starch in his shirts>.

Squeamish suggests an oversensitive or prudish readiness to be nauseated, disgusted, or offended <*squeamish* about erotic art>.

2. see CORRECT *adj.*

niggardly see STINGY.

night see NIGHTLY.

nightly, nocturnal, night mean of, relating to, or associated with the night.

Nightly may mean no more than this, but more often it carries a strong implication of recurrence and is appropriate when the reference is to something that happens night after night <awaited her *nightly* dreams>. ***ant*** daily

Nocturnal distinctively implies what is active at night <small creatures of *nocturnal* habit>. ***ant*** diurnal

Night, often interchangeable with *nocturnal,* may be preferred when a more casual term is desired <waiting for the *night* train> but distinctively describes a person who works at night <*night* nurses> and things that occur or are intended for use at night <*night* baseball>.

nimble see AGILE.

nobility see ARISTOCRACY.

noble see MORAL.

nocturnal see NIGHTLY.

noise see SOUND.

noiseless see STILL.

noisome see MALODOROUS.

nonchalant see COOL.
nonmoral see IMMORAL.
nonplus see PUZZLE.
nonsocial see UNSOCIAL.
norm see AVERAGE.
normal see REGULAR.
notable see NOTEWORTHY.
note *n* see SIGN 1.
note *vb* see SEE 1.
noted see FAMOUS.
noteworthy, notable, memorable mean having a quality that attracts attention.

Noteworthy implies a quality, especially of excellence, that merits or attracts attention <a *noteworthy* collection of stories>.

Notable is likely to connote a special feature, such as an excellence, a virtue, a value, or a significance, that makes the thing or person worthy of notice <a *notable* performance of Hamlet>.

Memorable stresses worthiness of remembrance, sometimes as an intrinsic quality, sometimes as a matter personal to the rememberer <a *memorable* occasion>.

notice see SEE 1.
noticeable, remarkable, prominent, outstanding, conspicuous, salient, signal, striking mean attracting notice or attention.

Noticeable applies to something unlikely to escape observation <a piano recital with no *noticeable* errors>. ***ant*** unnoticeable

Remarkable applies to something so extraordinary or exceptional as to demand attention or comment <a film of *remarkable* intelligence and wit>.

Prominent applies to something that commands notice by standing out against its surroundings or background <a doctor who occupies a *prominent* position in the town>. ***ant*** inconspicuous

Outstanding applies to something that rises above and excels others of the same kind <honored for her *outstanding* contributions to science>. ***ant*** commonplace

Conspicuous applies to something that is obvious and unavoidable to the sight or mind <the *conspicuous* waste of the corrupt regime>. ***ant*** inconspicuous

Salient applies to something of significance that thrusts itself into attention <list the *salient* points of the speech>.

Signal applies to what deserves attention as being unusually significant <a *signal* contribution to sculpture>.

Striking applies to something that impresses itself powerfully and deeply upon the mind or vision <the backwardness of the area is *striking* even to casual observers>.

notify see INFORM.

notion see IDEA.

notorious see FAMOUS.

novel see NEW.

novice, apprentice, probationer, postulant, neophyte mean one who is a beginner in something, such as a trade, a profession, a career, or a skill.

Novice stresses inexperience <a ski slope designed for *novices*>. ***ant*** doyen, old hand, old-timer, veteran

Apprentice applies to a beginner serving under a master or teacher and stresses subordination more than inexperience <bricklayer's *apprentice*>.

Probationer applies to a beginner on trial for a period of time in which he or she must demonstrate aptitude <among the graduate students who were *probationers* in the field>.

Postulant designates a candidate on probation, especially for admission to a religious order <gives advice to young *postulants* in the community>.

Neophyte usually suggests initiation and is applicable to one who is new to and learning the ways of something, such as an association, a science, or an art, and often connotes youthful eagerness and unsophistication <could easily tell the eager *neophytes* from the jaded professionals>.

noxious see PERNICIOUS.

nude see BARE.

nugatory see VAIN.

nullify, negate, annul, abrogate, invalidate mean to deprive of effective or continued existence.

Nullify implies counteracting completely the force, effectiveness, or value of something <his critical insights are *nullified* by tiresome puns>.

Negate implies the destruction or canceling out of one of two mutually exclusive things by the other <a relationship *negated* by petty jealousies>.

Annul suggests a neutralizing or a making ineffective or nonexistent often by legal or official action <the treaty *annuls* all previous agreements>.

Abrogate is like *annul* but more definitely implies a legal or official purposeful act <a law that would *abrogate* certain diplomatic privileges>. ***ant*** establish, fix

Invalidate implies a making of something powerless or unacceptable by a declaration of its logical or moral or legal unsoundness <the absence of witnesses *invalidates* the will>. ***ant*** validate

number see SUM.

nunnery see CLOISTER.
nuptial see MATRIMONIAL.

O

obdurate see INFLEXIBLE.

obedient, docile, tractable, amenable mean submissive to the will or control of another.

Obedient implies compliance with the demands or requests of one in authority <cadets must be *obedient* to their commanding officer>. ***ant*** disobedient, contumacious

Docile implies a predisposition to submit readily to control or guidance <a *docile* child who never caused trouble>. ***ant*** indocile, ungovernable, unruly

Tractable suggests having a character that permits easy handling or managing <Indian elephants are more *tractable* than their African cousins>. ***ant*** intractable, unruly

Amenable suggests a willingness to yield to or cooperate with advice, demands, or contrary suggestions <he's usually *amenable* to suggestions and new ideas>. ***ant*** recalcitrant, refractory

obey, comply, mind mean to follow the direction of another.

Obey is the general term and implies ready or submissive yielding to authority <*obeyed* her parents>. ***ant*** disobey, command, order

Comply, often used with *with,* is likely to imply complaisance, dependence, or lack of a strong opinion <willing to *comply* with the opinion of the majority>. ***ant*** command, enjoin

Mind is likely to be used in connection with children or juniors and in admonition or warning <children must *mind* their parents> or in a weaker sense can carry the implication of heeding or attending in order to conform or comply <*mind* you, he never spoke to me about it>.

object *vb* **Object, protest, remonstrate, expostulate, kick** mean to oppose by arguing against.

Object stresses dislike or aversion <*objected* to his sweeping generalizations>. ***ant*** acquiesce

Protest suggests an orderly presentation of objections in speech or writing <an open letter *protesting* the government's foreign policy>. ***ant*** agree

Remonstrate implies an attempt to persuade or convince by warning or reproving <*remonstrated* on his son's free-spending ways at college>.

Expostulate suggests an earnest explanation of one's objection and firm insistence on the merits of one's stand <*expostulated* at length on the reasons for her decision>.

Kick suggests more informally a strenuous protesting or complaining <everybody *kicks* when taxes are raised>.

object *n* **1.** see INTENTION. **2.** see THING.

objective *adj* **1.** see FAIR. **2.** see MATERIAL.

objective *n* see INTENTION.

oblige 1. see FORCE.

2. Oblige, accommodate, favor mean to do a service or courtesy.

Oblige implies the putting of someone into one's debt by doing something that is pleasing <ingenuous and eager to *oblige* everyone> and is commonly used in conventional acknowledgment of small courtesies <much *obliged* for their warm hospitality>. ***ant*** disoblige

Accommodate, when used of services, can replace *oblige* or can imply gracious compliance and consideration <a most *accommodating* host> or connote the intent to be of assistance <willing to *accommodate* their unusual requests>. ***ant*** discommode

Favor implies the rendering of a service out of goodwill and without imposing an obligation on or expecting a return from the one favored <luck *favored* him in all his enterprises>; it can sometimes carry a suggestion of gratuitousness or of patronizing <*favor* a friend with unsought advice>.

obliging see AMIABLE.

oblique see CROOKED.

obliterate see ERASE.

oblivious see FORGETFUL.

obloquy see ABUSE.

obnoxious see REPUGNANT.

obscene see COARSE.

obscure, dark, vague, enigmatic, cryptic, ambiguous, equivocal mean not clearly understandable.

Obscure implies a hiding or veiling of meaning through some inadequacy of expression or withholding of full knowledge <the poem is *obscure* to those unlearned in the classics>. ***ant*** distinct, obvious

Dark implies an imperfect or clouded revelation often with ominous, mysterious, or sinister overtones <muttered *dark* hints of revenge>. ***ant*** lucid

Vague implies a lack of clear definition or formulation because of inadequate conception or consideration <*vague* promises of reimbursement were made>. ***ant*** definite, specific, lucid

Enigmatic stresses a puzzling, mystifying quality <left behind *enigmatic* works on alchemy>. ***ant*** explicit

Cryptic implies a purposely concealed meaning and often an intent to perplex or challenge <a *cryptic* message only a spy could decode>.

Ambiguous applies to a difficulty of understanding arising from the use, usually inadvertent, of a word or words of multiple meanings <an *ambiguous* directive that could be taken either way>. ***ant*** explicit

Equivocal applies to the deliberate use of language open to differing interpretations with the intention of deceiving or evading <the prisoner would give only *equivocal* answers>. ***ant*** unequivocal

obsequious see SUBSERVIENT.

observe 1. see KEEP 1. **2.** see SEE 1.

observer see SPECTATOR.

obsolete see OLD.

obstinate, dogged, stubborn, pertinacious, mulish mean fixed and unyielding in course or purpose.

Obstinate implies usually a perverse or unreasonable persistence <a President who was resolute but never *obstinate*>. ***ant*** pliant, pliable

Dogged suggests a tenacious, and sometimes sullen and unwavering, persistence <pursued the story with *dogged* perseverance>. ***ant*** faltering

Stubborn implies innate sturdiness or immovability in resisting attempts to change or abandon a course or opinion <swallow your *stubborn* pride and admit that you are wrong>. ***ant*** docile

Pertinacious suggests an annoying or irksome persistence <a *pertinacious* salesman who wouldn't take no for an answer>.

Mulish implies a settled and thoroughly unreasonable obstinacy <a *mulish* determination to stick with a lost cause>.

obstreperous see VOCIFEROUS.

obstruct see HINDER.

obtain see GET.

obtrude see INTRUDE.

obtrusive see IMPERTINENT.

obtuse see DULL.

obviate see PREVENT 2.

obvious see EVIDENT.

occasion see CAUSE.

occupation see WORK 2.

occur see HAPPEN.

occurrence, event, incident, episode, circumstance mean something that happens or takes place.

Occurrence implies any happening without intent, volition, or plan <a meeting that was a chance *occurrence*>.

Event usually implies an occurrence of some importance and frequently one having evident antecedent causes <the sequence of *events* following the assassination>.

Incident suggests an occurrence of brief duration or relatively slight importance <one of the minor *incidents* of the war>.

Episode stresses the distinctiveness or apartness of an incident <recounted some amusing *episodes* from his youth>.

Circumstance implies a specific detail attending an action or event <couldn't remember the exact *circumstances*>.

odd see STRANGE.

odious see HATEFUL.

odor see SMELL.

odorous, fragrant, redolent, aromatic, balmy mean emitting and diffusing scent.

Odorous applies to whatever has a strong distinctive smell whether pleasant or unpleasant <*odorous* cheeses should be tightly wrapped>. ***ant*** malodorous, odorless, scentless

Fragrant applies to things such as flowers or spices with sweet or agreeable odors that give sensuous delight <roses that were especially *fragrant*>. ***ant*** fetid

Redolent applies usually to a place or thing that diffuses or is impregnated with odors <the kitchen was often *redolent* of garlic and tomatoes>.

Aromatic applies to things emitting pungent, often fresh odors <an *aromatic* blend of rare teas>. ***ant*** acrid

Balmy applies to things which have a delicate and soothing aromatic odor <the soft, *balmy* air of a summer evening>.

offend, outrage, affront, insult mean to cause hurt feelings or deep resentment.

Offend may indicate a violation, often inadvertent, of the victim's sense of what is proper or fitting <hoped that my remarks had not *offended* her>.

Outrage implies offending beyond endurance and calling forth extreme feelings <corruption that *outrages* every citizen>.

Affront implies treating with deliberate rudeness or contemptuous indifference to courtesy <a movie that *affronts* your intelligence>. ***ant*** gratify

Insult suggests a wanton and deliberate causing of humiliation, hurt pride, or shame <managed to *insult* every guest at the party>. ***ant*** honor

offense 1. Offense, resentment, umbrage, pique, dudgeon, huff mean an emotional response to a slight or indignity.

Offense implies a marked state of hurt displeasure <takes deep *offense* at racial slurs>.

Resentment suggests a longer lasting indignation or smoldering ill will <harbored a life-long *resentment* of his brother>.

Umbrage implies a feeling of being snubbed or ignored <took *umbrage* at a lecturer who debunked American legends>.

Pique applies to a transient feeling of wounded vanity <in a *pique* she foolishly declined the invitation>.

Dudgeon suggests an angry fit of indignation <walked out of the meeting in high *dudgeon*>.

Huff implies a peevish short-lived spell of anger, usually at a petty cause <in a *huff* she threw the ring in his face>.

2. Offense, sin, vice, crime, scandal mean a transgression of law or custom.

Offense applies to the infraction of any law, rule, or code <at that school no *offense* went unpunished>.

Sin implies an offense against moral or religious law or an offense of any sort that is felt to be highly reprehensible <the *sin* of blasphemy>.

Vice applies to a habit or practice that degrades or corrupts <gambling was traditionally the gentleman's *vice*>.

Crime implies a serious offense punishable by the law of the state <the *crime* of murder>.

Scandal applies to an offense that outrages the public conscience or damages the integrity of an organization or group <the affair was a public *scandal*>.

3. see ATTACK *n* 2.

offensive see ATTACK *n* 2.

offer, proffer, tender, present, prefer mean to lay, set, or put something before another for acceptance.

Offer implies a putting before one of something which may be accepted or rejected <*offer* a suggestion>.

Proffer suggests that one is at liberty to accept or reject what is offered, and stresses the voluntariness, spontaneity, and courtesy of the agent <*proffered* assistance to the elderly man>.

Tender implies modesty, humility, or gentleness on the part of the one who makes the offer <*tender* our thanks> and serves as an idiomatic or polite term in certain phrases <*tender* a resignation>.

Present suggests ceremonious exhibition <*presented* to the queen> or the offering of something for use or pleasure <a letter *presented* on a silver tray>.

Prefer retains a sense close to *offer* in legal usage <*prefer* an indictment>.

offhand see EXTEMPORANEOUS.

office 1. see FUNCTION. **2.** see POSITION 2.

officious see IMPERTINENT.

offset see COMPENSATE.

oft see OFTEN.

often, frequently, oft, oftentimes mean again and again in more or less close succession.

Often tends to stress the number of times a thing occurs without regard to the interval of recurrence <they *often* come to dinner>. ***ant*** seldom

Frequently usually emphasizes repetition, especially at short intervals <saw her as *frequently* as he could>. ***ant*** rarely, seldom

Oft, close to *often* in meaning, is used chiefly in compound adjectives <an *oft*-told tale> or occasionally in formal discourse <a man *oft* seen but seldom understood>.

Oftentimes may be preferred for intonational reasons or as a more florid word <a demeanor *oftentimes* vague and distracted>.

oftentimes see OFTEN.

oily see FULSOME.

old, ancient, venerable, antique, antiquated, antediluvian, archaic, obsolete mean having come into existence or use in the more or less distant past.

Old may apply to either actual or relative length of existence <an *old* sweater of mine>. ***ant*** new

Ancient applies to occurrence, existence, or use in or survival from the distant past <*ancient* accounts of dragons>. ***ant*** modern

Venerable stresses the hoariness and dignity of great age <the family's *venerable* patriarch>.

Antique applies to what has come down from a former or ancient time <collected *antique* Chippendale furniture>. ***ant*** modern, current

Antiquated implies that something is discredited or outmoded or otherwise inappropriate to the present time <*antiquated* teaching methods>. ***ant*** modernistic, modish

Antediluvian suggests that something is so antiquated and outmoded that it might have come from the time before the flood and Noah's ark <an *antediluvian* mode of travel>.

Archaic implies that something has the character or characteristics of a much earlier time <the play used *archaic* language to convey a sense of period>. ***ant*** up-to-date

Obsolete implies qualities that have gone out of currency or habitual practice <this nuclear missile will make all others *obsolete*>. ***ant*** current

oleaginous see FULSOME.

oligarchy, aristocracy, plutocracy mean government by, or a state governed by, the few.

Oligarchy is applicable to any government or state in which power is openly or virtually in the hands of a favored few <the many *oligarchies* of ancient Greece>.

Aristocracy basically and historically implies the rule of the best citizens, but in its more usual use it implies power vested in a privileged class, often regarded as superior in birth and breeding <a revolution that toppled the *aristocracy*>.

Plutocracy implies concentration of power in the hands of the wealthy and is regularly derogatory <successful attempts to prevent the state from becoming a *plutocracy*>.

ominous, portentous, fateful mean having a menacing or threatening aspect.

Ominous implies a menacing, alarming character foreshadowing evil or disaster <*ominous* rumbling from a dormant volcano>.

Portentous suggests being frighteningly big or impressive but not threatening <the *portentous* voice of the host of a televised mystery series>.

Fateful stresses momentousness or decisive importance <the *fateful* conference that led to war>.

omit see NEGLECT.

omnipresent, ubiquitous mean present or existent everywhere.

Omnipresent in its strict sense is a divine attribute equivalent to *immanent,* but more commonly it implies presence or prevalence <the residents of that neighborhood have an *omnipresent* sense of fear>.

Ubiquitous implies a quality being so active or so numerous as to seem to be everywhere <*ubiquitous* tourists toting their *omnipresent* cameras>.

onerous, burdensome, oppressive, exacting mean imposing hardship.

Onerous stresses laboriousness and heaviness and is likely to imply irksomeness and distastefulness <the *onerous* task of informing the family of his death>.

Burdensome suggests a quality that causes physical and especially mental strain <*burdensome* government regulations>. ***ant*** light

Oppressive implies extreme and often intolerable harshness or severity in what is imposed <found the pressure to conform socially *oppressive*>. ***ant*** unoppressive

Exacting implies rigor or sternness or extreme fastidiousness in the one demanding and extreme care and precision in the one who or thing that meets these demands <an *exacting* employer>. ***ant*** unexacting

onlooker see SPECTATOR.

onset see ATTACK *n* 1.

onslaught see ATTACK *n* 1.

onward, forward, forth mean in the act of advancing or going ahead, as in a movement, progression, series, or sequence.

Onward can stress progress or advance toward a definite goal, end, or place <struggled ever *onward* and upward>.

Forward more definitely implies movement or advance with reference to what lies before rather than behind <an event to which we all look *forward*> or in a succession as of incidents or steps <episodes that moved the plot slowly *forward*>. ***ant*** backward

Forth, often interchangeable with *forward,* may imply a bringing forward (as into knowledge, availability, or view) of something previously obscured <set *forth* the charges against them>.

open 1. see FRANK. **2.** see LIABLE.

opiate see ANODYNE 2.

opinion, view, belief, conviction, persuasion, sentiment mean a judgment one holds to be true.

Opinion implies a conclusion thought out yet open to dispute <each expert seemed to be of a different *opinion*>.

View suggests an opinion more or less colored by the feeling, sentiment, or bias of the holder <very assertive in stating his *views*>.

Belief implies deliberate acceptance and intellectual assent <a firm *belief* in a supreme being>.

Conviction applies to a firmly and seriously held belief <a *conviction* that she was right>.

Persuasion suggests a belief grounded on assurance often arising from feelings or wishes rather than from evidence or arguments of its truth <was of the *persuasion* that Republicans were better for business>.

Sentiment suggests a settled opinion reflective of one's feelings <her feminist *sentiments* were well-known>.

opponent, antagonist, adversary mean one who expresses or manifests an opposite position.

Opponent implies little more than position on the other side, as in a debate, election, contest, or conflict <*opponents* of the project cite cost as a factor>. ***ant*** exponent, proponent

Antagonist implies sharper, often more personal, opposition in a struggle for supremacy <a formidable *antagonist* in the struggle for corporate control>. ***ant*** supporter

Adversary may carry an additional implication of active hostility <two peoples that have been bitter *adversaries* for centuries>. ***ant*** ally

opportune see SEASONABLE.

oppose, combat, resist, withstand, antagonize mean to set oneself against someone or something.

Oppose can apply to a range, from mere objection to bitter hostility or active warfare <*opposed* the plan to build a nuclear power plant>.

Combat stresses the forceful or urgent nature of actively countering something <*combat* the disease by educating the public>. ***ant*** champion, defend

Resist implies an overt recognition of a hostile or threatening force and a positive effort to counteract, ward off, or repel it

<struggled valiantly to *resist* the temptation>. ***ant*** submit, abide

Withstand suggests a more passive, yet often successful, resistance <unable to *withstand* peer pressure>.

Antagonize implies an arousing of resistance or hostility in another <statements that *antagonized* even his own supporters>. ***ant*** conciliate

opposite, contradictory, contrary, antithetical mean being so far apart as to be or seem irreconcilable.

Opposite applies to things that stand in sharp contrast or in conflict <they held *opposite* views on foreign aid>. ***ant*** same

Contradictory applies to two things that completely negate each other so that if one is true or valid the other must be untrue or invalid <made *contradictory* predictions about the stock market>. ***ant*** corroboratory, confirmatory

Contrary implies extreme divergence or diametrical opposition of such things as opinions, motives, intentions, or ideas <*contrary* accounts of the late president's character>.

Antithetical stresses clear and unequivocally diametrical opposition <a law that is *antithetical* to the basic idea of democracy>.

oppress see WRONG.

oppressive see ONEROUS.

opprobrium see DISGRACE.

option see CHOICE *n*.

opulent 1. see LUXURIOUS. **2.** see RICH.

oracular see DICTATORIAL.

oral 1. see VOCAL.

2. Oral, verbal mean involving the use of words.

Oral, the narrower term, implies utterance and speech and is distinctively applicable to whatever is delivered, communicated, transacted, or carried on directly from one to another by word of mouth <an *oral* examination>.

Verbal stresses the use of words and may apply to what is either spoken or written <situations in which signals replace *verbal* communication>.

orbit see RANGE.

ordain see DICTATE.

order 1. Order, arrange, marshal, organize, systematize, methodize mean to put persons or things into their proper places in relation to each other.

Order suggests a straightening out so as to eliminate confusion <*ordered* her business affairs before going on extended leave>. ***ant*** disorder

Arrange implies a setting in a fit, suitable, or right sequence, relationship, or adjustment <a bouquet of elaborately *arranged* flowers>. ***ant*** derange, disarrange

Marshal suggests a gathering and arranging in preparation for a particular operation or for effective management or use <an argument won by carefully *marshalled* facts>.

Organize implies an arranging so that the whole aggregate works as a unit in which each element has a proper place and function <*organized* the volunteers into teams>. ***ant*** disorganize

Systematize implies an arranging according to a definite and predetermined scheme <billing procedures that have yet to be *systematized*>.

Methodize suggests the imposing of an orderly procedure rather than a fixed scheme <*methodizes* every aspect of her daily living>.

2. see COMMAND.

ordinance see LAW.

ordinary see COMMON.

organize see ORDER.

orifice see APERTURE.

origin, source, inception, root, provenance mean the point at which something begins its course or existence.

Origin applies to the things or persons from which something is ultimately derived and often to the causes operating before the thing itself comes into being <an investigation into the *origins* of baseball>.

Source applies more often to the point where something springs into being <the *source* of the Nile>. ***ant*** termination, outcome

Inception stresses the beginning of the existence of something without implying anything about causes <the business has been a success since its *inception*>. ***ant*** termination

Root suggests a first, ultimate, or fundamental source often not readily discerned <a need to find the real *root* of violence>.

original see NEW.

originate see SPRING.

ornament see ADORN.

oscillate see SWING.

ostensible see APPARENT.

ostentatious see SHOWY.

otiose see VAIN.

oust see EJECT.

out-and-out see OUTRIGHT.

outcome see EFFECT.

outdo see EXCEED.

outer, outward, outside, external, exterior mean being or placed without something.

Outer tends to retain its comparative force and apply to what is farther out from something described as *inner* <the *outer*

layer of skin is called the epidermis> or is farther than another thing from a center <shed one's *outer* garments>. ***ant*** inner

Outward commonly implies motion or direction away from, or the reverse of, what is inward <given to *outward* display> or implies what is apparent, as opposed to what is within or is spiritual or mental <an *outward* show of courage belied his inward terror>. ***ant*** inward

Outside usually implies a position on or a reference to the outer parts or surface of a thing <a shutter covered the *outside* of the window>; it also tends to apply to what is beyond some implied limit <looked for causes in *outside* influences>. ***ant*** inside

External, close to *outside* in meaning, may be preferred when location beyond or away from the thing under consideration is implied <directed their attention to *external* events>. ***ant*** internal

Exterior, also close to *outside,* may be preferred when location on the surface or outer limits of the thing is implied <gave the *exterior* of the building a fresh coat of paint>. ***ant*** interior

outfit see FURNISH.

outlandish see STRANGE.

outline, contour, profile, silhouette mean the line that bounds and gives form to something.

Outline applies to a continuous line marking the outer limits or edges of a body or mass <chalk *outlines* of the bodies on the sidewalk>.

Contour stresses the quality (such as smooth, curved, rough, or irregular) of an outline or a bounding surface <a car with smoothly flowing *contours*>.

Profile suggests a representation of something in side view in simple outline <drew a *profile* of his daughter> or a varied and sharply defined outline against a lighter background <a ship in *profile* against the sky> or sometimes a nonmaterial outline, such as one built up of data <furnished a *profile* of the operation>.

Silhouette suggests a shape, especially of a head or figure, with all detail blacked out in shadow and only the outline clearly defined <a photograph of two figures in *silhouette* on a mountain ridge>.

outlook see PROSPECT.

outrage see OFFEND.

outrageous, monstrous, heinous, atrocious mean enormously bad or horrible.

Outrageous implies exceeding the limits of what is right or decent or bearable or tolerable <*outrageous* terrorist acts against civilians>.

Monstrous applies to what is inconceivably, abnormally, or fantastically wrong, absurd, or horrible <a *monstrous* waste of the taxpayers' money>.

Heinous implies such flagrant evil or such conspicuous enormity as inevitably excites hatred or horror <*heinous* crimes that exceeded normal wartime actions>. ***ant*** venial

Atrocious implies such merciless cruelty, savagery, or contempt of ordinary values as excites condemnation <decent people cannot condone such *atrocious* treatment of prisoners>. ***ant*** humane, noble

outright, out-and-out, unmitigated, arrant mean without limit or qualification.

Outright implies that what is described has gone to the extreme and can be made neither better nor worse or is past recall <he is an *outright* fool>.

Out-and-out applies to what is completely as described at all times or in every part or from every point of view <this is an *out-and-out* fraud>.

Unmitigated applies to what is or seems to be so utterly what it is as to be beyond the possibility of being lessened, softened, or relieved <an *unmitigated* evil>.

Arrant applies to something that is all that is implied by the term, usually a term of abuse, that follows <an *arrant* coward>.

outside see OUTER.

outstanding see NOTICEABLE.

outstrip see EXCEED.

outward see OUTER.

outwit see FRUSTRATE.

overbearing see PROUD.

overcome see CONQUER.

overdue see TARDY.

overflow see TEEM.

overlook see NEGLECT.

oversight, supervision, surveillance mean a careful watching.

Oversight attributes the power or right to act to the watcher and implies the intent to assure the good condition or effective functioning of what is watched <a manager with *oversight* of all phases of the operation>.

Supervision carries a much stronger implication of authoritative powers and responsibilities <responsible for the *supervision* of the entire district>.

Surveillance implies a close, detailed, even prying watch kept on something and especially on a person felt likely to require unexpected or immediate attention <police *surveillance* of known criminals>.

overstatement see EXAGGERATION.

overthrow see CONQUER.

own 1. see ACKNOWLEDGE. **2.** see HAVE.
ozone see AIR.

P

pacific, peaceable, peaceful, irenic, pacifist, pacifistic mean affording or promoting peace.

Pacific applies chiefly to persons or to utterances, acts, influences, or ideas that tend to maintain peace or conciliate strife <adopted a *pacific* attitude at the conference>. ***ant*** bellicose

Peaceable stresses enjoyment of peace as a way of life and may imply absence of any intent to behave aggressively <a *peaceable* gathering>. ***ant*** contentious, acrimonious

Peaceful suggests absence of strife or contention as well as of all disturbing influences <*peaceful* solitude>.

Irenic, often used with relation to religious controversy, may describe attitudes and measures likely to allay dispute <issued an *irenic* interpretation of the canon>. ***ant*** acrimonious

Pacifist stresses opposition, and especially active opposition, to war or violence, typically on moral or conscientious grounds <a *pacifist* group on the campus>. ***ant*** combative

Pacifistic is close to *pacifist,* but ordinarily applies only to things <a determinedly *pacifistic* outlook>.

pacifist see PACIFIC.
pacifistic see PACIFIC.

pacify, appease, placate, mollify, propitiate, conciliate mean to ease or quiet the anger or disturbance of someone or something.

Pacify suggests a smoothing or calming or the quelling of insurrection <a sincere apology seemed to *pacify* his rage>. ***ant*** anger

Appease implies the quieting of agitation or insistent demands by making concessions <nothing seemed to *appease* their appetite for territorial expansion>. ***ant*** exasperate

Placate suggests a changing of resentment or bitterness to goodwill <bought flowers to *placate* his irate wife>. ***ant*** enrage

Mollify implies the softening of anger or the soothing of hurt feelings by positive action <a promise of a hearing *mollified* the demonstrators>. ***ant*** exasperate

Propitiate implies the averting of anger or malevolence or the winning of favor especially of a powerful person <*propitiated* his mother-in-law by getting the clean-cut look>.

Conciliate suggests the ending of an estrangement by persuasion, concession, or settling of differences <America's efforts to *conciliate* the nations of the Middle East>. ***ant*** antagonize

pains see EFFORT.

palatable, appetizing, savory, tasty, toothsome mean agreeable or pleasant to the taste.

Palatable often applies to something that is unexpectedly found to be agreeable <surprised to find Indian food quite *palatable*>. ***ant*** unpalatable, distasteful

Appetizing suggests a whetting of the appetite and applies to aroma and appearance as well as taste <select from a cart filled with *appetizing* desserts>. ***ant*** disgusting, nauseating

Savory applies to both taste and aroma and suggests piquancy and often spiciness <egg rolls filled with various *savory* fillings>. ***ant*** bland

Tasty implies a pronounced and appetizing taste <stale shrimp that were far from *tasty*>. ***ant*** bland

Toothsome stresses the notion of agreeableness and sometimes implies tenderness or lusciousness <a dazzling array of *toothsome* hors d'oeuvres>.

palate see TASTE 2.

pale 1. Pale, pallid, ashen, ashy, wan, livid mean deficient in natural or healthy color or in vividness or intensity of hue.

Pale implies relative nearness to white and deficiency of depth and brilliance of color <her dress was a very *pale* rose>.

Pallid is likely to suggest deprivation of natural color and connote abnormality <his *pallid* face reveals the strain he has been under>.

Ashen and *ashy* imply a pale grayish color suggestive of ashes and stress an unwholesome or portentous pallor <the *ashen* sky of a winter's afternoon> <hoping for color to return to his *ashy* cheeks>.

Wan suggests the blanched appearance associated with waning vitality and is likely to denote a sickly paleness <the *wan* paleness of the fading moon>.

Livid basically means leaden-hued and is used of things that have lost their normal coloring and assumed a dull grayish tinge <the *livid* red of the sun seen through fog>.

2. Pale, anemic, bloodless mean weak and thin in substance or vital qualities, as though drained of blood.

Pale stresses lack of color, character, vigor, force, or energy; it may also imply a failure to measure up to the requirements of a type or standard <a *pale* imitation of the original>. ***ant*** brilliant

Anemic implies deficiency in the elements that contribute especially to intellectual or spiritual vigor or richness <the *anemic* support of the arts in this country>. ***ant*** full-blooded, florid

Bloodless suggests the absence of such qualities as vitality, warmth, color, and human emotion that are necessary to life or lifelikeness <presented a *bloodless* portrait of the great national hero>. ***ant*** sanguine, plethoric

pall see SATIATE.

pallid see PALE 1.

palpable see PERCEPTIBLE.

palpate see TOUCH.

palter see LIE.

pamper see INDULGE.

pandemonium see DIN.

panegyric see ENCOMIUM.

panic see FEAR.

parade see SHOW 2.

parallel *adj* see SIMILAR.

parallel *n* **1.** see COMPARISON.

2. Parallel, counterpart, analogue, correlate mean one that corresponds to or closely resembles another.

Parallel implies that the two things being compared are so like that their lack of divergence suggests parallel lines <drew a *parallel* between their experiences>.

Counterpart suggests a complementary and sometimes an obverse relationship <gave the balls to her *counterpart* on the other team>.

Analogue usually implies a more remote likeness and may involve a comparison made to clarify, enlighten, or demonstrate <saw faith in technology as an *analogue* to earlier beliefs in supernatural forces>.

Correlate applies to what corresponds to something else from another point of view or in another order of viewing <debated whether higher interest rates are a *correlate* of economic prosperity>.

paramount see DOMINANT.

parasite, sycophant, toady, hanger-on, leech, sponge mean an obsequious flatterer or self-seeker.

Parasite applies to one who clings to a person of wealth, power, or influence or is useless to society <a jet-setter with the usual entourage of *parasites*>.

Sycophant adds to this a strong suggestion of fawning, flattery, or adulation <a military dictator who would only listen to *sycophants*>.

Toady emphasizes the servility and snobbery of the self-seeker <the president's own *toady* made others grovel>.

Hanger-on, usually contemptuous, refers to someone who habitually keeps company with or depends unduly on others for favors <kept tripping on her *hangers-on*>.

Leech stresses persistence in clinging to or bleeding another for one's own advantage <*leeches* who abandoned her when the money ran out>.

Sponge stresses the parasitic laziness, dependence, opportunism, and pettiness of the cadger <her brother, a shiftless *sponge,* often came by for a free meal>.

parcel see GROUP.

pardon *vb* see EXCUSE.

pardon *n* **Pardon, amnesty, absolution** mean a lifting of penalty or punishment.

Pardon, often ambiguous, denotes a release not from guilt but from a penalty imposed by an authority <received a *pardon* from the governor at the last moment>. ***ant*** punishment

Amnesty implies a pardon that is extended to a whole class or to a community <declared an *amnesty* for all tax evaders>.

Absolution in ecclesiastical and especially Roman Catholic use refers to a pardon extended for sins confessed and atoned for and implies that the eternal punishment for sin has been removed <asked for and was granted *absolution*>. ***ant*** condemnation

pardonable see VENIAL.

parley see CONFER.

parody see CARICATURE.

paroxysm see FIT *n*.

parsimonious see STINGY.

part *n* **Part, portion, piece, member, division, section, segment, fragment** mean something less than the whole to which it belongs.

Part is a general term appropriate when indefiniteness is required <they ran only *part* of the way>. ***ant*** whole

Portion implies an assigned or allotted part <cut the pie into six *portions*>.

Piece stresses separateness and applies to a separate or detached part of a whole <a puzzle with 500 *pieces*>.

Member suggests one of the functional units composing a body <an arm is a bodily *member*>.

Division applies to a large or diversified part made as if by cutting <the manufacturing *division* of the company>.

Section is like *division* but applies to a relatively small or uniform part <the entertainment *section* of the newspaper>.

Segment applies to a part separated or marked out by or as if by natural lines of cleavage <the retired *segment* of the population>.

Fragment applies to a part produced by or as if by breaking off or shattering or left after the rest has been used, eaten, worn away, or lost <only a *fragment* of the play still exists>.

part *vb* see SEPARATE.

partake see SHARE.

participate see SHARE.

particle, bit, mite, smidgen, whit, atom, iota, jot, tittle mean a very small or insignificant piece or part.

Particle implies an amount of a substance or quality that is within the range of visual or mental perception <a rumor without a *particle* of truth>.

Bit suggests the least feasible amount, extent, or degree <a movie that was a *bit* too violent>.

Mite may stress either smallness in size or minuteness in amount <doesn't have a *mite* of suspicion>.

Smidgen may go even further in stressing minuteness or scarcity <left them without even a *smidgen* of hope>.

Whit, used chiefly in negative phrases, implies the least conceivable amount <cared not a *whit* about their opinion>.

Atom suggests the very smallest size or amount possible <not an *atom* of dust escaped his attention>.

Iota and *jot* are used interchangeably to mean the smallest or most minute detail or amount <tried to remove the last *iota* of doubt> <added not a *jot* to their knowledge>.

Tittle has the same meaning as *iota* and *jot* but is usually used in the phrase *jot or tittle* <didn't care a jot or *tittle* about the opinions of others>.

particular *adj* **1.** see CIRCUMSTANTIAL. **2.** see NICE. **3.** see SINGLE. **4.** see SPECIAL.

particular *n* see ITEM.

partisan see FOLLOWER.

partner, copartner, colleague, ally, confederate mean an associate.

Partner implies an associate in business or one of two associates, as in some games, a dance, or marriage <now, all change *partners*>. ***ant*** rival

Copartner may add little to *partner,* or it may distinctively imply a fellow partner <the actions of one partner may commit his or her *copartners*>.

Colleague applies usually to an associate in office or in professional or academic relations <presented a lecture to her *colleagues*>.

Ally suggests an often temporary association in a common cause <agreed to act as *allies* for the duration of the conflict>. ***ant*** adversary

Confederate often suggests a closer or more permanent union for strength and solidarity <joined his *confederates* in a toast to the new undertaking>. ***ant*** adversary

pass see JUNCTURE.

passion 1. see FEELING.

2. Passion, fervor, ardor, enthusiasm, zeal mean intense emotion compelling action.

Passion applies to an emotion that is deeply stirring or ungovernable <developed a *passion* for reading>.
Fervor implies a warm and steady emotion <read the poem aloud with great *fervor*>.
Ardor suggests warm and excited feeling likely to be fitful or short-lived <the *ardor* of their honeymoon soon faded>. ***ant*** coolness, indifference
Enthusiasm applies to lively or eager interest in or admiration for a proposal or cause or activity <never showed much *enthusiasm* for sports>. ***ant*** apathy
Zeal implies energetic and unflagging pursuit of an aim or devotion to a cause <preaches with the *zeal* of the converted>. ***ant*** apathy

passionate see IMPASSIONED.
passive see INACTIVE.
pastoral see RURAL.
pat see SEASONABLE.
patch see MEND.
patent see EVIDENT.
pathetic see MOVING.
patrimony see HERITAGE.
pathos, poignancy, bathos mean a quality that moves one to pity or sorrow.
Pathos, common in critical and literary use, typically suggests the arousal of aesthetic rather than acute and personal emotional response <a drama more noted for its *pathos* than its plot>.
Poignancy may be preferred when the genuineness of the thing's emotional quality and of the emotions it arouses need to be stressed <felt the full *poignancy* of their last days together>.
Bathos is often applied to a false or pretentious pathos and typically implies a maudlin sentimentality more likely to arouse disgusted contempt than the emotion it seeks to elicit <could not tell the story of his last failed romance without descending into *bathos*>.

patois see DIALECT.
pattern see MODEL.
pause, recess, respite, lull, intermission mean a temporary cessation.
Pause stresses the fact of stopping and ordinarily implies an expectation of resumption, as of movement or activity <spoke during a *pause* in the music>.
Recess implies a temporary suspension of work or activity <children playing during the morning school *recess*>.
Respite implies a period of relief, as from labor, suffering, or

war, or of delay, as before being sentenced or before having to pay money due <enjoyed the brief *respite* between attacks>.
Lull implies a temporary cessation or, more often, marked decline, as in the violence of a storm or in business activity <the storm strengthened again after a *lull*>.
Intermission implies a break in continuity and is especially applicable to an interval available for some new or special activity <no one should work day after day without *intermission*>.

paw see TOUCH.

pay *vb* **Pay, compensate, remunerate, satisfy, reimburse, indemnify, repay, recompense** mean to give money or its equivalent in return for something.
Pay implies the discharge of an obligation incurred <we *pay* taxes in exchange for government services>.
Compensate implies a counterbalancing of services rendered or help given <an attorney well *compensated* for her services>.
Remunerate more clearly suggests a paying for services rendered and may extend to payment that is generous or not contracted for <promised to *remunerate* the searchers handsomely>.
Satisfy implies the paying of what is demanded or required by law <all creditors will be *satisfied* in full>.
Reimburse implies a return of money that has been expended for another's benefit <the company will *reimburse* employees for expenses incurred>.
Indemnify implies the promised or actual making good of a loss, injury, or damage suffered through accident, disaster, or warfare <the government cannot *indemnify* the families of military casualties>.
Repay stresses the paying back of an equivalent in kind or amount <*repay* a loan>.
Recompense suggests due return in amends, friendly repayment, or reward <the hotel *recompensed* us with a free bottle of champagne>.

pay *n* see WAGE.

peaceable see PACIFIC.

peaceful 1. see CALM. **2.** see PACIFIC.

peak see SUMMIT.

peculiar 1. see CHARACTERISTIC. **2.** see STRANGE.

pecuniary see FINANCIAL.

pedantic, academic, scholastic, bookish mean too narrowly concerned with learned matters.
Pedantic implies ostentation in learning and stodginess in expression and may connote absorption in scholarly matters to the exclusion of truly significant issues <gave an infuriatingly *pedantic* discourse on the matter>.

Academic is likely to stress abstractness and a lack of practical experience and interests that deprive one of the ability to deal with realities <the economist's concerns seemed more *academic* than practical>.

Scholastic is likely to imply aridity, formalism, adherence to the letter, and sometimes subtlety <presented a hopelessly *scholastic* argument>.

Bookish may suggest learning derived from books rather than actualities <had about him an effete, *bookish* air>.

peer see GAZE.

peeve see IRRITATE.

pejorative see DEROGATORY.

penalize, fine, amerce, mulct mean to punish by depriving of something.

Penalize usually presupposes a violation of an order, rule, or law intended to maintain discipline or ensure propriety; it also implies a penalty such as forfeiture of money, advantage, or privilege or imposition of a handicap <*penalize* late taxpayers by adding interest to their bills>.

Fine implies a monetary penalty fixed within certain limits by law <the library *fines* careless borrowers a few cents a day to encourage prompt return of books>.

Amerce implies a penalty left to the discretion of the judge and may refer to a nonpecuniary penalty <the judge *amerced* the offender in the sum of fifty dollars>.

Mulct implies subjection to a superior power that can legally or illegally enforce penalties and especially monetary penalties for failure to conform to its discipline or edicts and is likely to stress the helplessness of the victim and the arbitrariness of the penalizing power <a rash of arson designed to *mulct* the terrorized shopkeepers>.

penchant see LEANING.

penetrate see ENTER.

penetration see DISCERNMENT.

penitence, repentance, contrition, compunction, remorse mean regret for sin or wrongdoing.

Penitence implies sad and humble realization of and regret for one's misdeeds <willing to forgive when faced with the outward signs of *penitence*>.

Repentance adds the implication of an awareness of one's shortcomings and a resolve to change <a complete change of character accompanied his *repentance*>.

Contrition stresses the sorrowful regret that accompanies true penitence <the beatings were usually followed by tearful expressions of *contrition*>.

Compunction implies a painful sting of conscience for past or especially for contemplated wrongdoing <have no *compunctions* about taking back what is mine>.

Remorse suggests prolonged and insistent self-reproach and mental anguish for past wrongs and especially for those whose consequences cannot be remedied <swindlers are not usually plagued by feelings of *remorse*>.

pensive see THOUGHTFUL 1.

penurious see STINGY.

penury see POVERTY.

perceive see SEE 1.

perceptible, sensible, palpable, tangible, appreciable, ponderable mean apprehensible as real or existent.

Perceptible applies to what can be discerned, often to a minimal extent, by the senses <a *perceptible* difference in sound>. ***ant*** imperceptible

Sensible applies to whatever is clearly apprehended through the senses or impresses itself strongly on the mind <a *sensible* change in weather>. ***ant*** insensible

Palpable applies either to what has physical substance or to what is obvious and unmistakable <the tension in the air was almost *palpable*>. ***ant*** insensible, impalpable

Tangible suggests what is capable of being handled or grasped either physically or mentally <submitted the gun as *tangible* evidence>. ***ant*** intangible

Appreciable applies to what is distinctly discernible by the senses or definitely measurable <an *appreciable* increase in temperature>. ***ant*** inappreciable

Ponderable suggests having definitely measurable weight or importance especially as distinguished from what is so intangible as to elude such determination <exerted a *ponderable* influence on world events>.

perception see DISCERNMENT.

peremptory see MASTERFUL.

perennial see CONTINUAL.

perfect, whole, entire, intact mean not lacking or faulty in any respect.

Perfect implies the soundness and the excellence of every part, element, or quality of a thing, frequently as an unattainable or theoretical state <a *perfect* set of teeth>. ***ant*** imperfect

Whole suggests a completeness or perfection that can be sought and attained or lost and regained <an experience that made him feel a *whole* man again>.

Entire implies perfection deriving from integrity, soundness, or completeness <recorded the *entire* Beethoven corpus>. ***ant*** impaired

Intact implies retention of an original or natural perfection that might easily have been lost <somehow the building survived the storm *intact*>. ***ant*** defective

perfervid see IMPASSIONED.

perfidious see FAITHLESS.

perform, execute, discharge, accomplish, achieve, effect, fulfill mean to carry out or into effect.

Perform implies action that follows established patterns or procedures or fulfills agreed-upon requirements and often connotes special skill or experience <*performed* gymnastics on the parallel bars>.

Execute stresses the carrying out of what exists in design or in intent <*executed* the heist exactly as planned>.

Discharge implies execution and completion of appointed duties or tasks <*discharged* his duties promptly and effectively>.

Accomplish stresses the successful completion of a process rather than the means of carrying it out <*accomplished* in a year what had taken others a lifetime>. ***ant*** undo

Achieve adds to *accomplish* the implication of conquered difficulties <a nation struggling to *achieve* greatness>. ***ant*** fail

Effect adds to *achieve* an emphasis on the inherent force in the agent capable of surmounting obstacles <a dynamic personality who *effected* sweeping reforms>.

Fulfill implies a complete realization of implied responsibilities or plans or ends or possibilities <the rare epic that *fulfills* its ambitions>. ***ant*** frustrate, fail in

perfume see FRAGRANCE.

perilous see DANGEROUS.

perimeter, periphery, circuit, compass, circumference mean a continuous line enclosing an area.

Perimeter applies to the line bounding any area or the surface bounding a solid <walked the *perimeter* of the property every evening>.

Periphery, though sometimes interchangeable with *perimeter,* is likely to apply to the actual edge, border, or boundary of something concrete <explore the *periphery* of the island> or to limits which cannot be exceeded <the *periphery* of consciousness>.

Circuit applies to a route, or often a journey, around a periphery or sometimes to any path that comes back to its point of beginning <the hands of the clock made a *circuit* of the face>.

Compass is likely to refer to the area or space enclosed within a perimeter or to the ground that figuratively might be passed over by the leg of a compass in describing a circle <taxed all the land within the *compass* of the town>.

Circumference applies to the line that describes a circle or an ellipse or the length of such a line, or to something felt to have a center <built fires within the *circumference* of the camp>.

period, epoch, era, age mean a portion or division of time.

Period may designate an extent of time of any length <*periods* of economic prosperity>.

Epoch applies to a period begun or set off by some significant or striking quality, change, or series of events <the steam engine marked a new *epoch* in industry>.

Era suggests a period of history marked by a new or distinct order of things <the *era* of global communications>.

Age is used frequently of a fairly well-defined period dominated by a prominent figure or feature <the *age* of Samuel Johnson>.

periodic see INTERMITTENT.

periphery see PERIMETER.

perjure, forswear mean to violate one's oath or make a false swearer of oneself.

Perjure, in general as distinct from technical legal use, implies making a liar of oneself whether under oath or not <refused to *perjure* himself on anyone's behalf>.

Forswear implies a violation of an oath, promise, or vow or sometimes of something, such as one's principles or beliefs, that is as sacred as an oath <*forswore* the laws of her country in order to save the life of her child>.

permanent see LASTING.

permit see LET.

permission, leave, sufferance mean sanction granted by one in authority to act or to do something.

Permission implies the power or authority to grant or refuse what is asked <refused strangers *permission* to hunt on his land>. ***ant*** prohibition

Leave may be preferred to *permission* in conventionally courteous phrases <by your *leave,* we'll be going now> or in official reference to permission to leave one's duties <he was given *leave* to take care of emergency business>.

Sufferance implies a neglect or refusal to forbid or interfere and therefore suggests a tacit permission that may be withdrawn <you are here on *sufferance,* and must watch quietly if you are to stay>.

pernicious, baneful, noxious, deleterious, detrimental mean exceedingly harmful.

Pernicious implies irreparable harm done through evil or insidious corrupting or undermining <the claim that pornography has a *pernicious* effect on society>. ***ant*** innocuous

Baneful implies injury through poisoning or destroying influence <the *baneful* notion that discipline destroys creativity>. ***ant*** beneficial

Noxious applies to what is both offensive and injurious to the health of body or mind <*noxious* fumes emanating from a chemical plant>. ***ant*** wholesome, sanitary

Deleterious applies to what has an often unsuspected or unanticipated harmful effect, especially on the living body <megadoses of vitamins can have *deleterious* effects>. ***ant*** salutary

Detrimental implies something obviously, but not necessarily extremely, harmful to the thing it affects <the *detrimental* effects of prolonged fasting>. ***ant*** beneficial

perpendicular see VERTICAL.

perpetual see CONTINUAL.

perplex see PUZZLE.

persecute see WRONG.

persevere, persist mean to continue in a course in the face of difficulty or opposition.

Persevere implies an admirable determination and suggests both refusal to be discouraged, as by failure, doubts, or difficulties, and a steadfast pursuit of an end or undertaking <*persevered* doggedly in his efforts to get good grades>.

Persist often suggests a disagreeable or annoying quality, for it stresses pertinacity more than courage or patience and is likely to imply self-willed opposition to advice, remonstrance, disapproval, or conscience <the infuriating teasing that *persisted* despite all her attempts to stop it>. ***ant*** desist

persist 1. see PERSEVERE. **2.** see CONTINUE.

personality see DISPOSITION.

perspicacious see SHREWD.

perspicuous see CLEAR 2.

persuade see INDUCE.

persuasion see OPINION.

pert see SAUCY.

pertinacious see OBSTINATE.

pertinent see RELEVANT.

perturb see DISCOMPOSE.

perverse see CONTRARY.

pervert see DEBASE.

pessimistic see CYNICAL.

pester see WORRY.

pet see CARESS.

petite see SMALL.

pharisaical see HYPOCRITICAL.

phase, aspect, side, facet, angle mean one of the possible ways of viewing or being presented to view.

Phase implies a change in appearance often without clear reference to an observer <the second *phase* of the investigation>.

Aspect may stress the point of view of an observer and its limitation of what is seen or considered <an article that considers the financial *aspect* of divorce>.

Side stresses one of several aspects from which something may be viewed <a broadcast that told only one *side* of the story>.

Facet implies one of a multiplicity of sides that are similar to one another in some respect <explores the many *facets* of life in New York City>.

Angle suggests an aspect seen from a very restricted or specific point of view <find a fresh *angle* for covering the political convention>.

phenomenal see MATERIAL.

phlegm see EQUANIMITY.

phlegmatic see IMPASSIVE.

phrase, idiom, expression, locution mean a group of words which together express a notion and which may be used as part of a sentence.

Phrase is applicable to any group of words that recurs frequently but is likely to suggest some distinctive quality, such as triteness, pithiness, or pointedness <a poem made up of several trite *phrases* strung together>.

Idiom applies to a combination of word elements which is peculiar to the language in which it occurs either in its grammatical relationships or in its nonliteral meaning <"to keep house," "to catch cold," and "to strike a bargain" are *idioms*>.

Expression may be preferred when reference to a way of expressing oneself is accompanied by a qualifying adjective, phrase, or clause <that's an odd *expression*>.

Locution, a somewhat bookish word, may be chosen when reference is to phrases that are idiomatically peculiar to a language, a group, or a person <a pet *locution* of the author>.

physical 1. see BODILY. **2.** see MATERIAL.

physique, build, habit, constitution mean bodily makeup or type.

Physique applies to the structure, appearance, or strength of the body as characteristic of an individual or a race <a people of sturdy *physique*>.

Build, freely interchangeable with *physique,* may stress the body's conformation, calling attention to such qualities as size, structure, and weight <a horse of chunky *build*>.

Habit implies reference to the body as the outward evidence of characteristics that determine one's physical and mental capabilities and condition <a woman of tranquil mien and languorous *habit*>.

Constitution applies to the makeup of the body as affected by the complex of physical and mental conditions which collectively determine its state <a robust, healthy *constitution*>.

physiognomy see FACE.
picked see SELECT.
pickle see PREDICAMENT.
pictorial see GRAPHIC.
picturesque see GRAPHIC.
piece see PART.
pierce see ENTER.
pietistic see DEVOUT.
piety see FIDELITY.
pilfer see STEAL.
pillage *vb* see RAVAGE.
pillage *n* see SPOIL.
pilot see GUIDE.
pinch see JUNCTURE.
pine see LONG.
pinnacle see SUMMIT.
pious see DEVOUT.
piquant see PUNGENT.
pique *n* see OFFENSE 1.
pique *vb* **1.** see PROVOKE. **2.** see PRIDE.
pitch 1. see THROW. **2.** see PLUNGE.
piteous see PITIFUL.
pithy see CONCISE.
pitiable 1. see PITIFUL. **2.** see CONTEMPTIBLE.
pitiful, piteous, pitiable mean arousing or deserving pity or compassion.

Pitiful applies especially to what excites pity or sometimes commiseration because it is felt to be deeply pathetic <a long line of *pitiful* refugees>, but it can also apply to what excites pitying contempt <a *pitiful* excuse>. ***ant*** cruel

Piteous implies not so much the effect on the observer as the quality in the thing that may excite the pity <heard from afar their *piteous* cries for help>.

Pitiable, otherwise very close to *pitiful*, almost always implies a contemptuous commiseration, though contempt may be weakly or strongly connoted <faced a weak, *pitiable* resistance from the opposition party>.

pittance see RATION.
pity see SYMPATHY.
placate see PACIFY.
place 1. Place, position, location, situation, site, spot, station mean the point or portion of space occupied by or chosen for a thing.

Place, the most general of these terms, carries the implication of having dimensions in space, although the dimensions may be large or small and the limits may not be clearly defined <the *place* where I was born>.

Position can be used in relation to abstract as well as concrete things and usually implies place in relation to something in particular <an instrument used to indicate the *position* of the aircraft>.

Location is used in relation to concrete things and implies a fixed but not necessarily a clearly definite place <knows the *location* of every historical building in town>.

Situation adds to *location* a more specific note about the character of the surroundings <liked the *situation* of the house halfway up the hill>.

Site, close to *situation,* carries a clearer reference to the land on which something, such as a building, a group of buildings, or a town, is built <built the new factory on the *site* of the old one>.

Spot implies a restricted, particular place, clearly defined in extent <called back that she had found the perfect *spot* for the picnic>.

Station suggests the place where a person or thing stands or is set to stand and connotes the accompanying responsibility, as in performance of duty or participation <waiters standing expectantly at their *stations*>.

2. see POSITION 2.

placid see CALM.

plague see WORRY.

plain 1. see COMMON.

2. see EVIDENT.

3. Plain, homely, simple, unpretentious mean free from all ostentation or superficial embellishment.

Plain stresses lack of anything such as ornamentation or affectation likely to catch the attention <a *plain* house on a quiet street>, or it may suggest elegance <the furnishings were *plain* with very simple classic lines> or frugality <she set a *plain* but abundant table> or, with reference to personal appearance, lack of positive beauty that does not go to the extreme of ugliness <drawn to that *plain* and kindly face>. ***ant*** lovely

Homely may suggest easy familiarity or comfortable informality without ostentation <a comfortable, *homely* room>; in application to personal appearance, it implies something between *plain* and *ugly* <a *homely* mutt>. ***ant*** comely, bonny

Simple, very close to *plain* in its references to situations and things, may stress personal choice as the source of the quality described <lived the *simple* life> and regularly connotes lack of complication or ostentation <gave a *simple,* straightforward answer to the question>. ***ant*** elaborate

Unpretentious stresses lack of vanity or affectation and may praise a person <soft-spoken and *unpretentious*> but in reference to a thing may convey either praise or depreciation <an *unpretentious* and battered old car>. ***ant*** pretentious

4. see FRANK.

plan, design, plot, scheme, project mean a method devised for making or doing something or achieving an end.

Plan implies mental formulation and sometimes graphic representation of a method or course of action <studied the *plans* for the proposed industrial park>.

Design often suggests a definite pattern and some degree of achieved order or harmony <*designs* for three new gowns>.

Plot implies a laying out in clearly distinguished sections with attention to their relations and proportions <outlined the *plot* of the new play>.

Scheme stresses calculation of the end in view and may apply to a plan motivated by craftiness and self-interest <a *scheme* to swindle senior citizens of their savings>.

Project often stresses enterprise, imaginative scope, or vision but sometimes connotes ponderous or needless extension <a *project* to develop the waterfront>.

plane see LEVEL.

plastered see DRUNK.

plastic, pliable, pliant, ductile, malleable, adaptable mean susceptible of being modified in form or nature.

Plastic applies to substances soft enough to be molded yet capable of hardening into a final fixed form <*plastic* materials allow the sculptor greater freedom>.

Pliable suggests something easily bent, folded, twisted, or manipulated <headphones that are *pliable* and can be bent to fit>. ***ant*** unpliable

Pliant may stress flexibility and sometimes connote springiness or, in persons, submissiveness <select an athletic shoe with a *pliant* sole>. ***ant*** impliant

Ductile applies to what can be drawn out or extended with ease <copper is one of the most *ductile* of metals>.

Malleable applies to what may be pressed or beaten into shape <the *malleable* properties of gold enhance its value>. ***ant*** refractory

Adaptable implies the capability of being easily modified to suit other conditions, needs, or uses <computer hardware that is *adaptable*>. ***ant*** inadaptable, unadaptable

plausible, credible, believable, colorable, specious mean outwardly acceptable as true or genuine.

Plausible implies genuineness or reasonableness at first sight or hearing usually with some hint of a possibility of being deceived <a *plausible* excuse>. ***ant*** implausible

Credible implies apparent worthiness of belief especially because of support by known facts or sound reasoning <his story

is perfectly *credible* to one who knows his background>. ***ant*** incredible

Believable can apply to what seems true because within the range of possibility or probability or known facts <presented a play with *believable* characters>. ***ant*** unbelievable

Colorable refers to something which on its face seems true or that is capable to some extent of being sustained or justified <a theory supported by *colorable* evidence>.

Specious stresses plausibility usually with a clear implication of dissimulation or fraud <*specious* piety>. ***ant*** valid

play see FUN.

plea see APOLOGY.

pleasant, pleasing, agreeable, grateful, gratifying, welcome mean highly acceptable to or delighting the mind or senses.

Pleasant stresses a quality inherent in an object <a *pleasant* evening>. ***ant*** unpleasant, distasteful

Pleasing, close to *pleasant,* stresses the effect that something has on one <a *pleasing* arrangement of colors>. ***ant*** displeasing, repellent

Agreeable applies to what is in accord with one's tastes or liking <an *agreeable* companion>. ***ant*** disagreeable

Grateful implies satisfaction, relief, or comfort yielded by what is pleasing or agreeable <the fire threw a *grateful* warmth into the room>. ***ant*** obnoxious

Gratifying implies mental pleasure arising usually from a satisfying of one's hopes, desires, conscience, or vanity <a *gratifying* sense of accomplishment>.

Welcome is stronger than *pleasing* and *grateful* in stressing the pleasure given by satisfying a prior need or longing <as *welcome* as rain after a long drought>. ***ant*** unwelcome

pleasing see PLEASANT.

pleasure, delight, joy, delectation, enjoyment mean the agreeable emotion accompanying the possession or expectation of what is good or greatly desired.

Pleasure stresses a feeling of satisfaction or gratification rather than visible happiness <take *pleasure* in one's possessions>. ***ant*** displeasure

Delight usually reverses this emphasis and stresses lively expression of obvious satisfaction <the *delight* of grandparents in a new grandchild>. ***ant*** disappointment, discontent

Joy may imply a more deep-rooted rapturous emotion than either *pleasure* or *delight* <felt a profound *joy* at the sight>. ***ant*** sorrow, misery, abomination

Delectation suggests amusement, diversion, or entertainment in reaction to pleasurable experience <presented a variety of skits for their *delectation*>.

Enjoyment stresses a gratification or happiness resulting from a pleasurable experience <derived great *enjoyment* from her books and her music>. ***ant*** abhorrence

plenary see FULL.

plentiful, ample, abundant, copious mean more than sufficient without being excessive.

Plentiful implies a great or rich supply, often of something that is not regularly or universally available <peaches are *plentiful* this summer>. ***ant*** scanty, scant

Ample implies a generous sufficiency to satisfy a particular requirement <an *ample* amount of food to last the winter>. ***ant*** scant, meager

Abundant suggests an even greater or richer supply than does *plentiful* <has surprisingly *abundant* energy for a woman her age>. ***ant*** scarce

Copious stresses largeness of supply rather than fullness or richness <*copious* examples of bureaucratic waste>. ***ant*** meager

pliable see PLASTIC.

pliant see PLASTIC.

plight see PREDICAMENT.

plot 1. see PLAN.

2. Plot, intrigue, machination, conspiracy, cabal mean a plan secretly devised to accomplish an evil or treacherous end.

Plot implies careful foresight in planning a complex scheme <foiled an assassination *plot*>.

Intrigue suggests secret underhanded maneuvering in an atmosphere of duplicity <finagled the nomination by means of back-room *intrigues*>.

Machination implies a contriving of annoyances, injuries, or evils and imputes hostility or treachery to the contrivers <through *machinations* she pieced together a publishing empire>.

Conspiracy implies a secret agreement among several people, often, but not always, involving treason or great treachery <a *conspiracy* of oil companies to set prices>.

Cabal typically applies to intrigue, often involving persons of some eminence, to accomplish some end favorable to its members but injurious to those affected <the infamous *cabal* against General Washington>.

ploy see TRICK.

pluck see FORTITUDE.

plumb see VERTICAL.

plume see PRIDE.

plunder see SPOIL.

plunge, dive, pitch mean to throw oneself or to throw or thrust something forward and downward into or as if into deep water.

Plunge stresses the force of the movement and may imply entry into any penetrable substance or into a state or condition in which one is overwhelmed or immersed <he *plunged* eagerly into the new course of studies>.

Dive suggests intent and may imply more deliberateness and more skill than *plunge* <pilots trained to *dive,* climb, and bank in unison>.

Pitch is likely to stress lack of all intent or design <she caught her heel in a crack and *pitched* to the ground> or may imply the alternate forward and backward plunging of a ship or a spaceship <struggled to control the capsule as it *pitched* and yawed>.

plurality see MAJORITY.

plutocracy see OLIGARCHY.

pogrom see MASSACRE.

poignancy see PATHOS.

poignant 1. see MOVING. **2.** see PUNGENT.

poise see TACT.

poison, venom, virus, toxin, bane mean material that when present in or introduced into a living organism produces a deadly or injurious effect.

Poison is applicable to any deadly or noxious substance (such as strychnine, arsenic, or carbon monoxide) or to anything felt as having a comparable effect <a relationship destroyed by the *poison* of jealousy>.

Venom applies to a poison-containing fluid secreted by an animal such as a snake, bee, or spider and injected into another animal in defensive or predatory action; it may also imply a malignant hostility <a review full of *venom*>.

Virus applies to what is felt to have a corrupting quality poisonous to mind and spirit <the *virus* of apathy> or to a submicroscopic agent of infection working with insidious deadliness or destructiveness <the *virus* that causes AIDS>.

Toxin denotes a complex organic poison produced by a living organism, especially a bacterium or virus <the *toxins* causing the plague>; it may also imply an insidious undermining effect like that of a bacterial toxin <a nation undermined by the *toxin* of ethnic divisiveness>.

Bane may apply to any cause of ruin, destruction, or tribulation <the *bane* of his existence>.

polite see CIVIL.

politic 1. see EXPEDIENT. **2.** see SUAVE.

pollute see CONTAMINATE.

ponder, meditate, muse, ruminate mean to consider or examine attentively or deliberately.

Ponder implies a careful weighing of a problem or prolonged inconclusive thinking about a matter <*pondered* at length the various recourses open to him>.

Meditate implies a definite focusing of one's thoughts on something so as to understand it deeply <the sight of ruins prompted her to *meditate* upon human vanity>.

Muse suggests a more or less focused and persistent but languid and inconclusive turning over in the mind as if in a dream, a fancy, or a remembrance <*mused* upon the adventures of the heroines of gothic novels>.

Ruminate implies going over the same matter in one's thoughts again and again but suggests little of either purposive thinking or rapt absorption <the product of fifty years of *ruminating* on the meaning of life>.

ponderable see PERCEPTIBLE.

ponderous see HEAVY.

pool see MONOPOLY.

popular see COMMON.

portentous see OMINOUS.

portion 1. see FATE. **2.** see PART.

pose *n* **Pose, air, airs, affectation, mannerism** mean an adopted way of speaking or behaving.

Pose implies an attitude deliberately assumed in order to impress others or to call attention to oneself <her shyness was just a *pose*>.

Air may suggest natural acquirement through environment or way of life <years of living in Europe had given him a sophisticated *air*>.

Airs always implies artificiality and pretentiousness <a snobby couple much given to putting on *airs*>.

Affectation applies to a trick of speech or behavior that strikes the observer as insincere <his foreign accent is an *affectation*>.

Mannerism applies to an acquired peculiarity of behavior or speech that has become a habit <gesturing with a cigarette was her most noticeable *mannerism*>.

pose *vb* see PROPOSE.

posit see PRESUPPOSE.

position 1. Position, stand, attitude mean a point of view or way of regarding something.

Position implies reference to a question at issue or a matter about which there is a difference of opinion <the candidate discussed his *position* on the war>.

Stand is similar to *position* but connotes a strongly held or expressed opinion <took a *stand* against continuing any government subsidies>.

Attitude is likely to apply to a point of view colored by personal or party feeling and as much the product of temperament or emotion as of thought or conviction <he took a humorous *attitude* toward life>.

2. Position, place, situation, office, post, job mean employment for wages or salary.

Position may be preferred where the employment suggests higher status or more dignity in the work involved <my brother has a *position* as research director in the new company>.

Place often implies little more than employment for remuneration <she has lost her *place* as a cook>.

Situation adds an emphasis on a place needing to be filled <obtained a *situation* as clerk to the city council>.

Office applies to a position of trust or authority especially in public service <has held the *office* of county treasurer for many years>.

Post suggests a position involving some degree of responsibility <took a *post* as governess in an aristocratic household> or sometimes onerous duties <a new *post* in the foreign service>.

Job, a very general term, stresses the work involved <his first *job* was in public-school teaching> and is especially appropriate when physical labor is in question <seasonal *jobs*>.

3. see PLACE.

positive see SURE.

possess see HAVE.

possible 1. Possible, practicable, feasible mean capable of being realized.

Possible implies that a thing may certainly exist or occur given the proper conditions <contends that life on other planets is *possible*>. ***ant*** impossible

Practicable applies to something that may be easily or readily effected by available means or under current conditions <when television became *practicable*>. ***ant*** impracticable

Feasible applies to what is likely to work or be useful in attaining the end desired <commercially *feasible* for mass production>. ***ant*** unfeasible, infeasible, chimerical

2. see PROBABLE.

post see POSITION 2.

postpone see DEFER.

postulant see NOVICE.

postulate see PRESUPPOSE.

potential see LATENT.

pother see STIR *n.*

pour, stream, gush, sluice mean to send forth or come forth copiously.

Pour suggests abundant emission <it never rains but it *pours*> and may sometimes imply a coming in a course or stream from or as if from a spout <workers *poured* from the subway exits>.

Stream suggests a flowing through a channel or from an opening or the abundance or continuousness of that flow <tears *streamed* from her eyes>.

Gush implies a sudden and copious outpouring of or as if of something released from confinement <blood *gushed* from the wound>.

Sluice implies the operation of something like a sluice or flume for the control of the flow of water and regularly suggests a sudden abundant streaming <rainwater *sluicing* through the gutters>.

poverty, indigence, penury, want, destitution mean the state of one who is poor or with insufficient resources.

Poverty may cover a range from extreme want of necessities to a falling short of having comfortable means <the extreme *poverty* of many Americans>. ***ant*** riches

Indigence implies seriously straitened circumstances and the accompanying hardships <the *indigence* of her years as a graduate student>. ***ant*** affluence, opulence

Penury suggests a cramping or oppressive lack of resources, especially money <given the *penury* of their lifestyle, few suspected their wealth>. ***ant*** luxury

Want implies extreme poverty that deprives one of the basic necessities of life <lived in a constant state of *want*>.

Destitution suggests such utter lack of resources as threatens life through starvation or exposure <the widespread *destitution* in countries beset by famine>. ***ant*** opulence

power 1. Power, force, energy, strength, might mean the ability to exert effort.

Power may imply latent or exerted physical, mental, or spiritual ability to act or be acted upon <the incredible *power* of flowing water>. ***ant*** impotence

Force implies the actual effective exercise of power <used enough *force* to push the door open>.

Energy applies to power expended or capable of being transformed into work <a social reformer of untiring *energy*>.

Strength applies to the quality or property of a person or thing that makes possible the exertion of force or the withstanding of strain, pressure, or attack <use weight training to build your *strength*>. ***ant*** weakness

Might implies great or overwhelming power or force <all of his *might* was needed to budge the boulder>.

2. Power, faculty, function mean the ability of a living being to perform in a given way.

Power may apply to any such ability, whether acting primarily on a physical or a mental level <*power* to think clearly>.

Faculty applies to those powers which are the possession of every normal human being and especially to those that are associated with the mind <sensory *faculties*>.

Function applies to any special ability or capacity of a body part or system or to any special ability of the mind that contributes to the life of a living organism <the primary *function* of the eye is vision>.

3. Power, authority, jurisdiction, control, command, sway, dominion mean the right to govern or rule or determine.

Power implies possession of ability to wield coercive force, permissive authority, or substantial influence <the *power* of the President to mold public opinion>.

Authority implies the granting of power for a specific purpose within specified limits <gave her attorney the *authority* to manage her estate>.

Jurisdiction applies to official power exercised within prescribed limits <the bureau that has *jurisdiction* over Indian affairs>.

Control stresses the power to direct and restrain <you are responsible for students under your *control*>.

Command implies the power to make arbitrary decisions and compel obedience <the respect of the men under his *command*>.

Sway suggests the extent or scope of exercised power or influence <an empire that extended its *sway* over the known world>.

Dominion stresses sovereign power or supreme authority <a world government that would have *dominion* over all nations>.

powerless, impotent mean unable to effect one's purpose, intention, or end.

Powerless denotes merely lack of power or efficacy which is often temporary or relative to a specific purpose or situation <claimed he was *powerless* to make the change>. ***ant*** powerful, efficacious

Impotent implies powerlessness coupled with persistent weakness or complete ineffectiveness <stormed about in *impotent* rage>. ***ant*** potent

practicable 1. Practicable, practical mean capable of being put to use or turned to account.

Practicable applies to what has been proposed and seems feasible but has not been actually tested in use <the question of whether colonies in space are *practicable*>.

Practical applies to things and to persons and implies proven success in meeting the demands of actual living or use <the copier is the most *practical* machine in the office>. ***ant*** impractical, unpractical

2. see POSSIBLE.

practical see PRACTICABLE.

practically see VIRTUALLY.

practice *n* see HABIT.

practice *vb* **Practice, exercise, drill** mean to perform or make perform repeatedly.

Practice may imply a doing habitually or regularly <*practice* one's profession> or a doing over and over for the sake of acquiring proficiency or skill <*practice* on the piano each day>.

Exercise implies a keeping at work and often suggests the resulting strengthening or developing <*exercise* muscles by active play>.

Drill connotes an intent to fix as a habit and stresses repetition as a means of training and discipline <*drill* schoolchildren in pronunciation>.

precarious see DANGEROUS.

precedence see PRIORITY.

preceding, antecedent, foregoing, previous, prior, former, anterior mean being before.

Preceding usually implies being immediately before in time or in place <the last sentence of the *preceding* paragraph>. ***ant*** following

Antecedent applies to order in time and may suggest a causal or logical relation <study the revolution and its *antecedent* economic conditions>. ***ant*** subsequent, consequent

Foregoing applies to what has preceded, chiefly in discourse <a restatement of the *foregoing* paragraph>. ***ant*** following

Previous implies existing or occurring earlier <a *previous* marriage>. ***ant*** subsequent, consequent

Prior often adds to *previous* an implication of greater importance <the prices in this catalogue supersede all *prior* prices>.

Former implies always a definite comparison or contrast with something that is latter <the *former* name of the company>. ***ant*** latter

Anterior applies to position before or ahead of, usually in space, sometimes in time or order <the *anterior* lobe of the brain>. ***ant*** posterior

precept see LAW.

precious see COSTLY.

precipitate, headlong, abrupt, impetuous, sudden mean showing undue haste or unexpectedness.

Precipitate stresses lack of due deliberation and implies prematureness of action <the army's *precipitate* withdrawal>. ***ant*** deliberate

Headlong stresses rashness and lack of forethought of persons or acts <a *headlong* flight from arrest>.

Abrupt stresses curtness and a lack of warning or ceremony <an *abrupt* refusal>. ***ant*** deliberate, leisurely

Impetuous stresses extreme impatience or impulsiveness <it's a bit *impetuous* to propose marriage on the third date>.
Sudden stresses unexpectedness and sharpness or impetuousness of action <flew into a *sudden* rage>.

precipitous see STEEP.

précis see COMPENDIUM.

precise see CORRECT *adj*.

preciseness see PRECISION.

precision, preciseness mean the quality or state of being precise.
Precision regularly suggests a desirable or sought-for quality and connotes such contributing factors as exactitude, care, devoted workmanship, or thoughtful choice <chose her words with great care and *precision*>.
Preciseness more often suggests a less than desirable quality and is likely to connote such contributing factors as rigidity, severity and strictness, or overnicety in observance of rules or proprieties <spoke each sentence with an annoying and intimidating *preciseness*>.

preclude see PREVENT 2.

precursor see FORERUNNER.

predicament, dilemma, quandary, plight, fix, jam, pickle mean a situation from which escape is difficult.
Predicament suggests a difficult situation usually offering no satisfactory or easy solution <the *predicament* posed by increasing automation>.
Dilemma implies a predicament presenting a choice between equally unpleasant or unacceptable alternatives <faced with the *dilemma* of putting him in a nursing home or caring for him ourselves>.
Quandary stresses the puzzlement and perplexity of one faced by a dilemma <in a *quandary* about how to repair it>.
Plight suggests an unfortunate or trying situation <a study of the *plight* of the homeless>.
Fix and *jam* are informal equivalents of *plight* but are more likely to suggest involvement through some error, fault, or wrongdoing <constantly getting their son out of some *fix*> <in a real financial *jam* now that she's lost her job>.
Pickle implies a particularly distressing or sorry plight <conflicting obligations that put me in a real *pickle*>.

predict see FORETELL.

predilection, prepossession, prejudice, bias mean an attitude of mind that predisposes one to favor something or take a stand without full consideration or knowledge.
Predilection implies a strong liking deriving from one's temperament or experience <teenagers with a *predilection* for gory horror movies>.
Prepossession suggests a fixed conception likely to preclude

objective judgment of anything counter to it <a slave to his *prepossessions*>.

Prejudice usually implies an unfavorable prepossession and connotes a feeling rooted in suspicion, fear, or intolerance <strong *prejudices* that are based upon neither reason nor experience>.

Bias implies an unreasoned and unfair distortion of judgment in favor of or against a person or thing <society shows a *bias* against overweight people>.

predispose see INCLINE.

predominant see DOMINANT.

preempt see APPROPRIATE *vb*.

preen see PRIDE.

prefatory see PRELIMINARY.

prefer see OFFER.

preference see CHOICE *n*.

prejudice see PREDILECTION.

preliminary, introductory, preparatory, prefatory mean serving to make ready the way for something else.

Preliminary refers to what must be done or prepared or acquired before some other state or activity becomes possible <held a *preliminary* discussion to set up the agenda for the meeting>.

Introductory refers to the first steps in a process and usually applies to what sets something (such as an action, a work, or a process) going <the speaker's *introductory* remarks established his point of view>. ***ant*** closing, concluding

Preparatory comes close to *preliminary* in meaning but emphasizes preparedness for or against what is expected to ensue <take *preparatory* protective measures against a predicted hurricane>.

Prefatory usually implies a desire on the part of someone to prepare others for such activities as hearing, action, or understanding <made some *prefatory* remarks before introducing the speaker>.

premise see PRESUPPOSE.

preparatory see PRELIMINARY.

prepare, fit, qualify, condition, ready mean to make someone or something ready.

Prepare implies an often complicated process of making or getting ready <*prepare* the ground for a crop>.

Fit implies a making suitable to a particular end or objective <schools that don't *fit* students for further education>.

Qualify stresses the idea that fitness for a particular situation, such as an office, duty, or function, requires the fulfillment of necessary conditions, such as the taking of a course of study, an examination, or an oath <*qualified* for third grade by passing all subjects in second grade>.

Condition implies getting into or bringing to a state that is proper or necessary to satisfy a particular purpose or use <a program that *conditioned* him for the event> or sometimes merely a state that is the inevitable result of past events and impacts <*conditioned* to violence as a way of life>.

Ready emphasizes a putting or getting into order especially for use or action <*ready* a room for a committee meeting>.

preponderant see DOMINANT.

prepossession see PREDILECTION.

prerequisite see REQUIREMENT.

prescribe 1. see DICTATE.

2. Prescribe, assign, define mean to fix arbitrarily or authoritatively.

Prescribe implies an intent to provide explicit direction or clear guidance to those who accept or are bound by one's authority <the Constitution *prescribes* the conditions under which it may be amended>.

Assign implies an arbitrary but not despotic determination, allotment, or designation for the sake of an end such as harmonious functioning, smooth routine, or proper or efficient operation <*assign* a worker to the late shift>.

Define stresses an intent to mark boundaries so as to prevent confusion, conflict, or overlap <*defined* clearly the limits of their freedom>.

prescription see RECEIPT.

present 1. see GIVE. **2.** see OFFER.

presentiment see APPREHENSION.

presently, shortly, soon, directly mean after a little while.

Presently is a term of rather vague implications as to the extent of time indicated <the doctor will be here *presently*>.

Shortly typically implies a following quickly or without avoidable delay <you will receive the report *shortly* after the tests are completed>.

Soon may imply that the thing narrated or predicted happened or will happen without much loss of time <your sister should be home very *soon*>.

Directly implies something happening with little or a minimum of delay <*directly* after graduation he joined the family business>.

preserve see SAVE.

pressure see STRESS.

prestige see INFLUENCE.

presume see PRESUPPOSE.

presuppose, presume, assume, postulate, premise, posit mean to take something for granted as the basis for action or reasoning.

Presuppose may imply a hazy or imperfectly realized belief or an uncritical acceptance <a work which *presupposes* a knowledgeable readership>, or it may imply the necessity of accepting something that must logically be true <an effect *presupposes* a cause>.

Presume suggests that whatever is taken for granted is entitled to belief until it is disproved <*presumed* innocent until proven guilty>.

Assume indicates arbitrary or deliberate acceptance of something not proven or demonstrated <had *assumed* that the family would welcome his return>.

Postulate suggests advancing an assumption that cannot be proven but that is accepted as true because it serves as the basis for some thought or action <ordinary humans must *postulate* the reality of time and space>.

Premise indicates laying down a position from which an inference can be drawn or stating facts and principles fundamental to an argument <an argument *premised* on a belief in the value of a formal education>.

Posit suggests the selecting of a proposition on subjective or arbitrary grounds <a company that *posits* an eager consumer for each of its new products>.

pretend see ASSUME.

pretense, pretension, make-believe mean the offering of something false or deceptive as real or true.

Pretense may denote false show or the evidence of it <a person utterly devoid of *pretense*>, or it may apply to something such as an act, an appearance, or a statement intended to convince others of the reality of something that in fact lacks reality <gained their confidence under false *pretenses*>.

Pretension is often used in the sense of false show and implies an unwarranted belief in one's desirable qualities that results from conceit or self-deception <harbored *pretensions* to wealth and good breeding>.

Make-believe applies chiefly to pretenses that arise out of a strong or vivid imagination, as of a child or poet <delighted in her world of *make-believe*>.

pretension 1. see AMBITION. **2.** see PRETENSE.

pretentious see SHOWY.

pretext see APOLOGY.

pretty see BEAUTIFUL.

prevail see INDUCE.

prevailing, prevalent, rife, current mean generally circulated, accepted, or used in a certain time or place.

Prevailing stresses predominance <the *prevailing* medical opinion regarding smoking>.

Prevalent implies only frequency <dairy farms were once *prevalent* in the area>.

Rife implies a growing prevalence or rapid spread <during the epidemic rumors were *rife*>.

Current applies to what is subject to change and stresses prevalence at a particular time or present moment <the *current* migration towards the Sunbelt>. ***ant*** antique, antiquated, obsolete

prevalent see PREVAILING.

prevaricate see LIE.

prevent 1. Prevent, anticipate, forestall mean to deal with beforehand.

Prevent implies the taking of advance measures against something possible or probable <measures taken to *prevent* an epidemic>.

Anticipate may imply a getting ahead of another by being a precursor or forerunner or the checking of another's intention by acting first <*anticipated* the firing so she decided to quit first>. ***ant*** consummate

Forestall implies a getting ahead so as to stop or interrupt something in its course or to render something ineffective or harmless <a government order that effectively *forestalled* a free election>.

2. Prevent, preclude, obviate, avert, ward off mean to stop something from coming or occurring.

Prevent implies the existence of or the placing of an insurmountable obstacle <the blizzard *prevented* us from going>. ***ant*** permit

Preclude implies the existence of some factor that shuts out every possibility of a thing's happening or taking effect <an accident that *precluded* a career in football>.

Obviate suggests the use of forethought to avoid the necessity for unwelcome or disagreeable actions or measures <his resignation *obviated* the task of firing him>.

Avert implies the taking of immediate and effective measures to avoid, repel, or counteract threatening evil <deftly *averted* a hostile corporate takeover>.

Ward off suggests a close encounter and the use of defensive measures <a hot drink to *ward off* a chill>. ***ant*** conduce to

previous see PRECEDING.

prey see VICTIM.

price, charge, cost, expense mean what is given or asked in exchange for something.

Price designates what is asked, especially for goods and commodities <the *price* of vegetables has risen sharply>.

Charge is close to *price* but applies especially to services <what is the *charge* for hauling away a load of brush> and can apply additionally to what is imposed on one as a financial burden <*charged* them $3.00 each>.

Cost applies to what is given or surrendered for something, often specifically the payment of price asked <the *cost* of a new car>.

Expense often designates the aggregate amount actually disbursed for something <our *expenses* were higher last month>.

priceless see COSTLY.

pride *n* **Pride, vanity, vainglory** mean the quality or feeling of a person who is firmly convinced of his or her own excellence or superiority.

Pride may imply either justified or unjustified self-esteem, and it may refer to real or imagined merit or superiority or to feelings of proper respect for oneself and one's standards or to blatant and arrogant conceit <took *pride* in her marks>. ***ant*** humility, shame

Vanity implies an excessive desire to win notice, approval, or praise and connotes self-centeredness and may suggest concentration on trivia <a woman of enormous *vanity*>.

Vainglory suggests excessive boastful pride often manifested in an arrogant display of one's vaunted qualities <resorted to bragging and *vainglory* to get his own way>.

pride *vb* **Pride, plume, pique, preen** mean to congratulate oneself because of something one is, has, or has done or achieved.

Pride usually implies a taking of credit for something that brings honor or gives just cause for pride <he *prides* himself on his ancestry>.

Plume adds the implication of obvious, often vain display of one's satisfaction and commonly suggests less justification <*plumed* herself on the obedience of her staff>.

Pique differs from *plume* chiefly in carrying a hint of stirred-up pride, usually in some special accomplishment <*piques* himself on his ability to speak French well>.

Preen occasionally replaces *plume*, sometimes with a slight suggestion of adorning oneself with one's virtues or accomplishments <*preened* herself on her awards>.

prior see PRECEDING.

priority, precedence mean the act, the fact, or the right of being in front or going ahead of another.

Priority is the usual term in law and the sciences and in questions involving simple time relations of events <the right to inherit a title depends mainly on *priority* of birth>, but in questions involving things such as debts or cases or needs to be met which cannot be taken care of at one time, *priority* suggests a rule of arrangement that determines the order of procedure, often by relative importance <assigned teaching top *priority*>.

__Precedence__ is often close to *priority* <it is our intent to give them *precedence* over you>, but it most typically implies an established order which gives preference to those of superior rank, dignity, or position <a formal procession that observed the proper order of *precedence*>.

priory see CLOISTER.

prize *n* see SPOIL.

prize *vb* see APPRECIATE.

probable, possible, likely mean not currently certain but such as may be or become true or actual.

__Probable__ applies to what is supported by evidence that is strong but not conclusive <a *probable* cause of the accident>. *__ant__* certain, improbable

__Possible__ applies to what lies within the known limits of performance, attainment, nature, or mode of existence of a thing or person regardless of the chances for or against its actuality <it is *possible* that she went home without telling us>.

__Likely__ differs from *probable* in implying more superficial or more general grounds for judgment or belief and from *possible* in imputing much greater chance of being true or occurring <the *likely* result of their quarrel is continued bickering>. *__ant__* unlikely

probationer see NOVICE.

probe see ENTER.

probity see HONESTY.

problem see MYSTERY.

problematic see DOUBTFUL.

procedure see PROCESS.

proceed see SPRING.

proceeding see PROCESS.

process, procedure, proceeding mean the series of such things as actions, operations, or motions involved in the accomplishment of an end.

__Process__ is particularly appropriate when progress from a definite beginning to a definite end is implied and the sequence of events can be divided into a sequence of steps or stages <the *process* of digestion>.

__Procedure__ stresses the method followed or the routine to be followed <achieved success despite disdain for normal *procedure*>.

__Proceeding__ applies not only to the sequence of events, actions, or operations but also to any one of these events, actions, or operations and stresses the items involved rather than their relation or the end in view <had little patience with bureaucratic *proceedings*>.

proclaim see DECLARE.
proclivity see LEANING.
procrastinate see DELAY.
procure see GET.
prodigal *adj* see PROFUSE.
prodigal *n* see SPENDTHRIFT.
prodigious see MONSTROUS.
proffer see OFFER.
proficient, adept, skilled, skillful, expert mean having or manifesting the great knowledge and experience necessary for success in a skill, trade, or profession.

Proficient implies a thorough competence derived from training and practice <a translator thoroughly *proficient* in Russian>. ***ant*** incompetent

Adept implies special aptitude as well as proficiency <*adept* at handling large numbers in his head>. ***ant*** bungling, inapt, inept

Skilled stresses mastery of technique <a delicate operation requiring a *skilled* surgeon>. ***ant*** unskilled

Skillful implies individual dexterity in execution or performance <a shrewd and *skillful* manipulation of public opinion>. ***ant*** unskillful

Expert implies extraordinary proficiency and often connotes knowledge as well as technical skill <*expert* in the identification and evaluation of wines>. ***ant*** amateur

profile see OUTLINE.
profitable see BENEFICIAL.
profligate see SPENDTHRIFT.
profound see DEEP 2.
profuse, lavish, prodigal, luxuriant, lush, exuberant mean giving or given out in great abundance.

Profuse implies pouring forth without restraint or in a stream <uttered *profuse* apologies>. ***ant*** spare, scanty, scant

Lavish suggests an unstinted or unmeasured or extravagant profusion <a *lavish* wedding reception of obvious expense>. ***ant*** sparing

Prodigal implies reckless or wasteful lavishness threatening to lead to exhaustion of resources <*prodigal* spending exhausted the fortune>. ***ant*** parsimonious, frugal

Luxuriant suggest a rich and splendid abundance <the *luxuriant* vegetation of a tropical rain forest>.

Lush suggest rich, soft luxuriance at, or slightly past, the peak of perfection <nude portraits that have a *lush,* sensual quality>.

Exuberant implies marked vitality, vigor, or creative power in what produces abundantly or luxuriantly <a fantasy writer with an *exuberant* imagination>. ***ant*** austere, sterile

prognosticate see FORETELL.
progressive see LIBERAL 2.
prohibit see FORBID.
project see PLAN.
projection, protrusion, protuberance, bulge mean an extension beyond the normal line or surface.

Projection implies a jutting out especially at a sharp angle <those *projections* along the wall are safety hazards>.

Protrusion suggests a thrusting out so that the extension seems an excrescence or a deformity <the bizarre *protrusions* of a coral reef>.

Protuberance implies a growing or swelling out from a surface in rounded form <a skin disease marked by warty *protuberances*>.

Bulge suggests an expansion or swelling of a surface caused by pressure within or below <*bulges* soon appeared in the tile floor>.

prolific see FERTILE.
prolix see WORDY.
prolong see EXTEND.
prominent see NOTICEABLE.
promiscuous see MISCELLANEOUS.
promote see ADVANCE.
prompt see QUICK.
promulgate see DECLARE.
prone 1. see LIABLE.

2. Prone, supine, prostrate, recumbent mean lying down.

Prone implies a position with the front of the body turned toward the supporting surface <push-ups require the body to be in a *prone* position>. ***ant*** erect

Supine implies lying on one's back and suggests inertness or abjectness <lying *supine* upon a couch>.

Prostrate implies lying full-length as in submission, defeat, or physical collapse <a runner fell *prostrate* at the finish line>.

Recumbent implies the posture of one lying at ease or in comfortable repose <he was *recumbent* in his hospital bed>. ***ant*** upright, erect

propel see PUSH.
propensity see LEANING.
proper see FIT *adj*.
property see QUALITY 1.
prophesy see FORETELL.
propitiate see PACIFY.
propitious see FAVORABLE.
proportion see SYMMETRY.
proportional, proportionate, commensurate, commensurable mean in due ratio to something else.

Proportional may apply to several closely related things that change without altering their relations <medical fees are *proportional* to one's income>.
Proportionate applies to one thing that bears a reciprocal relationship to another <a punishment not at all *proportionate* to the offense>. ***ant*** disproportionate
Commensurate stresses an equality between things different from but in some way dependent on each other <the salary will be *commensurate* with experience>. ***ant*** incommensurate
Commensurable more strongly implies a common scale by which two quite different things can be shown to be significantly equal or proportionate <equal pay for jobs that are *commensurable* in worth>. ***ant*** incommensurable

proportionate see PROPORTIONAL.

propose, propound, pose mean to set before the mind for consideration.
Propose fundamentally implies an invitation to consider, discuss, settle, or agree upon some clearly stated question or proposition <*proposed* marriage> <*propose* a solution> or an offering of someone as a candidate <*proposed* his colleague for attorney general>.
Propound implies the stating of a question or proposition for discussion usually without personal bias or without any attempt to prove or disprove on the part of the propounder <*propounded* the thesis that all great music is inspired>.
Pose, very close to *propound*, is likely to imply that no attempt will be or can be made to seek an immediate answer <*pose* a question for your consideration>.

propound see PROPOSE.

propriety see DECORUM.

prorogue see ADJOURN.

prosaic, prosy, matter-of-fact mean having a plain, practical, unimaginative quality or character.
Prosaic implies an opposition to *poetic* and usually suggests a commonplace unexciting quality and the absence of everything that would stimulate feeling or awaken great interest <a downtown with a certain mundane, *prosaic* air>.
Prosy stresses dullness or tediousness and when applied to persons usually implies a tendency to talk or write at length in a boring and uninviting manner <wrote them a dull *prosy* letter>.
Matter-of-fact implies a disinterest in the imaginative, speculative, visionary, romantic, or ideal; it may connote down-to-earth practicality and accuracy in detail <a *matter-of-fact* account of their adventure> but often it suggests preoccupation with the obvious and a neglect of more subtle values <took a very *matter-of-fact* attitude toward her illness>.

prospect, outlook, anticipation, foretaste mean an advance realization of something to come.

Prospect implies expectation of a particular event, condition, or development of definite interest or concern <the appealing *prospect* of a quiet weekend>.

Outlook suggests a usually general forecasting of the future <a favorable *outlook* for the state's economy>.

Anticipation implies a prospect or outlook that involves advance suffering or enjoyment of what is foreseen <reviewing his notes in *anticipation* of the next meeting>. ***ant*** retrospect

Foretaste implies an actual though brief or partial experiencing of something that will come later in full force <the frost was a *foretaste* of winter>.

prosper see SUCCEED.

prostrate see PRONE.

prosy see PROSAIC.

protect see DEFEND 1.

protest 1. see ASSERT. **2.** see OBJECT.

protract see EXTEND.

protrusion see PROJECTION.

protuberance see PROJECTION.

proud, arrogant, haughty, lordly, insolent, overbearing, supercilious, disdainful mean showing superiority toward others or scorn for inferiors.

Proud may suggest a feeling or attitude of pleased satisfaction in oneself or one's accomplishments that may or may not be justified and may or may not be demonstrated offensively <a *proud* man, unwilling to admit failure>. ***ant*** humble, ashamed

Arrogant implies a claiming for oneself of more consideration or importance than is warranted and often suggests an aggressive, domineering manner <an *arrogant* business executive used to being kowtowed to>. ***ant*** meek, unassuming

Haughty suggests a blatantly displayed consciousness of superior birth or position <a *haughty* manner that barely concealed his scorn>. ***ant*** lowly

Lordly implies pomposity or an arrogant display of power <a *lordly* indifference to the consequences of their carelessness>.

Insolent implies insultingly contemptuous haughtiness <suffered the stares of *insolent* waiters>. ***ant*** deferential

Overbearing suggests a tyrannical manner or an intolerable insolence <wearied by demands from her *overbearing* in-laws>. ***ant*** subservient

Supercilious implies a cool, patronizing haughtiness <*supercilious* parvenus with their disdainful sneers>.

Disdainful suggests a more active and openly scornful superciliousness <*disdainful* of their pathetic attempts>. ***ant*** admiring, respectful

provide, supply, furnish mean to give or get what is desired by or needed for something.

Provide suggests foresight and stresses the idea of making adequate preparation by stocking or equipping <*provide* suitable accommodations>.

Supply may stress the idea of replacing, of making up what is needed, or of satisfying a deficiency <foods that *supply* needed protein and vitamins to the diet>.

Furnish may emphasize the idea of fitting with whatever is needed or, sometimes, normal or desirable <the porcupine, *furnished* by nature with a built-in defense>.

providential see LUCKY.

province see FUNCTION.

provisional, tentative mean not final or definitive.

Provisional applies to something that is adopted only for the time being and will be discarded when the final or definitive form is established or when the need for it otherwise comes to an end <a *provisional* government>. ***ant*** definitive

Tentative applies to something that is of the nature of a trial or experiment or serves as a test of practicability or feasibility <our plans are still *tentative*—subject to change without notice>. ***ant*** definitive

provoke 1. Provoke, excite, stimulate, pique, quicken mean to rouse someone or something into being, doing, or feeling.

Provoke directs attention to the response called forth and often applies to an angry or vexed or extreme reaction <my stories usually *provoke* laughter>.

Excite implies a stirring up or moving profoundly <news that *excited* anger and frustration>. ***ant*** soothe, quiet *(persons),* allay *(fears, anxiety)*

Stimulate suggests a rousing out of lethargy, quiescence, or indifference <the challenge *stimulated* them to work faster>. ***ant*** unnerve, deaden

Pique suggests stimulating by mild irritation or challenge <that remark *piqued* my interest>.

Quicken implies beneficially stimulating and making active or lively <the high salary *quickened* her desire to have the job>. ***ant*** arrest

2. see IRRITATE.

prowess see HEROISM.

prudent see WISE.

prying see CURIOUS.

publish see DECLARE.

pugnacious see BELLIGERENT.

pull, draw, drag, haul, tug mean to cause to move in the direction determined by an applied force.

Pull is the general term but may emphasize the force exerted rather than the resulting motion <to open the drawer, *pull* hard>.

Draw implies a smoother, steadier motion and generally a lighter force than *pull* <a child *drawing* his sled across the snow>.

Drag suggests great effort overcoming resistance or friction <*dragged* the dead body across the room>.

Haul implies sustained pulling or dragging, especially of heavy or bulky objects <a team of horses *hauling* supplies>.

Tug applies to strenuous often spasmodic efforts to move something <the little girl *tugged* at her mother's hand>.

punch see STRIKE 2.

punctilious see CAREFUL.

pungent, piquant, poignant, racy mean sharp and stimulating to the mind or the senses.

Pungent implies a sharp, stinging, or biting quality, especially of odors <a cheese with a *pungent* odor>. ***ant*** bland

Piquant suggests a power to whet the appetite or interest through a mildly pungent or provocative quality <grapefruit juice gave the punch its *piquant* taste>. ***ant*** bland

Poignant suggests something that is sharply or piercingly effective in stirring one's consciousness or emotions <upon her departure he felt a *poignant* sense of loss>. ***ant*** dull

Racy implies possession of a strongly characteristic natural quality that is fresh and unimpaired <the spontaneous, *racy* prose of the untutored writer>.

punish, chastise, castigate, chasten, discipline, correct mean to inflict a penalty on in requital for wrongdoing.

Punish implies the imposing of a penalty for violation of law, disobedience, or wrongdoing <*punished* for stealing>. ***ant*** excuse, pardon

Chastise may apply to either the infliction of corporal punishment or to verbal censure or denunciation <*chastised* his son for neglecting his studies>.

Castigate implies a severe, typically public lashing with words <an editorial *castigating* the entire city council>.

Chasten suggests any affliction or trial that leaves one humbled or subdued but improved and strengthened <a stunning election defeat that left him *chastened*>. ***ant*** pamper, mollycoddle

Discipline implies a punishing or chastising in order to bring or keep under control <the duty of parents to *discipline* their children>.

Correct implies a punishing aimed at reforming an offender <the function of prison is to *correct* the wrongdoer>.

pure see CHASTE.

purloin see STEAL.

purpose see INTENTION.
pursue see FOLLOW 2.
pursuit see WORK 2.
push, shove, thrust, propel mean to cause to move ahead or aside by the application of force.
Push implies the application of force by a body already in contact with the body to be moved <*push* the door open>.
Shove implies a strong and often fast, sudden, or rough pushing that forces something along or aside <*shoved* the man out of my way>.
Thrust suggest less steadiness and greater violence than *push* and implies the application of a single abrupt movement or action <*thrust* the money into my hand and ran away>.
Propel suggests a driving rapidly forward or onward by a force or power that imparts motion <ships *propelled* by steam>.
pushing see AGGRESSIVE.
pushy see AGGRESSIVE.
pusillanimous see COWARDLY.
putrefy see DECAY.
putrid see MALODOROUS.
put up see RESIDE.
puzzle *vb* **Puzzle, perplex, bewilder, distract, nonplus, confound, dumbfound** mean to baffle and disturb mentally.
Puzzle implies the presenting of a problem difficult to solve <a persistent fever which *puzzled* the doctor>.
Perplex adds a suggestion of worry and uncertainty especially about making a necessary decision <an odd change of personality that *perplexed* her friends>.
Bewilder stresses a confusion of mind that hampers clear and decisive thinking <the number of videotapes available *bewilders* consumers>.
Distract implies agitation or uncertainty induced by conflicting preoccupations or interests <a political scandal that *distracted* the country for two years>. ***ant*** collect *(one's thoughts, powers)*
Nonplus implies a bafflement that causes complete blankness of mind <she was utterly *nonplussed* by the abrupt change in plans>.
Confound implies temporary mental paralysis caused by astonishment or profound abasement <tragic news that *confounded* us all>.
Dumbfound suggests an intense but momentary confounding or astounding <*dumbfounded* by her rejection of his marriage proposal>.
puzzle *n* see MYSTERY.

Q

quail see RECOIL.
quaint see STRANGE.
quake see SHAKE 1.
qualified see ABLE.
qualify 1. see PREPARE. **2.** see MODERATE *vb.*
quality 1. Quality, property, character, attribute mean an intelligible feature by which a thing may be identified or understood.

Quality is a general term applicable to any trait or characteristic whether material or immaterial, individual or generic <a star whose acting had a persistently amateurish *quality*>.

Property implies a characteristic that belongs to a thing's essential nature and may be used to describe a type or species <asked them to name the basic *properties* of mammals>.

Character applies to a peculiar and distinctive quality of an individual or a class <each of the island's villages has a distinctive *character*>.

Attribute implies a quality ascribed to a thing or a being <a man with none of the traditional *attributes* of a popular hero>.

2. Quality, stature, caliber mean distinctive merit or superiority.

Quality, used in the singular, implies a complex of properties that together produce a high order of excellence, virtue, or worth <of a *quality* not often found anymore>.

Stature is likely to suggest height reached or development attained and to connote considerations of prestige and eminence <chose a new leader of great *stature*>.

Caliber suggests unusual but measurable extent or range of quality or powers, such as ability or intellect, or sometimes of deviation from a norm or standard <a man of very low moral *caliber*>.

qualm, scruple, compunction, demur mean a misgiving about what one is doing or going to do.

Qualm implies an uneasy fear that one is not following one's conscience or better judgment <no *qualms* about traveling in the Middle East>.

Scruple implies a doubt of the rightness of an act on grounds of principle <a lawyer totally devoid of *scruples*>.

Compunction implies a spontaneous feeling of responsibility and compassion for a potential victim <not likely to have *compunctions* about knocking out his opponent>.

Demur implies hesitation caused by objection or resistance to

an outside suggestion or influence <accepted her resignation without *demur*>.

quandary see PREDICAMENT.

quantity see SUM.

quarrel, wrangle, altercation, squabble, spat, tiff mean an angry dispute.

Quarrel implies a heated verbal clash followed by strained or severed relations <a bitter *quarrel* that ended their friendship>.

Wrangle suggests a noisy, insistent, often futile dispute <an ongoing *wrangle* over the town's finances>.

Altercation suggests noisy, heated verbal quarreling often with blows <a violent *altercation* between pro- and anti-abortion groups>.

Squabble implies childish and unseemly wrangling over a petty matter <the children constantly *squabble* over toys>.

Spat implies a lively but brief dispute over a trifle <the couple averages a *spat* a week>.

Tiff suggests a trivial dispute marked by ill humor or hurt feelings but without serious consequence <a *tiff* that was forgotten by dinnertime>.

quarrelsome see BELLIGERENT.

quarry see VICTIM.

quash see CRUSH.

quaver see SHAKE 1.

queer see STRANGE.

quell see CRUSH.

query see ASK 1.

question see ASK 1.

questionable see DOUBTFUL.

quick 1. see FAST.

2. Quick, prompt, ready, apt mean able to respond without delay or hesitation or indicative of such ability.

Quick stresses instancy of response and is likely to connote native rather than acquired power <a *quick* mind>. ***ant*** sluggish

Prompt is more likely to connote training and discipline that fits one for instant response <the *prompt* response of emergency medical technicians>.

Ready suggests facility or fluency in response <backed by a pair of *ready* assistants>.

Apt stresses the possession of qualities, such as high intelligence, a particular talent, or a strong bent, that make quick effective response possible <an *apt* student>.

quicken 1. Quicken, animate, enliven, vivify mean to make alive or lively.

Quicken stresses a sudden arousal or renewal of physical, spir-

itual, or intellectual life or activity especially in something inert <the arrival of spring *quickens* the earth>. ***ant*** deaden

Animate emphasizes the imparting of motion or vitality to what was previously deficient in or lacking such a quality <telling details that *animate* the familiar story>.

Enliven suggests a stimulating influence that arouses from dullness or torpidity <*enlivened* his lecture with humorous anecdotes>. ***ant*** deaden, subdue

Vivify implies a freshening or energizing through the imparting or renewal of vitality <her appearance *vivifies* a dreary drawing-room drama>.

2. see PROVOKE.

quick-witted see INTELLIGENT.

quiescent see LATENT.

quiet see STILL.

quip see JEST.

quit 1. see STOP. **2.** see GO.

quiver see SHAKE 1.

quixotic see IMAGINARY.

quote, cite, repeat mean to speak or write again something already said or written by another.

Quote usually implies precise repetition of the words of another for a particular purpose <illustrate the use of a word by *quoting* classical and modern authors>, but sometimes *quote* is applied to a more general referral to someone as author or source of information <don't *quote* me as your authority>.

Cite is likely to stress the idea of mentioning for a particular reason, such as proof of a thesis or substantiation of a position taken, with or without the idea of quoting another's exact words <his analysis of the causes of student unrest has been *cited* in several recent judicial opinions>.

Repeat stresses the mere fact of saying or writing again the words or presenting the ideas of another often with no reference to the source and little concern for precision <*repeat* a scandalous story told one in confidence>.

quotidian see DAILY.

R

rack see AFFLICT.

racket see DIN.

racy see PUNGENT.

radiant see BRIGHT.

radical see LIBERAL 2.

rage 1. see ANGER. **2.** see FASHION.

rail see SCOLD.

raise see LIFT.
rally see STIR *vb*.
ramble see WANDER.
rampant see RANK.
rancid see MALODOROUS.
rancor see ENMITY.
random, haphazard, chance, casual, desultory, hit-or-miss mean determined by accident rather than design.

Random stresses chance and lack of definite aim, fixed goal, or regular procedure <a *random* sampling of public opinion>. ***ant*** purposive

Haphazard applies to what is done without regard for regularity or fitness or ultimate consequence <his selection of college courses was entirely *haphazard*>.

Chance applies to what comes or happens to one or is done or made without prearrangement, foreknowledge, or preparation <a *chance* encounter> <a *chance* acquaintance>.

Casual suggests a leaving things to chance and a working or acting without deliberation, intention, or purpose <a *casual* tour of the sights>. ***ant*** deliberate

Desultory implies a jumping or skipping from one thing to another without method or system and a consequently inconsistent performance and lack of continuity <a *desultory* discussion of current events>. ***ant*** assiduous

Hit-or-miss applies to what is so haphazard as to lack all apparent plan, aim, system, or care <a real *hit-or-miss* operation>.

range *n* **Range, gamut, compass, sweep, scope, reach, orbit** mean the extent that lies within the powers of something to cover or control.

Range is a general term indicating the extent of one's perception or the extent of powers, capabilities, or possibilities <the entire *range* of human experience>.

Gamut suggests a graduated series running from one possible extreme to another <a performance that ran the *gamut* of emotions>.

Compass implies a sometimes limited or bounded extent of perception, knowledge, or activity <your concerns lie beyond the narrow *compass* of this study>.

Sweep suggests extent, often circular or arc-shaped, of motion or activity <the book covers the entire *sweep* of criminal activity>.

Scope is applicable to a predetermined and limited area of activity that is somewhat flexible within those limits <as time went on, the *scope* of the investigation widened>.

Reach suggests an extent of perception, knowledge, ability, or activity attained to or experienced by stretching out <a goal well within *reach*>.

Orbit suggests an often circumscribed range of activity or influence within which forces work toward accommodation <within that restricted *orbit* they tried to effect social change>.

range *vb* **1.** see LINE. **2.** see WANDER.

rank 1. Rank, rampant mean growing or increasing at an immoderate rate.

Rank implies vigorous, luxuriant, and often unchecked or excessive growth <the *rank* plant life of the tropics>.

Rampant implies rapid and often wild or unrestrained spreading and can be applied both to what literally grows and to what increases as if by physical growth <diseases that are *rampant* in the region>.

2. see FLAGRANT.

3. see MALODOROUS.

ransom see RESCUE.

rant see BOMBAST.

rap see TAP.

rapacious see VORACIOUS.

rapid see FAST.

rapture see ECSTASY.

rare 1. see CHOICE. **2.** see INFREQUENT.

rash see ADVENTUROUS.

rate see ESTIMATE.

ration, allowance, pittance mean the amount of food, supplies, or money allotted to an individual.

Ration implies apportionment and, often, equal sharing; basically, it applies to the daily supply of food provided for one individual, such as a prisoner or a milk cow, but it is freely extended to things in short supply that are made available either equally or equitably in accord with need <gasoline *rations* in wartime vary with the special needs of different individuals>.

Allowance stresses granting rather than sharing what is in restricted supply <each child was given an *allowance* as soon as he or she became old enough to handle money>.

Pittance stresses meagerness or miserliness and may apply indifferently to a ration, an allowance, an alms, a dole, or a wage <managed to survive on a mere *pittance*>.

rational, reasonable mean having or manifesting the power to reason or being in accordance with the dictates of reason.

Rational usually implies the power to make logical inferences and to draw conclusions that enable one to understand things <a *rational* being>; in applications to things conceived or formulated, it stresses satisfactoriness in terms of reason <engaged in *rational* discourse>. ***ant*** irrational, demented, absurd

Reasonable emphasizes the possession or use of practical sense, justice, and fairness and the avoidance of needless error <willing to grant any *reasonable* request>. ***ant*** unreasonable

rattle see EMBARRASS.

raucous see LOUD.

ravage, devastate, waste, sack, pillage, despoil mean to lay waste by plundering or destroying.

Ravage implies a violent, severe, and often cumulative depredation and destruction <a hurricane that *ravaged* the Gulf coast>.

Devastate implies the complete ruin and desolation of a wide area <the atomic bomb that *devastated* Hiroshima>.

Waste may imply a less complete destruction or one produced by a slower or less violent process <years of drought had *wasted* the area>. ***ant*** conserve, save

Sack implies the looting and destroying of a place <barbarians *sacked* ancient Rome>.

Pillage implies ruthless plundering at will but without the completeness suggested by *sack* <settlements *pillaged* by Vikings>.

Despoil applies to the looting or robbing of a place or person without suggesting accompanying destruction <the Nazis *despoiled* the art museums of Europe>.

ravenous see VORACIOUS.

ravish see TRANSPORT.

raw see RUDE.

rawboned see LEAN.

reach *n* see RANGE.

reach *vb* **Reach, gain, compass, achieve, attain** mean to arrive at a point or end by effort or work.

Reach may be used with reference to anything arrived at by any degree of effort <after a long climb we *reached* the top of the hill>.

Gain is likely to imply a struggle to reach a contemplated or desired goal or end <*gained* a measure of self-confidence from the experience>. ***ant*** forfeit, lose

Compass implies the exerting of efforts to get around difficulties and transcend limitation, and often connotes skill or craft in management <an actress taking on the most difficult role that her skills could *compass*>.

Achieve can stress the skill or endurance as well as the effort involved in reaching an end <*achieved* the success that was her due>. ***ant*** miss

Attain stresses the spur of aspiration or ambition and suggests a reaching for the extreme, the unusual, or the difficult <vowed not to relax his efforts until peace was *attained*>.

readiness, ease, facility, dexterity mean the power of doing something without evidence of effort.

Readiness emphasizes the quickness or promptitude with which something is done <indicated her *readiness* for the task>.

Ease implies absence of strain or care or hesitation with resulting smooth efficiency in performance <answer a series of questions with *ease*>. ***ant*** effort

Facility is often very close to *ease* but sometimes suggests a slick superficiality rather than true ease <a *facility* with words that was almost too glib>.

Dexterity implies proficient skill such as results from training and practice <handled the class with the *dexterity* of a master>. ***ant*** clumsiness

ready *adj* see QUICK.

ready *vb* see PREPARE.

real, actual, true mean corresponding to known facts.

Real is likely to stress genuineness and especially correspondence between appearance and essence <a *real* diamond>. ***ant*** unreal, apparent, imaginary

Actual stresses the fact of existence or fidelity to the existent as opposed to the nonexistent, abstract, or hypothetical <the *actual* tests of this missile have not yet been made>. ***ant*** ideal, imaginary

True can stress conformity to the real especially as a model or standard <the ladybug is not a *true* bug but a beetle> or conformity to the pertinent facts that are known or knowable <the *true* version of events>. ***ant*** false

realize see THINK 1.

reap, glean, gather, garner, harvest mean to do the work or a particular part of the work of collecting ripened crops.

Reap basically applies to the cutting down and usually collecting of ripened grain, and often suggests a return or requital <hoped to *reap* the rewards of hard work>.

Glean implies a stripping of a field or plant that has already been gone over once and applies to any gathering up of useful bits from here and there and especially of such as have been overlooked by others <*gleaned* new evidence from the site of the crime>.

Gather applies to any collecting or bringing together of material, such as the produce of a farm or garden, and stresses amassing or accumulating <*gathered* information>.

Garner implies the storing of produce reaped or gathered and can apply to any laying away of a store <a collection of maxims *garnered* from her neighbors>.

Harvest may imply any or all of these agricultural practices or may apply to any gathering in or husbanding <*harvested* a bumper crop>.

rear see LIFT.

reason *n* **1.** see CAUSE.

2. Reason, understanding, intuition mean the power of the intellect by which human beings attain truth or knowledge.

Reason refers to the faculty for order, sense, and rationality in thought, inference, and conclusion about perceptions <tried to approach each problem with calm and *reason*>.

Understanding may widen the scope of *reason* to include most thought processes leading to comprehension and also the resultant state of knowledge <research that led to a new *understanding* of the disease>.

Intuition stresses quick knowledge or comprehension without evident orderly reason, thought, or cogitation <responded on the basis of *intuition*>.

reason *vb* see THINK 2.

reasonable see RATIONAL.

rebellion, revolution, uprising, revolt, insurrection, mutiny mean an armed outbreak against powers in authority.

Rebellion implies an open, organized armed resistance that is often unsuccessful <the *rebellion* failed for lack of popular support>.

Revolution applies to a successful rebellion resulting in a major change in constituted authority <the American *Revolution*>.

Uprising implies a brief, limited, and often immediately ineffective rebellion <quickly put down the *uprising*>.

Revolt implies an armed uprising that quickly fails or succeeds <a *revolt* by the young Turks that surprised party leaders>.

Insurrection differs from *revolt* in suggesting more intransigence and less organized purpose <Nat Turner's unsuccessful slave *insurrection*>.

Mutiny applies to insubordination or insurrection especially against military or naval authority <the famous *mutiny* aboard the Bounty>.

rebuild see MEND.

rebuke see REPROVE.

rebut see DISPROVE.

recalcitrant see UNRULY.

recall 1. see REMEMBER. **2.** see REVOKE.

recant see ABJURE.

recede, retreat, retrograde, retract, back mean to move backward.

Recede implies a gradual withdrawing from a forward or high fixed point in time, space, or attitude <the flood waters gradually *receded*>. ***ant*** proceed, advance

Retreat implies a withdrawal from a point or position reached, typically in response to some pressure <under cross-examination he *retreated* from that statement>. ***ant*** advance

Retrograde implies a movement contrary to what is expected, normal, or natural, and is the reverse of progress <infant mortality rates *retrograding* to earlier levels>.

Retract implies a drawing back or in from an extended or outward position <a cat *retracting* its claws>. ***ant*** protract

Back is used with *up, down, out,* or *off* to refer to any retrograde or reversed motion <*backed* off when her claim was challenged>.

receipt, recipe, prescription mean a formula or set of directions for the compounding of ingredients especially in cookery and medicine.

Receipt often denotes a formula for a homemade or folk medical remedy <a family *receipt* for a cough syrup>.

Recipe is broadly applicable and can denote not only a formula or set of instructions for doing or making something but also a method or procedure for attaining some end <revealed their *recipe* for success>; in cookery it is the standard term for a set of directions for preparing a made dish <tried a new *recipe* for scalloped oysters>.

Prescription refers to a physician's instruction to a pharmacist for the compounding or dispensing of a medicine or to a medicine compounded or dispensed <wanted to get a *prescription* for a sleep aid>; it is sometimes extended to other formulas or formulations with a suggestion of the precision expected in medical directions <a candidate with a clear *prescription* for economic recovery>.

receive, accept, admit, take mean to permit to come into one's possession, presence, group, mind, or substance.

Receive can imply a welcoming recognition <*receive* guests with open arms>, but more often it implies that something comes or is allowed to come into one's possession or presence while one is passive <*received* the news without comment>.

Accept adds to *receive* an implication of some degree of positive acquiescence or consent even if tacit <refused to *accept* a valuable gift from a comparative stranger>. ***ant*** reject

Admit carries strong implications of permission, allowance, or sufferance <*admit* new members to a club>. ***ant*** eject, expel

Take carries the notion of accepting or at least of making no positive protest against receiving, and often of almost welcoming on principle, what is offered, conferred, or inflicted <a man who *took* whatever fortune sent him>.

recent see MODERN.

recess see PAUSE.

recipe see RECEIPT.

reciprocal, mutual, common mean shared or experienced by each of those concerned.

Reciprocal implies an equal return or counteraction by each of two sides toward or against or in relation to the other <allies with a *reciprocal* defense agreement>.

Mutual applies to feelings or actions shared or experienced by two and may suggest an accompanying reciprocity, equality, or interaction <two people with a *mutual* physical attraction>.

Common does not suggest reciprocity but merely a sharing with others <a couple with many *common* interests>. ***ant*** individual

reciprocate, retaliate, requite, return mean to give back usually in kind or in quantity.

Reciprocate implies a more or less equivalent exchange or a paying back of what one has received <*reciprocated* their hospitality by inviting them for a visit>.

Retaliate usually implies a paying back of injury in exact kind by way of vengeance <the enemy *retaliated* by executing their prisoners>.

Requite implies a paying back according to one's preference and often not equivalently <*requited* her love with cold indifference>.

Return implies a paying back of something usually in kind but sometimes by way of contrast <*returned* their kindness with ingratitude>.

reckless see ADVENTUROUS.

reckon 1. see CALCULATE. **2.** see RELY.

reclaim see RESCUE.

recognition, identification, assimilation, apperception mean a form of cognition that relates a perception of something new to knowledge already acquired.

Recognition implies that the thing now perceived has been previously perceived and that the mind is aware of the fact that the two things are the same thing or identical <encouraged by the patient's *recognition* of his mother>.

Identification adds to *recognition* the implication of such prior knowledge as permits one to recognize the thing as an individual member of a class <bird calls aid in the *identification* of species>.

Assimilation implies that the mind responds to new ideas, facts, and experiences by interpreting them in the light of what is already known, thereby making them an integral part of one's body of knowledge <proceeded rapidly with the *assimilation* of new material>.

Apperception implies that the mind responds to new facts, ideas, or situations when and only when it can relate them to what is already known <limited by my *apperceptions* of reality>.

recoil, shrink, flinch, wince, blench, quail mean to draw back in fear or distaste.

Recoil implies a start of a movement away prompted by shock, fear, or disgust <*recoils* at the sight of blood>. ***ant*** confront, defy

Shrink suggests an instinctive recoiling through sensitiveness, scrupulousness, or cowardice <refused to *shrink* from responsibilities>.

Flinch implies a failure to endure pain or to face something dangerous or frightening with resolution <faced her accusers without *flinching*>.

Wince suggests a slight involuntary physical recoiling from what pains, frightens, or disgusts <*winced* when the new secretary called him by his first name>.

Blench implies fainthearted, fearful flinching <never *blenched* even as his head was lowered on the guillotine>.

Quail suggests a shrinking and cowering in fear <*quailed* at the fury of the storm>.

recollect see REMEMBER.

recollection see MEMORY.

recompense see PAY.

reconcile see ADAPT.

recrudesce see RETURN.

rectify see CORRECT *vb*.

recumbent see PRONE.

recur see RETURN.

recurrent see INTERMITTENT.

redeem see RESCUE.

redolence see FRAGRANCE.

redolent see ODOROUS.

redound see CONDUCE.

redress see CORRECT *vb*.

reduce 1. see CONQUER. **2.** see DECREASE.

redundant see WORDY.

reel, whirl, stagger, totter mean to move or seem to move uncertainly and irregularly or with such loss of control as occurs in extreme weakness or in intoxication.

Reel usually suggests a turning round and round or a sensation of so turning or being turned, but it may also imply a being thrown off balance <a boxer *reeling* from the blow>.

Whirl is often used like *reel* <their heads *whirling* with confusion>, but it more frequently implies swiftness or impetuousness of movement <dancers *whirling* about the stage>.

Stagger stresses loss of control and uncertainty of movement, typically of a person walking while weak, intoxicated, or heavily burdened but sometimes simply of someone meeting with difficulty or adverse conditions <*staggered* by the sheer enormity of the task>.

Totter not only implies weakness or unsteadiness that causes uncertain movement but often also hints at the approach of complete collapse <watched closely as the oligarchy *tottered*>.

refer **1.** see RESORT.

2. Refer, allude, advert mean to call or direct attention to something.

Refer usually implies the intentional introduction and distinct and specific mention and sometimes judging <*referred* to her claims as fantasy>.

Allude suggests an indirect mention by a hint, roundabout expression, or figure of speech <*alluded* to incidents previously unknown>.

Advert usually implies a slight or glancing reference in a text or utterance <a theory *adverted* to here but discussed later>.

reflect see THINK 2.

reflective see THOUGHTFUL 1.

reform see CORRECT *vb.*

refractory see UNRULY.

refrain, abstain, forbear mean to keep oneself voluntarily from doing or indulging in something.

Refrain is likely to suggest the checking of a passing impulse <*refrain* from laughter in church>.

Abstain usually implies deliberate renunciation or self-denial on principle and often permanency of intent <a vegetarian who *abstains* from all meat>. ***ant*** indulge

Forbear usually implies self-restraint rather than self-denial, be it from patience, charity, or clemency or from discretion or stoicism <taught himself to *forbear* such expressions of anger>.

refresh see RENEW.

refuge see SHELTER *n.*

refuse see DECLINE.

refute see DISPROVE.

regard, respect, esteem, admire mean to recognize the worth of a person or thing.

Regard is a general term that is usually qualified <he is not highly *regarded* in the profession>. ***ant*** despise

Respect implies a considered evaluation or estimation as the basis of recognition or worth <after many years they came to *respect* her views>. ***ant*** abuse, misuse, scorn

Esteem implies a high valuation and a consequent warmth of feeling or attachment <no citizen of the town was more highly *esteemed*>. ***ant*** abominate

Admire suggests a usually enthusiastic but uncritical appreciation and often deep affection <*admired* the natural beauty of the scene>. ***ant*** abhor

regret see SORROW.

regular, normal, typical, natural mean being of the sort or kind that is expected as usual, ordinary, or average.

Regular stresses conformity to a rule, standard, or pattern <the *regular* monthly meeting of the organization>. ***ant*** irregular

Normal implies lack of deviation from what has been discovered or established as the most usual or expected <*normal* behavior for a two-year-old boy>. ***ant*** abnormal

Typical implies showing all important traits of a type, class, or group and may suggest lack of marked individuality <a *typical* small town in America>. ***ant*** atypical, distinctive

Natural applies to what conforms to a thing's essential nature, function, or mode of being <the *natural* love of a mother for her child>. ***ant*** unnatural, artificial, adventitious

regulation see LAW.

reimburse see PAY.

reiterate see REPEAT.

reject see DECLINE.

rejoin see ANSWER.

rejuvenate see RENEW.

relapse see LAPSE.

relate see JOIN.

related, cognate, kindred, allied, affiliated mean connected by or as if by close family ties.

Related can imply connection by blood or marriage or a correspondingly close connection <in separate but *related* incidents>. ***ant*** unrelated

Cognate applies to things that are generically alike, have a common ancestor or source, or derive from the same root or stock <*cognate* words in various languages, such as *pater*, *Vater*, and *father*>.

Kindred stresses family relations <an isolated community most of whose members were *kindred*> but in more common applications is likely to stress shared interests or tastes or congeniality <felt it to be the meeting of *kindred* souls>. ***ant*** alien

Allied may imply connection by marriage or voluntary association rather than by origin or blood <*allied* through his wife with several prominent English families> or remote biological relationship, but it is more likely to stress relationship based on common characters, qualities, aims, or effects <DDT and *allied* insecticides>. ***ant*** unallied

Affiliated, often close to *allied,* distinctively tends to stress a dependent relation like that of a child to a parent <all blood banks *affiliated* with the Red Cross> and may connote a loose union in which the associated elements are more or less independent <the network and its *affiliated* stations>. ***ant*** unaffiliated

relaxed see LOOSE.
release see FREE *vb.*
relegate see COMMIT.
relent see YIELD.
relevant, germane, material, pertinent, apposite, applicable, apropos mean relating to or bearing upon the matter at hand.

Relevant implies a traceable, significant, logical connection <use any *relevant* evidence to support your argument>. ***ant*** extraneous

Germane may additionally imply a fitness for or appropriateness to the situation or occasion <a topic not *germane* to our discussion>. ***ant*** foreign

Material implies so close a relationship that it cannot be altered without obvious deleterious effect <the scene is *material* to the rest of the play>. ***ant*** immaterial

Pertinent stresses a clear and decisive relevance <a *pertinent* observation that cut to the heart of the matter>. ***ant*** impertinent, foreign

Apposite suggests a marked and felicitous relevance <the anecdotes in his sermons are always *apposite*>. ***ant*** inapposite, inapt

Applicable applies to something such as a general rule or principle that may be brought to bear upon or used fittingly in reference to a particular case, instance, or problem <a precedent that is not *applicable* in this case>. ***ant*** inapplicable

Apropos suggests what is both relevant and opportune <for your term paper use only *apropos* quotations>. ***ant*** unapropos

relieve, alleviate, lighten, assuage, mitigate, allay mean to make something less grievous or more tolerable.

Relieve implies a lifting of enough of a burden to make it endurable or even temporarily forgotten <took drugs to *relieve* the pain>. ***ant*** intensify

Alleviate implies a temporary or partial lessening of pain or distress <new buildings that will help to *alleviate* the housing shortage>. ***ant*** aggravate

Lighten implies a reducing of a burdensome or depressing weight and often connotes a cheering influence <good news that *lightened* his worries>.

Assuage implies the softening or sweetening of what is harsh or disagreeable <hoped that a vacation would *assuage* the pain of the divorce>. ***ant*** exacerbate, intensify

Mitigate suggests a moderating or countering of the effects of something inflicting or likely to inflict pain or distress <ocean breezes *mitigated* the intense heat>. ***ant*** intensify

Allay implies an effective calming or soothing especially of fears or alarms <the encouraging report *allayed* their fears>. ***ant*** intensify

religious see DEVOUT.

relinquish, yield, resign, surrender, abandon, waive mean to give up completely.

Relinquish may suggest some regret, reluctance, or weakness in the giving up <*relinquished* her crown with bittersweet feelings>. ***ant*** keep

Yield implies a concession of compliance or submission to force <I *yield* to your greater expertise in this matter>.

Resign emphasizes a voluntary relinquishment or sacrifice without struggle <*resigned* rather than work under the new terms>.

Surrender implies a giving up to an external compulsion or demand after a struggle to retain or resist <forced to sign a document *surrendering* all claims to the land>.

Abandon stresses finality and completeness in giving up <*abandon* all hope>. ***ant*** cherish *(as hopes),* restain *(oneself)*

Waive implies a conceding or forgoing with little or no compulsion <*waived* the right to a trial by jury>.

relish see TASTE 2.

reluctant see DISINCLINED.

rely, trust, depend, count, reckon, bank mean to have or place full confidence.

Rely, used with *on* and *upon,* implies a judgment based on experience or association that someone or something will never fail in giving or doing what one expects <a man one can *rely* on in an emergency>.

Trust, used with *in* or *to,* implies assurance based on faith that another will not fail one <*trusted* in her own strength>.

Depend, used with *on* or *upon,* implies a resting on someone or something for support or assistance and often connotes weakness or lack of self-sufficiency <lost the compass on which their lives *depended*>.

Count and ***reckon,*** both used with *on,* imply a taking into one's calculations as certain or assured <*counted* on his sister for help> <a speaker who *reckons* on the intelligence of her audience>, or they may mean little more than *expect* <they *counted* on staying with friends> <*reckoned* they could always go home>.

Bank, used with *on,* expresses near or absolute certainty <you can *bank* on his honesty>.

remain see STAY 1.

remark 1. see SEE 1.

2. Remark, comment, commentate, animadvert mean to make observations or pass judgment.

Remark implies little more than a desire to notice and call attention to something <*remark* on a friend's taste in dress>.

Comment stresses often critical interpretation <refused to *comment* about the situation>.

Commentate is sometimes substituted for *comment* to suggest a purely expository or interpretive intent <*commentating* knowledgeably on current events>.

Animadvert implies a remarking or commentating usually of scholarly caliber or based on careful judgment <willing to *animadvert* at length on topics in her field> but often emphasizes the passing of an adverse judgment <elders *animadverting* on the content of rock music>.

remarkable see NOTICEABLE.

remedy 1. see CORRECT *vb*. **2.** see CURE.

remember, recollect, recall, remind, reminisce mean to bring an image or idea from the past into the mind.

Remember implies a keeping in memory that may be effortless or unwilled <*remembers* that day as though it were yesterday>. ***ant*** forget

Recollect implies bringing back to mind what is lost or scattered <as near as I can *recollect*>.

Recall suggests a summoning back to mind and often a telling of what is brought back <can't *recall* the words of the song>.

Remind suggests a jogging of one's memory by an association or similarity <that *reminds* me of a story>.

Reminisce implies a casual often nostalgic recalling of experiences long past and gone <old college friends like to *reminisce*>.

remembrance see MEMORY.

remind see REMEMBER.

reminisce see REMEMBER.

reminiscence see MEMORY.

remiss see NEGLIGENT.

remonstrate see OBJECT.

remorse see PENITENCE.

remote see DISTANT.

removed see DISTANT.

remunerate see PAY.

rend see TEAR.

renew, restore, refresh, renovate, rejuvenate mean to make like new.

Renew implies so extensive a remaking or replacing that what had become faded or disintegrated now seems like new <efforts to *renew* a failing marriage>. ***ant*** wear out

Restore implies a return to an original or perfect state after damage, depletion, or loss <*restored* a fine piece of furniture>.

Refresh implies the supplying of something necessary to restore lost strength, animation, or power <lunch *refreshed* my energy>. ***ant*** jade, addle

Renovate suggests a renewing by cleansing, repairing, or rebuilding <the apartment has been entirely *renovated*>.

Rejuvenate suggests the restoration of youthful vigor, powers, and appearance <the change in jobs *rejuvenated* her spirits>.

renounce 1. see ABDICATE. **2.** see ABJURE.

renovate see RENEW.

renowned see FAMOUS.

rent see HIRE.

renunciation, abnegation, self-abnegation, self-denial mean voluntary surrender or forgoing of something desired or desirable.

Renunciation commonly connotes personal sacrifice for a higher end <widely admired for his voluntary *renunciation* of power>.

Abnegation and ***self-abnegation*** both imply a high degree of unselfishness or a capacity for putting aside personal interest or desires <undertook all her duties with an air of *abnegation*> <modesty verging on *self-abnegation*>. ***ant*** indulgence, self-indulgence

Self-denial usually applies to an act or a practice and implies a forbearance from gratifying one's desires, whatever the motive <the *self-denial* involved in following a rigid diet>. ***ant*** self-indulgence

repair see MEND.

repartee see WIT.

repay see PAY.

repeal see REVOKE.

repeat 1. Repeat, reiterate, iterate mean to say or do again.

Repeat stresses the fact of uttering, presenting, or doing again one or more times <*repeated* the joke over and over>.

Reiterate usually implies one repetition after another especially of something that is said <*reiterated* her views on the matter at every opportunity>.

Iterate means the same as *reiterate* but is rarer and has a bookish feel <an ancient theme *iterated* by many noted authors>. **2.** see QUOTE.

repellent see REPUGNANT.

repentance see PENITENCE.

replace, displace, supplant, supersede mean to put someone or something out of a usual or proper place or into the place of another.

Replace implies a filling of a place once occupied by something lost, destroyed, or no longer usable or adequate <the broken window will have to be *replaced*>.

Displace implies an ousting or dislodging or crowding out, often preceding a replacement <thousands had been *displaced* by the floods>.

Supplant implies either a dispossessing or usurping of another's place, possessions, or privileges or an uprooting of something and its replacement with something else <discovered that he had been *supplanted* in her affections by another>.

Supersede implies the replacing of a person or thing that has become superannuated, obsolete, or otherwise inferior <the new edition *supersedes* all previous ones>.

replete see FULL.

replica see REPRODUCTION.

reply see ANSWER.

report, rumor, gossip, hearsay mean common talk or an instance of it that spreads rapidly.

Report is likely to suggest some ground for belief unless specifically qualified as being false, untrue, or wild <it was common *report* that they were living together>.

Rumor applies to a report that flies about, often gains in detail as it spreads, but lacks both an evident source and clear-cut evidence of its truth <unsubstantiated *rumors* that spread like wildfire>.

Gossip applies primarily to the idle, often personal, chatter that is the chief source and means of propagating rumors or reports <wrote a *gossip* column for the local paper>.

Hearsay stresses the source of a rumor or report as what is heard rather than what is seen or known directly <rumored by *hearsay* to have a personal stake in the deal> and in its application to evidence retains this implication of indirect and imperfect knowledge of the facts <based his prosecution on *hearsay* evidence>.

reprehend see CRITICIZE.

repress see SUPPRESS.

reprimand see REPROVE.

reproach see REPROVE.

reprobate see CRITICIZE.

reproduction, duplicate, copy, facsimile, replica mean something that closely resembles a thing previously made, produced, or written.

Reproduction implies an exact or close imitation of an existing thing <*reproductions* from the museum's furniture collection>. ***ant*** original

Duplicate implies a double or counterpart exactly corresponding to an original in all significant respects <make a *duplicate* of the key>.

Copy applies especially to one of a number of things reproduced mechanically <*copies* of the report were issued to all>. ***ant*** original

Facsimile suggests a close reproduction in the same materials that may differ in scale <a *facsimile* of an illuminated medieval manuscript>.

Replica emphasizes the closeness of likeness and is specifically used of a reproduction made exactly like the original <*replicas* of the ships used by Columbus>.

reprove, rebuke, reprimand, admonish, reproach, chide mean to criticize adversely.

Reprove implies an often kindly censuring or blaming intended to correct a fault <gently *reproved* her table manners>.

Rebuke suggests a sharp or stern reproof <the papal letter *rebuked* dissenting church officials>.

Reprimand implies a severe, formal, and often public or official rebuke <a general officially *reprimanded* for speaking out of turn>.

Admonish suggests an earnest or friendly warning and counseling <*admonished* by my parents to control expenses>. ***ant*** commend

Reproach connotes the conveying of dissatisfaction or displeasure through criticism or faultfinding <were severely *reproached* for their late return>.

Chide suggests the expression of disappointment or displeasure through mild reproof or scolding <*chided* by their mother for not keeping their room clean>. ***ant*** commend

repudiate 1. see DECLINE. **2.** see DISCLAIM.

repugnant, repellent, abhorrent, distasteful, obnoxious, invidious mean so unlikable as to arouse antagonism or aversion.

Repugnant applies to something that is so alien to one's ideas, principles, or tastes as to arouse resistance or loathing <regards boxing as a *repugnant* sport>. ***ant*** congenial

Repellent suggests a generally forbidding or unpleasant quality that causes one to back away <the public display of grief was *repellent* to her>. ***ant*** attractive, pleasing

Abhorrent implies a repugnance that causes active antagonism <practices that are *abhorrent* to the American political system>. ***ant*** congenial

Distasteful implies a contrariness to one's tastes or inclinations <a family to whom displays of affection are *distasteful*>. ***ant*** agreeable, palatable

Obnoxious suggests an objectionableness, often on personal grounds, too great to tolerate <the colonists found the tea tax especially *obnoxious*>. ***ant*** grateful

Invidious applies to what cannot be used or performed without creating ill will, odium, or envy <the *invidious* task of deciding custody of the child>.

request see ASK 2.

require 1. see DEMAND. **2.** see LACK.

requirement, requisite, prerequisite mean something regarded as necessary for success or perfection.

Requirement may imply something more or less arbitrarily demanded, especially by those with a right to lay down conditions <college entrance *requirements*>.

Requisite implies something indispensable for the end in view or otherwise essential and not arbitrarily demanded <education is a prime *requisite* of a free society>.

Prerequisite applies to a requisite that must be available in advance or acquired as a preliminary <a chemistry course that was a *prerequisite* to further study in biology>.

requisite see REQUIREMENT.

requite see RECIPROCATE.

rescind see REVOKE.

rescue, deliver, redeem, ransom, reclaim, save mean to set free from confinement, risk or danger.

Rescue implies a freeing from imminent danger by prompt or vigorous action <*rescue* the crew of a sinking ship>.

Deliver implies the releasing usually of a person from confinement, temptation, slavery, suffering, or something that distresses <*delivered* his people from bondage>.

Redeem implies a releasing from bondage or penalties by giving what is demanded or necessary as an equivalent <*redeemed* her from a life of boredom>.

Ransom specifically applies to a buying out of captivity <subjects forced to *ransom* their king>.

Reclaim suggests a bringing back to a former state or condition of someone or something abandoned or debased <*reclaimed* long-abandoned farms>. ***ant*** abandon

Save may replace any of the foregoing terms, or it may further imply a preserving or maintaining for usefulness or continued existence <a social worker who *saved* youths from life as criminals>. ***ant*** lose, waste, damn

resemblance see LIKENESS.

resentment see OFFENSE.

reserve see KEEP 2.

reserved see SILENT.

reside, live, dwell, sojourn, lodge, stay, put up mean to have as one's habitation or domicile.

Reside expresses the idea that a person keeps or returns to a particular place as his or her fixed, settled, or legal abode <*reside* happily in New Hampshire>.

Live may stress the idea of actually spending one's time and carrying out the activities of one's family life <*lived* for years in the house next door>.

Dwell, a close synonym of these words, is likely to appear in elevated language <longed to *dwell* amongst trees and hills>.

Sojourn distinctively implies a temporary habitation or abode or a more or less uncertain place or way of living <*sojourned* for a while in the south of France>.

Lodge also suggests a habitation for a time and may connote restricted accommodations such as in a hotel or rooming house <chose to *lodge* there for the night>.

Stay is the term commonly used in place of *sojourn* or *lodge* <*stayed* at that hotel for the entire week>.

Put up is the equivalent of *lodge* and usually suggests the status of a guest <decided to *put up* at her sister's house for the weekend>.

resign **1.** see ABDICATE. **2.** see RELINQUISH.

resilient see ELASTIC.

resist see OPPOSE.

resolute see FAITHFUL.

resolution see COURAGE.

resolve **1.** see DECIDE. **2.** see ANALYZE.

resort *vb* **Resort, refer, apply, go, turn** mean to have recourse to something when in need of help or relief.

Resort may imply that one has encountered difficulties impossible to surmount without help <found he could get no relief unless he *resorted* to the courts>.

Refer suggests a need for authentic information or authoritative action and recourse to a source of this <whenever you come to an unfamiliar word, *refer* to your dictionary>.

Apply suggests having direct recourse, as by a letter or in person, to one able to supply what is needed <*apply* to a bank for a loan>.

Go and *turn* are more general but often more picturesque or more dramatic terms that suggest action or movement in seeking aid or relief <the president *went* directly to the people with his plan> <*turned* to his mother for comfort>.

resort *n* see RESOURCE.

resource, resort, expedient, shift, makeshift, stopgap mean something one turns to in the absence of the usual means or source of supply.

Resource applies to anything one falls back upon <haven't exhausted all of my *resources* yet>.

Resort is like *resource* but is used mostly with *last* or in the phrase "to have *resort* to" <favor a sales tax only as a last *resort*>.

Expedient may apply to any device or contrivance used when the usual one is not at hand or not possible <the flimsiest of *expedients* ends the tale>.

Shift implies a tentative or temporary imperfect expedient and often connotes dubiousness or trickery <her desperate *shifts* and dodges fooled no one>.

Makeshift implies an inferior expedient adopted because of urgent need or countenanced through indifference <the space heater was supposed to be only a *makeshift*>.

Stopgap applies to something used temporarily as an emergency measure <the farm aid bill is no more than a *stopgap*>.

respect see REGARD.

respite see PAUSE.

resplendent see SPLENDID.

respond see ANSWER.

responsible, answerable, accountable, amenable, liable mean subject to an authority that may hold one to account.

Responsible implies the holding of a specific or formal office, duty, or trust <the bureau *responsible* for revenue collection>.

Answerable suggests a relationship between one having a moral or legal obligation and an authority charged with oversight of its observance <a fact-finding committee *answerable* only to the President>.

Accountable suggests the imminence of retribution for unfulfilled trust or violated obligation <in a democracy the politicians are *accountable* to the voters>. ***ant*** unaccountable

Amenable stresses the fact of subjection to review, censure, or control by a designated authority and a limitation of power <laws are *amenable* to judicial review>. ***ant*** independent *(of)*, autonomous

Liable implies an obligation under the law to answer in case of default <will not be *liable* for his ex-wife's debts> or may suggest merely a contingent obligation <all citizens *liable* for jury duty>.

restful see COMFORTABLE.

restive see CONTRARY.

restore 1. see RENEW.

2. Restore, revive, revivify, resuscitate mean to regain or cause to regain signs of life and vigor.

Restore implies a return to consciousness, health, or vigor often by the use of remedies or treatments <hearing can sometimes be *restored* by surgery>.

Revive may imply recovery from a deathlike state, such as a stupor or faint <*revive* him from a faint with cold water> but is widely applicable to restoration to a flourishing state <the showers *revived* the withering crops>.

Revivify tends to suggest adding of new life and carries a weaker suggestion than *revive* of prior depletion <a good night's sleep *revivifies* the strongest person>.

Resuscitate commonly implies a restoration to consciousness by arduous efforts to overcome a serious impairment <*resuscitate* a nearly drowned person with artificial respiration> and can suggest a restoring to vitality of someone or something in which life seems nearly or wholly extinct <labored to *resuscitate* her old interest in sports>.

restrain, check, curb, bridle mean to hold back from or control in doing something.

Restrain suggests a holding back by force or persuasion from acting or from going to extremes <*restrained* themselves from trading insults>. ***ant*** impel, incite, activate, abandon *(oneself)*

Check implies the restraining or impeding of a progress, activity, or impetus <deep mud *checked* our progress>. ***ant*** accelerate, advance, release

Curb suggests an abrupt or drastic checking or a restricting or restraining that tends to moderate <learn to *curb* your appetite>. ***ant*** spur

Bridle implies a keeping under control by subduing or holding in <they could no longer *bridle* their interest>. ***ant*** vent

restrict see LIMIT.

result see EFFECT.

resuscitate see RESTORE.

retain see KEEP 2.

retaliate see RECIPROCATE.

retard see DELAY.

reticent see SILENT.

retire see GO.

retort see ANSWER.

retract 1. see ABJURE. **2.** see RECEDE.

retreat *vb* see RECEDE.

retreat *n* see SHELTER.

retrench see SHORTEN.

retrograde see RECEDE.

return 1. Return, revert, recur, recrudesce mean to go or come back.

Return may imply a going back to a starting place or source or to a former or proper place or condition <*returned* home to an enthusiastic welcome>.

Revert is likely to imply a going back to a former, often a lower, condition <*reverted* to an earlier, less civilized state>, but it can also apply to a returning after interruption <after careful consideration he *reverted* to his first decision>.

Recur implies a return, often repeated returns, of something that has happened or been experienced before <suffered from *recurring* headaches>.

Recrudesce implies a returning to life or activity especially of something that has been suppressed or kept under control <af-

ter an initial subsidence the epidemic *recrudesced* with renewed vigor>.

2. see RECIPROCATE.

reveal, discover, disclose, divulge, tell, betray mean to make known what has been or should be concealed.

Reveal suggests an unveiling of what is not clear to human vision and may apply to a supernatural or inspired revelation <the belief that divine will is *revealed* in the Bible> or a simple disclosure <an act that *revealed* his true nature>. ***ant*** conceal

Discover implies an uncovering of matters kept secret and not previously known <a step-by-step comparison that *discovered* a clear case of plagiarism>.

Disclose may also imply a discovering but more often suggests an imparting of information previously kept secret <candidates must *disclose* their financial assets>.

Divulge implies a disclosure involving some impropriety or breach of confidence <refused to *divulge* confidential information>.

Tell implies an imparting of necessary or useful information <never *told* her that he was married>.

Betray implies a divulging that represents a breach of faith or an involuntary or unconscious disclosure <a blush that *betrayed* her embarrassment>.

revenge see AVENGE.

revengeful see VINDICTIVE.

revere, reverence, venerate, worship, adore mean to regard with profound respect and honor.

Revere stresses deference and tenderness of feeling <a tradition *revered* by generations of scholars>. ***ant*** flout

Reverence presupposes an intrinsic merit and inviolability in the one honored and a corresponding depth of feeling in the one honoring <the general *reverenced* the army's code of honor>.

Venerate implies a holding as holy or sacrosanct because of character, association, or age <national heroes who are still *venerated*>.

Worship implies homage usually expressed in words or ceremony to a divine being or to a person to whom exalted character or outstanding merit is imputed <*worships* the memory of her husband>.

Adore, close to *worship,* implies love and stresses the notion of an individual and personal attachment <a doctor who is practically *adored* by her patients>. ***ant*** blaspheme

reverence *n* **1.** see HONOR.

2. Reverence, awe, fear mean the emotion inspired by something that arouses one's deep respect or veneration.

Reverence stresses a recognition of the sacredness or inviolability of the person or thing which stimulates the emotion <demonstrated a lack of *reverence* for the truth>.

Awe fundamentally implies a sense of being overwhelmed or overcome by great superiority or impressiveness and may suggest such varied reactions as standing mute, adoration, profound reverence, terror, or submissiveness <stood in *awe* of his talent>.

Fear in the sense here considered occurs chiefly in religious use and implies awed recognition of divine power and majesty <lived in *fear* of the Lord>. ***ant*** contempt

reverence *vb* see REVERE.

reverse 1. Reverse, transpose, invert mean to change to the opposite position.

Reverse may imply change in order, side, direction, or meaning <*reversed* his position on the arms agreement>.

Transpose implies a change in order or relative position of units often through exchange of position <anagrams are formed by *transposing* the letters of a word or phrase>.

Invert applies to a change from one side to another by a turning upside down or inside out <a typo consisting of a whole line of *inverted* type>.

2. see REVOKE.

revert see RETURN 1.

revile see SCOLD.

revise see CORRECT *vb*.

revive see RESTORE.

revivify see RESTORE.

revoke, reverse, repeal, rescind, recall mean to undo something previously done.

Revoke implies a calling back that annuls or abrogates what was previously done <had his license *revoked* for ninety days>.

Reverse usually applies specifically to a high court's action in overthrowing a disputed law, decree, or court decision <the court of appeals *reversed* the opinion of the circuit court>; when applied to actions or judgments of a non-judicial nature, it implies an upsetting of what was previously done <convinced the umpire to *reverse* his decision>.

Repeal usually implies revocation of a law or ordinance by the legislative body that made it <*repealed* the parking ban>.

Rescind implies the exercise of proper authority in abolishing or making void <*rescinded* their earlier decision in a new vote>.

Recall, a less technical term, can replace any of the others <*recall* a bid in bridge>.

revolt see REBELLION.

revolution see REBELLION.
rhapsody see BOMBAST.
rhythm, meter, cadence mean the more or less regular rise and fall in intensity of sounds that is associated especially with poetry and music.
Rhythm implies movement and flow as well as an agreeable succession of rising and falling sounds and the recurrence at fairly regular intervals of a stress, such as a prolonged syllable or an accented note <moved gracefully to the *rhythm*>.
Meter implies the reduction of rhythm to system and measure and the establishment of a definite rhythmical pattern <an epic in hendecasyllabic *meter*>.
Cadence may be equivalent to *rhythm* or to *meter* or may stress variety in ordered sequence, often with falling or rising effects <the gentle *cadence* of the local dialect>.
ribald see COARSE.
rich, wealthy, affluent, opulent mean having goods, property, and money in abundance.
Rich implies having more than enough to gratify normal needs or desires <one of the *richest* nations in the world>. ***ant*** poor
Wealthy stresses the abundant possession of property and intrinsically valuable things <retired from politics a *wealthy* man>. ***ant*** indigent
Affluent suggests prosperity and increasing wealth <an *affluent* society>. ***ant*** impecunious, straitened
Opulent suggests lavish expenditure and ostentatious display of great wealth <*opulent* mansions>. ***ant*** destitute, indigent
riddle see MYSTERY.
ridicule, deride, mock, taunt, twit mean to make an object of laughter of.
Ridicule implies a deliberate often malicious belittling <consistently *ridiculed* everything she said>.
Deride suggests a contemptuous and often bitter ridiculing <*derided* their efforts to start their own business>.
Mock implies a scornful deriding often ironically expressed by mimicry or sham deference <youngsters began to *mock* the helpless old man>.
Taunt suggests a jeeringly reproachful insult or derisive challenging <terrorists *taunted* the hostages>.
Twit usually suggests mild or good-humored teasing <students *twitted* their teacher about his tardiness>.
ridiculous see LAUGHABLE.
rife see PREVAILING.
right see CORRECT *adj*.
righteous see MORAL.
rigid 1. see STIFF.

2. Rigid, rigorous, strict, stringent mean extremely severe or stern.
Rigid implies uncompromising inflexibility <the school's admission standards are *rigid*>. ***ant*** lax
Rigorous implies the imposition of hardship and difficulty <the *rigorous* training of recruits>. ***ant*** mild
Strict emphasizes undeviating conformity to rules, standards, or requirements <their doctor put them on a *strict* diet>. ***ant*** lenient
Stringent suggests restrictions or limitations that curb or coerce <the judge's ruling is a *stringent* interpretation of the law>.

rigor see DIFFICULTY.
rigorous see RIGID.
rile see IRRITATE.
rim see BORDER.
rip see TEAR.
ripe see MATURE *adj.*
ripen see MATURE *vb.*
rise 1. see SPRING.
2. Rise, arise, ascend, mount, soar mean to move or come up from a lower to a higher level.
Rise is used in reference to persons or animals that get up from a lying or sitting position <*rise* every morning at five> or to things that seem to come up into view or to lift themselves up <hills *rising* from the plain> or to fluid that is sent upward by some natural force <watched the river *rising*>. ***ant*** decline, set *(as the sun)*
Arise comes close to *rise* but is somewhat more rhetorical or poetic <*arose* slowly, brushing the dust of the street from his clothes>. ***ant*** recline, slump
Ascend suggests a continuous or progressive upward movement or climbing <the sun *ascends* the sky until noon>. ***ant*** descend
Mount, close to *ascend,* implies a gradual upward movement toward an even higher level or degree <felt her hopes *mount* as the race went on>. ***ant*** drop
Soar usually connotes a continuous, often swift, ascent into high altitudes especially intellectually, spiritually, or aesthetically <the brilliant product of a *soaring* imagination>.

risible see LAUGHABLE.
risky see DANGEROUS.
rival 1. see MATCH.
2. Rival, compete, vie, emulate mean to strive to equal or surpass.
Rival usually suggests an attempt to outdo each other <success that *rivaled* hers>.
Compete stresses a struggle for an objective that may be con-

scious but is typically a quite impersonal striving <athletes *competing* in college sports>.

Vie suggests a less intense effort but a more conscious awareness of an opponent than *compete* <*vied* with one another for her attention>.

Emulate implies a conscious effort to equal or surpass one that serves as a model <strove to *emulate* his teachers>.

rive see TEAR.

roam see WANDER.

robbery see THEFT.

robust see HEALTHY.

rock see SHAKE 2.

root see ORIGIN.

rot see DECAY.

rotate, alternate mean to succeed or cause to succeed each other in turn.

Rotate, which may be used of two or more, implies an indefinite repetition of the order of succession <farmers who learned to *rotate* crops>.

Alternate, which is referable only to two, implies repetition but does not carry as strong a suggestion of continuity as *rotate* <*alternate* heat and cold in treating a sprain>.

rough 1. Rough, harsh, uneven, rugged, scabrous mean not smooth or even.

Rough implies the presence of detectable inequalities on the surface, such as points, bristles, ridges, or projections <a *rough* wooden board>. ***ant*** smooth

Harsh implies a surface or texture distinctly unpleasant to the touch <the *harsh* fabric chafed his skin>. ***ant*** pleasant, mild

Uneven implies a lack of regularity in height, breadth, or quality <an old house with *uneven* floors>. ***ant*** even

Rugged implies irregularity or roughness of land surface and connotes difficulty of travel <follow the *rugged* road up the mountain>.

Scabrous implies scaliness or prickliness of surface and may connote an unwholesome, decayed, or diseased appearance <an allergic condition that results in *scabrous* hands>. ***ant*** glabrous, smooth

2. see RUDE.

rouse see STIR *vb*.

rout see CONQUER.

rove see WANDER.

rude, rough, crude, raw, callow, green, uncouth mean lacking in the qualities that make for finish or perfection in development or use.

Rude implies ignorance of or indifference to good form or materials <fashioned a *rude* structure> or may suggest intentional discourtesy <consistently *rude* behavior toward her in-laws>.

Rough is likely to stress lack of polish and gentleness <the *rough* manners of a man used to living in the outback>. ***ant*** gentle

Crude may apply to thought or behavior that is gross, obvious, or primitive or ignorant of what is highly developed or fully civilized <the *crude* antics of college students on spring break>. ***ant*** consummate, finished

Raw suggests being unprocessed, untested, inexperienced, or unfinished <charged with turning *raw* youths into young men>.

Callow applies to the immature and suggests such youthful qualities as naïveté, simplicity, and lack of sophistication <the insensitivity of *callow* youth>. ***ant*** full-fledged, grownup

Green implies inexperience and lack of assurance, especially in a new or complex situation and often simplicity or gullibility <tested the mettle of the *green* recruits>. ***ant*** experienced, seasoned

Uncouth implies strangeness in comparison to what is felt to be normal, finished, or excellent, whether because crude and clumsy or because lacking in polish and grace <behavior that was unbearably *uncouth*>.

rugged see ROUGH.

ruin *n* **Ruin, havoc, devastation, destruction** mean the bringing about of or the results of disaster.

Ruin suggests collapse and is applicable to whatever has given way or fallen apart through decay, corruption, neglect, or loss <the old house had fallen to *ruin*>.

Havoc suggests an agent that pillages, destroys, or ravages and the resulting confusion and disorder <the *havoc* left by the earthquake>.

Devastation implies a widespread laying waste, as by war or a natural catastrophe, but it is also applicable to something that overwhelms an individual with comparable decisiveness <tried to overcome the *devastation* of losing a spouse>.

Destruction suggests an utter undoing by or as if by demolition or annihilation <saw the rapid *destruction* of his entire life's work>.

ruin *vb* **Ruin, wreck, dilapidate** mean to subject to forces that are destructive of soundness, worth, or usefulness.

Ruin usually suggests the action of destructive agencies and the ending of the value, beauty, or well-being of something or someone or the loss of something vital <a reputation *ruined* by ugly rumors>.

Wreck implies a ruining by or as if by crashing or being shattered and is likely to suggest damage that is beyond repair <health *wrecked* by dissipation>.

Dilapidate historically implies ruin resulting from neglect or abuse but in more general use implies a shabby, run-down, or tumbledown condition without direct suggestion of culpability <drove a *dilapidated* car>.

rule *n* see LAW.

rule *vb* **1.** see DECIDE. **2.** see GOVERN.

ruminate see PONDER.

rumor see REPORT.

rural, rustic, pastoral, bucolic mean relating to or characteristic of the country.

Rural suggests open country and farming <a diminishing portion of the island remains *rural*>. ***ant*** urban, citified

Rustic suggests a contrast with city life and connotes rudeness and lack of polish <a hunting lodge filled with *rustic* furniture and decoration>.

Pastoral implies an idealized simplicity and peacefulness and apartness from the world <the *pastoral* setting of an exclusive health resort>.

Bucolic may refer to either the charming and desirable or the undesirable aspects of country life <fed-up city dwellers imagining a *bucolic* bliss> <trapped in a *bucolic* nightmare>.

ruse see TRICK.

rustic see RURAL.

ruth see SYMPATHY.

S

sack see RAVAGE.

sacred, sacrosanct, inviolate, inviolable mean protected by law, custom, or respect against abuse.

Sacred implies either a setting apart for a special use <the battered chair by the fireside that was *sacred* to father> or a special quality that leads to an almost religious reverence <a *sacred* memory>.

Sacrosanct in general use may retain its religious implication of the utmost of sacredness, or it may take on an ironic quality and suggest a supposed rather than a real sacredness <failed to accept that such public figures were *sacrosanct*>.

Inviolate applies to such things as laws, agreements, institutions, or persons which for one reason or another are secure from abuse or injury, and it stresses the fact of not having been violated <the *inviolate* beauty of the wilderness>. ***ant*** violated

Inviolable, while close to *inviolate*, implies a character that is secure from violation <the *inviolable* sanctity of the law>.

sacrosanct see SACRED.

sadness, depression, melancholy, melancholia, dejection, gloom mean the state of mind of one who is unhappy or low-spirited.

Sadness is a general term that carries no suggestion of the cause, extent, or exact nature of low spirits <a feeling of *sadness* marked the farewell dinner>. ***ant*** gladness

Depression suggests a condition in which one feels let down, disheartened, despondent, or enervated <under a doctor's care for severe *depression*>. ***ant*** bouyancy

Melancholy suggests a mood of sad and serious but not wholly unpleasant pensiveness <old love letters that gave her cause for *melancholy*>. ***ant*** exhilaration

Melancholia applies to a disordered mental state characterized by settled deep depression <fell into a state of *melancholia* after her husband's death>.

Dejection implies a usually passing mood of one who is downcast or dispirited from a natural or logical cause <a struggling actor used to periods of *dejection*>. ***ant*** exhilaration

Gloom applies to either the extreme sadness of the person afflicted by any of these moods or conditions or the atmosphere or the effect on others created by one so afflicted <a universal *gloom* engulfed the devastated town>. ***ant*** glee

safe, secure mean free from danger or risk.

Safe can imply that a risk has been run without incurring harm or damage <arrived home *safe* and sound> or can stress freedom from risk <kept her *safe* from harm> or can suggest a character that eliminates or minimizes risk <*safe* investments>. ***ant*** dangerous, unsafe

Secure usually stresses a freedom from anxiety or apprehension of danger or risk based on grounds that appear sound and sufficient <reached a *secure* harbor before the storm broke>. ***ant*** insecure, precarious, dangerous

safeguard see DEFEND.

saga see MYTH.

sagacious see SHREWD.

sage see WISE.

salary see WAGE.

salient see NOTICEABLE.

salubrious see HEALTHFUL.

salutary see HEALTHFUL.

same, selfsame, very, identical, equivalent, equal mean not different or not differing from one another or others.

Same may imply that the things under consideration are one thing or, although distinct, have no appreciable difference <we took the *same* route on the *same* day>. ***ant*** different

Selfsame always implies that the things under consideration are one thing and not two or more things <it was the *selfsame* ring I had lost years ago>. ***ant*** diverse

Very, like *selfsame,* implies identity <you're the *very* person I've been looking for>.

Identical may imply self-sameness or suggest absolute agreement in all details <their test answers were *identical*>. ***ant*** nonidentical, diverse

Equivalent implies amounting to the same thing in worth or significance <two houses of *equivalent* market value>. ***ant*** different

Equal implies correspondence in value, magnitude, or some specified quality and therefore equivalence <divided it into *equal* shares>. ***ant*** unequal

sample see INSTANCE.

sanctimonious **1.** see DEVOUT. **2.** see HYPOCRITICAL.

sanction see APPROVE.

sanctuary see SHELTER.

sane see WISE.

sangfroid see EQUANIMITY.

sanguinary see BLOODY.

sanguine see BLOODY.

sap see WEAKEN.

sapient see WISE.

sarcasm see WIT.

sarcastic, satiric, ironic, sardonic mean marked by bitterness and a power or intent to cut or sting.

Sarcastic applies to what intentionally inflicts pain by deriding, taunting, or ridiculing <a critic famous for his *sarcastic* remarks>.

Satiric implies an intent to censure by ridicule and reprobation <a *satiric* look at contemporary sexual mores>.

Ironic implies an attempt to be amusing or provocative by saying something startlingly or surprisingly different from, and often the opposite of, what is meant <made the *ironic* observation that the goverment could always be trusted>.

Sardonic implies a scornful, mocking, or derisive disbelief or doubt that is manifested by either verbal or facial expression <surveyed the scene with a *sardonic* smile>.

sardonic see SARCASTIC.

sate see SATIATE.

satiate, sate, surfeit, cloy, pall, glut, gorge mean to fill completely or to excess.

Satiate and **sate** may sometimes imply only complete satisfaction but more often suggest fullness that has destroyed interest or desire <movies that purported to *satiate* their appetite for violence> <audiences were *sated* with dizzying visual effects>.

Surfeit implies a fullness to the point of nausea or disgust <*surfeited* themselves with junk food>. ***ant*** whet
Cloy stresses the disgust or boredom resulting from such surfeiting <sentimental pictures that *cloy* after a while>. ***ant*** whet
Pall emphasizes the loss of ability to stimulate interest or appetite <even a tropical paradise begins to *pall* after ten trips>.
Glut implies an excess in feeding or supplying that chokes or impedes <bookstores *glutted* with diet books>. ***ant*** stint
Gorge suggests a glutting to the point of bursting or choking <*gorged* themselves with chocolate>.

satiny see SLEEK.

satire see WIT.

satiric see SARCASTIC.

satisfy 1. Satisfy, content mean to appease one's desires or longings.
Satisfy implies the full appeasement not only of desires or longings but of needs or requirements <*satisfied* her fondest desire>. ***ant*** tantalize
Content implies an appeasement to the point where one is not disquieted or disturbed even though every wish is not fully gratified <refused to *content* herself with the answer>.
2. see PAY.
3. Satisfy, fulfill, meet, answer mean to measure up to a set of criteria or requirements.
Satisfy implies adequacy to an end or need in view and often suggests a standard of comparison <*satisfied* all the requirements for her degree>.
Fulfill, often interchangeable with *satisfy*, may imply more abundance or richness in measuring up to a need that is less calculable, more immeasurable <a son who *fulfilled* his father's fondest hopes>.
Meet implies an exactness of agreement between a requirement and what is submitted to fill it <designed to *meet* the demands of today's students>.
Answer usually implies the simple satisfaction of a demand, need, or purpose often in a temporary or expedient manner <a solution that *answered* their immediate need>.

saturate see SOAK.

saturnine see SULLEN.

saucy, pert, arch mean flippant and bold in manner or attitude.
Saucy is likely to stress levity with a hint of smartness or amusing effrontery <made a *saucy* retort>. ***ant*** deferential
Pert implies a saucy freedom that may verge on presumption or affectation <amused by the boy's *pert* answers> and sometimes also suggests sprightliness or cleverness <held her head at a *pert* angle>. ***ant*** coy

Arch usually implies a coquettish or roguish audacity or mischievous mockery <known for sly wit and *arch* posturing>.

saunter, stroll, amble mean to walk slowly and more or less aimlessly.

Saunter suggests a leisurely pace and an idle and carefree mind <*sauntered* down the road>.

Stroll implies the pursuit of an objective, such as sight-seeing or exercise, without haste and often without predetermined path <*strolled* past shops and through the market>.

Amble can replace either *saunter* or *stroll* but distinctively suggests an easy effortless gait <*ambled* through the crowd, greeting each guest>.

savage 1. see FIERCE. **2.** see BARBARIAN.

save 1. see RESCUE.

2. Save, preserve, conserve mean to keep secure from injury, decay, or loss.

Save in this connection can imply the taking of measures to protect against danger of loss, injury, or destruction <*saved* his papers in a vault>. ***ant*** spend, consume

Preserve stresses a resistance to destructive agencies and implies the use of methods and efforts to keep something intact or in existence <*preserve* food for winter use>.

Conserve suggests a keeping sound and unimpaired and implies the avoidance of undue use or of waste or loss or damage <took every possible measure to *conserve* fuel>. ***ant*** waste, squander

savoir faire see TACT.

savor see TASTE 1.

savory see PALATABLE.

say, utter, tell, state mean to put into words.

Say basically means to articulate words <*say* each word carefully and clearly>, but it may be used in reporting something voiced <he *said* he would be home soon> or in implying the fact of putting in speech or writing <be careful what you *say* to that man>.

Utter stresses the use of the voice and the act of putting into spoken words <*uttered* a faint response> and is appropriate for reference to vocal sounds other than words <*utter* a hoarse laugh>.

Tell stresses the imparting of an idea or information and may refer to either spoken or written communication or other method to present an idea <an attempt to *tell* the story of her life>.

State may replace *say* when the added implication of clearness and definiteness is needed <*state* one's objections to a proposal>.

scabrous see ROUGH.

scale see SCALE ASCEND.
scan see SCRUTINIZE.
scandal see OFFENSE 2.
scant see MEAGER.
scanty see MEAGER.
scarce see INFREQUENT.
scathing see CAUSTIC.
scatter, disperse, dissipate, dispel mean to cause to separate or break up.
Scatter implies the action of a force that drives parts of units irregularly in many directions <the bowling ball *scattered* the pins>. ***ant*** gather
Disperse implies a wider separation of units and a complete breaking up of the mass or group <police *dispersed* the crowd>. ***ant*** assemble, congregate, collect
Dissipate stresses a complete disintegration or dissolution and final disappearance <the fog was *dissipated* by the morning sun>. ***ant*** accumulate, concentrate (*efforts, thoughts*)
Dispel stresses a driving away or getting rid of by or as if by scattering <an authoritative statement that *dispelled* all doubt>.
scent 1. see FRAGRANCE. **2.** see SMELL.
scheme see PLAN.
scholarly see LEARNED.
scholarship see KNOWLEDGE.
scholastic see PEDANTIC.
school see TEACH.
scoff, jeer, gibe, fleer, sneer, flout mean to show one's contempt through derision or mockery.
Scoff stresses a deriding motivated by insolence, disrespect, or incredulity <*scoffed* at the religious faith of others>.
Jeer suggests a coarser more undiscriminating derision <the crowd *jeered* the visiting team>.
Gibe implies a taunting either good-naturedly or in sarcastic derision <*gibed* at him for repeatedly missing the ball>.
Fleer suggests a grinning or grimacing derisively <some freshmen were greeted by *fleering* seniors>.
Sneer stresses an insulting by contemptuous facial expression, phrasing, or tone of voice <*sneered* at anything even remotely romantic>.
Flout stresses a showing of contempt by refusal to heed or by denial of a thing's truth or power <*flouted* the conventions of polite society>. ***ant*** revere
scold, upbraid, berate, rail, revile, vituperate mean to reproach angrily and abusively.
Scold implies a rebuking in irritation or ill temper justly or unjustly <relieved her frustrations by *scolding* the children>.

Upbraid implies a censuring on definite and usually justifiable grounds <the governor *upbraided* his aides for poor research>.

Berate suggests a prolonged and often abusive scolding <*berated* continually by a violent, abusive father>.

Rail, used with *at* or *against*, stresses an unrestrained berating <*railed* loudly at the whims of fate>.

Revile implies a scurrilous, abusive attacking prompted by anger or hatred <a President vehemently *reviled* in the press>. ***ant*** laud

Vituperate suggests a violent, abusive reviling <a preacher more given to *vituperating* than to inspiring>. ***ant*** acclaim

scope see RANGE.

scorn see DESPISE.

scout see DESPISE.

scowl see FROWN.

scrap see DISCARD.

scrawny see LEAN.

screen see HIDE.

scruple see QUALM.

scrupulous 1. see CAREFUL. **2.** see UPRIGHT.

scrutinize, scan, inspect, examine mean to look at or over carefully and usually critically.

Scrutinize stresses the application of close observation and attention to minute detail <closely *scrutinized* the bill from the hospital>.

Scan implies a surveying from point to point that often suggests a cursory overall observation <quickly *scanned* the wine list>.

Inspect implies a searching scrutinizing for errors or defects <*inspected* the restaurant for health-code violations>.

Examine suggests a scrutinizing or investigating in order to determine the nature, condition, or quality of a thing <*examined* the gems to see whether they were genuine>.

scurrility see ABUSE.

scurvy see CONTEMPTIBLE.

seasonable, timely, well-timed, opportune, pat mean peculiarly appropriate to the time or situation.

Seasonable implies appropriateness to the season or being perfectly fitted to the occasion or situation <*seasonable* weather>. ***ant*** unseasonable

Timely applies to what occurs or appears at the time or moment when it is most useful or valuable <a *timely* warning>. ***ant*** untimely

Well-timed applies to what is so timely as to suggest care, forethought, or design <a *well-timed* remark that stifled objections>. ***ant*** ill-timed

Opportune describes something that comes, often by chance, at the best possible moment and works to the advantage of those concerned <an idea that arose from an *opportune* remark>. ***ant*** inopportune

Pat may apply to what is notably apt, ready, or well-suited to the occasion <a *pat* remark> or to what is so very apt as to be suspect <offered an alibi that seemed too *pat*>.

seclusion see SOLITUDE.

secret, covert, stealthy, furtive, clandestine, surreptitious, underhanded mean existing or done without attracting observation or attention.

Secret implies concealment on any grounds for any motive <a *secret* meeting>.

Covert stresses the fact of not being open or declared <*covert* operations against guerrilla forces>. ***ant*** overt

Stealthy suggests taking pains to avoid being seen or heard especially in some misdoing <the *stealthy* movements of a cat burglar>.

Furtive implies a sly or cautious stealthiness <exchanged *furtive* smiles across the room>. ***ant*** forthright, barefaced, brazen

Clandestine implies secrecy usually for an evil or illicit purpose <a *clandestine* drug deal in a back alley>. ***ant*** open

Surreptitious applies to action or behavior done secretly often with skillful avoidance of detection and in violation of custom, law, or authority <compromised his diet with *surreptitious* snacking>. ***ant*** brazen

Underhanded stresses fraudulent or deceptive intent <a car dealership guilty of *underhanded* practices>. ***ant*** aboveboard

secrete see HIDE.

secretive see SILENT.

section see PART.

secure *adj* see SAFE.

secure *vb* **1.** see ENSURE. **2.** see GET.

sedate see SERIOUS.

seduce see LURE.

sedulous see BUSY.

see 1. See, behold, descry, espy, view, survey, contemplate, observe, notice, remark, note, perceive, discern mean to take cognizance of something by physical or sometimes mental vision.

See may be used to imply little more than the use of the organs of vision <he cannot *see* the crowd for he is blind> but more commonly implies a recognition or appreciation of what is before one's eyes <went to *see* a ballgame> or the exercise of other powers including a vivid imagination <I can *see* her plainly now, as she looked forty years ago> or mental sight <he was the only one who *saw* the truth> or powers of inference <though he appeared calm, I could *see* he was inwardly agitated>.

Behold carries a stronger implication of ocular impression and of distinct recognition and also suggests looking at what is seen <never *beheld* such beauty>.
Descry often suggests an effort to discover or a looking out for someone or something despite difficulties such as distance, darkness, or concealment <could barely *descry* his form in the gathering darkness>.
Espy usually implies skill in detection of what is small, or is not clearly within the range of vision, or is trying to escape detection <at last *espied* the narrow path along the cliff>.
View usually implies the mental or physical seeing of what is spread before one or what can be examined in detail and often implies a particular way of looking at a thing or a particular purpose in considering it <*view* a painting from various angles>.
Survey more often implies a detailed scrutiny or inspection by the eyes or the mind so that one has a picture or idea of something as a whole <carefully *surveyed* the scene before entering the room>.
Contemplate implies a fixing of the eyes upon something in abstraction, in enjoyment, or in reference to some end in view <a relaxed moment *contemplating* the sunset>.
Observe implies a heeding and not passing over and may carry an implication of directed attention <closely *observed* their reaction>.
Notice often implies some definite reaction to what is seen or sometimes heard, felt, or sensed, such as making a mental note of it or a remark about it <*noticed* with alarm that the door was unlocked>.
Remark is likely to suggest a registering mentally of one's impression and a judging or criticizing of what is noticed <disdainfully *remarked* the apparent camaraderie between them>.
Note often suggests a recording of one's impressions sometimes by a mental note, but sometimes in writing or in speech <he carried a map and *noted* every stream and every hill that we passed>.
Perceive carries a stong implication of the use of the mind in observation and implies an apprehension or obtaining of knowledge of a thing, not only though the sense of sight but through any of the senses <*perceived* the rock to be made of granite> and often connotes keen mental vision or special insight and penetration <was able to *perceive* the danger of their situation>.
Discern, like *descry,* often implies little more than a making out of something by means of the eyes <*discerned* an eagle high overhead> but more distinctively implies the powers of

deeply perceiving and of distinguishing or discriminating what the senses perceive <tried hard to *discern* her meaning>.

2. See, look, watch mean to perceive something by use of the eyes.

See stresses the fact of receiving visual impressions <she *sees* well with her new glasses>.

Look stresses the directing of the eyes to or the fixing of the eyes on something <*looked* long and hard at his receding form>.

Watch implies a following of something with one's eyes so as to keep it under constant observation <*watching* the clock as closely as a cat *watches* a mouse>.

seem, look, appear mean to give the impression of being as stated without necessarily being so in fact.

Seem is likely to suggest an opinion based on subjective impressions and personal reaction <*seemed* to be strong and healthy>.

Look implies an opinion based on general visual impression <*looked* exactly like his picture>.

Appear may convey the same implications as *look* but often it suggests an obviously distorted impression <an explanation that *appeared* to be true>.

seeming see APPARENT.

segment see PART.

seize see TAKE.

select, elect, picked, exclusive mean set apart by some superior character or quality.

Select refers to one chosen with discrimination in preference to others of the same class <the hotel caters to a *select* clientele> or may be used in the sense of *superior* or *exceptional* with little or no suggestion of choice <aimed at a *select* audience>. ***ant*** indiscriminate

Elect stresses the notion of being chosen and carries a strong implication of admission to a restricted or inner circle and often one of special privilege <considered herself among the *elect*>.

Picked commonly applies to what is conspicuously superior and may suggest the best available <the candidates were all *picked* citizens>.

Exclusive basically implies a character that sets apart or rules out whatever is not compatible or congruous <presented as a set of contradictory and mutually *exclusive* demands> but in respect to persons, groups, or institutions is likely to suggest a feeling of superiority as the basis for ruling out what is felt as beneath imposed standards or fastidious and critical requirements <membership in an *exclusive* club>. ***ant*** inclusive

selection see CHOICE *n*.

self-abnegation see RENUNCIATION.

self-assertive see AGGRESSIVE.
self-denial see RENUNCIATION.
self-possession see CONFIDENCE.
selfsame see SAME.
sensation, sense, feeling, sensibility mean the power to respond or the act of responding to stimuli.

Sensation may center attention on the fact of perception through or as if through the sense organs, with or without comprehension <felt a tingling *sensation*> but often suggests not only recognition but also intellectual and emotional reactions <bothered by the *sensation* that he was being ignored>.

Sense may differ little from *sensation* <as the fire burned lower a *sense* of chill crept over them> or it may be applied specifically to any one of the basic perceptive powers <the *sense* of smell>, but in its typical application to the power or act of responding to stimuli it tends to stress intellectual awareness and full consciousness <a *sense* of frustration>.

Feeling may apply to sensations such as touch, heat, cold, or pressure that are perceived through the skin <so cold she had no *feeling* in her fingers> or to a complex response to stimulation involving sensation, emotion, and a degree of thought <had a vague *feeling* of unease> or to the power to respond <a sentient, *feeling* being>.

Sensibility often replaces *feeling* in this last use, especially when a keenly impressionable nature is to be implied <a creature of gentle nature and great *sensibility*> or excessive or affected responsiveness suggested <made a great show of effete *sensibilities*>. ***ant*** insensibility

sense 1. see SENSATION.

2. Sense, common sense, gumption, judgment, wisdom mean ability to reach intelligent conclusions.

Sense implies a reliable ability to judge and decide with soundness, prudence, and intelligence <hasn't the *sense* to come in out of the rain>.

Common sense suggests an average degree of such ability often with native shrewdness but without sophistication or special knowledge <*common sense* tells me it's wrong>.

Gumption suggests a readiness to use or apply common sense and stresses initiative or drive <a shrewd businessman known for his *gumption*>.

Judgment implies sense tempered and refined by experience, training, and maturity <*judgment* is required of a camp counselor>.

Wisdom implies sense and judgment far above average <the *wisdom* that comes from years of experience>. ***ant*** folly, injudiciousness

3. see MEANING.

sensibility see SENSATION.
sensible 1. see AWARE. **2.** see MATERIAL. **3.** see PERCEPTIBLE. **4.** see WISE.
sensitive see LIABLE.
sensual 1. see CARNAL. **2.** see SENSUOUS.
sensuous, sensual, luxurious, voluptuous, sybaritic, epicurean mean relating to or providing pleasure through gratification of the senses.
Sensuous implies gratification for the sake of aesthetic pleasure <the *sensuous* delights of a Reubens painting>.
Sensual tends to imply the gratification of the senses or the indulgence of the physical appetites as ends in themselves <a man who indulged his *sensual* appetites>.
Luxurious suggests the providing of or indulgence in sensuous pleasure inducing bodily ease and languor and a grateful peace of mind <a vacation devoted to *luxurious* self-indulgence>. ***ant*** ascetic
Voluptuous implies more strongly an abandonment to sensual or sensuous pleasure for its own sake <promised a variety of *voluptuous* pleasures>. ***ant*** ascetic
Sybaritic suggests voluptuousness of an overrefined sort, especially with regard to food, drink, and surroundings <indulged in a *sybaritic* feast>.
Epicurean implies a catering to or indulging in the satisfaction of refined and fastidious physical pleasures <enjoyed a gently *epicurean* way of life>.
sentiment 1. see FEELING. **2.** see OPINION.
separate *vb* **Separate, part, divide, sever, sunder, divorce** mean to become or cause to become disunited or disjointed.
Separate may imply any of several causes such as dispersion, removal of one from others, or presence of an intervening thing <*separated* her personal life from her career>. ***ant*** combine
Part implies the separating of things or persons from close union or association <an argument that *parted* the friends permanently>. ***ant*** unite
Divide implies a separating into pieces, groups, or sections by cutting, breaking, or branching <civil war *divided* the nation>. ***ant*** unite
Sever implies violence especially in the removal of a part or member <his arm had been *severed* by a chain saw>.
Sunder suggests a violent rending or wrenching apart <a friendship *sundered* only by death>.
Divorce implies a separating of two things that commonly interact and belong together <would *divorce* scientific research from moral responsibility>.
separate *adj* **1.** see DISTINCT. **2.** see SINGLE.
serene see CALM.

serious, grave, solemn, sedate, staid, sober, earnest mean not light or frivolous.

Serious implies a concern for what really matters <prefers gothic romances to *serious* fiction>. ***ant*** light, flippant

Grave implies both seriousness and dignity in expression or attitude <read the pronouncement in a *grave* voice>. ***ant*** gay

Solemn suggests an impressive gravity utterly free from levity <the *solemn* occasion of a coronation>.

Sedate implies a composed and decorous seriousness <amidst the frenzy of activity the bride remained *sedate*>. ***ant*** flighty

Staid suggests a settled, accustomed sedateness and prim self-restraint <her dinner parties were *staid* affairs>. ***ant*** unstaid

Sober stresses a seriousness of purpose and absence of levity or frivolity <an objective and *sober* look at the situation>. ***ant*** gay

Earnest suggests a sincerity or often zealousness of purpose <an *earnest* attempt at dramatizing the Bible>. ***ant*** frivolous

servile see SUBSERVIENT.

servitude, slavery, bondage mean the state of being subject to a master.

Servitude, often vague or rhetorical in application, implies in general lack of liberty to do as one pleases <lived in *servitude* to the daily grind> or, more specifically, lack of freedom to determine one's course of action or way of life <a man sentenced to penal *servitude*>.

Slavery implies subjection to a master who owns one's person and may treat one as property <captured and sold into *slavery*> or sometimes a comparable subservience to something that dominates like a master <in *slavery* to his own ambition>.

Bondage implies a being bound by law or by other, usually physical, constraint in a state of complete subjection <the *bondage* of the Hebrews in Egypt>.

set *n* **Set, circle, coterie, clique** mean a more or less closed and exclusive group of persons.

Set applies to a comparatively large, typically social, group of persons bound together by common interests or tastes <the hunting *set*>.

Circle implies a common center of the group, such as a person, an activity, or a cause <a peaceful family *circle*>.

Coterie applies to a small, select, or exclusive circle <political aspirants, each with a *coterie* of advisors>.

Clique is likely to suggest a selfish or arrogant exclusiveness and is especially applicable to a small inner or dissident group within a larger set or circle <a high school made up of combative *cliques*>.

set *vb* **Set, settle, fix, establish** mean to put securely in position.

Set stresses the fact of placing in a definite, often final position or situation or relation <*set* food on the table>.

Settle carries a stronger suggestion of putting in a place or condition of stability, ease, or security <*settled* themselves gradually in their new home> and may imply a decisiveness or finality in ordering or adjusting something previously disturbed or unsettled <*settle* doubts with a clear explanation>. ***ant*** unsettle

Fix stresses permanence and stability <*fixed* the pole firmly in the ground>. ***ant*** alter, abrogate *(a custom, rule, or law)*

Establish is likely to give less stress to the fact of putting something in place than to subsequent fostering and care that helps it become stable and fixed <do not transplant a tree once it is *established*>. ***ant*** uproot, abrogate *(a right, privilege, or quality)*

setting see BACKGROUND.

settle 1. see DECIDE. **2.** see SET *vb.*

sever see SEPARATE.

several see DISTINCT.

severe, stern, austere, ascetic mean given to or marked by strict discipline and firm restraint.

Severe implies standards enforced without indulgence or laxity and may suggest harshness <the *severe* dress of the Puritans>. ***ant*** tolerant, tender

Stern stresses inflexibility and inexorability of temper or character <a *stern* judge who seemed immune to pleas for mercy>. ***ant*** soft, lenient

Austere stresses absence of warmth, color, or feeling and may imply rigorous restraint, simplicity, or self-denial <the view that modern architecture is *austere,* brutal, and inhuman>. ***ant*** luscious *(of fruits),* warm, ardent *(of persons, feelings),* exuberant *(of style, quality)*

Ascetic implies abstention from pleasure and comfort or self-indulgence as a measure of self- or spiritual discipline <the *ascetic* life of the monastic orders>. ***ant*** luxurious, voluptuous

shackle see HAMPER.

shade see COLOR.

shake 1. Shake, tremble, quake, totter, quiver, shiver, shudder, quaver, wobble, teeter, shimmy, dither mean to exhibit vibrating, wavering, or oscillating movement often as an evidence of instability.

Shake can apply to any such movement, often with a suggestion of roughness and irregularity <he *shook* with fear>.

Tremble applies specifically to a slight, rapid shaking <her body *trembling* with fear>.

Quake may be used in place of *tremble* but it commonly carries a stronger implication of violent shaking or of extreme agitation either from an internal convulsion, such as an earthquake, or from an external event that rocks a person or thing to its foundations <a stern lecture that made them *quake*>.

Totter usually suggests great physical weakness such as that associated with infancy, extreme old age, or disease and often connotes a shaking that makes movement extremely difficult and uncertain or that forebodes a fall or collapse <the mast *tottered* before it fell>.

Quiver may suggest a slight, very rapid shaking <aspen leaves *quiver* in the slightest breeze>, or it may suggest fear or passion and an implication of emotional tension <the little boy's lips *quivered* as he tried not to cry>.

Shiver typically suggests the effect of cold that produces a momentary quivering <came into the house snow-covered and *shivering*>, but it may apply to a quivering that results from an anticipation, a premonition, a foreboding, or a vague fear <*shivered* at the sight of the ancient gravestone>.

Shudder usually suggests a brief or temporary shaking that affects the entire body or mass and is the effect of something horrible or revolting <*shuddered* uncontrollably at the eerie shrieks>.

Quaver sometimes implies irregular vibration and fluctuation, especially as an effect of something that disturbs <the *quavering* flame of the candle> but often stresses tremulousness especially in reference to voices affected by weakness or emotion <made her plea in a voice *quavering* with fear>.

Wobble implies an unsteadiness that shows itself in tottering, or in a quivering characteristic of a mass of soft flesh or soft jelly, or in a shakiness characteristic of rickety furniture <his table *wobbles*>.

Teeter implies an unsteadiness that reveals itself in seesawing motions <an inebriated man *teetering* as he stands>.

Shimmy suggests the fairly violent shaking of the body from the shoulders down which is characteristic of the dance of that name and, therefore, may suggest vibrating motions of an abnormal nature <the *shimmying* of unbalanced front wheels of an automobile>.

Dither implies a shaking or a hesitant vacillating movement often as a result of nervousness, confusion, or lack of purpose <*dithered* incoherently>.

2. Shake, agitate, rock, convulse mean to move up and down or to and fro with some violence.

Shake often carries a further implication of purpose <*shake* well before using>.

Agitate suggests a violent and prolonged tossing or stirring <strong winds *agitated* the leaves on the trees>. ***ant*** quiet, lull, still

Rock suggests a swinging or swaying motion that is likely to result from violent impact or upheaval <the entire city was *rocked* by the explosion>.

Convulse suggests a violent pulling or wrenching as of a body in a paroxysm <we were *convulsed* with laughter>.

shallow see SUPERFICIAL.

sham *n* see IMPOSTURE.

sham *vb* see ASSUME.

shame see DISGRACE.

shameless, brazen, barefaced, brash, impudent mean characterized by boldness and a lack of a sense of shame.

Shameless implies a lack of effective restraints, such as modesty, an active conscience, or a sense of decency <told a *shameless* lie>.

Brazen adds to *shameless* an implication of defiant insolence <stood up to him with *brazen* arrogance>. ***ant*** bashful

Barefaced implies absence of all efforts to disguise or mask one's transgression and connotes extreme effrontery <a *barefaced* lie>. ***ant*** furtive

Brash stresses impetuousness and may imply heedlessness and temerity <won them over with his *brash* but charming manner>. ***ant*** wary

Impudent adds to *shameless* implications of bold or pert defiance of considerations of modesty or decency <a rude and *impudent* reply to a polite question>. ***ant*** respectful

shape *n* see FORM.

shape *vb* see MAKE.

share, participate, partake mean to have, get, or use in common with another or others.

Share may imply that one as the original holder grants to another the partial use, enjoyment, or possession of a thing, or may merely imply a mutual use or possession <*shared* my tools with the others>.

Participate implies a having or taking part in an undertaking, activity, or discussion <students are encouraged to *participate* in outside activities>.

Partake implies accepting or acquiring a share especially of food or drink <invited everyone to *partake* freely of the refreshments>.

sharp, keen, acute mean having or showing alert competence and clear understanding.

Sharp implies quick perception, clever resourcefulness, or sometimes devious cunning <*sharp* enough to know a con job when he saw one>. ***ant*** dull, blunt

Keen suggests quickness, enthusiasm, and a clear-sighted, penetrating mind <a *keen* observer of the political scene>. ***ant*** blunt

Acute implies a power to penetrate and may suggest subtlety and depth and sharpness of insight <an *acute* sense of what is linguistically effective>. ***ant*** obtuse

shed see DISCARD.

sheer see STEEP.

shelter *n* **Shelter, cover, retreat, refuge, asylum, sanctuary** mean the state or a place in which one is safe or secure from what threatens or disturbs.

Shelter implies temporary protection of a shield or roof from something that would harm or annoy <seek *shelter* from the storm in a cave>.

Cover stresses concealment and often applies to a natural shelter or something similarly protective <advanced under *cover* of darkness>. ***ant*** exposure

Retreat stresses usually voluntary retirement from danger or annoyance and escape to a safe, secure, or peaceful place <built themselves a country *retreat*>.

Refuge implies an attempt to flee from whatever threatens or harasses <sought *refuge* in the deserted house>.

Asylum adds to *refuge* the implication of the finding of safety and of exemption from seizure <asked for and was granted political *asylum*>.

Sanctuary stresses the claim of a refuge to reverence or inviolability <established a wildlife *sanctuary*>.

shelter *vb* see HARBOR.

shield see DEFEND.

shift see RESOURCE.

shimmer see FLASH.

shimmy see SHAKE 1.

ship see BOAT.

shiver see SHAKE 1.

shocking see FEARFUL 2.

shoot, branch, bough, limb mean one of the members of a plant that are outgrowths from a crown or from a main base or one of its divisions.

Shoot stresses actual growing and is applicable chiefly to new growth from a bud <allowed only the strongest *shoots* to grow>.

Branch suggests a spreading out by dividing and subdividing and applies typically to a matured member arising from a primary stem or trunk or from a division or subdivision of one of these <*branches* silhouetted against the sky>.

Bough may replace *branch*, in reference to a tree or shrub, especially when the notion of foliage or blossom or fruit is prominent <pine *boughs* for Christmas decoration>.

Limb is likely to apply to a main branch arising directly from a trunk <the great *limbs* of the old oak>.

shopworn see TRITE.
short see BRIEF.
shorten, curtail, abbreviate, abridge, retrench mean to reduce in extent.
Shorten implies a reduction in length or duration <*shorten* the speech to fit the allotted time>. ***ant*** lengthen, elongate, extend
Curtail adds an implication of cutting that in some way deprives of completeness or adequacy <ceremonies *curtailed* because of the rain >. ***ant*** prolong, protract
Abbreviate implies a making shorter usually by omitting or cutting off some part <hostile questioning that *abbreviated* the interview>. ***ant*** lengthen, extend
Abridge implies a reduction in compass or scope with retention of essential elements and relative completeness of the result <the *abridged* version of the novel>. ***ant*** expand, extend
Retrench suggests a reduction in extent of something felt to be excessive <falling prices forced the company to *retrench*>.
short-lived see TRANSIENT.
shortly see PRESENTLY.
shove see PUSH.
show 1. Show, manifest, evidence, evince, demonstrate mean to reveal outwardly or make apparent.
Show implies that what is revealed must be inferred from acts, looks, or words <careful not to *show* what he feels>.
Manifest implies a plainer, more direct, and more immediate revelation <*manifested* musical ability at an early age>. ***ant*** suggest
Evidence suggests a serving as proof of the actuality or existence of something <her deep enmity is *evidenced* by her silent glare>.
Evince implies a showing by outward marks or signs <he *evinced* no interest in the project>.
Demonstrate implies a showing by action or by display of feelings or evidence <*demonstrated* her appreciation in her own way>.
2. Show, exhibit, display, expose, parade, flaunt mean to present in such a way as to invite notice or attention.
Show implies a presenting to view so that others may see or look at <*showed* her snapshots to the whole group>. ***ant*** disguise
Exhibit stresses a putting forward prominently or openly <*exhibit* paintings at a gallery>.
Display emphasizes putting in a position so as to be seen to advantage or with great clearness <*display* sale items>.
Expose suggests a bringing forth from concealment and a displaying, often with a suggestion of unmasking <sought to *expose* the hypocrisy of the town fathers>.

Parade implies an ostentatious or arrogant displaying <*parading* their piety for all to see>.

Flaunt suggests a shameless, boastful, often offensive parading <nouveaux riches *flaunting* their wealth>.

showy, pretentious, ostentatious mean given to or making excessive outward display.

Showy inplies an imposing or striking appearance but usually suggests cheapness or poor taste <the *showy* costumes of the circus performers>.

Pretentious implies an appearance of importance not justified by the thing's value or the person's standing <for a family-style restaurant, the menu was far too *pretentious*>. ***ant*** unpretentious

Ostentatious stresses conspicuous or vainglorious display or parade that may or may not be showy or pretentious <very *ostentatious*, even for a debutante party>. ***ant*** unostentatious

shrewd, sagacious, perspicacious, astute mean acute in perception and sound in judgment.

Shrewd stresses the possession or effect of practical, hard-headed cleverness and wise, although sometimes selfish, judgment <a *shrewd* judge of character>.

Sagacious suggests wisdom, penetration, farsightedness, and mature keenness of judgment <a series of *sagacious* investments tripled her wealth>.

Perspicacious implies unusual power to see into and understand what is puzzling or hidden <the *perspicacious* counselor saw through his facade>. ***ant*** dull

Astute suggests shrewdness, perspicacity, and artfulness and, often, an incapacity for being fooled <an *astute* player of party politics>. ***ant*** gullible

shrink 1. see CONTRACT. **2.** see RECOIL.

shrivel see WITHER.

shudder see SHAKE 1.

shun see ESCAPE.

shy, bashful, diffident, modest, coy mean not inclined to be forward or obtrude oneself.

Shy implies a timid reserve and a shrinking from familiarity or contact with others <*shy* in front of total strangers>. ***ant*** bold, obtrusive

Bashful implies a frightened or hesitant shyness characteristic of immaturity <the *bashful* boy rarely told us how he felt about anything>. ***ant*** brash, forward

Diffident stresses a distrust of one's own ability, opinion, or powers that causes hesitation in acting or speaking <felt *diffident* about raising an objection>. ***ant*** confident

Modest suggests absence of undue confidence or conceit or of boldness or self-assertion <very *modest* about reciting his achievements>.

Coy implies an assumed or affected shyness <don't be misled by her *coy* demeanor>.

side see PHASE.

sign 1. Sign, mark, token, note, symptom mean a discernible indication of what is not itself directly perceptible.

Sign applies to any indication to be perceived by the senses or the reason <interpreted her smile as a good *sign*>.

Mark suggests something impressed on or inherently characteristic of a thing often in contrast to something outwardly evident <the bitter experience left its *mark* on him>.

Token applies to something that serves as a proof or offers evidence of something intangible <this gift is a *token* of our esteem>.

Note suggests a distinguishing mark or characteristic <a *note* of despair pervades her poetry>.

Symptom suggests detectable outward indication of an internal change or abnormal condition <rampant violence is a *symptom* of that country's decline>.

2. Sign, signal mean something, such as a gesture or action, by which a command or wish is expressed or a thought made known.

Sign is applicable to any means by which one conveys information without verbal communication <made a *sign* to the others to wait while he reconnoitered>.

Signal usually applies to a conventional and readily recognizable sign that conveys a command, a direction, or a warning <saw the coach's *signal*> or it may apply to a mechanical device that performs a comparable function <waiting for a traffic *signal* to change to green>.

signal *adj* see NOTICEABLE.

signal *n* see SIGN 2.

significance 1. see IMPORTANCE. **2.** see MEANING.

signification see MEANING.

silent 1. Silent, taciturn, reticent, reserved, secretive mean showing restraint in speaking.

Silent implies a habit of saying no more than is needed <her husband was the *silent* type, not given to idle chatter>. ***ant*** talkative

Taciturn implies a temperamental disinclination to speech and usually connotes unsociability <the locals are *taciturn* and not receptive to outsiders>. ***ant*** garrulous

Reticent implies a reluctance to speak out or at length, especially about one's own affairs <strangely *reticent* about his plans>. ***ant*** frank, unreticent

Reserved implies reticence and suggests the restraining influence of caution or formality in checking easy informal exchange <a *reserved* and distant demeanor>. ***ant*** effusive

Secretive, too, implies reticence but usually carries a disparaging suggestion of lack of frankness or of an often ostentatious will to conceal something that might reasonably be made known <a *secretive* public official usually stingy with news stories>.

2. see STILL.

silhouette see OUTLINE.

silken see SLEEK.

silky see SLEEK.

silly see SIMPLE.

similar, analogous, like, alike, akin, parallel, homogeneous, uniform, identical mean closely resembling each other.

Similar implies such likeness as allows the possibility of being mistaken for another <all the houses in the development are *similar*>. ***ant*** dissimilar

Analogous applies to things having many similarities but belonging to essentially different categories <*analogous* political systems>.

Like implies resemblance or similarity ranging from virtual identity to slight similarity <found people of *like* mind>. ***ant*** unlike

Alike implies having close resemblance even though obviously distinct <siblings who looked *alike*>. ***ant*** unlike, different

Akin suggests essential rather than apparent likeness <diseases *akin* to one another in their effects>. ***ant*** alien

Parallel suggests a marked likeness in the course of development of two things <the *parallel* careers of two movie stars>.

Homogeneous implies likeness of a number of things in kind, sort, or class <a *homogeneous* population>. ***ant*** heterogeneous

Uniform implies consistent likeness and lack of variation in existence, appearance, or operation <*uniform* application of the law>.

Identical indicates either essential sameness or exact correspondence without detectable or significant difference <shared *identical* concerns>. ***ant*** different

similarity see LIKENESS.

similitude see LIKENESS.

simple 1. see EASY.

2. see PLAIN.

3. Simple, foolish, silly, fatuous, asinine mean actually or apparently deficient in intelligence.

Simple implies a degree of intelligence inadequate to cope with anything complex or involving mental effort or implies a failure to use one's intelligence <*simple* peasants afraid of revolutionary ideas>. ***ant*** wise

Foolish implies the character of being or seeming unable to use judgment, discretion, or good sense <*foolish* people believed the ghost story>. ***ant*** smart

Silly suggests failure to act as a rational being by showing lack of common sense or by ridiculous behavior <the *silly* stunts of vacationing college students>. ***ant*** sensible

Fatuous implies contemptuous foolishness, inanity, and disregard of reality <the *fatuous* responses of over-ambitious politicians>. ***ant*** sensible

Asinine suggests utter and contemptible failure to use normal rationality or perception <a soap opera with an especially *asinine* plot>. ***ant*** judicious, sensible

simulate see ASSUME.

simultaneous see CONTEMPORARY.

sin see OFFENSE 2.

sincere, wholehearted, heartfelt, hearty, unfeigned mean genuine in feeling or expression.

Sincere stresses absence of hypocrisy, feigning, or any falsifying embellishment or exaggeration <offered a *sincere* apology>. ***ant*** insincere

Wholehearted suggests sincerity and earnest devotion without reservation or misgiving <promised our *wholehearted* support to the cause>.

Heartfelt suggests depth of genuine feeling outwardly expressed <a gift that expresses our *heartfelt* gratitude>.

Hearty suggests honesty, warmth, and exuberance in the display of feeling <received a *hearty* welcome at the door>. ***ant*** hollow

Unfeigned stresses spontaneity and absence of pretense or simulation <her *unfeigned* delight at receiving the award>.

single, sole, unique, separate, solitary, particular mean one as distinguished from two or more or all others.

Single implies being unaccompanied or unsupported by or not combined or united with any other <a *single* example will suffice>. ***ant*** multiple

Sole applies to the only one that exists, acts, has power or relevance, or should be considered <my *sole* reason for moving there>.

Unique applies to the only one of its kind or character in existence <the medal is *unique*, for no duplicates were made>.

Separate stresses discreteness and disconnectedness or unconnectedness from every other one <a country with a *separate* set of problems>.

Solitary implies being both single and isolated <television was her *solitary* link to the outside world>.

Particular implies singular or numerical distinctness from other instances, examples, or members of a class <a *particular* kind of wine>. ***ant*** general

singular see STRANGE.

sinister, baleful, malign mean seriously threatening evil or disaster.

Sinister applies to what threatens by appearance or reputation, and suggests a general or vague feeling of fear or apprehension on the part of the observer <a *sinister* aura surrounded the place>.

Baleful imputes perniciousness or destructiveness that works either openly or covertly <the *baleful* influence of superstition and fanaticism>. ***ant*** beneficent

Malign applies to something inherently evil or harmful <the *malign* effects of smoking on one's health>. ***ant*** benign

situation 1. see PLACE. **2.** see POSITION 2. **3.** see STATE.

site see PLACE.

skeleton see STRUCTURE.

skepticism see UNCERTAINTY.

sketch see COMPENDIUM.

skill see ART.

skilled see PROFICIENT.

skillful see PROFICIENT.

skimpy see MEAGER.

skinny see LEAN.

skulk see LURK.

slack 1. see LOOSE. **2.** see NEGLIGENT.

slacken see DELAY 1.

slander see MALIGN.

slang see DIALECT.

slant, slope, incline, lean mean to diverge or to cause to diverge from the vertical or horizontal.

Slant implies a noticeable physical divergence but implies nothing about the degree of divergence <handwriting that was characterized by *slanting* letters>.

Slope, often interchangeable with *slant,* may be preferred when reference is made to a gradual divergence of a side or surface <the land *slopes* to the east>.

Incline is likely to suggest the intervention of an external force, such as bending or tipping <graciously *inclined* her head in response to the cheers>.

Lean may stress a definite directing of an inclination <*leaned* the ladder against the wall> or a literal or figurative resting or intent to rest against a support <*lean* back in an easy chair>.

slap see STRIKE.

slatternly, dowdy, frowzy, blowsy mean deficient in neatness, freshness, and smartness, especially in dress or appearance.

Slatternly stresses notions of slovenliness, unkemptness, and sordidness <a run-down *slatternly* apartment>.

Dowdy is likely to suggest a complete lack of taste resulting from a combination of the untidy, drab, and tasteless <an old hotel with an imposing but *dowdy* appearance>. ***ant*** smart

Frowzy may describe a lazy lack of neatness, order, and cleanliness <a *frowzy* old office> or it may apply to a natural and not unwholesome disorder <a thicket *frowzy* with underbrush> or it may suggest drab misery and squalor <tried her best to overcome the *frowzy* circumstances under which she grew up>. ***ant*** trim, smart

Blowsy implies dishevelment or disorder <looked *blowsy* and dissolute> to which is often added a notion of crudity or coarseness or grossness <songs carelessly belted out by a *blowsy* singer>. ***ant*** smart, spruce, dainty

slaughter see MASSACRE.

slavery see SERVITUDE.

slavish see SUBSERVIENT.

slay see KILL.

sleazy see LIMP.

sleek, slick, glossy, silken, silky, satiny mean having a smooth bright surface or appearance.

Sleek suggests a smoothness or brightness resulting from attentive grooming or excellent physical condition <a *sleek* racehorse>.

Slick suggests extreme smoothness that results in an unsafe or slippery surface <slipped and fell on the *slick* floor>.

Glossy suggests a surface that is smooth and highly polished <photographs having a *glossy* finish>.

Silken and ***silky*** imply the smoothness and luster as well as the softness of silk <*silken* hair> <expensive dresses made of *silky* fabrics>.

Satiny applies to what is soft and smooth and shining <a flower's *satiny* petals>.

sleepy, drowsy, somnolent, slumberous mean affected by or inducing a desire to sleep.

Sleepy applies to whatever seems about to fall asleep or to whatever leads to such a state <a *sleepy* little town>.

Drowsy carries a stronger implication of the heaviness or languor associated with sleepiness than of an actual need for sleep <grew *drowsy* in the stuffy room>.

Somnolent is likely to suggest the sluggishness or inertness accompanying sleepiness more than the actual impulse to sleep <the *somnolent* air of a tropical noon>.

Slumberous may replace any of the other terms; distinctively it may connote quiescence or the repose of latent powers <felt the sea's *slumberous* power>.

slender see THIN.

slick see SLEEK.

slight *adj* see THIN.
slight *vb* see NEGLECT.
slighting see DEROGATORY.
slim see THIN.
sling see THROW.
slink see LURK.
slip see ERROR.
slope see SLANT.
slothful see LAZY.
slough see DISCARD.
slow see DELAY 1.
sluice see POUR.
slumberous see SLEEPY.

sly, cunning, crafty, tricky, foxy, artful mean attaining or seeking to attain one's ends by devious means.

Sly implies furtiveness, lack of candor, and skill in concealing one's aims and methods <a *sly* corporate-takeover scheme>.

Cunning suggests the inventive use of sometimes limited intelligence in overreaching or circumventing <relentlessly *cunning* in her pursuit of the governorship>. ***ant*** ingenuous

Crafty implies cleverness and subtlety of method <a *crafty* trial lawyer>.

Tricky suggests unscrupulous shiftiness and unreliability <a *tricky* interviewer who usually got what she wanted from her subject>.

Foxy implies a shrewd and wary craftiness usually based on experience in devious dealing <a *foxy* thief got away with her jewels>.

Artful implies insinuating or alluring indirectness in dealing and often connotes sophistication or coquetry or cleverness <*artful* matchmaker>. ***ant*** artless

small, little, diminutive, petite, minute, tiny, microscopic, miniature mean noticeably below average in size.

Small is often interchangeable with *little,* but it applies more to relative size determined by capacity, value, or number <a *small* amount>. ***ant*** large

Little is more absolute in implication and often connotes less magnitude that is usual, expected, or desired <your pathetic *little* smile>. ***ant*** big, great

Diminutive implies exceptional or abnormal smallness <the *diminutive* gymnast outshone her larger competitors>.

Petite applies chiefly to girls and women and implies marked smallness and trimness <specializing in clothing for *petite* women>.

Minute implies extreme smallness <a beverage with only a *minute* amount of caffeine>.

Tiny is an informal equivalent to *minute* <*tiny* cracks have formed in the painting>. ***ant*** huge

Microscopic applies to what is so minute it can only be seen under a microscope <found a *microscopic* defect>.

Miniature applies to an exactly proportioned reproduction on a very small scale <a doll house complete with *miniature* furnishings>.

smart see INTELLIGENT.

smell, scent, odor, aroma mean the quality that makes a thing perceptible to the olfactory sense.

Smell implies solely the sensation without suggestion of quality or character or source <an odd *smell* permeated the room>.

Scent applies to the characteristic smell given off by a substance, an animal, or a plant and stresses the source of the sensation <dogs trained to detect the *scent* of narcotics>.

Odor may imply a stronger or more readily distinguished scent or it may be equivalent to *smell* <a type of cheese with a very pronounced *odor*>.

Aroma suggests a somewhat penetrating, pervasive, or sometimes pungent, but usually pleasant odor <the *aroma* of freshly ground coffee>. ***ant*** stink, stench

smidgen see PARTICLE.

smite see STRIKE.

smog see HAZE.

smooth 1. see EASY. **2.** see LEVEL. **3.** see SUAVE.

smother see SUFFOCATE.

smuggled, bootleg, contraband mean transported in defiance of the law.

Smuggled applies to what is brought in or taken out of an area, especially to avoid payment of taxes or contravene the law <*smuggled* diamonds>.

Bootleg refers to a material substance offered for sale or distribution in defiance of prohibition or legal restrictions on its use <*bootleg* whiskey>.

Contraband, often interchangeable with *smuggled,* specifically applies to something whose exportation to belligerents is prohibited and which is therefore liable to seizure <seized a shipment of *contraband* merchandise at the border>.

snap see JERK.

snare see CATCH.

snatch see TAKE.

sneak see LURK.

sneer see SCOFF.

snug see COMFORTABLE.

soak, saturate, drench, steep, impregnate mean to permeate or be permeated with a liquid.

Soak implies a usually prolonged immersion that results in a thorough wetting, softening, or dissolving <*soak* the clothes to remove the stains>.

Saturate implies an absorption until no more liquid can be held <gym clothes *saturated* with sweat>.

Drench implies a thorough wetting by something that may pour down or may be poured <the cloudburst *drenched* us to the skin>.

Steep suggests an immersion and soaking that results in the extraction of an essence by the liquid <*steep* tea in boiling water>.

Impregnate implies a thorough interpenetration of one thing by another <a cake strongly *impregnated* with brandy>.

soar see RISE.

sober 1. Sober, temperate, continent, unimpassioned mean having or manifesting mastery of oneself and one's appetites.

Sober implies moderation in the use of food and especially drink and may suggest composure under stress and freedom from emotional excess <a calm *sober* disposition well-fitted to function in an emergency>. ***ant*** excited, drunk

Temperate stresses moderation and implies such control that one never exceeds the bounds of what is right or proper <maintained her equanimity and her *temperate* outlook>. ***ant*** intemperate

Continent stresses deliberate self-restraint especially in regard to expressing feelings or satisfying sexual desires <a nation known for its frugal and *continent* leaders>. ***ant*** incontinent

Unimpassioned may imply a subduing of feeling or passion by rationality <presented a reserved, *unimpassioned* appearance> but often it connotes a resulting coldness or hardness of heart <prosecuted the case with *unimpassioned* loathing>. ***ant*** impassioned

2. see SERIOUS.

sobriety see TEMPERANCE.

sociable see GRACIOUS.

society see ARISTOCRACY.

soft, bland, mild, gentle, lenient, balmy mean devoid of harshness, roughness, or intensity.

Soft implies a subduing of all that is vivid, intense, or forceful until it is agreeably soothing <took a walk in the *soft* evening air>. ***ant*** hard, stern

Bland implies the absence of anything that might disturb, stimulate, or irritate and may suggest insipidness <spent a week on a *bland* diet>. ***ant*** pungent, piquant, savory, tasty

Mild stresses moderation or restraint of force or intensity <*mild* weather> and is often applied to what induces a feeling of quiet beauty or serenity <spoke to the patient in a *mild* tone>. ***ant*** fierce, harsh

Gentle applies to things that are pleasant and agreeable rather than harsh, rough, fierce, strong, or irritating, and that produce a sense of placidity or tranquility or restrained power <a *gentle* rain>. ***ant*** rough, harsh

Lenient stresses a relaxing, softening, or calming influence <the *lenient* effect of lanolin>. ***ant*** caustic

Balmy suggests refreshment and sometimes exhilaration, frequently coupled with a suggestion of fragrance <an unusually *balmy* day in early spring>.

sojourn see RESIDE.

solace see COMFORT.

sole see SINGLE.

solemn see SERIOUS.

solicit **1.** see ASK 2. **2.** see INVITE

solicitor see LAWYER.

solicitude see CARE.

solid see FIRM.

solidarity see UNITY.

solitary **1.** see ALONE. **2.** see SINGLE.

solitude, isolation, seclusion mean the state of one who is alone.

Solitude stresses aloneness and a lack of contact and may imply being cut off by wish or compulsion from one's usual associates <the *solitude* enjoyed by the long-distance trucker>.

Isolation stresses often involuntary detachment or separation from others <the oppressive *isolation* of the village during winter>.

Seclusion suggests a shutting away or keeping apart from others and often connotes a deliberate withdrawal from the world or retirement to a quiet life <lived in bucolic *seclusion* surrounded by his art collection>.

somatic see BODILY.

somnolent see SLEEPY.

soon see PRESENTLY.

sophisticated, worldly-wise, worldly, blasé, disillusioned mean experienced in the ways of the world.

Sophisticated implies either refinement, urbanity, cleverness, and cultivation <guests at her salon were rich and *sophisticated*> or artificiality of manner, overrefinement, and absence of enthusiasm <too *sophisticated* to enjoy the carnival rides>. ***ant*** unsophisticated

Worldly-wise suggests a close knowledge of the affairs and manners of society and a concentration on material ends and aims <a *worldly-wise* woman with a philosophy of personal independence>.

Worldly, close to *worldly-wise,* stresses alienation from spiritual interests and dedication to happiness in this world <chose to focus on *worldly* concerns>. ***ant*** unworldly

Blasé implies a lack of responsiveness to common joys as a result of a real or affected surfeit of experience and cultivation <*blasé* travelers who claimed to have been everywhere>.

Disillusioned applies to someone who has lost all illusions and hope as a result of experience and who lacks enthusiasm or ideals <saw the world around him through scornful, *disillusioned* eyes>.

sordid see MEAN.

sorrow *n* **Sorrow, grief, anguish, woe, regret** mean distress of mind.

Sorrow implies a sense of loss or a sense of guilt and remorse <a nation united in *sorrow* upon the death of the President>. ***ant*** joy

Grief implies a poignant sorrow for an immediate cause <gave his father much *grief*>. ***ant*** joy

Anguish suggests a torturing often persistent grief or dread <the *anguish* felt by the hostages>. ***ant*** relief

Woe implies a deep or inconsolable distress or misery <cries of *woe* echoed throughout the bombed city>.

Regret implies a pain caused by deep disappointment, fruitless longing, or unavailing remorse <never felt a moment of *regret* following the divorce>.

sorrow *vb* see GRIEVE.

sorry see CONTEMPTIBLE.

sort see TYPE.

soul, spirit mean an immaterial entity distinguishable from the body.

Soul may be preferred when emphasis is on the entity as having functions, responsibilities, aspects, or destiny <praying for the *souls* of the dead> or when the emphasis is on relation or connection to a material entity to which it gives life or power <set out to save the *soul* of the nation>. ***ant*** body

Spirit may be chosen when the stress is upon the quality, the constitution, or the activity of the entity <a man fervent in *spirit*> or it may suggest an antithesis to something material <enforced the *spirit* rather than the letter of the law>.

sound *adj* **1.** see HEALTHY. **2.** see VALID.

sound *n* **Sound, noise** mean a sensation or effect resulting from stimulation of the auditory receptors.

Sound is applicable to anything that is heard and in itself is completely neutral in implication <loud *sounds* of laughter>. ***ant*** silence

Noise applies to a sound that is disagreeably loud or harsh or constantly or irritatingly perceptible <the constant *noise* and bustle of the city> or inappropriate to the situation and therefore disturbing <wakened by a *noise* at the door late at night>.

source see ORIGIN.

sovereign **1.** see DOMINANT. **2.** see FREE *adj*.

spacious, commodious, capacious, ample mean larger in extent or capacity than the average.

Spacious implies great length and breadth and sometimes height <a mansion with a *spacious* front lawn>. ***ant*** strait

Commodious stresses roominess and comfortable freedom from hampering constriction <a *commodious* and airy penthouse apartment>. ***ant*** incommodious

Capacious stresses the ability to hold, contain, or retain in exceptional quantity or to an exceptional degree <a *capacious* suitcase>. ***ant*** exiguous

Ample implies having a greater size, expanse, or amount than that deemed adequate and may suggest fullness or bulk or freedom from cramping restrictions <we have *ample* means to buy the house>. ***ant*** meager, circumscribed

spare 1. see LEAN. **2.** see MEAGER.

sparing, frugal, thrifty, economical mean careful in the use of one's money or resources.

Sparing stresses abstention and restraint <mother was *sparing* in the use of butter>. ***ant*** lavish

Frugal implies simplicity and temperance and suggests absence of luxury and display <carried on in the *frugal* tradition of the Yankees>. ***ant*** wasteful

Thrifty stresses good management and industry as well as frugality <the store prospered under his *thrifty* management>. ***ant*** wasteful

Economical stresses prudent management, lack of wastefulness, and efficient use of resources <trucking remains an *economical* means of transport>. ***ant*** extravagant

sparkle see FLASH.

sparse see MEAGER.

spasm see FIT *n.*

spasmodic see FITFUL.

spat see QUARREL.

speak, talk, converse mean to articulate words so as to express one's thoughts.

Speak may refer to any utterance, however coherent or disconnected, and with or without reference to hearers <too hoarse to *speak* clearly>.

Talk usually implies one or more listeners and related conversation or discourse <*talk* over a problem with an adviser>.

Converse implies an interchange in talk of thoughts and opinions <a multitude of subjects on which they happily *conversed*>.

special, especial, specific, particular, individual mean of or relating to one thing or class.

Special stresses having a distinctive quality, character, identity, or use <airline passengers who require *special* meals>.

Especial may add implications of preeminence or preference <a matter of *especial* importance>.

Specific implies a unique and peculiar relationship to a kind or category or individual <children with *specific* nutritional needs>. ***ant*** nonspecific, unspecific, generic

Particular stresses the distinctness of something as an individual <an Alpine scene of *particular* beauty>. ***ant*** general, universal

Individual implies unequivocal reference to one of a class or group <valued each *individual* opinion>. ***ant*** general

specific 1. see EXPLICIT. **2.** see SPECIAL.

specify see MENTION.

specimen see INSTANCE.

specious see PLAUSIBLE.

spectator, observer, beholder, looker-on, onlooker, witness, eyewitness, bystander, kibitzer mean one who sees or looks upon something.

Spectator can be used for one that attends an exhibition, performance, or entertainment which does not involve an appeal to the sense of hearing <*spectators* at a football game>; more broadly it denotes one who is felt to be wholly apart from whatever is presented to the attention <considered herself a *spectator* in the game of life>.

Observer may or may not imply an intent to see, but usually suggests that one attends closely to details and often keeps a record of them <earned a reputation as a keen *observer* of current mores>.

Beholder sometimes carries a strong implication of watching or regarding intently and is often applicable to one who has looked intently upon a person or thing and obtained a clear and accurate impression <a judgment left to the eye of the *beholder*>.

Looker-on and *onlooker* suggest casualness or detachment and lack of participation <there was a great crowd of *lookers-on* at the fire> <the surgeon refused to operate in the presence of *onlookers*>.

Witness specifically denotes one who has firsthand knowledge and therefore is competent to give testimony <presented a set of *witnesses* who had lived through the tragedy>.

Eyewitness more explicitly implies actual sight as the source of knowledge <there were no *eyewitnesses* of the collision>.

Bystander primarily denotes one who stands by when something is happening <the policeman took the names of all the *bystanders*> or as merely being present at a place <a *bystander* was injured by the explosion>.

Kibitzer specifically applies to one who watches a card game by looking over the shoulders of the players and who may annoy them by offering advice; it may also apply to an onlooker who meddles or makes unwelcome suggestions <a group composed equally of players and *kibitzers*>.

speculate see THINK 2.

speculative 1. see THEORETICAL. **2.** see THOUGHTFUL 1.

speed see HASTE.

speedy see FAST.

spend, expend, disburse mean to pay out for something received or expected.

Spend suggests the mere fact of paying out <*spend* a nickel for candy> or implies a draining or depleting or exhausting of what is used <*spent* months trying to find a satisfactory house>. ***ant*** save

Expend is likely to be chosen with reference to public or business rather than private spending and to imply an outlaying of large amounts <vowed to *expend* money on education if elected>.

Disburse implies a paying out of money from a fund, but it may also imply distribution, such as to pensioners or heirs, and often stresses an acting under authority <needed a court decree to *disburse* the funds>.

spendthrift, prodigal, profligate, waster, wastrel mean a person who dissipates resources foolishly and wastefully.

Spendthrift stresses lack of prudence in spending and usually implies imbalance between income and outgo <known in college as a real *spendthrift*>.

Prodigal suggests such lavish expenditure as can deplete the most abundant resources <a *prodigal* who squandered his parents' hard-earned money>.

Profligate may imply the habits of a spendthrift but stresses dissipation of resources and powers and suggests debauchery and dissoluteness more than waste <an aging rock star forced to abandon his life as a *profligate*>.

Waster may come close to *spendthrift* but carries a stronger implication of worthlessness and often suggests an idle ne'er-do-well <scorned by all as an idle *waster*>.

Wastrel stresses disreputable worthlessness and typically applies to one who has profligate and dissolute habits <worked hard to earn a reputation as a bounder and a *wastrel*>.

spirit 1. see COURAGE. **2.** see SOUL.

spite see MALICE.

spleen see MALICE.

splendid, resplendent, gorgeous, glorious, sublime, superb mean extraordinarily or transcendently impressive.

Splendid implies an outshining of the usual or customary <the royal wedding was a *splendid* occasion>. ***ant*** unimpressive

Resplendent suggests a glowing or blazing splendor <the church was *resplendent* in its Easter decorations>.

Gorgeous implies a rich or showy or elaborate splendor especially in display of color <a *gorgeous* red dress>.

Glorious suggests a radiance that heightens beauty or a state of being that is eminently worthy of admiration, renown, or distinction <a *glorious* sunset over the ocean>. ***ant*** inglorious

Sublime implies an exaltation or elevation almost beyond human comprehension <the *sublime* grandeur of the thunderous falls>.

Superb suggests a magnificence, brilliance, grandeur, splendor, or excellence of the highest conceivable degree <a three-star restaurant offering *superb* cuisine>.

splenetic see IRASCIBLE.

split see TEAR.

spoil *n* **Spoil, pillage, plunder, booty, prize, loot** mean something taken from another by force or craft.

Spoil, more commonly *spoils,* applies to what belongs by right or custom to the victor in war or political contest <a governor who relished doling out the *spoils* of office>.

Pillage applies to things taken with more open violence or lawlessness <filled his capital city with the *pillage* of Europe>.

Plunder applies to what is taken not only in war but in robbery, banditry, grafting, or swindling <a fortune that was the *plunder* of years of political corruption>.

Booty implies plunder that is to be shared among confederates <the thieves planned to divide their *booty* later>.

Prize applies to spoils captured on the high seas or in the territorial waters of the enemy <a pirate ship ruthlessly seizing *prizes*>.

Loot applies especially to what is taken from victims of a catastrophe <prowlers searched the storm-damaged cottages for *loot*>.

spoil *vb* **1.** see DECAY. **2.** see INDULGE.

sponge see PARASITE.

spontaneity see UNCONSTRAINT.

spontaneous, impulsive, instinctive, automatic, mechanical mean acting or activated without deliberation.

Spontaneous implies lack of prompting and connotes naturalness <a *spontaneous* burst of applause>. ***ant*** studied

Impulsive implies acting under stress of emotion or the spirit of the moment, seemingly without thought or volition <*impulsive* acts of violence>. ***ant*** deliberate

Instinctive stresses spontaneous action involving neither judgment nor will <blinking is an *instinctive* reaction>. ***ant*** intentional

Automatic implies prompt action engaging neither the mind nor the emotions and connotes a predictable and unvarying response <his denial was *automatic*>.

Mechanical stresses the lifeless, often perfunctory character of the response <over the years her style of teaching became *mechanical*>.

poradic see INFREQUENT.

port see FUN.

ports see ATHLETICS.

pot see PLACE.

prain see STRAIN.

prightly see LIVELY.

pring, arise, rise, originate, derive, flow, issue, emanate, proceed, stem mean to come up or out of something into existence.

Spring implies a rapid or sudden emergence <a brilliant idea that had *sprung* out of nowhere>.

Arise may convey the fact of coming into existence or notice often with no suggestion of prior state <a vicious rumor *arose*> or may imply causation <mistakes often *arise* from haste>.

Rise, sometimes interchangeable with *arise,* distinctively stresses gradual growth or ascent <as time passed legends about the house *rose*>. ***ant*** abate

Originate implies a definite source or starting point <the theory did not *originate* with Darwin>.

Derive implies a prior existence in another form <their system of justice *derives* from British colonial law>.

Flow adds to *spring* a suggestion of abundance or ease of inception <the belief that all good *flows* from God>.

Issue suggests an emerging from confinement or from a receptacle <shouts of joy *issued* from the team's locker room>.

Emanate applies to the passage of something immaterial such as a principle or thought but carries little suggestion of a causal force <serenity *emanated* from her>.

Proceed stresses place of origin, derivation, parentage, or logical cause <bitterness that *proceeded* from an unhappy marriage>.

Stem implies an originating by dividing or branching off from something as an outgrowth or subordinate development <a whole new industry *stemmed* from the discovery>.

springy see ELASTIC.

spry see AGILE.

spur see MOTIVE.

spurn see DECLINE.

squabble see QUARREL.

squalid see DIRTY.

squander see WASTE.
square see AGREE 3.
squat see STOCKY.
squeamish see NICE.
stable see LASTING.
stagger see REEL.
staid see SERIOUS.
stain see STIGMA.
stalwart see STRONG.
stammer, stutter mean to speak stumblingly.
Stammer implies a temporary inhibition from fear, embarrassment, or shock <*stammered* his thanks, overcome with embarrassment>.
Stutter is likely to suggest a habitual defect characterized by repetition of sounds, but it may apply to a similar manifestation due to a temporary cause <*stutters* when excited> or even, as may *stammer,* to something suggesting the pattern of a stutterer <the engine *stuttered* then came to life>.
stand *n* see POSITION 1.
stand *vb* see BEAR.
standard, criterion, gauge, yardstick, touchstone mean a means of determining what a thing should be.
Standard applies to any authoritative rule, principle, or measure by which the qualities, worth, or nature of something can be measured <the book is a classic by any *standard*>.
Criterion may apply to anything used as a test of quality whether formulated as a rule or principle or not <in art there are no hard-and-fast *criteria*>.
Gauge applies to a means of testing a particular dimension such as thickness, depth, or diameter, or a particular quality or aspect <congressional mail is not always an accurate *gauge* of public opinion>.
Yardstick is an informal substitute for *standard* or *criterion* that suggests quantity more often than quality <the movie was a flop by most *yardsticks*>.
Touchstone suggests a simple test of the authenticity or value of something intangible <fine service is one *touchstone* of a first-class restaurant>.
stare see GAZE.
start see BEGIN.
state *n* **State, condition, situation, status** mean the way in which one manifests existence or the circumstances under which one exists or by which one is given a definite character.
State most often implies the sum of the qualities involved in an existence at a particular time and place <the present *state* of the economy>.
Condition more distinctly implies the effect of immediate or

temporary influences <was left in a feeble *condition* after his illness>.

Situation implies an arrangement of circumstances that makes for a particular resulting condition, such as of embarrassment, advantage, or difficulty <struggled to keep abreast of the changing political *situation*>.

Status applies to one's state or condition as determined with some definiteness, especially for legal administrative purposes or by social or economic considerations <improved her *status* within the company>.

state *vb* see SAY.

stately see GRAND.

station see PLACE.

stature see QUALITY 2.

status see STATE.

statute see LAW.

staunch see FAITHFUL.

stay 1. Stay, remain, wait, abide, tarry, linger mean to continue to be in one place for a noticeable time.

Stay stresses continuance in a place or sometimes a situation and may connote the status of a visitor <*stayed* in the same job for over forty years>.

Remain is often used interchangeably with *stay* but distinctively means to stay behind or to be left after others have gone <only one *remained* in the building after the alarm was given>. ***ant*** depart

Wait implies a staying in expectation or in readiness <*wait* for an answer to a letter>.

Abide implies a prolonged staying or remaining behind and suggests either settled residence or patient waiting for some outcome <a culture whose influence will long *abide*>. ***ant*** depart

Tarry suggests a staying or a failing to proceed when it is time to do so <*tarried* too long and missed the train>.

Linger, close to *tarry,* may add an implication of deliberate delaying or unwillingness to depart <*lingered* over a second cup of coffee>.

2. see DEFER.

3. see RESIDE.

steadfast see FAITHFUL.

steady, even, equable mean not varying throughout a course or extent.

Steady implies regularity and lack of fluctuation or interruption of movement <ran the race at a *steady* pace> or fixity in position <*steady* as a rock>. ***ant*** unsteady, nervous, jumpy

Even suggests a levelness or lack of variation in quality or character <read the statement in an *even* voice>.

Equable implies a lack of extremes or of sudden sharp changes <an *equable* climate>. ***ant*** variable, changeable

steal, pilfer, filch, purloin mean to take from another without that person's knowledge or permission.

Steal may apply to any surreptitious taking of something either tangible or intangible <*steal* jewels> <*stole* a look at her>.

Pilfer implies a repeated stealing by stealth in small amounts <dismissed for *pilfering* from the company>.

Filch adds to *pilfer* a suggestion of quickness <*filched* an apple when the man looked away>.

Purloin stresses a removing or carrying off for one's own use or purposes <had *purloined* a typewriter and other office equipment>.

stealthy see SECRET.

steep *adj* **Steep, abrupt, precipitous, sheer** mean having an incline approaching the perpendicular.

Steep implies such sharpness of pitch that ascent or descent is very difficult <a *steep* staircase leading to the attic>.

Abrupt implies a sharper pitch and a sudden break in the level <a beach with an *abrupt* drop-off>. ***ant*** sloping

Precipitous applies to steepness approaching the vertical <the airplane went into a *precipitous* nosedive>.

Sheer suggests an unbroken perpendicular expanse <climbers able to ascend *sheer* cliffs>.

steep *vb* see SOAK.

steer see GUIDE.

stem see SPRING.

stentorian see LOUD.

stereotyped see TRITE.

sterile, barren, impotent, unfruitful, infertile mean lacking the power to produce offspring or bear fruit.

Sterile implies inability to reproduce or to bear literal or figurative fruit through or as if through an organic defect <a *sterile* imagination>. ***ant*** fertile

Barren, basically applicable to a female or a marriage that does not produce offspring, may imply a lack of normal or expected return or profit <a *barren* victory>. ***ant*** fecund

Impotent applies to the male and implies inability to copulate or reproduce <an operation that made him temporarily *impotent*>.

Unfruitful may replace *barren* in any of its applications with the emphasis on not bearing fruit <an *unfruitful* enterprise>. ***ant*** fruitful, prolific

Infertile is often interchanged with *sterile* <an *infertile* egg> but it may imply deficiency rather than absence of fertility <an *infertile* strain of beef cattle>. ***ant*** fertile

stern see SEVERE.

stick, adhere, cohere, cling, cleave mean to become closely attached.

Stick implies an attachment by affixing or by or as if by being glued together <the gummed label will *stick* when pressed>.

Adhere is often interchangeable with *stick* but sometimes implies a growing together of parts normally distinct <muscle fibers will *adhere* following surgery>.

Cohere suggests a sticking together of parts so that they form a unified mass <eggs will make the mixture *cohere*>.

Cling implies an attachment by or as if by hanging on with arms or tendrils <always *cling* to a capsized boat>.

Cleave stresses closeness and strength of attachment <barnacles *cleaving* to the hull of a boat>. ***ant*** part

stiff, rigid, inflexible, tense, wooden mean difficult to bend or enliven.

Stiff may apply to any degree of this condition <muscles will become *stiff* if they are not stretched>. ***ant*** supple, relaxed

Rigid applies to something so stiff that it cannot be bent without breaking <a *rigid* surfboard>. ***ant*** elastic

Inflexible stresses lack of suppleness or pliability <for adequate support, rock-climbers wear shoes with *inflexible* soles>. ***ant*** flexible

Tense suggests a stretching or straining to the point where elasticity or flexibility is lost <*tense* nerves>. ***ant*** expansive

Wooden suggests the hard inflexibility and dry rigidity of wood and connotes stiffness and lack of life and often clumsy or heavy deadness <moved in a stark *wooden* manner>.

stifle see SUFFOCATE.

stigma, brand, blot, stain mean a mark of shame or discredit.

Stigma may imply dishonor or public shame <tried to avoid the *stigma* of bankruptcy> but more often it applies to a negative attitude or judgment attached to something in order to bring discredit or disapproval <the increasing *stigma* attached to smoking in the workplace>.

Brand carries stronger implications of disgrace and infamy and may suggest the impossibility of removal or concealment or the resulting social ostracism and public condemnation <bore the *brand* of corruption and deceit>.

Blot and ***stain*** imply a blemish that diminishes but does not extinguish the honor of a name or reputation <a *blot* on the family name> <wanted there to be no *stain* on her record>.

still, quiet, silent, noiseless mean making no stir or noise.

Still applies to what is motionless and adds the implication of hush or absence of sound <the *still*, dark night>. ***ant*** stirring, noisy

Quiet, like *still*, may imply absence of perceptible motion or sound or of both but it is likely to stress absence of excitement or turbulence and connote tranquillity, serenity, or repose <a *quiet* town>. ***ant*** unquiet

Silent may apply to motion or stir unaccompanied by sound and carries a strong impression of silence <a submarine equipped for *silent* running>. ***ant*** noisy

Noiseless, also applicable to soundless motion, usually connotes absence of commotion or of sounds of activity or movement <a cat slowly advancing on *noiseless* feet>. ***ant*** noisy

stimulate see PROVOKE.

stingy, close, niggardly, parsimonious, penurious, miserly mean being unwilling or showing unwillingness to share with others.

Stingy implies a marked lack of generosity <a *stingy* child, not given to sharing>. ***ant*** generous

Close suggests keeping a tight grip on one's money and possessions <folks who are very *close* when charity calls>. ***ant*** liberal

Niggardly implies giving or spending the very smallest amount possible <gave his wife a *niggardly* household allowance>. ***ant*** bountiful

Parsimonious suggests a frugality so extreme as to lead to stinginess <a *parsimonious* attitude with no room for luxuries>. ***ant*** prodigal

Penurious implies niggardliness that gives an appearance of actual poverty <the *penurious* old woman left behind a fortune>.

Miserly suggests penuriousness motivated by obsessive avariciousness and a morbid pleasure in hoarding <a *miserly* man indifferent to the cries of the needy>.

stinking see MALODOROUS.

stint see TASK.

stipend see WAGE.

stir *n* **Stir, bustle, flurry, pother, fuss, ado** mean signs of excitement or hurry accompanying an act, action, or event.

Stir suggests brisk or restless movement or reaction, usually of a crowd <caused a great *stir*>. ***ant*** tranquillity

Bustle implies a noisy, obtrusive, often self-important activity <the hustle and *bustle* of city life>.

Flurry stresses nervous agitation and undue haste <a *flurry* of activity>.

Pother implies flurry and fidgety activity and may additionally stress commotion or confusion <the *pother* made by unexpected guests>.

Fuss is close to *pother* but adds the notion of needless worry or effort <wondered what all the *fuss* was about>.

Ado may suggest fussiness or waste of energy <go to work without more *ado*> or it may imply trouble or difficulty to be overcome <there was much *ado* before their affairs were sorted out>.

stir *vb* **Stir, rouse, arouse, awaken, waken, rally** mean to shift from acquiescence or torpor into activity or action.

Stir usually implies an exciting to action or expression of what is latent or dormant by something that agitates or disturbs <news events that *stirred* the public>; it may also imply the evocation of deep and agitating but usually pleasant emotion <a sight that *stirred* pity>.

Rouse suggests an incitement to vigorous activity and ensuing commotion from a state of rest by startling or frightening <*roused* from sleep by cries of panic>.

Arouse often means little more than to start into action with no hint of consequent action <made no effort to *arouse* their fears>. ***ant*** quiet, calm

Awaken and ***waken*** frequently imply an ending of sleep or connote the stimulating of spiritual or mental powers into activity <*awakened* the conscience of the nation> <gradually *wakening* to love's delights>. ***ant*** subdue

Rally implies a gathering together of diffused forces that stirs up or rouses from lethargy or inaction to action <*rallied* her strength to overcome the blow>.

stocky, thickset, thick, chunky, stubby, squat, dumpy mean being or having a body that is relatively compact in form.

Stocky suggests broad compact sturdiness <a *stocky*, powerful man>.

Thickset implies a thick, solid, burly body <a wrestler's *thickset* physique>.

Thick is more often used for body parts than of body build <*thick* legs>. ***ant*** thin

Chunky applies to a body type that is ample but robust and solid <a *chunky* fullback>.

Stubby stresses lack of height or length and real or apparent breadth <*stubby* fingers that seemed incapable of delicate precision>.

Squat is likely to suggest an unshapely lack of height <a *squat* little man in rumpled clothes>. ***ant*** lanky

Dumpy is likely to suggest short, lumpish gracelessness of body <an ill-fitting dress that made her look *dumpy*>.

stoic see IMPASSIVE.

stolid see IMPASSIVE.

stoop, condescend, deign mean to descend from one's level of rank or dignity to do something.

Stoop may imply a descent in dignity or from a higher moral plane to a lower one <how can you *stoop* to such childish name-calling>.

Condescend usually implies an assumed superiority and a patronizing stooping by one of high rank or position to interact with social inferiors <a plant manager *condescending* to mingle with the employees>. ***ant*** presume

Deign suggests a reluctant condescension of someone haughty, arrogant, or contemptuous <scarcely *deigned* to speak with her poor relations>.

stop, cease, quit, discontinue, desist mean to suspend or cause to suspend activity.

Stop applies to action or progress or to what is operating or progressing and may imply suddenness or definiteness <*stopped* the conversation>. ***ant*** start

Cease applies to states, conditions, or existence and may imply gradualness and a degree of finality <by nightfall the fighting had *ceased*>.

Quit may stress either finality or abruptness in stopping or ceasing <the engine faltered, sputtered, then *quit* altogether>.

Discontinue applies to the stopping of an accustomed activity or practice <we have *discontinued* the manufacture of that item>. ***ant*** continue

Desist implies forbearance or restraint as a motive for stopping or ceasing <*desisted* from further efforts to persuade them>. ***ant*** persist

stopgap see RESOURCE.

storm see ATTACK *vb*.

story, narrative, tale, anecdote, yarn mean a recital of happenings that is less elaborate than a novel.

Story is the most general term, applicable to legendary lore <the *story* of Arthur> or to an oral or written, factual or fictitious, prose or verse account, typically designed to inform or entertain and characteristically dealing with a series of related incidents or events <repeat the *story* of the opera>.

Narrative is more likely to imply factual than imaginative content <his journal is the only surviving *narrative* of the expedition>.

Tale may suggest a leisurely and loosely organized recital often of legendary or imaginative happenings <*tales* of the Greek heroes>.

Anecdote applies to a brief story featuring a small, discrete, and often humorous incident that may illustrate some truth or principle or illuminate some matter <a biography replete with charming *anecdotes*>.

Yarn is likely to suggest a rambling and rather dubious tale of exciting adventure, often marvelous or fanciful and without clear-cut outcome <*yarns* spun around the campfire>.

stout see STRONG.

straightforward, forthright, aboveboard mean free from all that is dishonest or secretive.

Straightforward applies to what is consistently direct and free from deviations or evasiveness <a *straightforward* answer> ***ant*** devious, indirect

Forthright applies to something that goes straight to the point without swerving or hesitating <a *forthright* approach to the problems on campus>. ***ant*** furtive

Aboveboard describes an action or method that is free of all traces of deception or duplicity <a chief executive who managed to be honest and *aboveboard* in all her dealings>. ***ant*** underhand, underhanded

strain 1. see STRESS.

2. Strain, sprain mean an injury to a part of the body through overstretching.

Strain, the more general and less technical term, usually suggests overuse, overexercise, overexertion, or overeffort as a cause and implies injury that may vary from slight soreness or stiffness to a disabling damage <slipped and got a bad *strain* in his back>.

Sprain regularly implies injury to a joint, usually from a wrenching that stretches and tears its ligaments or enclosing membrane, resulting in swelling, pain, and disablement of the joint <twisted her ankle and suffered a bad *sprain*>.

straits see JUNCTURE.

strange, singular, unique, peculiar, eccentric, erratic, odd, queer, quaint, outlandish mean departing or varying from what is ordinary, usual, or to be expected.

Strange stresses unfamiliarity and may apply to the foreign, the unnatural, the unaccountable, or the new <immigrants adjusting to *strange* new customs>. ***ant*** familiar

Singular suggests individuality or puzzling strangeness <a *singular* feeling of impending disaster>.

Unique implies an absence of peers and the fact of being without a known parallel <a career that is *unique* in the annals of science>.

Peculiar implies a marked distinctiveness <problems *peculiar* to inner-city areas>.

Eccentric suggests a divergence from the usual or normal especially in behavior <the *eccentric* eating habits of young children>.

Erratic stresses a capricious and unpredictable wandering or deviating from the normal or expected <disturbed by his friend's *erratic* behavior>.

Odd applies to a possibly fantastic departure from the regular or expected <an *odd* sense of humor>.

Queer suggests a dubious sometimes sinister oddness <puzzled by the *queer* happenings since her arrival>.

Quaint suggests an old-fashioned but pleasant oddness <a *quaint* and remote village in the mountains>.

Outlandish applies to what is uncouth, bizarre, or barbaric <islanders having *outlandish* customs and superstitions>.

strangle see SUFFOCATE.

stratagem see TRICK.

strategy, tactics, logistics mean an aspect of military science.

Strategy applies to the art or science of fundamental military planning for the overall effective use of forces in war <sought a *strategy* that would maximize the use of air power>.

Tactics applies to the handling of forces in the field or in action and suggests the actual presence of an enemy force <known for their daring *tactics* in battle>.

Logistics is the art or science of military supply and transportation, both planning and implementation in all their aspects <wrestled with the *logistics* of the campaign>.

stray see WANDER.

stream see POUR.

strength see POWER.

strenuous see VIGOROUS.

stress, strain, pressure, tension mean the action or effect of force exerted upon or within a thing

Stress and *strain* are the most comprehensive terms and apply to a force tending to deform a body <the weight of the snow put *stress* on the roof> <bolts snapping under the tremendous *strain* of the impact>.

Pressure commonly applies to a stress characterized by a weighing down upon or a pushing against a surface <normal atmospheric *pressure*>.

Tension applies to either of two balancing forces causing or tending to cause elongation of an elastic body or to the stress resulting in the body <tested the *tension* on the tightrope>.

strict see RIGID.

strident 1. see LOUD. **2.** see VOCIFEROUS.

strife see DISCORD.

strike 1. Strike, hit, smite, slap, swat, punch mean to come or bring into contact with a sharp blow.

Strike basically may imply the aiming and dealing of a blow with the hand or with a weapon or tool and usually with moderate or heavy force <*strike* a nail with a hammer>.

Hit is likely to stress the impact of the blow or the reacting of the target aimed at <*hit* a snake with a stick>.

Smite, somewhat rhetorical or bookish, is likely to stress the injuriousness or destructiveness of the contact and to suggest such motivations as hot anger or a desire for vengeance <fell as if *smitten* by a heavy blow>.

Slap primarily applies to a striking with the open hand and implies a sharp or stinging blow with or as if with the palm of the hand <waves *slapped* against the boat>.

Swat suggests a forceful slapping blow with an instrument such as a flyswatter or a bat <*swat* a baseball out of the ballpark>.

Punch implies a quick sharp blow with or as if with the fist <*punch* a man in the nose>.

2. see AFFECT.

striking see NOTICEABLE.

stringent see RIGID.

strive see ATTEMPT.

stroll see SAUNTER.

strong, stout, sturdy, stalwart, tough, tenacious mean showing power to resist or to endure.

Strong may imply power derived from muscular vigor, large size, structural soundness, or intellectual or spiritual resources <a *strong* desire to succeed>. ***ant*** weak

Stout suggests an ability to endure stress, pain, or hard use without giving way <wear *stout* boots when hiking>.

Sturdy implies strength derived from vigorous growth, determination of spirit, or solidity of construction <people of *sturdy* independence>. ***ant*** decrepit

Stalwart suggests an unshakable dependability and connotes great physical, mental, or spiritual strength <*stalwart* supporters of the environmental movement>.

Tough implies great firmness and resiliency <a *tough* political opponent>. ***ant*** fragile

Tenacious suggests strength in seizing, retaining, clinging to, or holding together <*tenacious* of their right to privacy>.

structure, anatomy, framework, skeleton mean the parts of or the arrangement of parts in a whole.

Structure, the most general term, refers to any whole, natural or artificial, material or immaterial, and may be used specifically of the parts or arrangements that give a whole its characteristic form or nature <studied the *structure* of the atom>.

Anatomy applies principally to the structure of an organism or any of its parts <the *anatomy* of the heart> but is likely to stress examination of parts and study of their relation to a whole <described the *anatomy* of a political campaign>.

Framework is used chiefly with reference to an artificial supporting construction that serves as a prop or guide but is not visible in the finished whole <the *framework* of a sofa>.

Skeleton applies to the bony framework of the animal body <found only the *skeleton* of a mouse> or may imply either a carefully developed and articulated design or a sketchy conception of the whole that serves as a starting point <roughed out the *skeleton* of the novel>.

strut, swagger, bristle, bridle mean to assume an air of dignity or importance.

Strut suggests a pompous affectation of dignity, especially in gait or bearing <*strutted* like a peacock>.

Swagger implies an ostentatious conviction of one's own superiority, often manifested in insolent gait and overbearing manner <*swaggered* onto the field>.

Bristle implies an aggressive manifestation sometimes of anger or of zeal but often of an emotion that causes one to show one's sense of dignity or importance <an accusation that made her *bristle*>.

Bridle usually suggests an awareness of a threat to one's dignity or state and a reaction of hostility or resentment <local government leaders who *bridled* against interference>.

stubborn see OBSTINATE.

stubby see STOCKY.

study see CONSIDER.

stupendous see MONSTROUS.

stupid, dull, dense, crass, dumb mean lacking in or seeming to lack power to absorb ideas or impressions.

Stupid implies a slow-witted or dazed state of mind that may be either congenital or temporary <you're too *stupid* to know what's good for you>. ***ant*** intelligent

Dull suggests a slow or sluggish mind such as results from disease, depression, or shock <monotonous work that left his mind *dull*>. ***ant*** clever, bright, sharp

Dense implies a thickheaded imperviousness to ideas or impressions <was too *dense* to take a hint>. ***ant*** subtle, bright

Crass suggests a grossness of mind precluding discrimination or delicacy <a *crass*, materialistic people>. ***ant*** brilliant

Dumb applies to an exasperating obtuseness or lack of comprehension <too *dumb* to figure out what's going on>.

stupor see LETHARGY.

sturdy see STRONG.

stutter see STAMMER.

style see FASHION.

suave, urbane, diplomatic, bland, smooth, politic mean pleasantly tactful and well-mannered.

Suave suggests a specific ability to deal with others easily and without friction <a luxury restaurant with an army of *suave* waiters>. ***ant*** bluff

Urbane implies high cultivation and poise coming from wide social experience <the *urbane* host of a television series>. ***ant*** rude, clownish, bucolic

Diplomatic stresses an ability to deal with ticklish situations tactfully and effectively <be *diplomatic* in asking them to leave>. ***ant*** undiplomatic

Bland emphasizes mildness of manner and absence of irritating qualities <a *bland* manner suitable for early morning radio>. ***ant*** brusque

Smooth suggests often an excessive, deliberately assumed suavity <the *smooth* sales pitch of a car dealer>. ***ant*** bluff

Politic implies a shrewd as well as tactful and suave handling of people and situations <an ambassador's wife must be *politic* and discreet>.

subdue see CONQUER.

subdued see TAME.

subject *n* see CITIZEN.

subject *adj* see LIABLE.

subjugate see CONQUER.

sublime see SPLENDID.

submission see SURRENDER.

submissive see TAME.

submit see YIELD.

subscribe see ASSENT.

subservient, servile, slavish, menial, obsequious mean showing or characterized by extreme compliance or abject obedience.

Subservient implies the compliant or cringing manner of one conscious of a subordinate position <domestic help was expected to be properly *subservient*>. ***ant*** domineering, overbearing

Servile suggests lowly status and mean or fawning submissiveness <a political boss and his entourage of *servile* hangers-on>. ***ant*** authoritative

Slavish suggests abject or debased servility <the *slavish* condition of migrant farm workers>. ***ant*** independent

Menial stresses humbleness and degradation associated with one who works at an economically or socially inferior occupation <wanted to escape from a life of *menial* jobs>.

Obsequious implies fawning or sycophantic compliance and exaggerated deference of manner <waiters who are *obsequious* in the presence of celebrities>. ***ant*** contumelious

subside see ABATE.

substantiate see CONFIRM.

subterfuge see DECEPTION.

subtle see LOGICAL.

succeed 1. see FOLLOW 1.

2. Succeed, prosper, thrive, flourish mean to attain or be attaining a desired end.

Succeed implies an antithesis to *fail* and is widely applicable to persons and things <*succeeded* in her third try for public office>. ***ant*** fail

Prosper carries an implication of continued or long-continuing and usually increasing success <*prosper* in business>.

Thrive adds the implication of vigorous growth often because of or in spite of specified conditions <plants that *thrive* in acid soil>. ***ant*** languish

Flourish implies a state of vigorous growth and expansion without signs of decadence or decay but also without any suggestion of how long this state will be maintained <attitudes that *flourished* in the Middle Ages>. ***ant*** languish

successive see CONSECUTIVE.

succinct see CONCISE.

succumb see YIELD.

sudden see PRECIPITATE.

suffer 1. see BEAR. **2.** see LET.

sufferance see PERMISSION.

suffering see DISTRESS.

sufficient, enough, adequate, competent mean being what is necessary or desirable.

Sufficient suggests a quantity or scope that closely meets a need <had supplies *sufficient* to last a month>. ***ant*** insufficient

Enough is less exact and more approximate than *sufficient* <do you have *enough* food?>.

Adequate may imply barely meeting a requirement <the room was *adequate,* no more>. ***ant*** inadequate, unadequate

Competent suggests measuring up to all requirements without question or being adequately adapted to an end <a *competent* income for their way of life>.

suffocate, asphyxiate, stifle, smother, choke, strangle mean to interrupt the normal course of breathing.

Suffocate is likely to imply the impossibility of breathing because of the absence of oxygen, the presence of noxious gases, or interference with the passage of air to and from the lungs <*suffocating* under the sand which had fallen upon him>.

Asphyxiate is likely to refer to situations involving death through lack of oxygen or presence of toxic gas <several people were *asphyxiated* by chlorine escaping from the wrecked train>.

Stifle is appropriately used to refer to situations where breathing is difficult or impossible because of inadequate fresh air <the room's *stifling* atmosphere>.

Smother is usable in situations in which the supply of oxygen is or seems inadequate for life and often suggests a deadening pall of smoke, dust, or impurities in the air <*smothered* by a blanket of volcanic ash>.

Choke suggests positive interference with breathing, for example by compression, obstruction, or severe inflammation of the throat <*choke* on a bit of apple>.

Strangle, similar to *choke*, more consistently implies a serious or fatal interference <*strangled* to death by the assailant>.

suffuse see INFUSE.

suggest, imply, hint, intimate, insinuate mean to convey an idea indirectly.

Suggest may stress a putting into the mind by an association of ideas, an awakening of a desire, or an initiating of a train of thought <an actress who can *suggest* a whole character with one gesture>. ***ant*** express

Imply is close to *suggest* but may indicate a more definite or logical relation of the unexpressed idea to the expressed <pronouncements that *imply* he has lost touch with reality>. ***ant*** express

Hint implies the use of slight or remote suggestion with a minimum of overt statement <*hinted* that she might have a job lined up>.

Intimate stresses delicacy of suggestion without connoting any lack of candor <*intimated* that he was ready to pop the question>.

Insinuate applies to the conveying of a usually unpleasant idea in a sly underhanded manner <*insinuated* that the neighbors were not what they appeared to be>.

suitable see FIT *adj.*

sulky see SULLEN.

sullen, glum, morose, surly, sulky, crabbed, saturnine, dour, gloomy mean showing a forbidding or disagreeable mood.

Sullen implies a silent ill humor and a refusal to be sociable or cooperative <remained *sullen* throughout the party>.

Glum suggests a silent dispiritedness <the whole team was *glum* following the defeat>. ***ant*** cheerful

Morose adds to *glum* an element of bitterness <became *morose* after the death of his wife>. ***ant*** blithe

Surly implies sullenness, gruffness, and churlishness of speech or manner <a *surly* young man>. ***ant*** amiable

Sulky suggests childish resentment expressed in peevish sullenness <a period of *sulky* behavior followed every argument>.

Crabbed applies to a forbidding, ill-natured harshness of manner <his *crabbed* exterior was only a pose>.

Saturnine describes a heavy, forbidding, taciturn gloom or suggests a bitter, sardonic manner <a *saturnine* wit>. ***ant*** genial, mercurial

Dour suggests a superficially severe, obstinate, and grim bitterness <a disposition to match the landscape, *dour* and unfriendly>.

Gloomy implies a depression in mood making for seeming sullenness, dourness, or glumness <bad news that put everyone in a *gloomy* mood>. ***ant*** cheerful

sum, amount, number, aggregate, total, whole, quantity mean all that is present in a group or mass.

Sum applies to the result of addition of numbers or particulars <thought of his car as more than the *sum* of its parts>.

Amount implies the result of combining sums or weights or measures into a whole <the *amount* of cotton raised last year>.

Number suggests a countable aggregate of persons or things <a large *number* of apples>.

Aggregate implies a counting or considering together of all the distinct individuals or particulars of a group or collection <errors that are individually insignificant but that in their *aggregate* destroy confidence>.

Total suggests the completeness or inclusiveness of the result and may stress magnitude in the result <counted a *total* of 328 paying customers>.

Whole, close to *total,* emphasizes unity in what is summed up <wanted the individual elements to create a cohesive *whole*>.

Quantity applies to things measured in bulk, even though they can be counted <a *quantity* of carrots> or to anything that is measurable in extent, duration, volume, magnitude, intensity, or value <the *quantity* of work performed>.

summary see CONCISE.

summative see CUMULATIVE.

summit, peak, pinnacle, climax, apex, acme, culmination mean the highest point attained or attainable.

Summit implies the topmost level attainable <a singer at the *summit* of his career>.

Peak suggests the highest point reached in a course or during a specific length of time <an artist working at the *peak* of her powers>.

Pinnacle suggests a dizzying and often insecure height <the *pinnacle* of success>.

Climax implies the highest point in an ascending series <the moon landing marked the *climax* of the program>.

Apex implies the point where all ascending lines or processes converge and in which everything is concentrated <Dutch culture reached its *apex* in the 17th century>. ***ant*** nadir

Acme implies a level of quality representing the perfection of a thing <a statue that was once deemed the *acme* of beauty>.

Culmination suggests an apex that is the outcome of a growth or development <the bill marked the *culmination* of the civil rights movement>.

summon, call, cite, convoke, convene, muster mean to demand the presence of.

Summon implies the exercise of authority and may imply a mandate, an imperative order, or urgency <*summoned* by the court to appear as a witness>.

Call may be used less formally and less emphatically for *summon* <the President *called* Congress for a special session>.

Cite implies a summoning to court usually to answer a charge <*cited* to answer the charge of drunken driving>.

Convoke implies a summons to assemble, especially for deliberative or legislative purposes <*convoked* an assembly of the world's leading scientists>.

Convene is somewhat less formal or emphatic than *convoke* <*convened* the students in the school auditorium>.

Muster suggests a calling up of a number of things that form a group in order that they may be exhibited, displayed, or utilized as a whole for some purpose <*muster* the troops for an inspection>.

sumptuous see LUXURIOUS.

sunder see SEPARATE.

superb see SPLENDID.

supercilious see PROUD.

supererogatory, gratuitous, uncalled-for, wanton mean done without need, compulsion, warrant, or provocation.

Supererogatory implies a giving above or beyond what is required by rule and may suggest the adding of something not needed or not wanted <an abrupt man who regarded the usual pleasantries as *supererogatory*>.

Gratuitous may apply to a voluntary giving without expectation of return <provided *gratuitous* services> but usually applies to something offensive or unpleasant given or done without provocation <a *gratuitous* insult>.

Uncalled-for implies a gratuitous impertinence or logical absurdity <resented her *uncalled-for* advice>. ***ant*** required

Wanton implies not only a lack of provocation but a malicious, arbitrary, or sportive motive <the *wanton* destruction of property by vandals>.

superficial, shallow, cursory, uncritical mean lacking in depth, comprehensiveness, or solidity.

Superficial implies a concern only with obvious or surface aspects or an avoidance of fundamental matters <a *superficial* examination of the wound>. ***ant*** exhaustive, radical

Shallow is more generally derogatory in implying lack of depth in knowledge, reasoning, emotions, or character <a *shallow* interpretation of the character Hamlet>. ***ant*** deep

Cursory suggests haste and casualness that lead to a lack of thoroughness or a neglect of details <even a *cursory* reading of the work will reveal that>. ***ant*** painstaking

Uncritical implies a superficiality or shallowness unbefitting to a critic or sound judge <her *uncritical* acceptance of his excuses>. ***ant*** critical

supersede see REPLACE.

supervene see FOLLOW 1.

supervision see OVERSIGHT.

supine 1. see INACTIVE. **2.** see PRONE.

supplant see REPLACE.

supple 1. see ELASTIC.

2. Supple, limber, lithe, lithesome, lissome mean showing freedom and ease in bodily movements.

Supple stresses flexibility of muscles and joints and perfect coordination, ease, and rapidity in movement <the light *supple* spring of a cat>. ***ant*** stiff

Limber implies flexibility and ease and quickness in moving but does not stress excellence of coordination or grace <her long *limber* fingers moved over the keyboard>.

Lithe suggests a slender supple body and nimble graceful movements <the *lithe* form of a tiger>.

Lithesome may suggest a strength and vigor that makes for sure graceful movement <drew back the bow with a single *lithesome* effort>.

Lissome may imply a light easy supple grace in bearing or movement <*lissome* as a bird in flight>.

supplicate see BEG.

supply see PROVIDE.

support, uphold, advocate, back, champion mean to favor actively someone or something that meets opposition.

Support is least explicit about the nature of the assistance given <people who *support* the development of the area>. ***ant*** buck

Uphold implies extended support given to something attacked <*upheld* the legitimacy of the military action>. ***ant*** contravene, subvert

Advocate stresses a verbal urging or pleading <*advocated* a return to basics in public school education>. ***ant*** impugn

Back suggests a supporting by lending assistance to one failing or falling <allies refused to *back* the call for sanctions>.

Champion suggests the public defending of those who are unjustly attacked or too weak to advocate their own cause <*championed* the rights of pregnant women>.

suppress 1. see CRUSH.

2. Suppress, repress mean to hold back more or less forcefully one that seeks an outlet.

Suppress implies a putting down or keeping back completely, typically by the exercise of great or oppressive power or violence <*suppressed* the revolt> <*suppress* an impulse>.

Repress implies little more than a checking or restraining and often suggests that the thing restrained may break out anew or in a different way <had difficulty in *repressing* his curiosity>.

supremacy, ascendancy mean the position of being first, as in rank, power, or influence.

Supremacy implies superiority over all others that is usually perfectly apparent or generally accepted <the *supremacy* of Shakespeare among English dramatists>.

Ascendancy sometimes implies supremacy, but its chief idea is either that of emerging domination or of autocratic use of power <struggled to maintain their *ascendancy* over the other teams in the league>.

sure, certain, positive, cocksure mean having no doubt or uncertainty.

Sure usually stresses a subjective or intuitive feeling of assurance <felt *sure* that he had forgotten something>. ***ant*** unsure

Certain may apply to a basing of a conclusion or conviction on definite grounds or indubitable evidence <scientists are now *certain* what caused the explosion>. ***ant*** uncertain

Positive intensifies sureness or certainty and may imply opinionated conviction or the forceful expression of it <she is *positive* that he is the killer>. ***ant*** doubtful

Cocksure implies presumptuous or careless positiveness <you're always so *cocksure* about everything>. ***ant*** dubious, doubtful

surfeit see SATIATE.

surly see SULLEN.

surmise see CONJECTURE.

surmount see CONQUER.

surpass see EXCEED.

surprise 1. Surprise, waylay, ambush mean to attack unawares.

Surprise in technical military use may imply strategic planning and secrecy in operations intended to catch an enemy unawares <*surprised* an enemy camp>, but general use is more likely to suggest a chance catching unawares <police *surprised* a burglar leaving the house>.

Waylay commonly implies a lying in wait along a public way, often in concealment <highwaymen who *waylaid* all travelers>, but sometimes it merely implies an intercepting and detaining <a teacher *waylaid* by questioning students>.

Ambush tends to evoke the image of would-be attackers concealed in a thicket and is often used with reference to guerrilla warfare <he had been *ambushed* by rebel forces> but is equally applicable to other situations where the primary image is pertinent <*ambushed* by joy>.

2. Surprise, astonish, astound, amaze, flabbergast mean to impress forcibly through unexpectedness.

Surprise stresses the causing of surprise, amazement, or wonder through being unexpected or unanticipated at a particular time or place <*surprised* to find his mother in a bar>.

Astonish implies a surprising so great as to seem incredible <the young player *astonished* the chess masters>.

Astound stresses a stunning or overwhelming emotional effect resulting from unprecedented or unbelievable but true occurrences <news of the atomic bomb *astounded* everyone>.

Amaze suggests an effect of bewilderment, perplexity, or wonder <*amazed* by the immense size of the place>.

Flabbergast may suggest a dumbfounding astonishment and bewilderment or dismay <*flabbergasted* by his daughter's precocious comments>.

surrender *n* **Surrender, submission, capitulation** mean the yielding up of one's person, forces, or possessions to another person or power.

Surrender in both military and general use is likely to imply a complete yielding and a dependence on the mercy or humanity of a stronger power <called for the unconditional *surrender* of all enemy forces>.

Submission stresses the acknowledgment of the power or authority of another and often suggests loss of independence <hung his head in a gesture of *submission*>. ***ant*** resistance

Capitulation may stress conditions elaborated between parties to a surrender but is likely to stress completeness or finality of yielding <forced their *capitulation* to her demands>.

surrender *vb* see RELINQUISH.

surreptitious see SECRET.

surveillance see OVERSIGHT.

survey *n* see COMPENDIUM.

survey *vb* see SEE 1.

susceptible see LIABLE.

suspend 1. see DEFER 1. **2.** see EXCLUDE.

suspicion see UNCERTAINTY.

suture see JOINT.

swagger see STRUT.

swarm see TEEM.

swat see STRIKE.

sway *vb* **1.** see AFFECT. **2.** see SWING 2.

sway *n* see POWER 3.

sweep see RANGE.

sweeping see INDISCRIMINATE.

sweet, engaging, winning, winsome, dulcet mean distinctly pleasing or charming and free of all that is irritating or distasteful.

Sweet is likely to be a term of mild general approval for what pleases or attracts without stirring deeply <what a *sweet* little

cottage> but can sometimes suggest a cloying excess of what is pleasing in moderation <a *sweet,* overpowering aroma>. ***ant*** sour, bitter

Engaging is likely to stress the power of attracting and often of holding favorable attention <an *engaging* smile>. ***ant*** loathesome

Winning, otherwise close to *engaging,* is likely to stress the power of a person to please or delight <a girl with a ready smile and very *winning* ways>.

Winsome implies a generally pleasing and engaging quality and often a childlike charm and innocence <had an indefinably *winsome* quality>.

Dulcet suggests an appealing and gratifying or soothing quality <the *dulcet* tones of a harp>. ***ant*** grating

swell see EXPAND.

swerve, veer, deviate, depart, digress, diverge mean to turn aside from a straight course.

Swerve suggests a usually somewhat abrupt physical, mental, or moral turning <suddenly *swerved* to avoid hitting an animal>.

Veer implies a major change in direction often under an outside influence <at that point the road *veers* to the right>.

Deviate implies a turning from a customary or prescribed course and often implies irregularity <the witness never *deviated* from her story>.

Depart suggests a deviation from a traditional or conventional course or type <a book that *departs* from the usual memoirs of a film star>.

Digress applies to a departing from the subject at hand <frequently *digressed* during his lecture>.

Diverge may equal *depart* but usually suggests a branching of a single path into two or more leading in different directions <after medical school their paths *diverged*>. ***ant*** converge

swift see FAST.

swindle see CHEAT.

swing 1. Swing, wave, flourish, brandish, thrash mean to wield or cause to move to and fro or up and down.

Swing implies a regular or uniform movement usually to and fro <*swing* the rope back and forth>.

Wave usually implies a smooth or continuous motion <a flag *waving* in the breeze>.

Flourish suggests a vigorous, ostentatious, or graceful movement of something held in the hand <*flourishing* her racket, she challenged me to a match>.

Brandish implies a threatening or menacing motion <*brandishing* his fist, he vowed vengeance>.

Thrash suggests a vigorous, abrupt, violent movement <a child *thrashing* about in a tantrum>.

2. Swing, sway, oscillate, vibrate, fluctuate, waver, undulate mean to move to and fro, up and down, or back and forth.

Swing implies a movement through an arc of something attached at one end or one side <the door suddenly *swung* open>.

Sway implies a slow swinging or teetering movement <the bridge *swayed* a little and then fell>.

Oscillate stresses a usually rapid alternation between extremes of direction <a fan that *oscillates* will cool more effectively>.

Vibrate suggests the rapid oscillation of an elastic body under stress or impact <the *vibrating* strings of a piano>.

Fluctuate suggests a constant irregular changing of level, intensity, or value <monetary exchange rates *fluctuate* constantly>.

Waver stresses an irregular motion suggestive of reeling or tottering <his whole body *wavered* as he crossed the finish line>.

Undulate suggests a gentle wavelike motion <an *undulating* sea of grass>.

sybaritic see SENSUOUS.

sycophant see PARASITE.

syllabus see COMPENDIUM.

symbol, emblem, attribute mean a perceptible thing that stands for something unseen or intangible.

Symbol is applicable to an outward sign of something spiritual or immaterial <a king's crown is the *symbol* of his sovereignty and his scepter the *symbol* of his authority>.

Emblem may apply to a pictorial device or representation chosen as the symbol of a person, a nation, a royal line, or other institution that has adopted it <the fleur-de-lis is the *emblem* of French royalty>.

Attribute, with *emblem,* may apply to an object that is conventionally represented in art as an accompanying symbol of a character or of a personified abstraction <the blindness that is the *attribute* of Justice>.

symmetry, proportion, balance, harmony mean a quality in design that gives aesthetic pleasure and which depends on the proper relating of parts to each other and to the effect of the whole.

Symmetry implies a median line or axis on either side of which the details correspond in size, form, and placement <the *symmetry* of a Greek temple>.

Proportion implies a grace or beauty that stems from the measured fitness of every detail and the consequent perfection of the whole <a statue of perfect *proportion*>. ***ant*** disproportion

Balance is sometimes equivalent to *symmetry* but distinctively suggests equality of values and a massing of different things such as light and shade or contrasting colors that offset each other <a painting in which light and dark were in perfect *balance*>. ***ant*** imbalance

Harmony suggests the pleasing aesthetic impression produced by something that manifests symmetry, proportion, or balance, singly or in combination <achieved *harmony* through the imaginative use of color>.

sympathetic see CONSONANT.

sympathy 1. see ATTRACTION.

2. Sympathy, pity, compassion, ruth, empathy mean a feeling for or a capacity for sharing in the interests or distress of another.

Sympathy is the most general term, ranging in meaning from friendly interest or agreement in taste to emotional identification <felt *sympathy* for his political beliefs>.

Pity implies tender or sometimes slightly contemptuous sympathy or sorrow for one in distress <he felt a tender *pity* for her>.

Compassion implies tenderness and understanding and a desire to aid or spare <treated the sick with great *compassion*> but can be quite impersonal in its reference <justice tempered with *compassion*>.

Ruth is likely to suggest pity or compassion resulting from the softening of a stern or indifferent spirit <an old man ignorant of the healing effects of *ruth*>.

Empathy implies a capacity for vicarious feeling, but the feeling need not be one of sorrow nor involve agreement <lacked capacity for *empathy* for the plight of others>.

symptom see SIGN 1.

synchronous see CONTEMPORARY.

syndicate see MONOPOLY.

synopsis see ABRIDGMENT.

synthetic see ARTIFICIAL.

system see METHOD.

systematize see ORDER.

T

taciturn see SILENT.

tact, address, poise, savoir faire mean skill and grace in dealing with others.

Tact implies delicate and considerate perception of what is fit or appropriate under given circumstances <use *tact* when inquiring about the divorce>. ***ant*** awkwardness

Address stresses dexterity and grace in dealing with new and trying situations and may imply success in attaining one's ends <brought off her first dinner party with remarkable *address*>. ***ant*** maladroitness, gaucherie

Poise may imply both tact and address but stresses self-possession and ease in meeting difficult situations <the *poise* of one who has been officiating all his life>.

Savoir faire is likely to stress worldly experience and a sure awareness of what is proper or expedient in various situations <has little of the *savoir faire* expected of a Washington hostess>.

tactics see STRATEGY.

taint see CONTAMINATE.

take 1. Take, seize, grasp, clutch, snatch, grab mean to get hold of by or as if by catching up with the hand.

Take is a general term applicable to any manner of getting something into one's possession or control <*take* some salad from the bowl>.

Seize implies a sudden and forcible effort in getting hold of something tangible or in apprehending something fleeting or elusive when intangible <*seized* the crook as he tried to escape>.

Grasp stresses a laying hold of so as to have firmly in possession <firmly *grasp* the handle and pull>.

Clutch suggests avidity or anxiety in seizing or grasping and may imply failure in taking or holding <frantically *clutching* the bush at the edge of the cliff>.

Snatch suggests a more sudden or quick action <*snatched* a doughnut before running out the door> and may carry a connotation of stealth <*snatch* a purse>.

Grab implies roughness or rudeness and often implies arrogant or vulgar disregard for the rights of others <roughly *grabbed* her by the arm>.

2. see RECEIVE.

tale see STORY.

talent see GIFT.

talisman see FETISH.

talk see SPEAK.

talkative, loquacious, garrulous, voluble mean given to talk or talking.

Talkative may imply a readiness to engage in talk or a disposition to enjoy conversation <not the *talkative* type who would enjoy a party>. ***ant*** silent

Loquacious suggests fluency and ease in speaking or an undue talkativeness <the corporation needs a spokesperson who is *loquacious* and telegenic>.

Garrulous implies prosy, rambling, or tedious loquacity

<forced to endure a *garrulous* companion the whole trip>. ***ant*** taciturn

Voluble suggests a free, easy, and unending loquacity <the Italians are a *voluble* people>. ***ant*** curt

tall see HIGH.

tally see AGREE 3.

tame, subdued, submissive mean docilely tractable or incapable of asserting one's will.

Tame implies a lack of independence and spirit that permits or results from domination by others <a friendship that rendered her uncharacteristically *tame*>. ***ant*** fierce, untamed, wild

Subdued generally implies a loss of vehemence, intensity, or force and may suggest the quietness or meekness of one dependent, chastised, or timorous <a meek, *subdued* attitude>. ***ant*** unsubdued

Submissive implies the state of mind of one who has yielded his or her will to control by another and who unquestioningly obeys or accepts <*submissive* to authority>. ***ant*** rebellious

tamper see MEDDLE.

tang see TASTE 1.

tangent see ADJACENT.

tangible see PERCEPTIBLE.

tantalize see WORRY.

tap, knock, rap, thump, thud mean to strike or hit audibly.

Tap implies making a light blow usually repeated <*tap* on the window to attract a friend's attention>.

Knock implies a firmer blow, sometimes amounting to a pounding or hammering, and a correspondingly louder sound <the messenger *knocked* loudly to awaken us>.

Rap suggests a smart vigorous striking on a hard surface that produces a sharp quick sound or series of sounds <the chairman *rapped* for order>.

Thump implies a solid pounding or beating that produces a dull booming sound <heard the *thumping* and banging of carpenters working on the floor below>.

Thud places more emphasis on the sound and often implies the result of something falling or striking rather than of something being struck <heard the severed tree limbs *thud* as they fell>.

tardy, late, behindhand, overdue mean not arriving or doing or occurring at the set, due, or expected time.

Tardy implies a lack of promptness or punctuality or a lateness that results from slowness in progress or, more often, from delay in starting <made excuses for his *tardy* arrival>. ***ant*** prompt

Late usually stresses a failure to come or take place at the time due because of procrastination, slowness, or interference <he

was *late* for work most mornings>. ***ant*** early, punctual, prompt

Behindhand applies to the situation of persons who have fallen into arrears or whose development, progress, or action is slower than normal <*behindhand* in their mortgage payments>.

Overdue may apply to what has become due but not been dealt with <an *overdue* library book> or what has been expected or scheduled but has not arrived <our guests are long *overdue*> or what might logically have occurred or appeared long before <produced *overdue* tax reform>. ***ant*** early

tarry see STAY.

task, duty, job, chore, stint, assignment mean a piece of work to be done.

Task implies usually a specific piece of work imposed by a person in authority or by circumstance <performed a variety of *tasks* for the company>.

Duty implies an obligation to perform or a responsibility for performance <the *duties* of a lifeguard>.

Job applies to a piece of work voluntarily performed or to an assigned bit of menial work and may sometimes suggest difficulty or importance <took on the *job* of turning the company around>.

Chore implies a minor routine activity necessary for maintaining a household or farm and may stress the drabness of such activity <every child had a list of *chores* to do>.

Stint implies a carefully allotted or measured quantity of assigned work or service <during his *stint* as governor>.

Assignment implies a definite limited task assigned by one in authority <your *assignment* did not include interfering with others>.

taste **1. Taste, flavor, savor, tang** mean that property of a substance which makes it perceptible to the gustatory sense.

Taste merely indicates the property <the fundamental *tastes* are acid, sweet, bitter, and salt>.

Flavor suggests the interaction of the senses of taste and smell <a head cold seems to spoil the *flavor* of most foods>.

Savor suggests delicate or pervasive flavor appealing to a sensitive palate <sipping slowly to get the full *savor* of the wine>.

Tang implies a sharp penetrating flavor or savor <there was a *tang* of vinegar in the dressing>.

2. Taste, palate, relish, gusto, zest mean a liking for or enjoyment of something because of the pleasure it gives.

Taste implies a specific liking or interest, whether natural or acquired <had a *taste* for music> or a discerning appreciation based on informed aesthetic judgment <excellent *taste* in wines>. ***ant*** antipathy

Palate implies a liking based on pleasurable sensation <the discriminating *palate* of a tea taster>.

Relish suggests a capacity for keen gratification <seemed to utter the denunciation with great *relish*>.

Gusto implies a hearty relish that goes with high spirits and vitality <sang all the old songs with *gusto*>.

Zest implies eagerness and avidity in doing, making, encountering, or experiencing <possessed a *zest* for life>.

tasty see PALATABLE.

taunt see RIDICULE.

taut see TIGHT.

tawdry see GAUDY.

teach, instruct, educate, train, discipline, school mean to cause to acquire knowledge or skill.

Teach applies to any manner of imparting information or skill so that others may learn <*taught* them how to ski>.

Instruct suggests a methodical or formal teaching <*instruct* the recruits in calisthenics at boot camp>.

Educate implies an attempting to bring out and develop latent capabilities <*educate* students so that they are prepared for the future>.

Train stresses an instructing and drilling with a specific end in view <*trained* foreign pilots to operate the new aircraft>.

Discipline implies a subordinating to a master or a subjection to control <*disciplined* herself to exercise daily>.

School implies a training or disciplining especially in what is hard to master or to bear <*schooled* myself not to flinch at the sight of blood>.

tear, rip, rend, split, cleave, rive mean to separate forcibly.

Tear implies a pulling apart by force that leaves jagged edges <*tear* up lettuce for a salad>.

Rip implies a pulling apart in one rapid uninterrupted motion often along a seam or joint <*ripped* the jacket along the seams>.

Rend, often rhetorical in tone, implies violent or ruthless severing or sundering <an angry mob *rent* his clothes>.

Split implies a cutting or breaking apart in a continuous, straight, and usually lengthwise direction or in the direction of grain or layers <*split* logs for firewood>.

Cleave implies a forceful splitting or cutting with a blow of an edged weapon or tool <a bolt of lightning *cleaved* the giant oak>.

Rive suggests action rougher and more violent than *split* or *cleave* <a friendship *riven* by jealousy>.

tease see WORRY.

tedium, boredom, ennui, doldrums mean a state of dissatisfaction and weariness.

Tedium is likely to suggest dullness and lowness of spirits resulting from irksome inactivity or sameness or monotony of occupation <could scarcely bear the *tedium* of listening to one long lecture after another>.

Boredom adds suggestions of listlessness, dreariness, and unrest that accompany an environment or situation or company that fails to stimulate or challenge <seeks distraction from the *boredom* of housework>.

Ennui stresses profound dissatisfaction or weariness of spirit and often suggests physical depression as well as boredom <a life of self-indulgence that later left him subject to feelings of *ennui*>.

Doldrums applies to a period of depression marked by listlessness, lagging spirits, and despondency <failed to rouse her from the *doldrums*> or implies a dull inactive state <the stock market has been in the *doldrums* lately>.

teem, abound, swarm, overflow mean to be plentifully supplied with or rich in.

Teem implies productiveness or fecundity <the rivers *teemed* with fish and the woods with game>.

Abound implies plenitude in numbers or amount and usually stresses profusion <the sturdy maples with which the local forests *abound*>. ***ant*** fail, fall short

Swarm usually stresses motion and thronging, but it may suggest infestation <tenements that *swarmed* with rats and other vermin>.

Overflow adds to *abound* the notion of glutting or of exceeding something's or someone's capacity to contain or use <*overflowing* with human kindness>.

teeter see SHAKE 1.

tell 1. see REVEAL. **2.** see SAY.

telling see VALID.

temerity, audacity, hardihood, effrontery, nerve, cheek, gall, chutzpah mean conspicuous or flagrant boldness.

Temerity suggests presumptuous boldness arising from rashness and contempt of danger <had the *temerity* to ask for a favor after that insult>. ***ant*** caution

Audacity implies a disregard of restraints commonly imposed by convention or prudence <an entrepreneur with *audacity* and vision>. ***ant*** circumspection

Hardihood suggests firmness of purpose in daring and defiance <no serious scientist has the *hardihood* to claim that>. ***ant*** cowardice, timidity

Effrontery implies shameless and arrogant disregard of propriety or courtesy <had the *effrontery* to tell me how to do my job>.

Nerve, an informal equivalent for *effrontery,* stresses hardihood <the *nerve* of that guy>.

Cheek, also a substitute for *effrontery,* implies impudent self-assurance <has the *cheek* to bill herself as a singer>.

Gall is like *nerve* and *cheek* but emphasizes insolence <had the *gall* to demand some evidence>.

Chutzpah adds to *nerve* and *gall* the notion of supreme self-confidence <her *chutzpah* got her into the exclusive party>.

temper *n* **1.** see DISPOSITION. **2.** see MOOD.

temper *vb* see MODERATE *vb.*

temperament see DISPOSITION.

temperance, sobriety, abstinence, abstemiousness, continence mean self-restraint in the gratification of appetites and desires.

Temperance implies habitual moderation and the exercise of discretion in any activity; in reference to the use of intoxicating beverages it implies not moderation but abstention <exercise *temperance* in all activities>. ***ant*** excess

Sobriety suggests avoidance of excess, often specifically of the excess of drinking that leads to intoxication; it may also connote seriousness and the avoidance of ostentation <a sect noted for its *sobriety* of dress>. ***ant*** insobriety, drunkenness, excitement

Abstinence implies voluntary deprivation <practiced *abstinence* when it came to dessert>. ***ant*** self-indulgence

Abstemiousness implies habitual self-restraint, moderation, and frugality, especially in eating or drinking <lived a life of frugality and *abstemiousness*>. ***ant*** gluttonous

Continence emphasizes self-restraint in regard to impulses and desires <a style of writing marked by *continence* and craft>; it finds its typical application in regard to sexual indulgence where it may imply either complete chastity or avoidance of excess <a society that encouraged sexual *continence* in all its members>. ***ant*** incontinence

temperate **1.** see SOBER. **2.** see MODERATE *adj.*

tempt see LURE.

tenacious see STRONG.

tenacity see COURAGE.

tend, attend, mind, watch mean to take charge of or look after someone or something.

Tend suggests the need for constant or recurring attention <a shepherd *tending* his flock>.

Attend is more likely to stress a taking charge and is, therefore, appropriate when a professional service or skilled activity is involved <the doctor who *attended* his mother>.

Mind, otherwise close to *tend,* distinctively suggests a guarding or protecting from injury or harm or failure <a neighbor who *minds* their children after school>.

Watch, often close to *mind,* may imply a more constant or more professional relationship or suggest an actual need to forestall danger <a guard hired to *watch* the store at night>.

tendency, trend, drift, tenor, current mean movement in a particular direction or with a particular character.

Tendency implies an inclination sometimes amounting to an impelling force <the *tendency* to expand the limits of what is art>.

Trend applies to the general direction maintained by a winding or irregular course <the long-term *trend* of the stock market is upward>.

Drift may apply to a tendency whose direction or course may be determined by external forces <the *drift* of the population away from large cities>, or it may apply to an underlying or obscure trend of meaning or discourse <a racist *drift* runs through all of his works>.

Tenor stresses a clearly perceptible direction and a continuous, undeviating course <a suburb seeking to maintain its *tenor* of tranquility>.

Current implies a clearly defined but not necessarily unalterable course or direction <an encounter that altered forever the *current* of my life>.

tender see OFFER.

tenet see DOCTRINE.

tenor see TENDENCY.

tense **1.** see STIFF. **2.** see TIGHT.

tension see STRESS.

tentative see PROVISIONAL.

tenuous see THIN.

tergiversation see AMBIGUITY.

terminal see LAST.

terminate see CLOSE *vb.*

termination see END.

terminus see END.

terrible see FEARFUL 2.

terrific see FEARFUL 1.

terror see FEAR.

terse see CONCISE.

testy see IRASCIBLE.

thankful see GRATEFUL.

theatrical see DRAMATIC.

theft, larceny, robbery, burglary mean the act or crime of stealing.

Theft implies the taking and removing of another's property without the person's consent and usually by stealth <the *theft* of an idea may hurt far more than the *theft* of money>.

Larceny, chiefly in legal use, applies to simple direct theft in which the property of one person is taken into the possession of another <*larceny* is "grand" or "petty" according to the value of the goods taken>.

Robbery in strict use implies violence or the threat of violence employed in the taking of another's property <the messenger was attacked and seriously injured in the course of a *robbery*>.

Burglary implies a forced and unlawful entering of enclosed premises for the purpose of committing a felony, usually that of larceny or robbery <lived in constant fear of *burglary*>.

then see THEREFORE.

theoretical, speculative, academic mean concerned principally with abstractions and theories.

Theoretical may apply to branches of learning which deal with the inferences drawn from observed facts and the laws and theories which explain these <the discoveries of *theoretical* physics that form the bases for applied physics>, but it may often imply a divorce from reality or actuality that gives a distorted view of things or a lack of testing and experience in actual use <considered both the *theoretical* and the practical aspects of the problem>. ***ant*** applied

Speculative may go beyond *theoretical* in stressing a concern with theorizing and often implies a daring use of the imagination in the manipulation of ideas <proposed a startling new theory that was fascinating but highly *speculative*>.

Academic in this use is likely to be derogatory and regularly stresses a tendency to concentrate, often overconcentrate, on the abstract to the neglect of reality or practical concerns <a knowledge of human nature that was purely *academic*>.

theory see HYPOTHESIS.

therefore, hence, consequently, then, accordingly mean as a result or concomitant.

Therefore stresses the logically deduced conclusion that it introduces <it was raining hard and *therefore* we stayed inside>.

Hence, though often interchangeable with *therefore,* is more likely to stress the importance of what precedes <a meal badly overcooked and *hence* inedible>.

Consequently tends to suggest good and reasonable grounds or a strong logical possibility <he said he would come; *consequently* we will wait for him>.

Then, when used to indicate logical sequence, is employed chiefly in the consequent clause or conclusion in a conditional sentence <if A and B are mutually exclusive possibilities and A is true, *then* B is false>.

Accordingly usually indicates logical or causal sequence but connotes naturalness or usualness in the consequence rather than necessity or inevitability <knew where the edges of the driveway were and plowed the snow *accordingly*>.

thick 1. see CLOSE *adj.* **2.** see STOCKY.

thickset see STOCKY.

thin, slender, slim, slight, tenuous mean not thick, broad, abundant, or dense.

Thin implies comparatively little extension between surfaces or in diameter <*thin* wire>, or it may suggest lack of substance, richness, or abundance <soup that was *thin* and tasteless>. ***ant*** thick

Slender implies leanness or spareness often with grace and good proportion <the *slender* legs of a Sheraton chair>.

Slim applies to a slenderness that suggests fragility or scantiness <a *slim* chance of success>. ***ant*** chubby

Slight implies smallness as well as thinness <the *slight* build of a professional jockey>.

Tenuous implies extreme thinness, sheerness, or lack of substance and firmness <the sword hung by a few *tenuous* threads>. ***ant*** dense

thing 1. see AFFAIR.

2. Thing, object, article mean something considered as having actual, distinct, and demonstrable existence.

Thing may apply not only to whatever can be known directly through the senses but also to something whose existence may be inferred from its signs and effects; in more restricted use it may refer to an entity existing in space and time as opposed to one existing only in thought <virtue is not a *thing* but an attribute of a *thing*> or to an inanimate entity as opposed to living beings and especially persons <she treasures each *thing* she buys>.

Object stresses existence separate from the observer and typically applies to something that is or can be set before one to be viewed, considered, or contemplated <concentrated on the atom as an *object* of study> or that has body and usually substance and shape <stumbled over some unseen *object* in the dark room>.

Article is used chiefly of objects that are thought of as members of a group or class <picked up several *articles* of clothing that the boy had dropped>.

think 1. Think, conceive, imagine, fancy, realize, envisage, envision mean to form an idea of something.

Think implies the entrance of an idea into one's mind with or without deliberate consideration or reflection <I just *thought* of a good story>.

Conceive suggests the forming and bringing forth and usually developing of an idea, plan, or design <*conceive* of a plan to rescue the hostages>.

Imagine stresses a visualization <*imagine* a permanently operating space station>.

Fancy suggests an imagining often unrestrained by factual reality but spurred by desires <*fancied* himself a super athlete>.

Realize stresses a grasping of the significance of what is vividly conceived or imagined <*realized* the enormity of the task ahead>.

Envisage and ***envision*** imply a conceiving or imagining that is especially clear or detailed <*envisaged* a totally computerized operation> <*envisioned* a world free from hunger and want>.

2. Think, cogitate, reflect, reason, speculate, deliberate mean to use one's powers of conception, judgment, or inference.

Think is general and may apply to any mental activity, but used alone it often suggests the attainment of clear ideas or conclusions <a course that really teaches you to *think*>.

Cogitate implies a deep or intent thinking <quietly sitting and *cogitating*>.

Reflect suggests the unhurried consideration of something called or recalled to the mind <*reflected* on fifty years of married life>.

Reason stresses a consecutive logical thinking <*reasoned* that the murderer and victim knew each other>.

Speculate implies a reasoning about things that are theoretical or problematic <historians have *speculated* about the fate of the Lost Colony>.

Deliberate suggests a slow or careful reasoning and consideration before forming an opinion or idea or reaching a conclusion or decision <the jury *deliberated* for five hours>.

3. see KNOW.

thirst see LONG.

though, although, albeit mean in spite of the fact.

Though can be used to introduce an established fact <*though* we have put men on the moon, we have not stopped wars> or a hypothesis or admission of possibility or probability <they decided to go on, *though* rain seemed likely> and is the usual term to introduce a contrary-to-fact or imaginary condition <*though* they may come, we will never give in>.

Although, in most uses interchangeable with *though*, may introduce an assertion of fact <*although* she ran faster than ever before, she did not win>.

Albeit is especially appropriate when the idea of admitting something that seems or suggests a contradiction is to be stressed <a thorough, *albeit* slow, examination>.

thought see IDEA.

thoughtful 1. Thoughtful, reflective, speculative, contemplative, meditative, pensive mean characterized by or showing the power to engage in thought, especially concentrated thinking.

Thoughtful may imply either the act of thinking in a concentrated manner or the disposition to apply oneself to careful and serious thought about specific problems or questions <demonstrated his *thoughtful* mind>. ***ant*** thoughtless

Reflective suggests the use of analysis or logical reasoning with a definite aim <a philosopher of *reflective* bent>.

Speculative suggests a tendency to think about things so abstract or unknowable that any conclusions are bound to be uncertain; the term often implies theorizing with little consideration of the evidence <theories about the origins of the universe that are as yet *speculative*>.

Contemplative implies an attention fixed on the object of thought or a habit of mind <hoped for a calmer, more *contemplative* life in retirement>.

Meditative suggests a tendency to ponder or muse over something but without necessarily any purpose other than pleasure <allowed himself the luxury of a few *meditative* minutes every day>.

Pensive, not always distinguishable from *meditative,* may carry suggestions of dreaminess, wistfulness, or melancholy <a rainy day conducive to *pensive* reflection>.

2. Thoughtful, considerate, attentive mean mindful of others.

Thoughtful usually implies unselfish concern for others and a capacity for anticipating another's needs or wants <the thank-you note was a *thoughtful* gesture>. ***ant*** thoughtless, unthoughtful

Considerate stresses concern for the feelings or distresses of others <a manner both courtly and *considerate*>. ***ant*** inconsiderate

Attentive emphasizes continuous thoughtfulness often shown by repeated acts of kindness <a wonderfully *attentive* host>. ***ant*** inattentive, neglectful

thrash see SWING 1.

threadbare see TRITE.

threaten, menace mean to announce or forecast impending danger or evil.

Threaten may imply an attempt to dissuade or influence by promising punishment for failure to obey <*threaten* a child with a spanking if he teases the baby>, or it may apply to an impersonal warning of something dire, disastrous, or disturbing <heavy clouds that *threaten* rain>.

Menace stresses a definitely hostile or alarming quality in what portends <conditions that *menace* the stability of society>.

thrifty see SPARING.

thrill, electrify, enthuse mean to fill with emotions that stir or excite.

Thrill suggests being pervaded by usually agreeably stimulating emotion that sets one atingle with pleasure, horror, or excitement <a *thrilling* detective story>.

Electrify suggests a sudden, violent, startling stimulation comparable to that produced by an electric current <the news *electrified* the community>.

Enthuse implies an arousing or experiencing of enthusiasm <was *enthused* about the new vacuum cleaner>.

thrive see SUCCEED.

throng see CROWD.

throw, cast, toss, fling, hurl, pitch, sling mean to cause to move swiftly through space by a propulsive movement or a propelling force.

Throw is general and interchangeable with the other terms but may specifically imply a distinctive propelling motion with the arm <*throws* the ball with great accuracy>.

Cast usually implies lightness in the thing thrown and sometimes a scattering <*cast* bread crumbs to the birds>.

Toss suggests a light or careless or aimless throwing and may imply an upward motion <*tossed* her racket on the bed>.

Fling stresses a vigorous throwing with slight aim or control <*flung* the ring back in his face>.

Hurl implies a powerful and forceful driving as in throwing a massive weight <*hurled* the intruder out the window>.

Pitch suggests a throwing carefully at a target <*pitch* horseshoes> or lightness and casualness <*pitch* trash in the basket>.

Sling suggests propelling with a sweeping or swinging motion, usually with force and suddenness <*slung* the bag over his shoulder>.

thrust see PUSH.

thud see TAP.

thump see TAP.

thwart see FRUSTRATE.

tidy see NEAT.

tie, bind mean to make fast or secure.

Tie implies the use of a line, such as a rope or chain or strap, to attach one thing that may move to another that is stable <*tie* the boat securely to the dock>. ***ant*** untie

Bind implies the use of a band or bond to attach two or more things firmly together <used wire to *bind* the gate to the fence post>. ***ant*** loose, unloose, unbind

tiff see QUARREL.

tight 1. Tight, taut, tense mean drawn or stretched to the limit or to the point where there is no looseness or slackness.

Tight implies a drawing together or around something in such a way that there is little or no slack or a binding or constricting results <a *tight* belt> or stresses the idea of squeezing or restraining unmercifully <found themselves in unbearably *tight* quarters>. ***ant*** loose

Taut suggests the pulling of a rope or fabric to the limit or until there is no give or slack <walked across the *taut* rope to safety> or is likely to stress especially nervous strain <nerves that were *taut* and on edge>. ***ant*** slack

Tense may be preferred when the tightness or tautness results in or manifests itself in severe physical or mental tension or strain <the crouching cat, *tense* and ready to spring>. ***ant*** relaxed

2. see DRUNK.

timely see SEASONABLE.

timid, timorous mean so fearful and apprehensive as to hesitate or hold back.

Timid stresses lack of courage and daring and implies extreme cautiousness and a fear of venturing into the unfamiliar or the uncertain <a *timid* investor impairing his capital in a vain search for complete security>. ***ant*** bold

Timorous stresses a usually habitual domination by fears and apprehensions of often imaginary risks that leads one to shrink terrified from any exhibition of independence or self-assertion <a *timorous* personality unsuited to door-to-door selling>. ***ant*** assured

timorous see TIMID.

tinge see COLOR.

tint see COLOR.

tiny see SMALL.

tipsy see DRUNK.

tire, weary, fatigue, exhaust, jade, fag mean to make or become unable or unwilling to continue.

Tire implies a draining of one's strength or patience <the long ride *tired* us out>.

Weary stresses a tiring until one is unable to endure more <*wearied* of the constant arguing>.

Fatigue suggests the causing of great lassitude through excessive strain or undue effort <*fatigued* by the long, hard climb>. ***ant*** rest

Exhaust implies the complete draining of physical or mental strength by hard exertion <shoveling snow *exhausted* him>.

Jade suggests a weariness or fatiguing that deprives one of all freshness and eagerness <*jaded* with the endless round of society parties>. ***ant*** refresh

Fag implies a drooping with fatigue <arrived home, all *fagged* out by a day's shopping>.

tireless see INDEFATIGABLE.

tittle see PARTICLE.
toady *n* see PARASITE.
toady *vb* see FAWN.
toil see WORK 1.
token see SIGN 1.
tolerant see FORBEARING.
tolerate see BEAR.
tool see IMPLEMENT.
toothsome see PALATABLE.
torment see AFFLICT.
torpor see LETHARGY.
torture see AFFLICT.
toss see THROW.
total *adj* see WHOLE.
total *n* see SUM.
totter **1.** see REEL. **2.** see SHAKE 1.
touch **1. Touch, feel, palpate, handle, paw** mean to get or produce or affect with a sensation by or as if by bodily contact.

Touch stresses the act and may imply bodily contact or the use of an implement <*touch* paint with a finger to see if it is dry>, or it may imply immaterial contact <we were *touched* by his concern>.

Feel stresses the sensation induced or experienced <*felt* to see that no bones were broken>.

Palpate stresses the feeling of the surface of a body as a means of examining its internal condition <the doctor *palpated* the abdomen and detected a swollen mass>.

Handle implies examination or exploration with hands or fingers to determine qualities such as texture, weight, or condition <heavier fabrics can be appreciated better by actually *handling* them, feeling the substance and texture>.

Paw is likely to imply clumsy or offensive handling <*pawed* eagerly through the box of prizes>.

2. see AFFECT.
3. see MATCH.

touching see MOVING.
touchstone see STANDARD.
touchy see IRASCIBLE.
tough see STRONG.
toxin see POISON.
toy see TRIFLE.
trace, vestige, track mean a perceptible sign made by something that has passed.

Trace may suggest any line, mark, or discernible effect left behind <an animal species believed to have vanished without a *trace*>.

Vestige applies to a tangible reminder such as a fragment or remnant of what is past and gone <boulders that are *vestiges* of the last ice age>.

Track implies a continuous line of marks or footprints or scent that can be followed <the fossilized *tracks* of dinosaurs>.

track see TRACE.
tractable see OBEDIENT.
trade see BUSINESS.
traduce see MALIGN.
traffic see BUSINESS.
trail see FOLLOW 2.
train see TEACH.
traipse see WANDER.
traitorous see FAITHLESS.
trammel see HAMPER.
tranquil see CALM.
transcend see EXCEED.
transfigure see TRANSFORM.

transform, metamorphose, transmute, convert, transmogrify, transfigure mean to change a thing into a different thing or form.

Transform implies a major change in form, nature, or function <*transformed* a small company into a corporate giant>.

Metamorphose suggests an abrupt or startling change induced by or as if by magic or a supernatural power or the proceeding of a process of natural development <*metamorphosed* awkward girls into graceful ballerinas>.

Transmute implies a fundamental transforming into a higher element or thing <*transmuted* a shopworn tale into a psychological masterpiece>.

Convert implies a change fitting something for a new or different use or function <*converted* the boys' room into a guest bedroom>.

Transmogrify suggests an extreme, often grotesque or preposterous metamorphosis <the prince was *transmogrified* into a frog>.

Transfigure implies a change that exalts or glorifies <ecstasy *transfigured* her face>.

transgression see BREACH.

transient, transitory, ephemeral, momentary, fugitive, fleeting, evanescent, short-lived mean lasting or staying only a short time.

Transient applies to what is actually short in its duration or stay <a hotel catering primarily to *transient* guests>. ***ant*** perpetual

Transitory applies to what is by its nature or essence bound to change, pass, or come to an end <fame in the movies is *transitory*>. ***ant*** everlasting, perpetual

Ephemeral implies brevity of life or duration <much slang is *ephemeral*>. ***ant*** perpetual

Momentary suggests coming and going quickly, often merely as a brief interruption of a more enduring state or course <my feelings of guilt were only *momentary*>. ***ant*** agelong

Fugitive implies passing so quickly as to make apprehending difficult <in winter the days are short and sunshine is *fugitive*>.

Fleeting is close to *fugitive* but stresses the difficulty or impossibility of holding back from flight <a life with only *fleeting* moments of joy>. ***ant*** lasting

Evanescent suggests momentary existence, a quick vanishing, and an airy or fragile quality <the story has an *evanescent* touch of whimsy that is lost on stage>.

Short-lived implies extreme brevity of life or existence, often of what might be expected to last or live longer <*short-lived* satisfaction>. ***ant*** agelong, long-lived

transitory see TRANSIENT.

translucent see CLEAR 1.

transmogrify see TRANSFORM.

transmute see TRANSFORM.

transparent see CLEAR 1.

transpire see HAPPEN.

transport *n* see ECSTASY.

transport *vb* **1.** see CARRY.

2. Transport, ravish, enrapture, entrance mean to carry away by strong and usually pleasurable emotion.

Transport implies the fact of being intensely moved by an emotion, as delight or rage, that exceeds ordinary limits and agitates or excites <children *transported* with delight at the thought of Christmas>.

Ravish can imply a seizure by emotion and especially by joy or delight <*ravished* by the sight of the tropical sunset>.

Enrapture implies a putting into a state of rapture and usually suggests an intense, even ecstatic, delight, often in one of the arts <young girls *enraptured* with the ballet before them>, but sometimes it stresses the bemusing aspects of rapture and then suggests a bedazzling or suppressing of the powers of clear thinking <a campaign that failed to *enrapture* the voters>.

Entrance usually suggests being held as spellbound as if in a trance by something that awakens an overmastering emotion <a naive ingenuousness that *entranced* them>.

3. see BANISH.

transpose see REVERSE.

trap see CATCH.

travail see WORK 1.

traverse see DENY.

travesty see CARICATURE.
treacherous see FAITHLESS.
treasure see APPRECIATE.
treat 1. see CONFER 1.
2. Treat, deal, handle mean to have to do with in a specified manner.
Treat in the sense of doing about, serving, or coping with is usually accompanied by context indicating attitude, temperament, or point of view that determines behavior or manner <*treat* the subject realistically in an essay>.
Deal, used with *with,* may suggest a managing, controlling, or authoritative disposing <*dealt* with each problem as it arose>.
Handle usually suggests manipulation and a placing, using, directing, or disposing with or as if with the hand <*handle* an ax skillfully>.
tremble see SHAKE 1.
tremendous see MONSTROUS
trenchant see INCISIVE.
trend see TENDENCY.
trepidation see FEAR.
trespass *n* see BREACH.
trespass *vb* **Trespass, encroach, entrench, infringe, invade** mean to make inroads upon the property, territory, or rights of another.
Trespass implies an unwarranted, unlawful, or offensive intrusion <warned people about *trespassing* on their land>.
Encroach suggests gradual or stealthy intrusion upon another's territory or usurpation of rights or possessions <on guard against laws that *encroach* upon our civil rights>.
Entrench suggests establishing and maintaining oneself in a position of advantage or profit at the expense of others <opposed to regulations that *entrench* upon free enterprise>.
Infringe implies an encroachment clearly violating a right or prerogative of another <a product that *infringes* upon another's patent>.
Invade implies a definite, hostile, and injurious entry into the territory or sphere of another <practices that *invade* our right to privacy>.
tribute see ENCOMIUM.
trick *n* **Trick, ruse, stratagem, maneuver, gambit, ploy, artifice, wile, feint** mean an indirect means to gain an end.
Trick may imply deception, roguishness, illusion, and either an evil or harmless intent <used every *trick* in the book to get the teacher's attention>.
Ruse stresses an attempt to mislead by giving a false impression <secured a papal audience through a clever *ruse*>.
Stratagem implies a ruse used to entrap, outwit, circumvent, or

surprise an opponent or enemy <a series of *stratagems* that convinced both sides he was their agent>.

Maneuver suggests adroit and skillful manipulation of persons or things to solve a problem or avoid difficulty <a bold *maneuver* that won him the nomination>.

Gambit applies to a trick or tactic used to gain an advantage, often by harassing or embarrassing an opponent <tried a new *gambit* in the peace negotiations>.

Ploy may add to *gambit* a suggestion of finesse or roguishness <tried a new *ploy* in order to gain entrance>.

Artifice implies ingenious contrivance or invention <his fawning smile was just an *artifice*>.

Wile suggests an attempt to entrap or deceive with false allurements <used all his *wiles* to win his uncle's favor>.

Feint implies a diversion or distraction of attention away from one's real intent <ballcarriers use *feints* to draw defensemen out of position>.

trick *vb* see DUPE.

trickery see DECEPTION.

tricky see SLY.

trifle, toy, dally, flirt, coquet mean to deal with or act toward someone or something without serious purpose.

Trifle may imply such varied attitudes as playfulness, unconcern, indulgent contempt, or light amorousness <*trifled* with her boyfriend's feelings>.

Toy implies an acting without full attention or serious exertion of one's powers <*toying* with the idea of taking a cruise>.

Dally suggests an indulging in thoughts or plans or activity merely as an amusement or pastime <likes to *dally* with the idea of writing a book someday>.

Flirt implies a superficiality of interest or attention that soon passes to another object <*flirted* with one college major after another>.

Coquet implies an attracting of interest or admiration or a trifling in love without serious intention <brazenly *coquetted* with the husbands of her friends>.

trim see NEAT.

trite, hackneyed, stereotyped, threadbare, shopworn mean lacking the freshness that evokes attention or interest.

Trite applies to a once effective phrase or idea spoiled by too long familiarity <"you win some, you lose some" is a *trite* expression>. ***ant*** original, fresh

Hackneyed applies to what has been worn out by overuse as to become dull and meaningless <all of the metaphors and images in the poem are *hackneyed*>. ***ant*** unhackneyed

Stereotyped implies falling invariably into the same imitative pattern or form <views of American Indians that are *stereotyped* and out-of-date>. ***ant*** changeful

Threadbare applies to what has been used or exploited until its possibilities of interest have been totally exhausted <a mystery novel with a *threadbare* plot>.

Shopworn suggests a loss from constant use of qualities that appeal or arouse interest <used phrases too *shopworn* to generate any interest or convey any praise>.

triumph see VICTORY.

trouble *n* see EFFORT.

trouble *vb* **Trouble, distress, ail** mean to cause to be uneasy or upset.

Trouble suggests a loss of tranquillity and implies a disturbing element that interferes with efficiency, convenience, comfort, health, or peace of mind <*troubled* by sleeplessness>.

Distress implies subjection to strain or pressure and resulting tension, pain, worry, or grief <*distressed* by the sight of suffering>.

Ail implies that something unspecified has gone wrong and often suggests a will to find the cause with an eye to aid or correction <what *ails* that naughty child?>.

truckle see FAWN.

true see REAL.

trust *n* see MONOPOLY.

trust *vb* see RELY.

truth, veracity, verity, verisimilitude mean the quality of keeping close to fact or reality and avoiding distortion or misrepresentation.

Truth may apply to an ideal abstraction that conforms to a universal or generalized reality or quality of statements, acts, or feelings that adhere to reality and avoid error or falsehood <swore to the *truth* of the statement he had made>. ***ant*** untruth, lie, falsehood

Veracity implies rigid and unfailing adherence to, observance of, or respect for truth <a politician not known for his *veracity*>. ***ant*** unveracity

Verity designates the quality of a state or thing that is exactly what is purports to be or accords completely with the facts <test the *verity* of his remarks> or refers to things felt to be of lasting, ultimate, or transcendent truth <a teacher still believing in the old *verities* of school pride and loyalty>.

Verisimilitude implies the quality of an artistic or literary representation that causes one to accept it as true to life or to human experience <a novel about contemporary marriage that was praised for its *verisimilitude*>.

try 1. see AFFLICT. **2.** see ATTEMPT.

tug see PULL.

tumescent see INFLATED.
tumid see INFLATED.
tumor, neoplasm, malignancy, cancer mean an abnormal growth or mass of tissue.
Tumor is applicable to any such growth on or in the body of a person, animal, or plant and to various other enlargements <removed a benign *tumor* from his skull>.
Neoplasm is likely to replace *tumor*, especially in technical use, when reference is to a more or less unrestrained growth of cells without evident function or to a mass formed by such growth <identified the growth as a *neoplasm*>.
Malignancy applies to a neoplasm that because of unrestrained proliferation and tendency to invade tissues constitutes a menace to life <X rays revealed a *malignancy* in the lung>.
Cancer is the usual popular and technical term for a malignant neoplasm <kept her worries about the *cancer* to herself>.
tumult see COMMOTION.
tune see MELODY.
turgid see INFLATED.
turmoil see COMMOTION.
turn 1. see CURVE. **2.** see RESORT.
twist see CURVE.
twit see RIDICULE.
twitch see JERK.
type, kind, sort, nature, ilk, description, character mean a number of individuals thought of as a group because of a common quality or qualities.
Type may suggest strong and clearly marked similarity throughout the items included so that the distinctiveness of the group is obvious <one of three basic body *types*>.
Kind may be indefinite and involve any criterion of classification whatever <that *kind* of ice cream> or may suggest natural or intrinsic criteria <a zoo with animals of every *kind*>.
Sort, often close to *kind,* may suggest a note of disparagement <the *sort* of newspaper dealing in sensational stories>.
Nature may imply inherent, essential resemblance rather than obvious or superficial likenesses <two problems of a similar *nature*>.
Ilk may suggest grouping on the basis of status, attitude, or temperament <cynics of that *ilk*>.
Description implies a group marked by agreement in all details of a type as described or defined <not all individuals of that *description* are truly psychotic>.
Character stresses the distinguishing or individualizing criteria that mark the group <a society with little of the *character* of an advanced culture>.
typical see REGULAR.

tyrannical see ABSOLUTE.
tyro see AMATEUR.

U

ubiquitous see OMNIPRESENT.

ugly, hideous, ill-favored, unsightly mean neither pleasing nor beautiful, especially to the eye.

Ugly may apply not only to what is not pleasing to the eye but to what offends another sense or gives rise to repulsion, dread, or moral distaste in the mind <a street of small drab *ugly* houses>. ***ant*** beautiful

Hideous stresses personal reaction and the horror of loathing induced by something felt as outwardly or inwardly extremely ugly <a hurricane that caused *hideous* destruction>. ***ant*** lovely

Ill-favored applies especially to personal appearance and implies ugliness to the sense of sight without in itself suggesting a resulting distaste or dread <self-conscious about his *ill-favored* features>. ***ant*** well-favored, fair

Unsightly is likely to refer to a material thing on which the eye dwells with no pleasure and connotes a suggestion of distaste <a dump that sat as an *unsightly* blot on the landscape>. ***ant*** sightly

ultimate see LAST.
umbrage see OFFENSE.
unafraid see BRAVE.
unbecoming see INDECOROUS.

unbelief, disbelief, incredulity mean the attitude or state of mind of one who does not believe.

Unbelief stresses absence of belief especially in respect to something above or beyond one's experience or capacity <received news of the disaster with an attitude of *unbelief*>. ***ant*** belief

Disbelief implies a positive rejection of something stated or advanced <regarded his explanation with *disbelief*>. ***ant*** belief

Incredulity suggests a disposition to refuse belief or acceptance <greeted her announcement with *incredulity*>. ***ant*** credulity

unbiased see FAIR.
uncalled-for see SUPEREROGATORY.
uncanny see WEIRD.

uncertainty, doubt, dubiety, skepticism, suspicion, mistrust mean lack of sureness about someone or something.

Uncertainty stresses lack of certitude that may range from a mere falling short of certainty to an almost complete lack of definite knowledge especially about an outcome or result

<general *uncertainty* about the program's future>. ***ant*** certainty

Doubt suggests both uncertainty and inability to make a decision <plagued by *doubts* about his upcoming marriage>. ***ant*** certitude, confidence

Dubiety stresses a lack of sureness that leads to a wavering between conclusions <in times of crisis a leader must be free of all *dubiety*>. ***ant*** decision

Skepticism implies a habitual state of mind or customary reaction characterized by unwillingness to believe without conclusive evidence <an economic forecast that was met with *skepticism*>. ***ant*** gullibility

Suspicion stresses lack of faith in the truth, reality, fairness, or reliability of something or someone <viewed the new neighbors with *suspicion*>.

Mistrust implies a genuine doubt based upon suspicion <had a great *mistrust* of all doctors>. ***ant*** assurance, trust

uncommon see INFREQUENT.

unconcerned see INDIFFERENT.

unconstraint, abandon, spontaneity mean a free and uninhibited expression of thoughts or feelings or a mood or style marked by this.

Unconstraint expresses the fact of freely yielding to impulse and can replace either of the other terms though it is less positive in implication <lived a life of complete *unconstraint*>. ***ant*** constraint

Abandon may add an implication of loss of self-control <weep with *abandon*> or of the absence or impotence of any check on full, free, or natural expression of feeling <ate with *abandon* the whole time we were on vacation>. ***ant*** self-restraint

Spontaneity suggests an unstudied naturalness and may connote freshness, lack of deliberation, or obedience to the impulse of the moment <a welcome full of warm *spontaneity*>.

uncouth see RUDE.

uncritical see SUPERFICIAL.

unctuous see FULSOME.

underhanded see SECRET.

undermine see WEAKEN.

understand, comprehend, appreciate mean to have a clear or complete idea of.

Understand may stress the fact of having attained a mental grasp of something <*understood* the instructions>.

Comprehend stresses the mental process of arriving at a result <failed to *comprehend* the entire process>.

Appreciate implies a just estimation of a thing's value and is often used in reference to what is likely to be misjudged <failed to *appreciate* the risks involved>.

understanding see REASON.
undulate see SWING.
unearth see DISCOVER.
unerring see INFALLIBLE.
uneven see ROUGH.
unfeigned see SINCERE.
unflagging see INDEFATIGABLE.
unfruitful see STERILE.
ungovernable see UNRULY.
uniform see SIMILAR.
unimpassioned see SOBER.
union see UNITY.
unique 1. see SINGLE. **2.** see STRANGE.
unite see JOIN.
unity, solidarity, integrity, union mean a combining of parts or elements or individuals into an effective whole or the quality of a whole made up of closely associated parts.

Unity implies oneness especially of what is varied and diverse in its elements or parts <a multiplicity of styles effectively combined into a *unity* of architectural design>.

Solidarity implies a unity in a group or class that enables it to manifest its strength and exert its influence as one <an ethnic minority with a strong sense of *solidarity*>.

Integrity implies unity that indicates exactitude of association and interdependence of the parts and completeness and perfection of the whole <a farcical scene that destroys the play's *integrity*>.

Union implies a thorough integration and harmonious cooperation of the parts or the body or organization that results from such a uniting <the *union* of thirteen diverse colonies to form one nation>.

universal, general, generic mean characteristic of, relating to, comprehending, or affecting all or the whole.

Universal implies reference to every one without exception in the class, category, or genus considered <declared *universal* amnesty>. ***ant*** particular

General implies reference to all or nearly all <the theory has met *general* acceptance> or, in reference to such things as words, language, ideas, or notions, suggests lack of precision <got the *general* idea>.

Generic implies reference to every member of a genus and is applicable especially to items such as qualities, characteristics, or likenesses that serve as identifying guides <*generic* likenesses among all dogs>. ***ant*** specific

unlawful, illegal, illegitimate, illicit mean not being in accordance with law.

Unlawful implies lack of conformity with law of any sort <*unlawful* conduct>. ***ant*** lawful

Illegal often stresses lack of conformity to what is sanctioned by the law as defined by statute and administered by courts <an *illegal* U-turn>. ***ant*** legal

Illegitimate tends to be narrow in reference and usually applies to children born out of wedlock or to a relation leading to such a result <their union was *illegitimate*>, but it may refer to something that is not proper according to rules of logic or to authorities or to precedent <an *illegitimate* inference>. ***ant*** legitimate

Illicit may imply lack of conformance with a regulatory law <*illicit* distilling>, but it is also applied to something obtained, done, or maintained unlawfully, illegally, or illegitimately <an *illicit* affair>. ***ant*** licit

unlearned see IGNORANT.

unlettered see IGNORANT.

unman see UNNERVE.

unmindful see FORGETFUL.

unmitigated see OUTRIGHT.

unmoral see IMMORAL.

unnatural see IRREGULAR.

unnerve, enervate, unman, emasculate mean to deprive of strength or vigor and the capacity for effective action.

Unnerve implies a marked often temporary loss of courage, self-control, or power to act <*unnerved* by the near midair collision>.

Enervate suggests a gradual physical or moral weakening through such debilitating influences as climate, disease, luxury, or indolence until one is too feeble to make an effort <totally *enervated* after a week's vacation>. ***ant*** harden, inure

Unman implies a loss of manly vigor, fortitude, or spirit <the sight of blood usually *unmanned* him>.

Emasculate stresses a depriving of characteristic force by removing something essential <an amendment that *emasculates* existing gun-control laws>.

unpremeditated see EXTEMPORANEOUS.

unpretentious see PLAIN.

unreasonable see IRRATIONAL.

unruffled see COOL.

unruly, ungovernable, intractable, refractory, recalcitrant, willful, headstrong mean not submissive to government or control.

Unruly implies unwillingness to submit to discipline or incapacity for discipline and often connotes waywardness or turbulence of disposition <*unruly* children>. ***ant*** tractable, docile

Ungovernable implies either incapacity for or escape from control or guidance by oneself or others or a state of being unsubdued <*ungovernable* rage>. ***ant*** governable, docile

Intractable suggests stubborn resistance to guidance or control <the farmers were *intractable* in their opposition to the hazardous-waste dump>. ***ant*** tractable

Refractory stresses resistance to attempts to manage or to mold <special schools for *refractory* children>. ***ant*** malleable, amenable

Recalcitrant suggests determined resistance to or rebellious and deliberate defiance of the will or authority of another <acts of sabotage by a *recalcitrant* populace>. ***ant*** amenable

Willful implies an obstinate and often capricious determination to have one's own way <a *willful* disregard for the rights of others>. ***ant*** biddable

Headstrong suggests self-will that is impatient of restraint, advice, or suggestion <a *headstrong* young army officer bent on engaging the enemy>.

unseemly see INDECOROUS.

unsightly see UGLY.

unsocial, asocial, antisocial, nonsocial mean not social and therefore opposed to what is social.

Unsocial implies a distaste for the society of others or an aversion to close association and interaction with others <a very *unsocial* temperament>. ***ant*** social

Asocial applies more often to behavior, thoughts, or acts viewed objectively and implies a lack of all the qualities conveyed by the word *social*, and rather stresses a self-centered, individualistic, egocentric orientation <dreaming is an *asocial* act>. ***ant*** social

Antisocial applies to things such as acts, ideas, or movements that are felt as harmful to or destructive of society or the social order or institutions <tried to discourage *antisocial* behavior among her students>. ***ant*** social

Nonsocial applies to what cannot be described as *social* in any relevant sense <*nonsocial* bees>.

unsophisticated see NATURAL.

unstable see INCONSTANT.

untangle see EXTRICATE.

untiring see INDEFATIGABLE.

untruthful see DISHONEST.

untutored see IGNORANT.

unwearied see INDEFATIGABLE.

upbraid see SCOLD.

upheaval see COMMOTION.

uphold see SUPPORT.

upright, honest, just, conscientious, scrupulous, honorable mean having or showing a strict regard for what is morally right.

Upright implies a strict adherence to moral principles <ministers of the church must be *upright* and unimpeachable>.

Honest stresses recognition of and adherence to such virtues as truthfulness, candor, and fairness <doctors must be *honest* with the terminally ill>. ***ant*** dishonest

Just stresses a conscious choice and regular practice of what is right or equitable <a reputation for being entirely *just* in business dealings>.

Conscientious implies an active moral sense governing all one's actions and stresses painstaking efforts to follow one's conscience <*conscientious* in doing all of her chores>. ***ant*** unconscientious, conscienceless

Scrupulous, like *conscientious,* connotes the action of a moral sense in all one's doings, but distinctively it stresses meticulous attention to details of morality or conduct <*scrupulous* in carrying out the terms of the will>. ***ant*** unscrupulous

Honorable suggests a firm holding to codes of right behavior and the guidance of a high sense of honor and duty <the *honorable* thing would be to resign my position>. ***ant*** dishonorable

uprising see REBELLION.

uproar see DIN.

uproot see EXTERMINATE.

upset see DISCOMPOSE.

urbane see SUAVE.

usage see HABIT.

use *n* **1. Use, usefulness, utility** mean a capacity for serving an end or purpose.

Use implies little more than suitability for employment for some purpose specified or implied <she hated to throw away anything that might have some *use*>.

Usefulness is employed chiefly with reference to definite concrete things that serve or are capable of serving a practical purpose <demonstrated the *usefulness* of the gadget>. ***ant*** uselessness

Utility may differ from *usefulness,* especially in technical use, by implying a measurable property or one that can be viewed as an abstraction <a college major of no immediate *utility*>.

2. see HABIT.

use *vb* **Use, employ, utilize, apply** mean to put into service especially to attain an end or to give a practical value.

Use implies availing oneself of something as a means or instrument to an end <willing to *use* any means to achieve her goals>.

Employ suggests the using of a person or thing that is available but idle, inactive, or disengaged by putting him, her, or it to some work or profitable activity <your time might have been better *employed* by reading>.

Utilize may suggest the discovery of a new, profitable, or practical use for something that might be overlooked or wasted <meat processors *utilize* every part of the animal>.

Apply stresses the bringing of one thing into contact or relation with something else in such a way that it proves useful or acquires practical value <*applied* specific rules to the situation>.

usefulness see USE.

usual, customary, habitual, wonted, accustomed mean familiar through frequent or regular repetition.

Usual stresses the absence of strangeness or unexpectedness and is applicable to whatever is normal <my *usual* order for lunch>. ***ant*** unusual

Customary applies to what accords with the practices, conventions, or usages of an individual or community <a *customary* waiting period before remarrying>. ***ant*** occasional

Habitual suggests a practice settled or established by much repetition <an *habitual* exercise regime that served her well>. ***ant*** occasional

Wonted stresses habituation but usually applies to what is favored, sought, or purposefully cultivated <his *wonted* pleasures had lost their appeal>. ***ant*** unwonted

Accustomed is less emphatic than *wonted* or *habitual* in suggesting fixed habit or invariable custom <accepted the compliment with her *accustomed* modesty>. ***ant*** unaccustomed

usurp see APPROPRIATE.

utensil see IMPLEMENT.

utility see USE *n.*

utilize see USE *vb.*

utter 1. see EXPRESS. **2.** see SAY.

V

vacant see EMPTY.

vacillate see HESITATE.

vacuous see EMPTY.

vagary see CAPRICE.

vague see OBSCURE.

vain 1. Vain, nugatory, otiose, idle, empty, hollow mean being without worth or significance.

Vain implies either absolute or relative absence of value or worth <it is *vain* to think that we can alter destiny>.

Nugatory suggests triviality or insignificance <a monarch with *nugatory* powers>.
Otiose suggests that something serves no purpose and is either an encumbrance or a superfluity <not a single scene in the film is *otiose*>.
Idle suggests a lack of capacity for worthwhile use or effect <it is *idle* to speculate on what might have been>.
Empty and *hollow* suggest a deceiving lack of real substance, soundness, genuineness, or value <an *empty* attempt at reconciliation> <a *hollow* victory that benefited no one>.
2. see FUTILE.

vainglory see PRIDE *n*.
valiant see BRAVE.
valid, sound, cogent, convincing, telling mean having such force as to compel serious attention and usually acceptance.
Valid implies being supported by objective truth or generally accepted authority <absences will be excused for *valid* reasons>. ***ant*** invalid, fallacious, sophistic
Sound implies a basis of flawless reasoning or solid grounds <a *sound* proposal for combatting terrorism>. ***ant*** unsound, fallacious
Cogent may stress either weight of sound argument and evidence or lucidity of presentation <the prosecutor's *cogent* summation won over the jury>.
Convincing suggests a power to overcome doubt, opposition, or reluctance to accept <a documentary that makes a *convincing* case for court reform>.
Telling stresses an immediate and crucial effect striking at the heart of a matter and may or may not imply soundness and validity <a *telling* example of the bureaucratic mentality>.

validate see CONFIRM.
valor see HEROISM.
valorous see BRAVE.
valuable see COSTLY.
value 1. see APPRECIATE. **2.** see ESTIMATE.
vanity see PRIDE *n*.
vanquish see CONQUER.
vapid see INSIPID.
variance see DISCORD.
various see DIFFERENT.
vary see CHANGE.
vast see ENORMOUS.
vaunt see BOAST.
veer see SWERVE.
vein see MOOD.
venerable see OLD.
venerate see REVERE.

vengeful see VINDICTIVE.

venial, pardonable mean not warranting punishment or the imposition of a penalty.

Venial usually implies an opposition to *grave, serious,* or *grievous* <*venial* acts as opposed to truly criminal ones> or, in theological use, to *mortal,* and consequently it applies to what is trivial, harmless, or unwitting <mistakes that were *venial* and easily overlooked>. ***ant*** heinous, mortal

Pardonable implies that there is excuse of justification that makes the fault or error unworthy of consideration <spoke with *pardonable* pride of his daughter's success>. ***ant*** unpardonable

venom see POISON.

vent see EXPRESS.

venturesome see ADVENTUROUS.

veracity see TRUTH.

verbal see ORAL.

verbose see WORDY.

verge see BORDER.

verify see CONFIRM.

verisimilitude see TRUTH.

veritable see AUTHENTIC.

verity see TRUTH.

vernacular see DIALECT.

versatile, many-sided, all-around mean marked by or showing skill or ability or capacity or usefulness of many kinds.

Versatile, applied to persons, stresses variety of aptitude and facility that allows one to turn from one activity to another without loss of effectiveness or skill <a skilled and *versatile* performer>; applied to things, it stresses their multiple and diverse qualities, uses, or possibilities <needed a vehicle that was *versatile* and reliable>.

Many-sided, applied to persons, stresses breadth or diversity of interests or accomplishments <a *many-sided* scholar, critically aware of yesterday, today, and tomorrow>; applied to things, it stresses diversity of aspects, attributes, or uses <a *many-sided* public-policy debate>.

All-around implies completeness or symmetry of development and connotes general competence more often than special or outstanding ability <an *all-around* athlete and sportsman>.

vertical, perpendicular, plumb mean being at right angles to a baseline.

Vertical suggests a line or direction rising straight upward toward a zenith <the side of the cliff is almost *vertical*>. ***ant*** horizontal

Perpendicular may stress the straightness of a line making a right angle with any other line, not necessarily a horizontal one <the parallel bars are *perpendicular* to the support posts>.

Plumb stresses an exact verticality determined by the earth's gravity (as with a plumb line) <make sure that the wall is *plumb*>.

very see SAME.

vessel see BOAT.

vestige see TRACE.

vex see ANNOY.

vibrate see SWING 2.

vice 1. see FAULT. **2.** see OFFENSE 2.

vicious, villainous, iniquitous, nefarious, infamous, corrupt, degenerate mean highly reprehensible or offensive in character, nature, or conduct.

Vicious may directly oppose *virtuous* in implying moral depravity, or it may connote malignancy, cruelty, or destructive violence <a *vicious* gangster wanted for murder>. ***ant*** virtuous

Villainous applies to any evil, depraved, or vile conduct or characteristic <*villainous* behavior that must be punished>.

Iniquitous implies absence of all signs of justice or fairness <an *iniquitous* tyrant, ruling by fear and intimidation>. ***ant*** righteous

Nefarious suggests flagrant breaching of time-honored laws and traditions of conduct <pornography, prostitution, and organized crime's other *nefarious* activities>. ***ant*** exemplary

Infamous suggests shameful and scandalous wickedness <*infamous* for their crimes>. ***ant*** illustrious

Corrupt stresses a loss of moral integrity or probity causing betrayal of principle or sworn obligations <city hall was filled with *corrupt* politicians>.

Degenerate suggests having sunk from a higher to an especially vicious or enervated condition <a *degenerate* regime propped up by foreign support>. ***ant*** regenerate

vicissitude see DIFFICULTY.

victim, prey, quarry mean one killed or injured for the ends of the one who kills or injures.

Victim basically applies to a living being killed as a sacrifice to a divinity, but in more general use it applies to one killed, injured, ruined, or badly treated either by a ruthless person or by an impersonal power that admits of no effective resistance <*victims* of wars and disasters>.

Prey basically applies to animals hunted and killed for food by other animals and is often extended to a victim of something suggestive of a rapacious predator <consumers who are easy *prey* for advertisers>.

Quarry basically applies to a victim of the chase and in more general use may apply to one pursued intensely as well as to one actually taken by the hunter or pursuer <the private investigator stalked her *quarry* relentlessly>.

victory, conquest, triumph mean a successful outcome in a contest or struggle.

Victory stresses the fact of winning against an opponent or against odds <won an upset *victory* in the election>. ***ant*** defeat

Conquest stresses the subjugation or mastery of a defeated opponent, be it a personal antagonist or a difficult undertaking <the *conquest* of space>.

Triumph suggests a brilliant or decisive victory or an overwhelming conquest and usually connotes the acclaim and personal satisfaction accruing to the winner <crossed the finish line, her arms aloft in *triumph*>. ***ant*** defeat

vie see RIVAL.

view *n* see OPINION.

view *vb* see SEE 1.

vigilant see WATCHFUL.

vigorous, energetic, strenuous, lusty, nervous mean having great vitality and force.

Vigorous further implies showing undepleted or undiminished capacity for activity or freshness or robustness <still *vigorous* and sharp in her seventieth year>. ***ant*** languorous, lethargic

Energetic suggests a capacity for intense, sometimes bustling or forced, activity <an *energetic* wife, mother, and career woman>. ***ant*** lethargic

Strenuous suggests what is arduous or challenging and evokes a consistently vigorous response <moved to Alaska in search of the *strenuous* life>.

Lusty implies exuberant energy and capacity for enjoyment <a huge meal to satisfy their *lusty* appetites>. ***ant*** effete

Nervous suggests especially the forcibleness and sustained effectiveness resulting from mental vigor <a *nervous* energy informs his sculptures>.

vile see BASE *adj*.

vilify see MALIGN.

villainous see VICIOUS.

vindicate 1. see EXCULPATE. **2.** see MAINTAIN.

vindictive, revengeful, vengeful mean showing or motivated by a desire for vengeance.

Vindictive tends to stress the reaction as inherent in the nature of the individual and is appropriate when no specific motivating grievance exists <not a *vindictive* bone in his body>, but sometimes it implies a persistent emotion, based on real or fancied wrongs, that may manifest itself in implacable malevolence or in mere spiteful malice <a *vindictive* person plotting revenge>.

Revengeful and *vengeful* are more likely to suggest the state of one specifically provoked to action and truculently ready to seek or take revenge; both terms may also apply to an agent or weapon by which vengeance can be attained <an insult that provoked a *revengeful* spirit in its target> <trained his children to be his *vengeful* agents>.

violation see BREACH.

virile see MASCULINE.

virtually, practically, morally mean not absolutely or actually, yet so nearly so that the difference is negligible.

Virtually may imply a merely apparent difference between outward seeming and inner reality <the prime minister is *virtually* the ruler of his country>.

Practically implies a difference between what meets ordinary or practical demands and what qualifies in some formal or absolute way <the road is *practically* finished; cars can use it all the way>.

Morally implies a difference between what satisfies one's judgment and what constitutes legal or logical proof <the jurors were *morally* certain of the defendant's guilt but the lack of conclusive evidence demanded a verdict of "not guilty">.

virtuous see MORAL.

virus see POISON.

visage see FACE.

visionary see IMAGINARY.

visit, visitation, call mean a coming to stay with another temporarily and usually briefly.

Visit applies to any such coming, be it long or short, and whatever its nature or cause or purpose <spent the summer on a *visit* to her English cousins>.

Visitation applies chiefly to a formal or official visit made by one in authority often for a special purpose such as inspection or couseling <parochial *visitations* of a bishop>.

Call applies to a brief, usually formal visit for social or professional purposes <the salesmen were expected to make at least ten *calls* each day>.

visitation see VISIT.

vital 1. see ESSENTIAL. **2.** see LIVING.

vitalize, energize, activate mean to arouse to activity, animation, or life.

Vitalize may stress the arousal of something more or less inert or lifeless, often by communicating an impetus or force <took steps to *vitalize* the local economy> or an imparting of significance or interest to something <a set of images that *vitalize* the story>. ***ant*** atrophy

Energize implies an arousing to activity or a readying for activity by an imparting of strength or a providing with a source of energy <a speech that *energized* the sales force for what lay ahead>.

Activate implies a passing from an inactive to an active state and stresses the influence of an external agent in arousing to activity <a switch in the office *activates* all the outdoor lights>. ***ant*** arrest

vitiate see DEBASE.

vituperate see SCOLD.

vituperation see ABUSE.

vivacious see LIVELY.

vivid see GRAPHIC.

vivify see QUICKEN.

vocal 1. Vocal, articulate, oral mean uttered by the voice or having to do with such utterance.

Vocal implies the use of the voice, but not necessarily of speech or language <preferred *vocal* to instrumental music>.

Articulate implies the use of distinct intelligible language <so enraged that he was scarcely capable of *articulate* speech>. ***ant*** inarticulate

Oral implies the use of the voice rather than the hand (as in writing or signaling in communication) <legend is the *oral* transmission of tradition>. ***ant*** written

2. Vocal, articulate, fluent, eloquent, voluble, glib mean being able to express oneself clearly or easily.

Vocal usually implies ready responsiveness to an occasion for expression or free and usually forceful, insistent, or emphatic voicing of one's ideas or feelings <one of the president's most *vocal* critics>.

Articulate implies the use of language which exactly and distinctly reveals or conveys what it seeks to express <questioned the validity of literary criticism coming from those who are themselves hardly *articulate*>. ***ant*** inarticulate

Fluent stresses facility in speaking or writing and copiousness in the flow of words <seemed to be *fluent* on any subject>; it can also apply to facility and ease in the use of a foreign language <had a *fluent* command of idiomatic French>.

Eloquent usually implies fluency but it suggests also the stimulus of powerful emotion and its expression in fervent and moving language <moved by the *eloquent* words of the Gettysburg Address>.

Voluble is usually somewhat derogatory and suggests a flow of language that is not easily stemmed <indulge in *voluble* explanations>. ***ant*** stuttering, stammering

Glib is also usually derogatory and implies superficiality or emptiness in what is said or slipperiness or untrustworthiness in the speaker <a *glib* reply> <known for his *glib* tongue>.

vociferous, clamorous, blatant, strident, boisterous, obstreperous mean so loud or insistent as to compel attention.

Vociferous implies a vehement deafening shouting or calling out <*vociferous* cries of protest and outrage> or an insistent, urgent presentation of requests, excuses, or demands <made *vociferous* demands>.

Clamorous may imply insistency as well as vociferousness in demanding or protesting <*clamorous* demands for prison reforms>. ***ant*** taciturn

Blatant implies an offensive bellowing or insensitive, conspicuous, or vulgar loudness <a *blatant* and abusive drunkard>. ***ant*** decorous, reserved

Strident suggests a harsh and discordant noise <heard the *strident* cry of the crow>.

Boisterous suggests a noisiness and turbulence due to high spirits and release from restraint <a *boisterous* crowd of partygoers>.

Obstreperous suggests unruly and aggressive noisiness and resistance to restraint or authority <the *obstreperous* demonstrators were removed from the hall>.

vogue see FASHION.

voice see EXPRESS.

void see EMPTY.

volatility see LIGHTNESS.

voluble 1. see TALKATIVE. **2.** see VOCAL 2.

volume see BULK.

voluntary, intentional, deliberate, willful, willing mean done or brought about of one's own will.

Voluntary implies freedom and spontaneity of choice or action without external compulsion <*voluntary* enlistment in the armed services>. ***ant*** involuntary, instinctive

Intentional stresses an awareness of an end to be achieved <the *intentional* concealment of vital information>. ***ant*** unintentional, instinctive

Deliberate implies full consciousness of the nature of one's act and its consequences <the *deliberate* sabotaging of a nuclear power plant>. ***ant*** impulsive

Willful adds to *deliberate* the implication of an obstinate determination to follow one's own will or choice <*willful* ignorance>.

Willing implies a readiness and eagerness to accede to or anticipate the wishes of another <a *willing* accomplice in a bank robbery>. ***ant*** unwilling

voluptuous see SENSUOUS.

voracious, gluttonous, ravenous, rapacious mean excessively greedy.

Voracious applies especially to habitual gorging with what satisfies an appetite <teenagers are often *voracious* eaters>.

Gluttonous applies to delight in eating or acquiring things especially beyond the point of necessity or satiety <an admiral who had a *gluttonous* appetite for glory>. ***ant*** abstemious

Ravenous implies excessive hunger and suggests violent or grasping methods of dealing with whatever satisfies an appetite <football practice usually gives them *ravenous* appetites>.

Rapacious often suggests excessive and utterly selfish acquisitiveness or avarice <*rapacious* land developers indifferent to the ruination of the environment>.

vouch see CERTIFY.

vouchsafe see GRANT.

vulgar 1. see COARSE. **2.** see COMMON.

W-Z

wage, salary, stipend, pay, fee mean the price paid for services or labor.

Wage, often used in the plural *wages,* applies to an amount paid usually on an hourly basis and chiefly at weekly intervals especially for physical labor <dirty and difficult jobs should command a higher *wage*>.

Salary applies to compensation at a fixed, often annual, rate that is paid in installments at regular intervals and suggests that the services performed require training or special ability <negotiated for a higher *salary*>.

Stipend adds to *salary* the notion of a regular income such as a pension or scholarship paid without concurrently performed service <received a fellowship that included a small *stipend*>.

Pay can replace any of the foregoing and is the one of these terms freely used in combination or as a modifier <waiting for *pay* day> <lost his *pay* envelope>.

Fee applies to the price asked, usually in the form of a fixed charge, for a specific professional service <a pianist's *fee* for a concert>.

wait see STAY.

waive see RELINQUISH.

waken see STIR *vb.*

wallow, welter, grovel mean to move heavily or clumsily because or as if impeded or out of control.

Wallow basically implies a lurching or rolling to and fro, as of a hog in the mire or a ship in a troubled sea, and may imply complete self-abandonment <*wallowing* in self-pity> or absorption <*wallowed* in the romantic music>.

Welter is likely to carry a stronger implication of being helplessly at the mercy of outside forces <a tide of refugees, many of whom *weltered,* adrift on the sea, for days>.

Grovel implies a crawling or wriggling close to the ground in abject fear, self-abasement, or utter degradation <*grovelled* for forgiveness>.

wan see PALE 1.

wander, stray, roam, ramble, rove, range, traipse, meander mean to move about more or less aimlessly from place to place.

Wander implies an absence of or an indifference to a fixed course <found her *wandering* about the square>.

Stray carries a stronger suggestion of a deviation from a fixed or proper course and may connote a being lost <*strayed* into the underbrush>.

Roam suggests a wandering about freely and often far afield and often connotes enjoyment <liked to *roam* through the woods>.

Ramble stresses carelessness and indifference to one's course or objective and suggests a straying beyond bounds or an inattention to guiding details <the speaker *rambled* on without ever coming to the point>.

Rove suggests vigorous and sometimes purposeful roaming <armed brigands *roved* through the countryside>.

Range adds to *rove* an emphasis on the extent of territory covered and is often used when literal wandering is not implied <a lecture that *ranged* over much of both Eastern and Western philosophy>.

Traipse implies an erratic if purposeful and vigorous course <*traipsed* all over town looking for the right dress>.

Meander implies a winding or intricate course suggestive of aimless or listless wandering <the river *meanders* for miles through rich farmland>.

wane see ABATE.

want *n* see POVERTY.

want *vb* **1.** see DESIRE. **2.** see LACK.

wanton see SUPEREROGATORY.

warlike see MARTIAL.

ward off see PREVENT 2.

warn, forewarn, caution mean to let one know of approaching or possible danger or risk.

Warn may range in meaning from simple notification of something to be watched for or guarded against to admonition or threats of violence or reprisal <the weather bureau *warned* coastal areas to prepare for a hurricane>.

Forewarn stresses timeliness and regularly implies warning in advance of a foreseen risk or danger <they had been *forewarned* of the danger, and were prepared when it arose>.

Caution stresses giving advice that puts one on guard or suggests precautions against either a prospective or a present risk or peril <the doctor *cautioned* him against overeating>.

warp see DEFORM.

warrant see JUSTIFY.

wary see CAUTIOUS.

waste 1. see RAVAGE.

2. Waste, squander, dissipate, fritter, consume mean to spend or expend futilely or without gaining a proper or reasonable or normal return.

Waste usually implies careless or prodigal expenditure <*wasted* her money on frivolous items>, but it may also imply fruitless or useless expenditure <why *waste* time trying to help people who want no help?>. ***ant*** save, conserve

Squander stresses reckless and lavish expenditure that tends to exhaust resources <*squandered* all their time and energy playing tennis>.

Dissipate implies loss by extravagance and commonly stresses exhaustion of the store or stock <eventually realized they had *dissipated* all their resources>.

Fritter, usually used with *away,* implies expenditure on trifles, bit by bit, or without commensurate return <*frittered* away the entire afternoon on aimless pursuits>.

Consume can imply a wasting or squandering as entirely as if by devouring <built a fire that *consumed* the entire stock of wood>.

waster see SPENDTHRIFT.

wastrel see SPENDTHRIFT.

watch 1. see SEE 2. **2.** see TEND.

watchful, vigilant, wide-awake, alert mean being on the lookout especially for danger or opportunity.

Watchful is the least explicit term <played under the *watchful* eyes of their mothers>. ***ant*** unwatchful

Vigilant suggests intense, unremitting, wary watchfulness <*vigilant* taxpayers forestalled all attempts to raise taxes>.

Wide-awake stresses keen awareness of and watchfulness for opportunities and developments more often than for dangers <*wide-awake* observers will recall other summit meetings>.

Alert stresses readiness or promptness in meeting a problem or a danger or in seizing an opportunity <*alert* traders anticipated the stock market's slide>.

wave see SWING 1.

waver 1. see HESITATE. **2.** see SWING 2.

way see METHOD.

waylay see SURPRISE 1.

wayward see CONTRARY.

weak, feeble, frail, fragile, infirm, decrepit mean not strong enough to endure strain, pressure, or strenuous effort.

Weak applies to deficiency or inferiority in strength or power of any sort <a *weak* government likely to topple soon>. ***ant*** strong

Feeble suggests extreme weakness inviting pity or disdain <a *feeble* attempt to resist the enemy attack>. ***ant*** robust

Frail implies delicacy and slightness of constitution or structure and liability to failure or destruction <a once-robust man now *frail* with disease>. ***ant*** robust

Fragile suggests frailty, inability to resist rough usage, and liability to destruction <a *fragile* beauty that the camera cannot convey>. ***ant*** durable

Infirm suggests instability, unsoundness, and insecurity due to loss of strength from old age, crippling illness, or temperamental vacillation <an *infirm* old woman confined to her home>. ***ant*** hale

Decrepit implies being worn-out or broken down from long use or old age <the *decrepit* butler had been with the family for years>. ***ant*** sturdy

weaken, enfeeble, debilitate, undermine, sap, cripple, disable mean to lose or cause to lose strength, energy, or vigor.

Weaken may imply the loss of physical strength, health, soundness, or stability or of quality, intensity, or effective power <a disease that *weakens* the body's defenses against infection>. ***ant*** strengthen

Enfeeble implies an obvious and pitiable weakening to the point of helplessness <so *enfeebled* by arthritis that he requires constant care>. ***ant*** fortify

Debilitate suggests a less marked or more temporary impairment of strength or vitality <the operation has a temporary *debilitating* effect>. ***ant*** invigorate

Undermine suggests a weakening by something working surreptitiously and insidiously and implies a caving in or breaking down <a poor diet *undermines* your health>. ***ant*** reinforce

Sap is close to *undermine* but adds a suggestion of a draining of strength <drugs had *sapped* his ability to think>.

Cripple implies the causing of a serious loss of functioning power through damaging or removing an essential part or element <inflation had *crippled* the economy>.

Disable suggests a usually sudden crippling or enfeebling of strength or competence <*disabled* soldiers received an immediate discharge>. ***ant*** rehabilitate

wealthy see RICH.

wean see ESTRANGE.

weary see TIRE.

weigh see CONSIDER.

weight **1.** see IMPORTANCE. **2.** see INFLUENCE.

weighty see HEAVY.

weird, eerie, uncanny mean mysteriously strange or fantastic.

Weird may imply an unearthly or supernatural strangeness or it may stress queerness or oddness <*weird* creatures from another world>.

Eerie suggests an uneasy or fearful consciousness that mysterious and malign powers are at work <an *eerie* calm preceded the bombing raid>.

Uncanny implies an unpleasant or disquieting strangeness or mysteriousness <bore an *uncanny* resemblance to his dead wife>.

welcome see PLEASANT.

well see HEALTHY.

well-nigh see NEARLY.

well-timed see SEASONABLE.

welter see WALLOW.

wet, damp, dank, moist, humid mean more or less covered or soaked with liquid.

Wet usually implies saturation but may suggest a covering of a surface with water or something such as paint not yet dry <slipped on the *wet* pavement>. ***ant*** dry

Damp implies a slight or moderate absorption and often connotes an unpleasant degree of moisture <clothes will mildew if stored in a *damp* place>.

Dank implies a more distinctly disagreeable or unwholesome dampness and often connotes a lack of fresh air and sunshine <a prisoner in a cold, *dank* cell>.

Moist applies to what is slightly damp or not entirely dry <treat the injury with *moist* heat>.

Humid applies to the presence of an oppressive amount of water vapor in warm air <the hot, *humid* conditions brought on heatstroke>.

wheedle see COAX.

whim see CAPRICE.

whirl see REEL.

whit see PARTICLE.

whiten, blanch, bleach, decolorize, etiolate mean to change from an original or natural color to white or nearly white.

Whiten implies a making white or whiter, often by a surface application <the snow fell softly, *whitening* the roofs and streets>. ***ant*** blacken

Blanch implies a whitening either by the removal of color <*blanched* when she saw the accident> or by preventing it from developing <*blanch* celery by covering the stalks with earth>.

Bleach implies the action of light or chemicals in removing or reducing color <*bleach* hair with peroxide>.

Decolorize implies the deprivation of color by a process such as bleaching or blanching <a process to *decolorize* raw sugar>. ***ant*** color

Etiolate is a scientific term chiefly in reference to plants from which sunlight has been excluded and the natural coloring of chlorophyll has not been formed <*etiolated* plants look sickly>.

whole *adj* **1. Whole, entire, total, all** mean including everything or everyone without exception.

Whole implies that nothing has been omitted, ignored, abated, or taken away <read the *whole* book>. ***ant*** partial

Entire may suggest a state of completeness or perfection from which nothing has been taken or to which nothing can be added <the *entire* population was wiped out>. ***ant*** partial

Total implies that everything has been counted, weighed, measured, or considered <the *total* number of people present> or may suggest the absence of all reservation <a *total* eclipse>. ***ant*** partial

All may equal *whole, entire,* or *total* <*all* their money went to pay the rent>. ***ant*** part *(of)*

2. see PERFECT.

whole *n* see SUM.

wholehearted see SINCERE.

wholesale see INDISCRIMINATE.

wholesome 1. see HEALTHFUL. **2.** see HEALTHY.

wicked see BAD.

wide see BROAD.

wide-awake see WATCHFUL.

wield see HANDLE.

wile see TRICK.

willful 1. see UNRULY. **2.** see VOLUNTARY.

willing see VOLUNTARY.

win see GET.

wince see RECOIL.

winning see SWEET.

winsome see SWEET.

wipe out see EXTERMINATE.

wisdom see SENSE.

wise, sage, sapient, judicious, prudent, sensible, sane mean having or showing sound judgment.

Wise suggests great understanding of people and of situations and unusual discernment and judgment in dealing with them and may imply a wide range of experience, knowledge, or learning <*wise* enough to know what really mattered in life>. ***ant*** simple

Sage suggests wide experience, great learning, and wisdom <sought the *sage* advice of her father in times of crisis>.

Sapient suggests great sagacity and discernment <the *sapient* observations of a veteran foreign correspondent>.

Judicious stresses a capacity for weighing and judging and for reaching wise decisions or just conclusions <*judicious* parents using kindness and discipline in equal measure>. ***ant*** injudicious, asinine

Prudent applies to someone who is rich in practical wisdom and hence able to exercise self-restraint and sound judgment <a *prudent* decision to wait out the storm>. ***ant*** imprudent

Sensible applies to action guided and restrained by good sense and rationality <a *sensible* woman who was not fooled by flattery>. ***ant*** absurd, foolish

Sane stresses mental soundness, prudent rationality, and levelheadedness <remained *sane* even as the war raged around him>. ***ant*** insane

wisecrack see JEST.

wish see DESIRE.

wishy-washy see INSIPID.

wit, humor, irony, sarcasm, satire, repartee mean a mode of expression intended to arouse amused interest or evoke laughter.

Wit suggests the power to evoke laughter by remarks showing verbal felicity or ingenuity and swift perception especially of the incongruous <appreciate the *wit* of Wilde and Shaw>.

Humor implies an ability to perceive the ludicrous, the comical, and the absurd in human life and to express these usually with keen insight and sympathetic understanding and without bitterness <a person with a finely honed sense of *humor*>.

Irony applies to a manner of expression in which the intended meaning is the opposite of the expressed meaning <with wry *irony,* he said, "Thank God I'm an atheist!">.

Sarcasm applies to savagely humorous expression frequently in the form of irony that is intended to cut or wound <a cynic much given to heartless *sarcasm*>.

Satire applies to writing that exposes or ridicules conduct, doctrines, or institutions either by direct criticism or more often through irony, parody, or caricature <the play is a *satire* on contemporary living arrangements>.

Repartee implies the power or art of answering quickly, pointedly, or wittily or to an interchange of such responses <a partygoer well known for razor-sharp *repartee*>.

withdraw see GO.

wither, shrivel, wizen mean to lose or cause to lose freshness and smoothness of appearance.

Wither implies a loss of vital moisture, such as sap or tissue fluids, with consequent fading or drying up <*withered* leaves> or suggests a comparable loss of vigor, vitality, or animation <interest that *withered* as the hard work increased>. ***ant*** flourish

Shrivel carries a stronger impression of a becoming wrinkled or crinkled or shrunken <leaves *shrivel* in the hot sun>.

Wizen may be preferred when the notions of shrinking in size and accompanying wrinkling of the surface are stressed, especially if the shrinking is caused by aging, deprivation, or failing vitality <the *wizened* old man> <the *wizened* face of the starving child>.

withhold see KEEP 2.

withstand see OPPOSE.

witness *n* see SPECTATOR.

witness *vb* see CERTIFY.

witticism see JEST.

witty, humorous, facetious, jocular, jocose mean provoking or intended to provoke amusement or laughter.

Witty suggests cleverness and quickness of mind and often a caustic tongue <a film critic remembered for his *witty* reviews>.

Humorous applies broadly to anything that evokes usually genial laughter and may contrast with *witty* in suggesting whimsicality or eccentricity <laced her lectures with *humorous* anecdotes>.

Facetious stresses a desire to produce laughter and may be derogatory in implying clumsy, dubious, or ill-timed attempts at wit or humor <*facetious* comments that were not appreciated at the funeral>. ***ant*** lugubrious

Jocular implies a usually habitual, often temperamental fondness for jesting and joking <a *jocular* fellow whose humor often brightened spirits>.

Jocose suggests habitual waggishness or playfulness that is often clumsy or inappropriate <the dim-witted took his *jocose* proposals seriously>. ***ant*** lugubrious

wizen see WITHER.

wobble see SHAKE 1.

woe see SORROW.

woebegone see DOWNCAST.

womanish see FEMALE.

womanlike see FEMALE.

womanly see FEMALE.

wont see HABIT.

wonted see USUAL.

wooden see STIFF.

wordy, verbose, prolix, diffuse, redundant mean using more words than necessary to express thought.

Wordy may also imply loquaciousness or garrulousness <a *wordy* speech that said nothing>. ***ant*** laconic

Verbose suggests a resulting dullness, obscurity, or lack of incisiveness or precision <*verbose* position papers that no one reads>. ***ant*** concise, laconic

Prolix suggests unreasonable and tedious dwelling on details <habitually transformed brief anecdotes into *prolix* sagas>.

Diffuse stresses lack of the organization and compactness that make for pointedness of expression and strength of style <*diffuse* memoirs that are so many shaggy-dog stories>. ***ant*** succinct

Redundant implies superfluity resulting from needless repetition or overelaboration <emended the text by removing whatever was *redundant*>. ***ant*** concise

work 1. Work, labor, travail, toil, drudgery, grind mean activity involving effort or exertion.

Work may imply activity of body, of mind, of a machine, or of a natural force, or it may apply to effort expended or to the product of such effort <too tired to do any *work*>. ***ant*** play

Labor applies to physical or intellectual work involving great and often strenuous, onerous, or fatiguing exertion <believes that farmers are poorly paid for their *labor*>.

Travail is a somewhat bookish term for labor involving pain or suffering <years of *travail* were lost when the building burned>.

Toil implies prolonged and fatiguing labor <his lot would be years of back-breaking *toil*>.

Drudgery suggests dull and irksome labor <a job with a good deal of *drudgery*>.

Grind implies dreary, monotonous labor exhausting to mind or body <the *grind* of performing the play eight times a week>.

2. Work, employment, occupation, calling, pursuit, métier, business mean a specific sustained activity engaged in especially in earning one's living.

Work may apply to any purposeful activity whether remunerative or not <her *work* as a hospital volunteer>.

Employment implies work for which one has been engaged and for which one is being paid <*employment* will be terminated in cases of chronic tardiness>.

Occupation implies work in which one engages regularly or by preference, especially as a result of training or experience <his *occupation* as a trained auto mechanic>.

Calling applies to an occupation viewed as a vocation or profession to which one has been drawn by one's nature, tastes, or aptitudes <I feel the ministry is my true *calling*>.

Pursuit suggests a trade, profession, or avocation followed with zeal or steady interest <her family considered medicine the only proper *pursuit*>.

Métier implies a calling or pursuit for which one believes oneself to be especially fitted <from childhood I considered acting my *métier*>.

Business may be used in the sense of *work* or *occupation* but often suggests activity in commerce or the management of money and affairs <the *business* of managing a hotel>.

worldly 1. see EARTHLY. **2.** see SOPHISTICATED.

worldly-wise see SOPHISTICATED.

worry *vb* **Worry, annoy, harass, harry, plague, pester, tease, tantalize** mean to torment to the point of destroying one's peace of mind or to disturb or irritate acutely by persistent acts.

Worry implies an incessant goading or attacking that drives one to desperation or defeat <pursued a policy of *worrying* the enemy>.

Annoy implies a disturbing of one's composure or peace of mind by intrusion, interference, or petty attacks <you're doing that just to *annoy* me>.

Harass implies petty persecutions or burdensome demands that wear down, distract, or weaken <*harassed* on all sides by creditors>.

Harry may imply a heavy, driving oppression or maltreatment <*harried* mothers trying to cope with small children>.

Plague implies a painful, persistent, and distressing affliction <*plagued* all her life by poverty>.

Pester implies a continuous harassment with petty, persistent attacks <the bureau was constantly *pestered* with trivial complaints>.

Tease suggests an attempt to break down one's resistance or rouse to wrath by persistent raillery or petty tormenting <malicious children *teased* the dog>.

Tantalize stresses the repeated awakening of expectation and then its frustration <*tantalizing* clues as to the origins of the universe>. ***ant*** satisfy

worry *n* see CARE.

worship see REVERE.

wrangle see QUARREL.

wrath see ANGER.

wreck see RUIN *vb*.

wretched see MISERABLE.

wrong *n* see INJUSTICE.

wrong *vb* **Wrong, oppress, persecute, aggrieve** mean to injure unjustly or outrageously.

Wrong implies inflicting injury either unmerited or out of proportion to what one deserves <a penal system that had *wronged* him>.

Oppress suggests inhumane imposing of burdens one cannot endure or exacting more than one can perform <a people *oppressed* by a warmongering tyrant>.

Persecute implies a relentless and unremitting subjection to annoyance or suffering <a boy with a clubfoot *persecuted* by his playmates>.

Aggrieve implies suffering caused by an infringement or denial of rights <a legal aid society representing *aggrieved* minority groups>.

yank see JERK.

yardstick see STANDARD.

yarn see STORY.

yearn see LONG.

yield **1.** see RELINQUISH.

2. Yield, submit, capitulate, succumb, relent, defer mean to give way to someone or something that one can no longer resist.

Yield in reference to a person implies being overcome by force or entreaty <*yielded* to their pleas for popcorn> but in reference to a thing implies such qualities as elasticity or weakness that facilitate a giving way <a mattress that *yielded* to pressure>. ***ant*** withstand

Submit suggests a full surrendering after resistance or conflict to the will or control of another <voluntarily *submitted* to an inspection of the premises>. ***ant*** resist, withstand

Capitulate stresses the fact of ending all resistance and may imply either a coming to terms, as with an adversary, or submission to an irresistible opposing force <the college president *capitulated* to the protesters' demands>.

Succumb implies weakness and helplessness in the one that gives way or an overwhelming power in the one that overcomes <a stage actor *succumbing* to the lure of Hollywood>.

Relent implies a yielding through pity or mercy by one who holds the upper hand <finally *relented* and let the children stay up late>.

Defer implies a voluntary yielding or submitting out of respect or reverence for or deference and affection toward another <I *defer* to your superior expertise in these matters>. ***ant*** withstand

zeal see PASSION.

zest see TASTE 2.